THE STORY OF THE
WESTBURY TO WEYMOUTH LINE

No. 5900 *Hinderton Hall*, with a faint haze of smoke issuing from the chimney, heads past the 'down' home signal at Brewham at 11.35am on 2nd July 1955 with the 8am Birmingham–Weymouth.

R.C. Riley

Class U 2-6-0 No. 31802 with the Yeovil Town shedplate (72C) on the smokebox door travels along the 'down' main line at Yeovil Pen Mill on 6th September 1964. The Sykes banner repeaters for Yeovil South Junction are both at danger, indicating that the engine is probably the station pilot for the day and is pulling a long string of wagons out of the 'down' yard. When the points have been cleared the engine will then set back into the yard under the directions of the shunter. I have done this many a time when shunting at the station, nipping out between 'down' trains to pull a long raft of wagons out of the yard.

Gerald T. Robinson

THE STORY OF THE
WESTBURY TO WEYMOUTH LINE

From the battle of the gauges to the present day

Derek Phillips

OPC

Oxford Publishing Co.

'Modified Hall' No. 7921 *Edstone Hall* rolls through Witham with the 2.15pm Weymouth Town–Westbury parcels on 27th October 1962. No. 7921 was built to Lot 376 in September 1950, and withdrawn in 1963.

C. L. Caddy

ISBN 0 86093 514 0

Oxford Publishing Co.
is an imprint of Haynes Publishing,
Sparkford, near Yeovil, Somerset, BA22 7JJ

Printed in Great Britain by Butler & Tanner Ltd, Frome and London.

Typeset in Times Roman Medium by Character Graphics (Taunton) Ltd.

Notes: Train times are as per BR timetables, therefore the 24-hour clock has been used for 1964 and onwards.
The signal box diagrams and track plans do not always show lines as viewed from the same direction.

The 'boards' are against 'Hymek' No. D7054 with the 9.15am Swindon–Weymouth parcels on 21st March 1964. The Yeovil Pen Mill station staff are busy on the 'down' platform loading and unloading the train; 2-6-2T No. 82044 steam heats its coaches in the goods yard before the next trip to Taunton via Langport West and Durston.

John Day

Contents

Acknowledgements

Whilst preparing this book I have been fortunate in having the assistance of many people, with their memories of the line, and excellent photographs etc, I would like to thank everyone who has helped me: George Pryer for his excellent track plans and signalling history, R. C. Riley, Hugh Ballantyne, Colin Caddy, R. E. Toop, Gerald T. Robinson, S. C. Nash, D. E. Canning, John Day, John Scrace, Lens of Sutton, Peter and Heather Foster, P. Rendall, Richard Woodley, Norman Kibby, Derek Gill, Gerald Quartley, Peter and Pauline Nicholson, Michael McGarvie, Les Sayers, Mrs B. Darch, H. Trim, R. Bartlett, Miss D. Penny, the Signalling Record Society, John Morris, Michael Marshall, Mr & Mrs Higgins, John Liffen and The National Railway Museum, Tom Whittle, Jack Gardiner, Adrian Vaughan, John Miller, Albert White, H. B. Priestley, G. March, P. J. Marden, Chester Denby, John Cornelius, Fred Martin, S. P. J. A. Derek, Barry Eagles, and everbody who has been kind enough to assist.

It is with sadness that I have to inform you that Tom Whittle, who gave me his recollections of the bombing of Castle Cary, has since passed away; my condolences are with his family. As a personal thank you for his kindness, I would therefore like to dedicate this book to Tom Whittle.

Bibliography

An Historical Survey of Great Western Engine Sheds 1947 E. T. Lyons – Oxford Publishing Company 1974.
An Historical Survey of Great Western Engine Sheds 1837–1947 E. Lyons and E. Mountford. Oxford Publishing Company.
The Weymouth Quay Tramway C. L. Caddy – Dorset Transport Circle.
Rails Around Frome Steve McNicol – Becknell Books 1984.
The Bath To Weymouth Line Colin Maggs – The Oakwood Press 1982.
Locomotives of The Great Western Railway Parts 1–13 RCTS.
The Complete BR Diesel & Electric Locomotive Directory Colin J. Marsden – Oxford Publishing Company 1993.
GWR Engines Names, Numbers, Types & Classes – David & Charles 1971.
An Outline of Great Western Locomotive Practice 1837–1947 H. Holcroft – Locomotive Publishing Company 1957.
The Devizes Branch Nigel S. M. Bray – Picton Publishing 1984.
Great Western Railway Halts Volume One Kevin Robertson – Irwell Press 1990.
The Book of Frome Michael McGarvie – Barracuda Books Ltd 1984.
The Bridport Branch B. L. Jackson & M. J. Tattershall – Oxford Publishing Company 1976.
History of the Great Western Railway E. T. MacDermot/C. R. Clinker/O. S. Nock – Ian Allan.
GWR Locomotive Allocations. First & Last Sheds 1922–1967 J. W. P. Rowledge – David & Charles 1986.
BR Steam Motive Power Depots WR Paul Bolger – Ian Allan 1985.
Signal Box Diagrams of the Great Western & Southern Railways. Vol. 1 G.W.R. Lines in Dorset – G. A. Pryer.

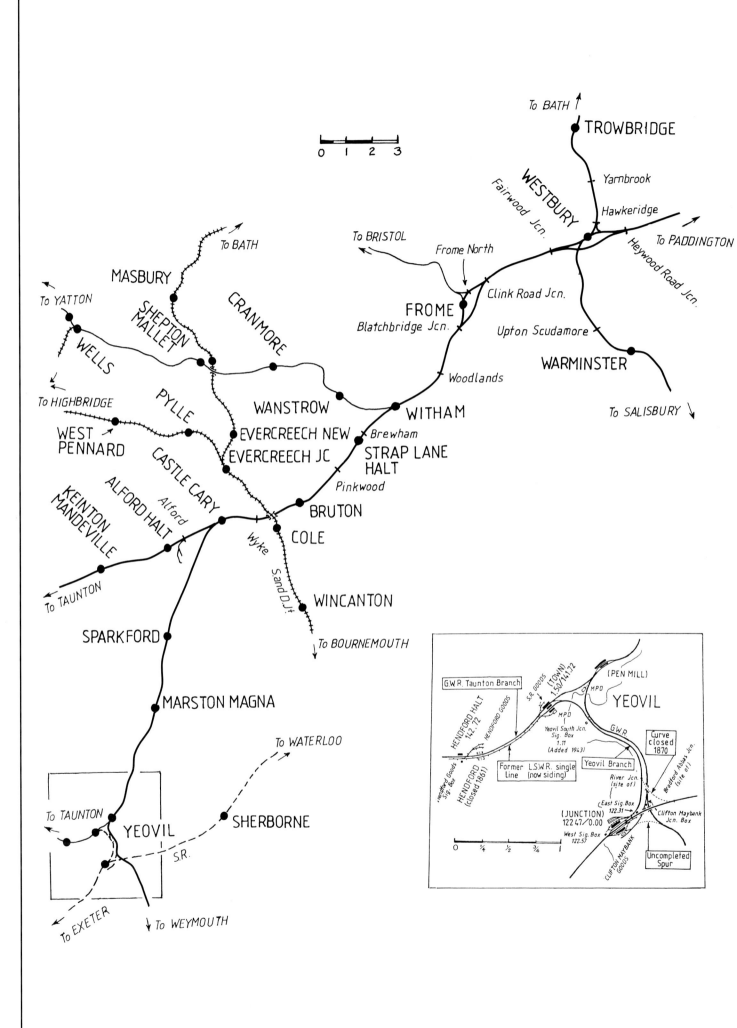

Introduction

The line from Westbury to Weymouth brings back many memories to myself, who as a young boy in the late 1940s, travelled regulary on the route with its copper capped locomotives, and diesel railcars of the Great Western Railway. Lower quadrant signals, grimy pannier tanks, smoky engine sheds at Westbury, Frome, Yeovil and Weymouth, coal and limestone trains from the Somerset mines and quarries, branch passenger trains awaiting their main line connections at the respective main line stations, banking engines at Westbury, Evershot and Castle Cary: The "Cornish Riveria Express" storming westwards along the Frome avoiding line with a gleaming 'King' or 'Castle' at the head – all come to mind.

On the busy summer Saturdays, the place to be was at the summit of Brewham bank by the signal box, as train after train would pound up the bank heading east from the West of England and Weymouth lines, and just as many trains would head west, storming past the signal box and running down the bank with whistles screaming through Bruton, heading for the junction at Castle Cary. The "Channel Islands Boat Express", the "Mayflower", and the "Torbay Express" are just a few of the names that have gone forever. Anyone who has heard the crisp beat of a main line GWR locomotive echoing around Evershot or Brewham will never forget that sound, that resounding exhaust, so typical of the Swindon built engines, each one hand built by craftsmen from an age that has passed into history.

The line today is of course vastly different from my boyhood days. Many stations, and all of the old working signal boxes, except one, have been swept away, but a few gems remain; my boyhood station at Frome is still in place, complete with its Brunel type overall roof. It is well worth a visit, even now, to walk along the platform under that vast roof, and it takes me back to when I was a boy, waiting with my parents for the Bristol train. With a mighty roar and a hissing of steam, a gleaming 'Hall' or 'Grange' would run in and stop with a squeal of brakes at the platform. As we entered our carriage, the heavy doors would slam behind us, and we would settle in our seats in the compartment with its old sepia photographs of places to visit.

Another anachronism of the modern railway age is Yeovil Pen Mill, still complete with its mechanical signal box and lower quadrant signalling, especially when the West of England main line only a few miles to the north, is controlled by colour light signals from Paddington to Plymouth. But the old Wilts, Somerset & Weymouth line from Castle Cary to Dorchester West, now singled and but a shadow of its former self is still there, and open with its stations and halts echoing to the sound of 'Sprinters' and Class 37s, instead of 'Castles' and 'Halls'.

Derek Phillips,
Yeovil,
Somerset.

No. 4917 *Crosswood Hall*, in immaculate condition and not showing even the slightest breath of steam from her front end, runs into Castle Cary on 2nd July 1955 with the 11.12am Weymouth–Paddington. No. 4917 with ten coaches behind the tender had to pull up twice at the platform in order to unload its passengers. The three signals on the gantry to the left, read from left to right: 'down' refuge, 'down' Weymouth, 'down' main, while the ring signal in the background controls the exit from the 'down' goods loop.
R. C. Riley

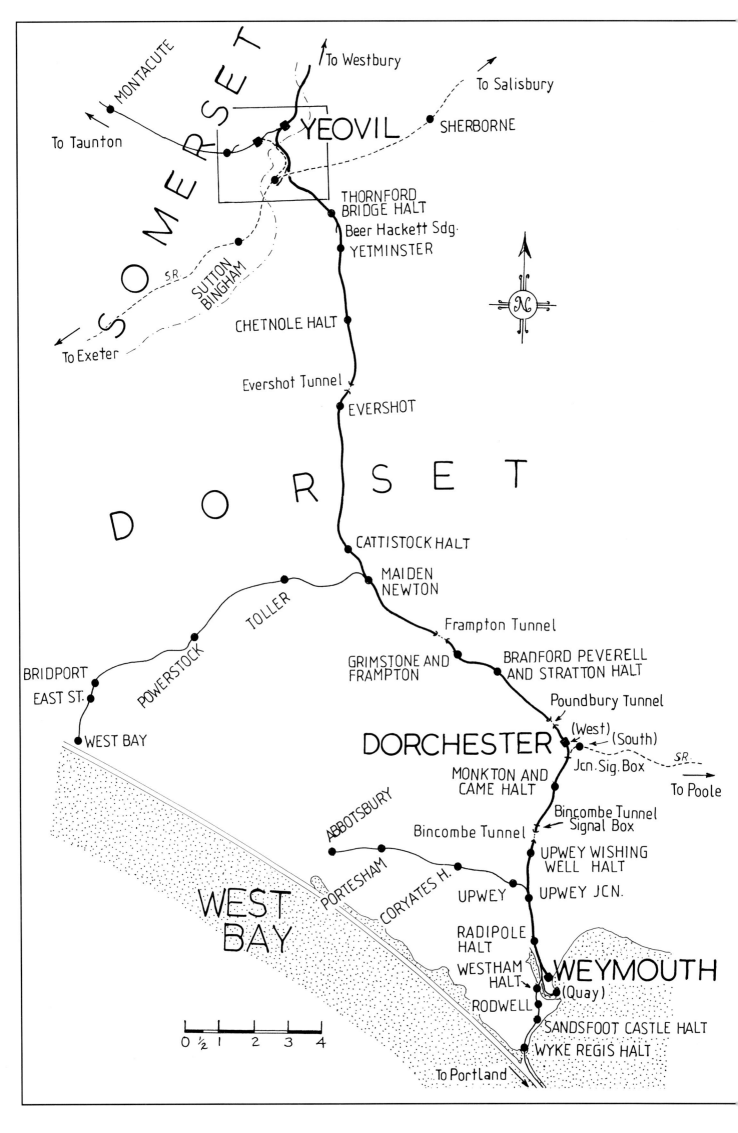

History

Although this book is concerned primarily with one fairly short section of railway it is necessary to describe many events elsewhere in order to explain why the line came into being in the first place. This would be true of most lines, but in this instance a wider view becomes essential because 'Westbury to Weymouth' was never a complete railway in itself, but rather part of a sprawling broad gauge enterprise known as the Wilts, Somerset & Weymouth.

For the purposes of this book it can be treated as a self contained unit because Westbury always seemed something of a frontier – particulary in late GWR and BR days – beyond which Weymouth and Yeovil train crews and traffic relief staff, such as signalmen seldom worked. To begin with, let us take a look at the area before the railway age.

The whole district cannot have been very attractive to railway promoters, the population being scattered thinly in isolated villages and farms, and the prospects of revenue from heavy freight negligible. As an additional disincentive, the fashionable watering-place of Weymouth showed no interest in trains, the belief being that a polite resort which was still basking in the glow of King George III's patronage had no need for such novelties. It was not until it became obvious to some businessmen of the town that trade was beginning to decline, as people favoured resorts on the railway map, that there was any enthusiasm whatsover, but at no stage did this enthusiasm extend to investing money! In short, it was not the sort of country through which an expensive railway line could be built with much hope of profit.

The Formative Years

It is important for the purposes of any railway history to look at the background in the heady days of the 'Railway Mania' when many railway schemes were projected. Many of the plans foundered, either due to lack of vision with regard to the routes proposed, or lack of financial backing. However, nearly a year before the opening of the Stockton & Darlington Railway, the first proposals for a railway between London and Bristol originated with the Merchants of Bristol as early as the autumn of 1824, and at a meeting on December 27th that year the 'London & Bristol Rail-Road Company' was formed. One of the directors was a famous road engineer of the day, John Loudon McAdam, and he was employed as the engineer of the line. Within a fortnight he had produced plans for a railway from Bristol to Brentford. No attempt was made to take the railway right into London, but as it was envisaged solely as a goods line this did not matter as merchandise could readily be distributed to most central areas of the Metropolis by river from the wharves at Brentford.

McAdam recommended that a turnpike road should also be made on the same line but, 'passing through the towns instead of near them, as the railroad must necessarily do'. At a meeting on 2nd February 1825, the directors adopted the plan and resolved to apply for an Act of Parliament for both the railway and turnpike schemes, but no application to parliament was made and we hear no more of the London & Bristol Rail-Road Company. Many other schemes were projected in 1825, but they did not come to fruition. For seven years there was a lull in railway activities in the Bristol area, but with the success of the Liverpool & Manchester (opened in 1830), and the Stockton & Darlington (1825), and lines proposed and surveyed between London and Birmingham and Liverpool and Birmingham, the idea of a railway link between Bristol and London was revived again in 1832 by two engineers, William Brunton and Henry Habberly Price. The route proposed was from Bristol, via Bath, Bradford and Trowbridge, then passing near Devizes and through the Pewsey Vale to Hungerford, thence through Newbury and Reading, Datchet, Colnbrook and Southall 'to a vacant site within three or four hundred yards of Edgware Road, Oxford Street, and the Paddington and City Road turnpike'.

A short branch was planned to unite this line with the intended Birmingham Railway, and thereby proceed towards the City as far as Battle Bridge. This project was announced by a circular headed 'Bristol and London Railway' and dated from 7th May 1832, and repeated by another letter in the following month, but although the planned railway project was still extant in January 1833, due to lack of financial support we hear no more of it. However, with railway fever still holding Bristol in its grip, and with much discussion in the press and between influential commercial groups, other persons were quick to adopt the idea. Four successful businessmen started the ball rolling in the autumn of 1832, with the result that, by the end of the year a committee of prominent merchants and others representing the five corporate bodies of Bristol – Bristol Corporation, Society of Merchant Venturers, Bristol Dock Company, Bristol Chamber of Commerce and the Bristol & Gloucestershire Railway – was appointed to investigate the practicability of a railway to London. Here indeed was a body with both teeth and financial support!

The first meeting was held on 21st January 1833, and the committee considered the matter generally and advertised for information. During the following month the constituent public bodies, having received favourable prospects for the intended line, provided funds for a preliminary survey and estimate, and this involved the selection of an engineer. On 7th March 1833, Isambard Kingdom Brunel was appointed to this important post at the age of 27. He, in company with W. H. Townsend, a land surveyor and valuer, set about surveying the country between Bristol and London. First, they inspected the route between Bath and Reading via Bradford, Devizes, the Pewsey Vale and Newbury, in the footsteps of the previous project, then the second route, north of the Marlborough Downs, via Chippenham, Swindon, the Vale of the White Horse and the Thames Valley. This latter being the route selected.

East of Maidenhead two or three lines of approach to the Capital were surveyed and left for later decision. With the surveys and estimates drawn up, a public meeting was held in the Guildhall at Bristol on 30th July 1833, at which it was declared that, 'a company should be resolved for the establishment of railway communication between Bristol and London'. At the same meeting it was proposed that a body of directors be appointed to represent Bristol in conjunction with a similar group in London, to constitute a General Body of Management for securing subscriptions and obtaining an Act of Parliament. The first joint meeting of the London and Bristol committees was held in London on 19th August 1833, the title 'Great Western Railway' being adopted instead of the 'Bristol and London Railroad' by which the scheme had originally been known. The capital was stated as £3,000,000 in shares of £100 each, deposit £5 per share. The cost of the 120-mile line was estimated at £2,805,330, and the prospective revenue at £747,752 per annum. A map showing the course of the railway, includes three 'probable branches' – from Didcot to Oxford, Swindon to Gloucester, and Chippenham to Bradford. The second reading of the Bill in the House of Commons was carried by 182 votes to 92 on 10th March 1834 and referred to Committee, but due to the violent opposition of the Eton College authorities the proposed branch to Windsor was dropped. The Committee met on 16th April with the proceedings taking 57 days to complete, with Brunel himself being cross-examined for eleven days! Chief objectors to the Bill included the many landowners of Middlesex, Buckinghamshire and Berkshire, plus Eton College, while further opposition came from the promoters of the 'narrow gauge' (4ft 8$\frac{1}{2}$in) London & Southampton Railway. This company was also looking for their own Act of Incorporation in the same session of Parliament and they attacked the GWR Bill by stating that Bristol and Bath could be equally well served by a branch from their line. This was the start of the bitter hostility between the two companies. However, the Committee approved the GWR Bill, and it passed the Commons only to be defeated in the House of Lords by 47 votes to 30 on 25th July.

The Company began making preparations for a new Bill the following year, and in September a supplementary prospectus, signed by the two secretaries of the Company, was issued inviting subscriptions for 10,000 additional shares, which, with the 10,000 already subscribed, would enable the directors to carry a Bill for the whole line through Parliament in the next session. Meanwhile, the London & Southampton, having obtained their Act, began another attack on the Great Western by promoting a 'narrow gauge' line from Basingstoke to Bristol via Newbury, Hungerford, Devizes, Trowbridge and Bradford. There was little support for the 'narrow gauge' scheme from either Bath or Bristol, and at a public meeting held in Bath in September by the London & Southampton, Brunel successfully demolished their arguments and the resolution was carried in the favour of the GWR. The London & Southampton, although rebuffed, was not put off by this result and proceeded with their Bill for the Basingstoke, Bath & Bristol Railway. The GWR, sensing that trouble could be looming with the proposed L&S line from Basingstoke, added a forked branch from Chippenham to Bradford and Trowbridge into their new Bill.

By the end of February 1835, the GWR was able to announce to the public that the whole of the 10,000 additional shares required by Parliament for the entire railway from London to Bristol, making, with the previous 10,000, a capital of £2 million, had been subscribed and that the petition for the Bill had been presented to the House of Commons. At long last, on 31st August 1835, the Bill received the Royal Assent, and the Great Western Railway was incorporated and empowered to make its line, the route being as follows: 'Commencing at or near a certain field called Temple Mead within the parish of Temple otherwise Holy Cross in the City and County of the City of Bristol, adjoining or near to the new cattle market there' and passing through specified parishes in the counties of Gloucester, Somerset, Wiltshire, Berkshire, Oxfordshire, Buckinghamshire, and Middlesex, 'and terminating by a junction with the London and Birmingham Railway in a certain field lying between the Paddington Canal and the Turnpike Road leading from London to Harrow on the western side of the General Cemetery in the Parish or Township of Hammersmith in the said County of Middlesex'. Also, a branch railway from near Thingley Farm, in the parish of Corsham, to a field near the Gas Works in the part of the parish of Trowbridge called Islington, with another branch thereout from the south western extremity of the village of Holt in the parish of Bradford, to the farmyard of Kingston Farm adjoining the town of Bradford. So at last the Great Western had succeeded where others had failed. It is interesting to note that the clauses in the Bill referring to the branches "from near Thingley Farm to Trowbridge" and "from Holt to Bradford" had been inserted especially to thwart the London & Southampton's ambition to construct a line from Basingstoke to Bristol. Once the Company had received Parliamentary authority it lost no time in making a start on the work, construction being commenced simultaneously at both the London and Bristol ends. The building of the original GWR main line has been well documented elsewhere, so for the purposes of this book we now return to Wiltshire and Somerset.

The rather grand-sounding Bath & Great Western Union Railway, which had emerged in 1836 with a scheme to link Weymouth with Bath by way of Cerne Abbas and Wincanton, had failed to materialise, and nothing further happened in the area until 1844 when Dorset and southern Somerset suddenly found themselves in the front line of the "Battle of the Gauges".

The Battle of the Gauges in the South 1844–1854

At the time the large and wealthy railway companies were establishing their territories, the 'narrow' (standard) gauge London & South Western was laying claim to Hampshire with a westernmost outpost at Salisbury in Wiltshire, the broad gauge alliance of the GWR and the Bristol & Exeter Railway were seeking a monopoly in the remainder of Wiltshire, Somerset and Devon. There were several undercurrents to all this planning, the GWR casting covetous eyes at Southampton and Portsmouth and the L&SWR yearning to reach Exeter or even further west. With the Parliamentary session of 1844 came the first signs of the coming battles between the GWR and its 'narrow gauge' enemy, the former London and Southampton which had been renamed the London & South Western in 1839. The first skirmish occurred at Newbury, with both companies intending to provide a railway connection to that town. The GWR proposed a branch from Pangbourne whilst the LSWR wanted a line from Basingstoke, with a possible extension to Swindon. In the event the result was a draw, both Bills being thrown out. The GWR Bill was defeated in the Commons by landowners' opposition, and the LSWR was rejected by the Lord's Committee.

The Great Western Chairman, Charles Russell, then communicated with William Chapman – his counterpart on the South Western, suggesting that a joint line be constructed from the South Western at Basingstoke to join the GWR between Pangbourne and Reading with a branch being laid from it to Newbury, the whole line being laid with a third rail to take both companys' stock. This suggestion was rejected by the South Western and swords were again drawn in preparation for the following parliamentary session. The battle lines were now drawn, with the Great Western proposing lines from Reading to Basingstoke and Newbury (known as the Berks & Hants Railway), and from Corsham to Salisbury with branch lines to Devizes, Bradford, Frome and a coal line to Radstock, the whole to be known as the Wilts & Somerset Railway.

The GWR had formulated the Wilts & Somerset at a meeting in Warminster on 9th July 1844. Brunel, in company with other officers of the Company, was present, and he presented his scheme for a line from Thingley Junction to Salisbury via Trowbridge and the Wylye Valley with branches to Bradford-on-Avon and Frome, and a branch from Melksham to Devizes. The GWR directors' report of August 1844 stated that the main object of the Corsham and Salisbury line was to afford, in conjunction with the London & South Western's authorized branch from Bishopstoke to Salisbury, a means of communication between Bristol and Bath, Southampton, Portsmouth and the Isle of Wight, 'superior in every respect to any railway which could be made between Basingstoke and Swindon'. This was not the only broad gauge project to worry the LSWR as the Bristol & Exeter Railway was striking out from the west with a line from near Taunton to Yeovil and onwards to Weymouth. In the autumn of the same year, the plans of the Great Western were altered, with the Newbury branch of the Berks & Hants being extended to Hungerford. However, at a meeting held in the George Inn, Frome, on 23rd October 1844 it was announced that the Bristol & Exeter was no longer interested in proceeding beyond Yeovil, and that public support should be given instead to an extension of the projected Wilts & Somerset line to Weymouth. An amended scheme was hastily prepared by the latter Company which left the original proposals undisturbed but extended the 'Frome Branch' to Weymouth with branches to Sherborne and Bridport. The branch from Trowbridge to Bradford-on-Avon was also extended through the Avon Valley to make another junction with the GWR main line at Bathampton. Despite these wide ranging extensions the 'Main Line' was still seen as running to Salisbury, but the name of the undertaking was amended to 'Wilts, Somerset & Weymouth Railway'.

It was these expansionist ideas that made Dorset, as yet unclaimed, something of a buffer zone. The time was right for a clever man to start the ball rolling with a locally funded railway scheme and then play the two major companies off against each other to obtain either a ready cash sale at a profit or very advantageous working arrangements. Such a man was Charles Castleman, a Wimborne solicitor, who was the moving spirit and principal promoter behind the Southampton & Dorchester Railway, a line to be constructed at minimal cost through easy country. This project linked the towns named in the title by way of Ringwood, Wimborne and Wareham. Bournemouth did not then exist, and the ancient port of Poole was to be served by a branch. Castleman was realistic enough to know that it might prove difficult to raise capital for a more ambitious plan, but made no secret of his ultimate aim of being a through line between Southampton and Exeter via Bridport and Axminster.

Castleman's westward extension from Dorchester was actually surveyed, and so sure was he of its excellence that he made the mistake of trying to dictate future LSWR policy over lines to the West. But the larger company was not inclined to dance to Castleman's tune and declined to come to terms over the project, so an approach was made to the GWR. Paddington was quick to realise that control of the Southampton & Dorchester would not only safeguard the whole of Dorset from L&SWR invasion but also open up a possible broad gauge route to Southampton, albeit a circuitous one. So, not only did they show interest in Castleman's offer by agreeing to take a lease of the line, but stated their willingness to promote a line that would connect with his, namely the Wilts, Somerset & Weymouth. Meanwhile, the London & South Western had placed their irons in the fire with two projected branches from Basingstoke – one to Didcot and the other to Swindon via Newbury – a cut-off line known as the 'Hookpit Deviation' from a point about two miles north of Winchester to join the Salisbury branch at Dunbridge, and extensions from Salisbury to Yeovil and Salisbury to Dorchester and Weymouth with a branch serving Poole. The South Western also supported the Cornwall & Devon Central Railway – a 'narrow gauge' project from Exeter, via Okehampton, Launceston and Bodmin to Truro and Falmouth. Due to lack of finance, a proposed line between Yeovil and Exeter was abandoned.

In 1844 a special committee of the Board of Trade, known in railway circles as 'The Five Kings' and headed by Lord Dalhousie, was appointed to examine all new railway Bills to weed out obvious non starters, thereby saving much valuable parliamentary time. The projected ideas from the two rival companies now went before the 'Five Kings'. On 31st December 1844, these worthies pronounced their judgement in favour of the Great Western and other broad gauge projects, and against the proposals of the London & South Western, including the Southampton & Dorchester's coastal line to Exeter. The GWR and the LSWR thereupon reached an uneasy truce not to invade each others' territory, and in an agreement between the two rivals dated 16th January 1845, the GWR with the assent of the Southampton & Dorchester, surrendered their interest in that line to the South Western and pledged not to promote any competing lines from Basingstoke.

The South Western for their part undertook to abide by the decision of the Board of Trade by withdrawing their own projects, all connection with the Cornwall & Devon Central Railway, and their opposition to the broad gauge lines sanctioned by the Board. They further promised not to promote extension lines from Salisbury or Dorchester which would compete with the Great Western, including its branches and the lines now sanctioned. The agreement was approved by both groups of shareholders at their respective General Meetings in February 1845. Peace therefore reigned between the two rival camps for the 1845 session, and the GWR forged ahead with projects in other parts of its empire.

The Bill incorporating the Wilts, Somerset & Weymouth Railway was passed on 30th June 1845, powers to lease the line being granted to the Great Western, who also appointed four of the twelve directors for the new company. Other Bills to pass through Parliament included the Berks & Hants, and the Bristol & Exeter Railway's Yeovil branch. Whilst considering the WS&W Bill the Lords Committee became convinced of the need for a direct line between the West of England and London, and obtained a pledge from the promoters counsel that any powers granted would not be used at some future date to oppose such a line being made through the district. The Southampton & Dorchester also received their Act of Incorporation with powers to lease or sell the railway to the South Western, and poor Castleman had perforce to go cap-in-hand to the LSWR Board in order to regain their support for his line. With the standard gauge company taking the place of the GWR in line with the January agreement, the intended broad gauge of the Southampton & Dorchester was now altered to standard, and provision had therefore to be made for laying mixed gauge track over the eight miles between Dorchester and Weymouth.

Construction work on the Southampton & Dorchester went ahead with some vigour, and the line was opened on 1st June 1847. It had always been the intention of the GWR that the Wilts & Somerset should form part of a main line to Exeter, and with Parliament attaching importance to a direct line to the West, Brunel was instructed by his directors to prepare proposals for the coming 1846 session. As the proposed line would inflict unfair competition upon the Bristol & Exeter the GWR decided that it was honour bound to make an arrangement with that company before actively promoting the direct line. The Great Western approached the B&E with terms considered favourable to both parties for the purchase of the Bristol & Exeter, but this proposal was rejected by the Board of the B&E by a sizeable majority. The Great Western, despite this rebuff, felt that they had done their best to appease the B&E, and carried on with their plans which can be summarised thus: To extend the Berks & Hants Railway from Hungerford to Westbury, with branch lines to Marlborough and Devizes, and to move the junction between the Weymouth and Salisbury lines to Westbury instead of Upton Scudamore. Furthermore, to promote a company entitled 'The Exeter Great Western Railway' to run from the Wilts & Somerset line at Yeovil to Exeter via Crewkerne, Axminster, Honiton, Ottery St Mary and Stoke Canon with branches to Bridport, Chard and Sidmouth.

As soon as the news of the intended GWR direct line reached the ears of the LSWR all hell was let loose and swords were drawn again! The uneasy truce of 1845 was quickly forgotten, the South Western rounding upon its broad gauge foe and seizing upon the proposed route as a pretext for breaking the agreement. The South Western protested to the Board of Trade that the agreement had been materially altered by the Great Western's new proposal, and requested that the Board of Trade receive a deputation to discuss a new line from Salisbury to Yeovil and Exeter which had been forbidden under the 1845 agreement, but which the Company now considered they were at liberty to promote in view of the GWR's apparent

breach of faith. The Board of Trade refused to become involved – a neutral stance, which greatly annoyed the LSW Board, who voted to press on with their West of England line with or without their blessing! They went on to signal the end of the truce by informing Paddington that they . . . "had come to the conclusion that in the present state of circumstances the London and South Western Railway Company are at liberty to act in such a manner as shall seem best for the interests of this Company". This brought forth a letter of protest from the GWR, in which the conduct of the 'narrow gauge' company was condemmed as "an unexampled breach of faith", but the gauge war had started again with a vengeance, and the 1846 session of Parliament saw the LSWR either promoting or actively supporting lines to Yeovil, Exeter and Dorchester plus the Devon & Cornwall Central lines. Of these, only the Basingstoke and Yeovil was to be immediately successful. The Devon & Cornwall failed standing orders, and the remainder were defeated by GWR opposition. However, Bills for the GWR proposals faced a two pronged attack from both the South Western and the Bristol & Exeter, and their Bills were thrown out by the Commons with the exception of the Cornwall and West Cornwall railways.

We now move on to the 1847 session of Parliament. The gauge battle was as bitter as ever with no quarter given on either side. The GWR reintroduced the Berks & Hants extension, and the Exeter Great Western – although the latter was now altered somewhat to include branches to Charmouth and Crewkerne, plus various plans for a central station in Exeter with connecting spurs to both the Bristol & Exeter and South Devon Railways. The GWR also promoted the Compton & Wilton line connecting Yeovil with Salisbury from a point on the Weymouth line north east of Yeovil to Wilton on the Salisbury line. The Exeter Great Western Bill was again opposed by the Bristol & Exeter, who in turn were promoting their own Bill for a railway from Durston to Castle Cary on the WS&W. The London & South Western, in the same session, requested powers to construct the Salisbury & Yeovil line, and supported the Exeter, Yeovil & Dorchester and Cornwall & Devon Central companies. Eventually, after a lengthy 53-day fight in the Committee stage, the Berks & Hants extension, the B&E Durston to Castle Cary line, and the 'narrow gauge' lines from Salisbury to Yeovil, and Exeter, Yeovil & Dorchester, passed through the Commons. The Cornwall & Devon Central, and the Exeter Great Western were again thrown out. As it was late in the session, the passed Bills entered the House of Lords the following year, and after another lengthy battle they were passed by the Upper House.

Having opened both the Southampton and Dorchester line, and the branch from Bishopstoke to Salisbury (Milford) in 1847, and having completed some construction work on the section between Basingstoke and Salisbury, the LSWR allowed the other powers obtained in the 1846 session to lapse. This was much to the displeasure of the citizens of Salisbury, who set about the creation of an independent company to build the line westward to Yeovil and to take over the uncompleted works of the direct line from Basingstoke via Andover to their city. This well-intentioned idea came to grief in the Parliamentary sessions of 1851 and 1852, but the following year the LSWR decided to give it support lest the promoters became involved with the GWR. On that occasion the Bill was successful, a penalty clause suspending the LSWR's dividends in the event of late completion of the line, being inserted. At this time all was not well with the LSWR, various factions on the Board being at odds with each other over the western extension of the system. Castleman and his Engineer, Moorson, were actively pushing their 'coastal' line to Exeter from Dorchester – a scheme favoured by some LSW directors – whilst an influential group headed by Locke (by that time MP for Honiton) favoured the 'Central Line' from Yeovil.

The Great Western, witnessing the infighting of the rival camp – and perhaps seeing a chink in the enemy armour – prepared themselves for one last mighty battle against their rival. Their plan was set out at the GWR half-yearly meeting on 12th August 1852, and the battleground was set once again in Dorset. A proposed joint line (Great Western and the Bristol & Exeter) known as the Devon & Dorset Railway, would run from a triangular junction at Maiden Newton on the Wilts, Somerset & Weymouth, through Powerstock, Netherbury, Bettiscombe and Chardstock to Axminster, thence via Honiton and Ottery St Mary to join the B&E south of Stoke Canon. Two branch lines were proposed on the new line: Netherbury to Bridport Harbour, and Ottery to Sidmouth.

In view of the financial plight of the WS&W at the time, owing to its non-completion, and lawsuits flying everywhere from citizens disenchanted with the progress of the undertaking, one has to ask if this scheme was put forward solely to spike both of the rival companies' projects. The Bill for the said line was placed before Parliament in 1853, and by the time it had been read for a second time there was an uneasy stirring in the enemy camp. Sensing that the combined GWR and B&E forces might be on to a winner, the South Western held a special meeting of the shareholders in May of the same year. They had to face the stark choice of pledging themselves to back the coastal scheme from Dorchester, or risk losing the whole district to the broad gauge. When the vote was taken it authorised the directors to apply for powers at the earliest moment for the coastal route from Dorchester to Exeter via Bridport and Axminster. Such was the urgency to proceed with this venture it was agreed the capital should be raised by the L&SWR itself, and not through an independent company.

On 17th June 1853 the House of Commons Committee sat to hear evidence for and against the Devon & Dorset Bill. The London & South Western had organized a massive lobby of landowners with petitions against the proposed line, and doubtless to the pleasure of that company, and the dismay of the Great Western, there were also petitions from the inhabitants of the towns which were disenchanted – to put it mildly – with the GWR for delays in constructing the authorized lines in their area, namely the Wilts, Somerset & Weymouth. At the hearing the GWR witnesses, Brunel and Saunders, faced severe criticism over the non-completion of the WS&W which added great weight to their rival's argument. The Bristol & Exeter did not attend the meeting. The Hon. Francis Scott, MP Chairman of the London & South Western Railway, pledged that if the Devon & Dorset Bill was defeated, his company would forthwith apply to Parliament for the powers to construct the coastal route from Dorchester. To bolster his argument he had a formidable backing, including the Home Secretary, Lord Palmerston, Secretary of War and MP for South Wilts, the Hon Sidney Herbert, former Foreign Secretary, Lord Malmesbury, Commander in Chief of the Army, General Lord Hardinge, and First Lord of the Admiralty, Sir James Graham. The two latter gentlemen gave witness to the fact that the defence of the country from Dover to Plymouth would be best served by a railway without a break of gauge, but if this was unavoidable then it should be as far west as possible. In view of this weight of argument and the pledge given by the South Western that they would apply for powers in the following session to proceed with the coastal route, the committee found in favour of the L&SWR and the Devon & Dorset Bill was defeated. As far as further endeavours in the South West were concerned, the broad gauge cause in the disputed areas of the South was smashed beyond repair with the defeat of the Devon & Dorset Bill. Although more skirmishes were to follow in other areas in the years ahead, the GWR now abandoned any ideas of advancing in the area between Salisbury and Exeter via Dorchester.

Construction of the Wilts, Somerset & Weymouth

Construction work on the WS&W was put in hand fairly quickly as soon as the Act of Parliament of 30th June 1845 was received, and the first meeting of the directors was held on 1st August 1845. Isambard Kingdom Brunel was duly appointed engineer of the line, with Mr Ward becoming resident engineer for the sections from Thingley Junction to Salisbury and from Frome to Radstock, whilst Mr Peniston was employed in a similar capacity for the Frome to Weymouth section. Brunel stated that the land between Thingley and Westbury had been pegged out for an immediate start on construction, and by October of the same year the line was marked out as far as Salisbury and almost to Bruton. Work started at the northern end of the route and land was purchased and contracts let out along the length of the line. By February 1846, contractors had erected their workshops at Melksham and were 'to break ground' immediately, whilst on the Weymouth section at Holywell, at the summit of the Evershot bank, working shafts had been sunk to the crown of the tunnel, and by August of the same year the Melksham and Trowbridge contracts were in full operation and also at seven different places near Sparkford and Yeovil, and also at Evershot where the heaviest engineering works took place.

By a supplementary Act of 1846, the Company was authorized to alter the junction of the Salisbury & Weymouth lines from Upton Scudamore to Westbury, and the junction of the Devizes branch from Melksham to Holt, short deviations at Thingley, Frome and near Dorchester, and extensions to the quays at Weymouth, and a line from Bradford to join the GWR main line at Bathampton were authorized by this same Act. A further Act of 1847 allowed an improved line between Frome and Bruton. But in 1847/8 came the depression. Loans were almost unobtainable and calls on shares went unpaid. Many railway schemes were now in trouble, and the WS&W itself ran out of money after completing just under 14 miles of double track from the junction with the GWR main line at Thingley to Westbury. Stations were provided at Melksham and Trowbridge. This section (the only one completed by the independent WS&W) was opened on 5th September 1848, but the financial outlook was so bleak that all further work was suspended and the contractors were dismissed.

Some of the land was re-let, much of it to the previous owners and the countryside for many miles along the route was punctuated with stretches of half-completed earthworks and bridges. The branch from Staverton to Bradford was completed and Bradford station built, but the rails were not laid on this section, much to the annoyance of the local populace! On 4th June 1849 the WS&W directors were advised by the Great Western to suspend all the workings of the line except the section from Westbury to Frome. In a report to the shareholders presented with the half-yearly accounts in January 1850, the GWR advised that the lines should not be extended for the present beyond Frome and Warminster.

Although the WS&W was a nominally independent concern it had always in reality been a creature of the GWR, the hope being entertained that a seemingly local company would make better progress with raising subscriptions. By now it was obvious that this was untrue, so the pretence was ended by the GWR taking over the WS&W and its unfinished line of railway on 14th March 1850. The GWR gave the shareholders of the now defunct company 4% guaranteed stock in lieu of their ordinary shares – a purely paper transaction since the GWR had, from the line's inception, guaranteed 4% on the capital and invested £545,000 in the project. Transfer of the former company to the GWR was confirmed by Parliament on 3rd July 1851, and the erstwhile Wilts, Somerset & Weymouth Company was dissolved.

Times were still hard, but the greater resources available to the mighty Great Western enabled some further work to be done. Construction forged ahead to Warminster on the Salisbury line, and the section from Westbury to Frome was given top priority in the hope that bringing the line close to the Somerset coalfield would attract lucrative freight traffic. The station at Frome was in the course of construction by 5th August

1850 and was virtually complete by the 25th of that month. Trackwork was being laid at Clink on 8th September, but although the trackbed and bridges between Westbury and Frome were set out for double track, this 5 mile 61 chain section was laid as a single line and eventually opened on 7th October 1850.

The 4 mile 73 chain section from Westbury to Warminster was opened as a single line on 9th September 1851. The coal branch from Frome to Radstock was started, but there was some difficulty in purchasing the land, and again money ran out and all work ceased. The people of Bradford-on-Avon, who had seen their station completed in every detail apart from the laying of track, had good reason to be furious that no attempt was made to finish their part of the line. Indeed, there was a general disenchantment with the GWR throughout the district, and many towns – including Devizes, which was pressing for the completion of its branch, served Bills of Mandamus upon the GWR which culminated in a lawsuit at Somerset Assizes in the Michaelmas Term of 1852; a writ against the railway company being sought to compel them to complete and open the whole system. This action met with only limited success. The GWR, being able to prove that their financial position was far from strong, was successful in defeating many of the lawsuits, but Mandamus was made absolute for the Avon Valley section through Bradford-on-Avon to Bathampton. The GWR lodged an appeal against the order, but it was dismissed, with the Exchequer Chamber deciding that under the terms of the 1845 Act, the Company could be compelled to make the branch.

With land being purchased beyond Frome for the continuation of the line, and the company entering negotiations with various local bodies in order to obtain the capital for finishing the railway, the GWR, under an Act of 1852 made another attempt to stimulate local interest by floating a separate company under the title 'Frome, Yeovil & Weymouth Railway'. The Act contained a clause that the agreement with the GWR should be void unless the the whole capital was subscribed within three months, but this was not

An old postcard view of Adderwell, Frome. Three Dean clerestory coaches, and a six-wheeled van stand on the sidings west of Frome station. To the left of the coaches can be seen the old Frome South signal box standing near the engine shed. This signal box was closed on 17th September 1933 and replaced by a new South box located at the Westbury end of the 'down' platform.

Gerald Quartley Collection

successful and the Frome, Yeovil & Weymouth Railway Company was dissolved. This left the Great Western with no option but to finance the line itself, which it was not happy to do, but at the same time they did not want the area to fall into the hands of its rival, the London & South Western. At this time the Great Western allowed the powers to lapse regarding construction of the Sherborne and Bridport branches.

On 31st July 1854 the GWR obtained another Act of Parliament, granting an extension of time to complete the unfinished sections of the WS&W, the Act containing a penalty clause that allowed for suspension of the Company's dividends if the works were not finished within two years. The Bill also contained details of arrangements with the LSWR at Dorchester, of which more anon. Although Mandamus had been granted for the Avon Valley line and some work had recommenced on that section, cutting through the great embankments of the Kennet & Avon Canal was proving a tedious and costly business, and this was destined to be the last part of the WS&W system to be opened for traffic. Elsewhere a little construction was being done as finances permitted, the 8 mile 19 chain mineral branch from Frome to Radstock being opened on 14th November 1854. By this time there was little enthusiasm for the lines beyond Frome. The railway had been so long in the building that times had changed completely since the original scheme had been drawn up, and the long section into Dorset, never tremendously attractive from a revenue point of view, offered even less prospect of paying a return on the investment. Early in 1855 the GWR found itself having to raise more capital, to the sum of £1,325,000, to complete various works, including the Wilts, Somerset & Weymouth. In the shareholders' report of January 1856 it was revealed that £1,433,000 had already been spent on the WS&W, £750,000 of this sum being used on land and works on the unfinished parts of the line beyond Frome and Warminster. At the time only 31½ miles of the project were open for traffic.

Yeovil, the only intermediate place of any consequence, already had a broad gauge branch from the Bristol & Exeter at Durston which had opened to a station at Hendford (on the western edge of the town) on 1st October 1853, and the 'narrow gauge' Salisbury & Yeovil looked certain to succeed. Further south, the Southampton & Dorchester had opened on 1st June 1847, and this line was bound to attract most of the London traffic by virtue of its considerably shorter route, no matter what service the GWR was able to provide. Indeed, the GWR now viewed the completion of the WS&WR as nothing but a necessary evil to protect their empire in the west from standard gauge expansionism, for despite the truce of 1844, the L&SWR had made some advances into Great Western territory, and were again showing interest in the extension from Dorchester to Exeter. Castleman's Dorchester terminus had been laid out as a through station with this extension in mind, and the project remained a serious threat to the GWR until 1856, when it was killed off by the passing of the Bill for the L&SWR Yeovil to Exeter line.

Despite the political urgency of completing the WS&W it was another two years before any of it was brought into service, the 19½-mile section from Warminster to Salisbury opening on 30th June 1856. This was followed by the 26-mile section between Frome and Yeovil, with stations at Witham, Bruton, Castle Cary, Sparkford, Marston (renamed Marston Magna in 1895), and Yeovil Pen Mill, on 1st September of the same year. Of these stations only Marston was not equipped with a passing loop, but there is evidence

Staff and passengers pose for the camera in the gloomy interior of Yeovil Pen Mill station. The internal footbridge connecting the platforms can be seen at the far end, and boxes of gloves on the porter's barrow await collection by the next 'up' train. Yeovil was once famous for its glove making industry and many local factories produced gloves for export and delivery around the country. The overall roof was removed in 1934.

Lens of Sutton

15

A view of Marston Magna station looking west and taken before the First World War. The footpath leading down from the Rimpton road to the 'up' platform can be seen to the right, loaded milk churns stand on barrows on the 'up' platform awaiting collection by the next train, and empty churns await collection on the 'down' platform. The Station Master walks along the platform, whilst a young child watches the cameraman. Oil lamps grace the platforms and the footpath, and the signal arms are 'off' for the 'up' and 'down' lines. Note the carefully tended hedge rows in the lane behind the 'down' platform. The fields to the left were to form part of the huge ammunition depot constructed there during the Second World War.

L. Sayers

to suggest that the loops were infrequently used in the early years – especially that at Bruton. Both of these extensions were single track, although the bridges and earthworks were wide enough for double line.

The 27½-mile Yeovil to Weymouth section was laid as a single line using bridge rails, varying from 61 to 68lb per yard, on longitudinal sleepers. Here again the earthworks were constructed for double track. This section contained the heaviest engineering works, including nine viaducts varying in length from 22 yards to 102 yards, and constructed variously of stone or timber. There were four tunnels, (Holywell 311 yards, Frampton 660 yards, Poundbury 264 yards and Bincombe 814 yards) plus two lesser tunnels of 40 yards and 20 yards.

Stations were provided at Yetminster, Evershot, Maiden Newton, Grimstone (renamed Grimstone & Frampton in 1858), Dorchester and Weymouth. (Upwey was not opened until 1871.) The line opened on 20th January 1857 and a sharply-curved single mixed gauge connecting spur was laid between the two rival's lines at Dorchester Junction, with double mixed gauge track between that point and Weymouth. On the same day as the Yeovil to Weymouth section was opened, 'narrow gauge' trains from the Southampton & Dorchester station were also extended to Weymouth. The Act of Parliament dated 31st July 1854 enforced a curious arrangement between the two companies whereby the GWR laid an additional rail over their property for eight miles, between Dorchester Junction and Weymouth, for use by LSWR traffic in return for a similar distance of broad gauge track on the Southampton & Dorchester line. This was complied with to the letter, the broad gauge rail fizzling out in empty heathland about halfway between Moreton and Wool! It was certainly of no operational use whatsoever, and one wonders what the GWR Board had in mind when asking for it. Perhaps it was still seen as offering a broad gauge approach to Southampton! Apart from the double-track section from Dorchester to Weymouth, the remainder of the WS&W was single, except for the original section from Thingley Junction to Westbury. The Bristol & Exeter opened a spur from their station at Hendford (Yeovil), to the GWR station at Yeovil Pen Mill on 2nd February 1857, this opening up a broad gauge communication between Westbury and Taunton via Durston.

The initial service of five trains per day each way was not generous, but no doubt adequate for the available traffic. In any case, the long stretches of single track, coupled to the heavy gradients on the southern section, made anything more ambitious impossible. The last section to be opened was, ironically, that for which the Assize Court had issued a writ of Mandamus back in 1852, namely the 9½-mile Avon Valley line from Bradford Junction (north of Trowbridge) to Bathampton which opened on 2nd February 1857. The long suffering residents of Bradford-on-Avon, who had been waiting for over seven years for rails to reach their completed station, received some reward for their patience in the form of a free excursion train to Weymouth. Having regard to the time of year, most of those who availed themselves of this offer probably did so for the novelty of the journey rather than the appeal of visiting a cold seaside town out of season! Also in 1857, the 8-mile branch from Holt Junction to Devizes was opened on 1st July. The WS&W had only been operational as a through line from Westbury to Weymouth for a short time, when the Bridport Railway Company, incorporated on 5th May 1855, made connection with it at Maiden Newton.

The Permanent Way Gang pose proudly for the camera at Marston Magna before the First World War. True to the tradition of the early railway navvies, each man wears the hallmark of his trade, namely the waistcoat. The railway navvies in the early days, when railways were being built all over the country at the time of the railway mania, wore a purple waistcoat to distinguish themselves from other types of labourers. The old gentleman in the middle of the group must have started in the days of the broad gauge and the youngest member of the gang, standing to the far left, is wielding a fearsome looking shovel. Milk churns are being sorted on the 'down' platform and school children look on curiously.

Miss D. Penny

The busy little market town of Bridport, long famous for the manufacture of rope, nets and twine, had featured in several early railway projects, perhaps the most interesting being Castleman's "Dorchester and Exeter Coast Extension" of 1851 which promised the town the security of being placed on an important trunk line. In the end, however, Bridport had to settle for a locally promoted branch line from Maiden Newton which opened on 12th November 1857. The 9-mile branch was worked by the GWR from the start. It was laid with MacDonnell patent permanent way, which consisted of 51lb bridge rails on longitudinal

Witham station, looking east in the early 1900s. The nameboard on the 'up' platform reads: 'WITHAM SHEPTON MALLET and WELLS JUNCTION'. A Dean clerestory is stabled in the branch bay awaiting the next trip along the 'Strawberry line'. Note the platform awning which is extended from the bay platform overall roof, while oil lamps and milk churns abound. The main station buildings are grouped on the 'up' platform, with a stone waiting shelter provided on the 'down' platform.

Lens of Sutton

rolled iron sleepers secured to each other by screw bolts and nuts, the gauge being maintained by angle cross ties situated 9ft apart. A strip of wood was inserted between the rails and sleepers to maintain flexibility. Although the harbour had been seen as a valuable source of traffic by most of the previous schemes, the Bridport Railway as built made no attempt to reach it, the terminus being over a mile inland. This railway did eventually reach the coast, in 1884, by means of the West Bay Extension, but this was intended to foster holiday traffic rather than freight business and no physical connection with the harbour was made.

It is not surprising that the Somerset town of Shepton Mallet and the neighbouring cathedral city of Wells, both places of considerable local importance, were early candidates for railway connection. The East Somerset Railway Company, which made a junction with the WS&W at Witham, opened a 9-mile branch to Shepton Mallet on 9th November 1858, the line being extended by a further $4^1/2$ miles to Wells on 1st March 1862. Nine years later the railway from Yatton also reached Wells, but although both of these lines were broad gauge through running was impossible because the distance between the two stations in the city, about 500 yards, was owned by the standard gauge Somerset Central who had established their terminus at Priory Road in March 1859. Although an agreement was reached to mix the gauge over this short section to facilitate through broad gauge running, the Board of Trade objected to the arrangements and the two lines were worked as separate units until January 1878. From that time the East Somerset station in Wells was relegated to goods traffic, passenger business for GWR trains being concentrated at Tucker Street station. Great Western trains, although passing through the platform at Priory Road station, did not call there until October 1934. The Cheddar Valley line – as the whole route from Witham to Yatton soon became known – was one of the more successful branch lines, serving several small towns and developing a healthy excursion business between Bath, Bristol, and Cheddar and Wookey caves. There was also a good level of freight traffic, the area being noted for its limestone quarries.

At first there was no rail connection to the harbour at Weymouth, despite the existence of a well established steam packet service between that port and the Channel Islands. Indeed, the prospectus of the WS&W made no mention of shipping traffic, and it fell to a local company, the Weymouth & Portland Railway, to provide the necessary link. This company was incorporated in June 1862 to build a single-track line from a junction just outside Weymouth station to Portland, with a tramway through the streets to the quay. It was no coincidence that the Weymouth & Portland's secretary, Joseph Maunders, held a similar post with the Weymouth & Channel Islands Steam Packet Company! Both lines were completed in 1864, but the opening was delayed until 18th October the following year because the Board of Trade was unhappy about the stability of two viaducts on the Portland line. The lines were leased jointly by the GWR and the LSWR from the outset, although the harbour tramway was used solely by horse drawn goods traffic until 1880.

The standard gauge competitor at Yeovil had become a reality in 1860 with the opening of the line from Salisbury, which at first terminated at the Bristol & Exeter station at Hendford, but was extended to Exeter within a few weeks. All goods traffic between this line and the WS&W had to be exchanged via the congested depot at Hendford until 13th June 1864, when the GWR opened a branch which ran directly from their line to exchange sidings and a transhipment shed adjoining Yeovil Junction station, known as Clifton Maybank Goods.

On 21st June 1871 a station was opened at Upwey in response to a memorial from local residents. At first only GWR trains called, those of the LSWR not doing so until February the following year. The station at Upwey was to be the last development of the broad gauge era which came to a close on the WS&W on the weekend of 18th–22nd June 1874. In those few hectic days the entire WS&W system was converted to standard gauge, and over the next 25 years most of it was doubled. This paved the way for faster and more frequent services. The standardisation of gauge also opened up an alternative route to Bristol. As previously stated, Radstock had been given a branch from the WS&W at Frome in 1854, but this was seen as a mineral line and no attempt was made to introduce a passenger service. Passenger facilities arrived at Radstock on 3rd September 1873 with the opening of the standard gauge Bristol & North Somerset Railway. This new line also won much of the coal traffic because it opened up a new mining area around Pensford and Clutton, and avoided transhipment for Radstock coal consigned to destinations off the broad gauge map – the break of gauge at Radstock required all through traffic to be transhipped. However, this state of affairs ended when the Frome to Radstock branch was converted to standard gauge in 1874, but passenger services were not introduced over the Frome–Radstock section until 5th July 1875, after the west curve was laid north from Frome station to join the former mineral branch, thereby creating a triangular junction.

The year 1885 saw the emergence of the last, and least important branch line – that from Upwey Junction to Abbotsbury – which despite its purely local character, raised once again the spectre of the coastal line to Exeter. This railway, which opened on 9th November 1885, made extravagant claims about opening up vast mineral deposits in the Waddon Valley, and offering a short route from Plymouth and Exeter to France by building a costly extension from Abbotsbury to Axminster via Bridport which would allow through running between the West of England and Weymouth Quay. One has only to view the hilly country west of Abbotsbury to realise the enormous expense involved in such a project, and anyway 1885 was too late in the railway age for a scheme of this nature to succeed. The mineral traffic also proved to be largely illusary, and the line was never profitable. At first there were no exchange facilities between the main line and this branch, all traffic circulating via Weymouth, but on 19th April 1886 the existing Upwey station was closed and a new junction station opened 35 chains to the south. This, like its predecessor, had no sidings for goods traffic, although public goods facilities for the district were available at Upwey station on the branch itself.

The Line in the Twentieth Century

The early years of the twentieth century were to see part of the WS&W transformed from a sluggish backwater into a first class main line, although the impetus for this work came from well outside the area. The

The staff pose for the camera as a 'down' train approaches Sparkford station in June 1915. The Station Master stands on the platform, whilst the shunter leans on his shunting pole and the signalman looks out of the box window. Barrels stand outside the former broad gauge goods shed which contains plenty of freight traffic, with more freight wagons standing on the 'down' sidings to the right.

H. Trim

GWR and LSWR were in hot competition for the lucrative West of England traffic, especially the prestigious ocean liner business between the docks at Plymouth and London, but the Great Western was somewhat disadvantaged by the circuitous route via Bristol which had earned it the nickname "Great Way Round". It was therefore decided to provide a much shorter route which involved three totally new lengths of railway and the upgrading of three existing sections. New lines, with moderate gradients and easy curves suitable for fast running, were to be constructed between Patney and Chirton and Westbury, Castle Cary and Curry Rivel, and Athelney and Cogload. East of Patney the existing Berks & Hants line from Newbury was to be improved, as was that section of the WS&W between Westbury and Castle Cary. The old Bristol & Exeter Railway Yeovil branch was to be doubled and realigned between Curry Rivel and Athelney. This was no mean undertaking, and it took several years to complete. The first section, through the Stert Valley from Patney to Westbury, was opened for goods on 29th July 1900, with a local passenger service commencing on 1st October.

Westbury station was rebuilt in its present form of two island platforms, and the track layout was considerably enlarged and remodelled in anticipation of the extra traffic. Westward of Castle Cary the new line was brought into use in stages. Somewhat oddly, the section to Charlton Mackerell was opened as soon as it was ready on 1st July 1905, although business must have been extremely thin. A local goods service was extended to Somerton on 20th May the following year, and on 11th June, through freight services between London and the West began running over the new route. A few weeks later on 2nd July, some expresses began running "via Castle Cary", and with the introduction of the next timetable, all daytime trains were

switched to this line, although some of the overnight services continued to run via Bristol.

The year 1905 also saw the introduction of a railmotor service between Weymouth and Dorchester, three new halts – Upwey Wishing Well (28th May), Came Bridge and Radipole (1st July) – being opened for the occasion. Came Bridge was intended to serve the golf club on Came Down, but was of more value to the residents of Winterborne Monkton and was renamed Monkton and Came Halt after only a few months. At the same time a similar local service was provided on the original section of the WS&W between Trowbridge and Chippenham, with new halts at Lacock, Beanacre, Broughton Gifford and Staverton. The Great War certainly brought much additional traffic onto the WS&W although it left little lasting impression except for on the Westbury–Salisbury section. Large tracts of downland had been purchased by the War Office in 1895, and a number of military camps established along the western edge of Salisbury Plain. These camps brought considerable traffic onto the line, even in peacetime, but the outbreak of war increased it to the extent that many additional sidings had to be provided, together with goods running loops between Codford and Sherrington Crossing, and branch lines from Heytesbury to Sutton Veny Camp and from Codford to Codford Camp. Both of these branch lines were to vanish after the end of hostilities, never to reappear, but the goods loops at Codford, although removed at the same time, were reinstated during the Second World War.

The inter-war years were not easy for the railways. Heavy industry was in depression with a consequent loss of freight revenue, and this was further eroded by the emergence of a serious competitor in the form of the road haulier. The private motor car remained the province of the wealthy and was not a very serious

19

Mr George Foot stands in front of a wagon of Somerset coal, which he has unloaded into sacks at Marston Magna; the scales for weighing the bagged coal can be seen in the truck. Mr Foot worked for the Somerset Trading Company in their yard at the station, attending to customers who called for goods, coal or bricks, which could be taken away in their wagons and wheelbarrows. The wooden four-plank coal wagon, No. 93, has come from the Somerset coalfield via Radstock and Frome, and is marked 'Empty to Radstock GWR.' Mr George Foot died at Marston Magna in 1960 aged 95.

G. March

threat, but local passenger traffic was under attack from bus services which could penetrate into the very hearts of villages and drop their customers off at any convenient point en route. In an effort to combat this bus competition the GWR embarked on a programme of new halts – unstaffed platforms, cheaply constructed and offering minimal facilities, at which local trains could pause briefly to pick up or set down (sometimes by request only). Although the large village of Cattistock was situated close to the railway, the populace had always been obliged to walk to Maiden Newton until a halt was opened to serve the village on 3rd August 1931. Other halts soon followed – Strap Lane (18th July 1932), Bradford Peverell and Stratton (22nd May 1933), Chetnole (11th September 1933), and finally Thornford Bridge (23rd March 1936), and to cater for the new halts the railmotor service was extended from Dorchester to Maiden Newton or Yeovil. Strap Lane was the odd one out, being situated on the main line between Bruton and Witham and was served by a few Westbury to Taunton stopping trains.

Another development of the time was holiday traffic. Holidays with pay were now becoming the norm, and the ordinary working man was becoming sufficiently affluent to take his family to the seaside for a week or two, but not yet affluent enough to purchase his own transport. Summer weekends therefore witnessed a tremendous rush of additional trains, many of them very heavily loaded. The section between Westbury and Castle Cary, which had to contend not only with the extra Weymouth traffic but also the many holiday expresses bound for the West Country, was worked to saturation level, and delays were often caused by congestion at Westbury and by the severe speed restrictions through Frome station. The GWR therefore decided to bypass the two bottlenecks by constructing avoiding lines which came into use on 1st January 1933. At first only goods trains used them, but express trains were booked over the new lines with the

Yeovil Pen Mill looking east pre 1934. A 'down' express headed by a 'Bulldog' 4-4-0 stands at the island platform. Freight wagons are lined up in the goods yard to the right. The timber all-over roof can be seen in the background, straddling the two platforms. An extension awning covers the main part of the 'down' platform, and the curving 'dog leg' preventing fast through running on the 'up' line can be seen in the foreground.

Lens of Sutton

The bridge over the Frome to Warminster road is seen under construction for the new Frome avoiding line, pictured here on 6th July 1931. Two level crossing gates have been erected to the left, these being for the contractor's trains (the tops of the rails can be seen in front of the fence at the bottom of the embankment) to travel over the road from one end of the new workings to the other without disturbing work on the new bridge.

National Railway Museum

start of the summer timetable that year. Four new signal boxes were opened to control the junctions between the new avoiding lines and the original route – which of course remained open for local freight and passenger traffic – Heywood Road Junction and Fairwood Junction at Westbury, and Clink Road Junction and Blatchbridge Junction at Frome.

It is impossible to say whether many of the halts were actually a success in their own right because within a few years the outbreak of World War II and the subsequent rationing of petrol brought to them, and indeed to the railways as a whole, an artificially inflated level of traffic. Once again the WS&W line became busy with military traffic, although by far the greatest flow was over the Salisbury line. A few new features appeared in connection with the Second World War, most notably additional signal boxes to control War Department sidings at Lacock and Beanacre on the Thingley to Westbury section, and at Beechgrove on the Salisbury line. The goods loops were also reinstated between Codford and Sherrington with a new signal box being opened at the latter location. On the Weymouth section a siding at Beer Hackett serving a government buffer store, and operated by a ground frame released by Yetminster signal box was brought into use. Long goods loops were provided at Castle Cary after the bombing in 1942, a long reception loop serving a War Department supply depot was installed at Marston Magna, and a new connection between the Southern Railway Yeovil Town branch and the WS&W line at Yeovil South Junction. The Clifton Maybank goods branch had closed in 1937, and the exchange of traffic had again been via Yeovil Town station or Hendford goods from that time. It was obvious that the great increase in freight traffic generated by wartime conditions would lead to problems, and anyway, the government was anxious to see alternative routes made available in case a line was knocked out by enemy action. The new junction at Yeovil offered through running between the Paddington line at Castle Cary and Exeter via the Southern Railway main line at Yeovil Junction, a valuable escape route if the Taunton line was out of commission. The lever frame in Yeovil South Junction was actually laid out to allow for another junction from

the Weymouth direction towards Yeovil Town station, but this was never installed. The signal box and connections were constructed by Canadian troops over a period of three days, and came into service on 13th October 1943.

Government sidings were opened at Sparkford in May 1944 and a new signal box was opened in 1940 at Alford Halt, on the West of England main line between Castle Cary and Keinton Mandeville. This controlled access to the vast ammunition depot at Dimmer Camp. Also on the main line at Somerton, up and down loops each capable of holding 86 wagons plus locomotive and brake van, were installed in 1943. The Weymouth line certainly did its share for the War Effort, huge tonnages of supplies being carried in connection with various stores depots, military camps, airfields, and other important establishments in the area, as well as that for the strategic Naval base at Portland.

Nationalisation of the railways after the war made little difference at first, but soon the end of petrol rationing and the growing popularity of the private car were making it obvious that the future must bring contraction. In 1950, the line south of Castle Cary, including the Yeovil to Taunton branch as far as Langport, and the Bridport, Abbotsbury and Portland branch lines, were transferred to Southern Region control, but this was purely an administrative matter and made little impact upon the train services. The only visible signs of new management arrived slowly over a period of years, and included a sprinkling of upper quadrant signals and green paint on the stations. Just two years after this transfer came the first signs of retrenchment, with the Portland branch closing to passengers on 2nd March, and the Abbotsbury line closing completely on 1st December, 1952. Actually, closure of the latter was not quite complete, a section of about half a mile between Upwey Junction and Upwey being retained for goods traffic. Upwey Junction subsequently became Upwey & Broadwey, and Upwey became Upwey Goods. The Westbury to Salisbury line, which had also been placed under Southern Region control south of Dilton Marsh, was next to witness economies, with all stations between Warminster and Salisbury being closed from 19th September 1955.

On the sections of the WS&W still administered from Paddington, the 1950s brought few changes, the only one of note being the closure of Strap Lane Halt on 5th June 1950. This halt had already undergone a period of closure as a wartime economy, and its early demise was not surprising. The end of the decade brought many changes which were a mixture of cuts and improvements. Many of the cuts were not very significant, although the Frome to Bristol line via Radstock lost its passenger service on 2nd November 1959. Two years prior to this the halts at Upwey Wishing Well and Monkton & Came had closed on 7th January 1957, but on 4th April that year a more positive note was sounded by the opening of a new signal box at Weymouth to replace the two delapidated ex-GWR boxes. In connection with this work two new platforms capable of dealing with twelve-coach trains were brought into use, and the layout was improved to allow all six platforms to be used by either arrivals or departures. The winter timetable of 1959 introduced dmus on many of the local services, but steam remained in charge of freight and parcels traffic as well as some of the longer distance trains.

An unexpected boost to traffic came in 1960 with the Southern Region withdrawing shipping facilities between Southampton and the Channel Islands and concentrating the traffic on Weymouth. Long fully-fitted trains conveying tomatoes, potatoes, green vegetables, or flowers (according to season) laboured over the gradients of the WS&W with ever increasing frequency, and additional sidings were provided both at Weymouth station and on the quay tramway. The future looked secure, and the general feeling of prosperity was enhanced by the reconstruction of two of the halts, Cattistock, and Bradford Peverell & Stratton in modern precast concrete. At that time nobody had heard of Dr Beeching, and it was unthinkable that within a few years the situation would change entirely.

When the Beeching Report was published it cast grave doubts on the future not only of the WS&W line but of all railways in Dorset. As an area of thin population and a conspicuous lack of heavy industry, the counties of Dorset and Somerset were to feel the full force of Beeching's economies. The original proposal was to close most of the intermediate stations together with the Bridport branch, and surprisingly Dorchester West, leaving only Weymouth and Yeovil Pen Mill as points of access for passengers. This was naturally the subject of strong objections from various bodies, including the county councils, and was modified to some extent. The Bridport branch was to stay because the narrowness of the lanes between that town and Maiden Newton made a replacement bus service impossible, and Dorchester West, Maiden Newton, Chetnole, Thornford Bridge and Bruton were also to remain open. While all this was being discussed the regional boundaries were again altered to return the whole line north of Dorchester West to Western Region control, although the Salisbury line remained within the Southern Region. The arguments raging throughout Britain over the Beeching proposals tended to obscure an important closure that would have otherwise have attracted more attention. The Cheddar Valley line from Witham to Yatton lost its passenger service on 9th September 1963, but general freight remained for a long time. Later, the eastern end of the branch was to become a major scource of

revenue for the railway with the development of Foster Yeoman's massive quarry at Merehead.

Three years later came the big cuts, first to go being the general freight trains over the section from Castle Cary to Weymouth with the introduction of the 1966 summer timetable. Some Channel Islands fruit trains continued to use the route, but many of these were diverted via Bournemouth, Southampton and Reading. Then, on 3rd October that year the halts and stations at Witham, Sparkford, Marston Magna, Evershot, Cattistock, Grimstone & Frampton and Bradford & Peverell were closed. With this reduction in traffic it became possible to obtain further economies by singling much of the line between Castle Cary and Dorchester West. This work was carried out in three stages: Castle Cary to Yeovil Pen Mill on 13th May 1968, Yeovil Pen Mill to Maiden Newton (including the connecting line to Yeovil Junction) on 26th May, and Maiden Newton to the north end of Dorchester West station on 9th June. The Thingley Junction to Bradford Junction section had received this treatment the previous year, but the line from Bathampton through to Salisbury via Trowbridge and the main line section between Westbury and Castle Cary and the new cut off line through to Cogload Junction were to remain double, as was the Dorchester to Weymouth section which also had to cater for traffic off the Southern Region route from Waterloo and Bournemouth.

Since this big reorganisation in the 1960s there have been few alterations, the most noteworthy being the closure of the Bridport branch on 5th May 1975. Maiden Newton then lost its importance as a junction and was subsequently unstaffed. The Southern Region eventually electrified its route to Weymouth, with the third rail being laid over the Dorchester Junction to Weymouth section, the current being switched on from 10th February 1988, although the full service did not commence until 16th May. Upwey was given a more frequent service with the electrification, but this has not benefited the WS&W line generally. In connection with the modernisation the terminus at Weymouth was rebuilt by making use of the two 'new' platforms of 1957 and building one new short one, a total of three, instead of the original six!

At present the service from Westbury to Weymouth survives on a total of about seven trains a day, many of which only call at the smaller stations by request. Traffic is light for much of the year, but a fine summer weekend can still bring in a remnant of the once thriving excursion business. By contrast the Bathampton to Salisbury line enjoys an improved service of hourly 'Sprinters', and there are still some freight trains over this route. The West of England expresses continue to run via Castle Cary and the cut off line to Cogload Junction, but many of them do not call anywhere on the WS&W system, even Westbury. A few Paddington HSTs call at Castle Cary at commuter times, but for much of the day they simply speed through the area. It is doubtful that an argument based purely on economic grounds could be advanced for the retention of the Castle Cary to Dorchester line, and it will be interesting to see what place such a service can have in a privatised rail system. It is to be hoped that some way will be found to keep the trains running well into the next century, by which time perhaps a shortage of oil and a true understanding of the damage inflicted upon the environment by the internal combustion engine will ensure its future.

The Gauge Conversion

June 1874. The End of the Broad Gauge on the Wilts, Somerset & Weymouth

It was as early as November 1864 that the Board of the GWR had resolved to lay the 'narrow gauge' from Bristol to Salisbury 'at an early date', and an agreement had been made with the Bristol & North Somerset Company in 1866 (incorporated in 1863), to make a line from Bristol to Radstock. This involved laying a 'narrow gauge' rail from Radstock via Frome to a junction with the Somerset & Dorset Railway near Bruton, but this work was never carried out due to the collapse of the North Somerset Company. However, in 1870 a new agreement was substituted, and the GWR undertook to provide 'narrow gauge' communication between Radstock and Salisbury. The directors of the GWR in 1871 proposed in the Company's own interests, to construct an additional 'narrow gauge' line beside the single existing broad gauge track from Frome to the London & South Western Railway beyond Yeovil, at an estimated cost of £54,000. This very interesting idea did not come to fruition. At Yeovil, the Bristol & Exeter whilst awaiting completion of the Joint station at Yeovil Town, laid an independent 'narrow gauge' line for the LSWR alongside the B&E broad gauge branch from Hendford to Pen Mill in order for the LSWR to reach the Bristol & Exeter station at Hendford. But the days of the broad gauge on the Wilts & Somerset were drawing to a close as the directors' report to the shareholders in February 1874 confirms.

"By the terms of an Agreement with the Bristol and North Somerset Company and the principal Colliery Proprietors of the Radstock District, this Company is under engagement to lay the Narrow Gauge between Radstock and Salisbury on or before the 3rd September next.

In view of this obligation, the Directors have had to consider the best mode of dealing with the question of the Gauge on the Wilts, Somerset & Weymouth, and the Berks and Hants Railways, and they are of the opinion that the convenience of the public will be best met, and the interest of the Proprietors best secured, by the alteration from Broad to Narrow Gauge of all the Lines in the District which these Railways accommodate. This alteration will necessitate the extension of the Mixed Gauge over a portion of the Main Line between Swindon and Bristol, and the Directors recommend that at the same time a second line of rails should be laid on the Wilts, Somerset & Weymouth Railway between Frome and Witham and between Westbury and Warminster, where the earthworks and bridges have already been constructed for a double line. In connection with the conversion of the Gauge, the Station accommodation on the Lines referred to will be enlarged and improved to meet the requirements of the increasing traffic. The cost of carrying out the alterations and additions to the Permanent Way, Stations, and Works involved in this arrangement is estimated at £290,000. In anticipation of the operation now recommended, provision has already to some extent been made for the supply of Narrow Gauge Rolling Stock, and a further outlay of about £70,000 will cover the cost of the Locomotive, Carriage, and Wagon Stock necessary to work the traffic of the district."

The Engineers in the meantime proceeded to lay the third rail on the main line between Swindon and Thingley Junction, beyond Chippenham, and between Bristol and Bathampton. The lines in the Wilts & Somerset district to be converted consisted of Thingley Junction to the junction with the London & South Western Railway at Dorchester, from Bathampton to Bradford Junction, Westbury to Salisbury, the mineral branch from Frome to Radstock, (traffic on the branch had been suspended on 13th June), Witham to Wells, the goods branch from Yeovil to Clifton Maybank, and the branch from Maiden Newton to Bridport. A total of 131⅓ miles of railway not including the sidings, all of the track consisting of single lines, except between Thingley Junction and Frome, Bradford and Bradford Junction, Yeovil and Evershot, and Dorchester station to Dorchester Junction. The conversion was to be carried out in June, giving the engineers the benefit of long daylight hours and hopefully, good weather. Except for the section from Bradford to Bathampton which was laid on cross sleepers, and the Bridport branch which was laid on MacDonnell iron plates, the whole of the permanent way consisted of longitudinal timbers and transoms.

Following the lessons of earlier conversions much preparation work was done on the lines before the actual conversion date, the track being prepared for slewing by clearing away ballast, and marking the transoms for cutting. The transoms were laid to the usual practice at intervals of 11ft and every second one had been disconnected and partially sawn to the new 'narrow gauge' length and all the nuts and bolts were oiled for quick removal. The 'narrow gauge' pointwork and crossing work would be laid in or, failing this, be framed up and ready to be hauled into place before the stoppage of traffic. Sufficient short rails were provided at curves to save time when cutting the outer rail of the curve to be moved inwards. Every detail was worked out beforehand with numerous meetings between the traffic officers and engineers with detailed instructions to all staff, timetables of train services to be maintained whilst the work was in progress etc. So as not to waste time in moving men and materials from place to place, the line was divided into lengths, averaging about four miles each and varying according to the amount of work to be done, a central depot was allocated to each length. This was equipped with tools and materials, blacksmiths, and cooking and sleeping accommodation, although if working near a town, the company would pay lodging money. The depots were in the charge of two gangers with a gang of 20 men under them, with an inspector supervising the work of every two gangs. Vast armies of platelayers from other districts and their equipment were drafted in by special trains in order to start work early on Tuesday, 16th

June. Each ganger received four shillings and six pence, plus one shilling and three pence ration money and six pence per hour overtime pay for work in excess of nine hours. Straw for bedding, coal and oatmeal were provided by the company. The oatmeal was used for making a drink similar to barley water, (the famous Skilly!), this drink being popular with the railway navvies of the day as alcohol was banned by the railway company. Everything was now ready for the conversion. The first to be tackled were the down sections on the double parts of the lines, ie Thingley to Frome, Bradford to Bathampton (this was known as the up line for this stretch of line), and Yeovil to Evershot. The up line was used for a reduced train service and worked as a single line on these sections with pilotmen and pilot engines between Chippenham and Weymouth, and Bristol to Salisbury, plus the branch lines. Thursday, 18th June was the final day of broad gauge working south of Frome, and on all of the branches.

When the last down trains had completed their journeys on that final Thursday, they were despatched as empty trains from Weymouth, and from the Bridport and Wells branch lines, and Salisbury. What a spectacle this must have been as the long trains of broad gauge empty stock passed through Westbury on their way to Swindon for the last time! At 11pm a special engine with an inspector on board left Weymouth, the engine stopping at all stations to check that all rolling stock had been cleared from the sidings and yards. The inspector distributed notices at all stations that the broad gauge could no longer be used south of Frome. The single lines were then handed over to the engineers and traffic suspended, the exception to this being the section between Chippenham and Frome, and the double section from Dorchester to Weymouth. This latter portion of the line had always been mixed gauge from the outset for the London & South Western Railway. The down line between Dorchester and Weymouth was converted on the Thursday and the up line was put into temporary use as a single line whilst the work was carried out. The GWR carried out a local service on the Friday throughout the period of conversion using stock which had been despatched from Swindon to Weymouth via Basingstoke and the London & South Western Railway, the up line from Weymouth to Dorchester being converted on the

Friday. Converting mixed gauge sections like this was swiftly accomplished.

On the broad gauge sections the work was hard but the platelayers had it down to a fine art. The permanent way was of the usual bridge rail laid on longitudinal sleepers and transoms. In order to narrow the gauge, the bolts had to be disconnected from one end of each transom, and then about 2ft 3½in had to be sawn off from one end of each transom. The longitudinal sleepers, with the rails still attached were then slewed across to the now shortened transoms and refixed. The work was accomplished by a very hardy breed of men who had built the railway system in the new railway age through fair weather and foul. The final broad gauge train had departed from Frome on Sunday 21st June, and the up line to Thingley Junction was now closed for conversion. Strict timing was adhered to with the well laid plans of the GWR again swinging into action later on the same day with trains of 'narrow gauge' stock being despatched from Swindon to Weymouth, Wells, Bridport, Salisbury and to Bristol via Bathampton. The new stock must have looked magnificent as train after train rumbled through Westbury to their respective destinations, with coaches and engines absolutely gleaming in their fresh paintwork ready to start the limited service on the following day. The double sections were completed by the following Thursday, and the ordinary service of passenger and goods trains was now put back to normal. The broad gauge was now extinct from the Wilts, Somerset & Weymouth.

The gauge conversion of the old Wilts, Somerset & Weymouth lines, by the Great Western Railway, was a magnificent engineering achievement – a virtual masterpiece of planning by the railway company, together with the manual skills of the railway navvies, of whom a total of 1,800 workmen were employed, most of whom were drafted in by the GWR from districts far and wide. Even the much vaunted final conversion of 1892, pales into significance when compared with the conversion of the 131½ miles of the WS&W in June 1874. The gauge of the lines between Southcote Junction through to Newbury, Devizes and Holt Junction, plus the branch from Savernake to Marlborough, a total of 62 miles was also converted between 27th June and 4th July of the same year.

Signals and Telegraph

The Wilts, Somerset & Weymouth lines pre-dated block working and signalling as most people understand it. The double-line sections (Thingley Junction–Westbury and Dorchester Junction–Weymouth) were operated under the 'Time Interval' system, whilst the single lines were controlled by double-needle telegraph instruments located in the station offices and worked by the clerks. All passing places for each train were set out in the timetable, and any departure from this brought about by late running or last minute special traffic, involved great caution on the part of the telegraph operators to ensure that a clear understanding had been reached.

These revised crossing arrangements had to be set out in a written train order given to the crew of the train(s) affected. The telegraph was not actually complete in time for the opening of the line, the Yeovil to Dorchester Junction section being worked by two pilotmen, with a crossing place at Evershot only for the first few weeks of operation. It appears to have been fully operative through to Weymouth in the spring of 1857 (certainly by 7th May), and thereafter Maiden Newton was also used as a crossing station. A policeman's hut was erected at the northern end of Bincombe Tunnel, and special telegraph working introduced between that point and Weymouth. This was a difficult section to work, involving a heavy gradient and a lengthy tunnel, and handling the standard gauge trains of the LSWR as well as the broad gauge WS&W traffic, so no doubt additional precautions were thought necessary. At the lonely outpost of Bincombe, and also at the junctions at Dorchester and Bradford, the telegraph instruments were under the policeman's control as there were no other staff.

At the small intermediate stations, the policemen were responsible for setting the points and signals, but they also had other, more general duties, such as the ejection of trespassers, control of crowds on platforms, and the security of goods and parcels. There is evidence to suggest that at most places, they also unofficially worked the telegraph, leaving the clerks free to conduct other business. At larger stations there were both police and switchmen, the former working the signals and giving instructions to the latter who walked (or ran) about setting the points. This arrangement applied at Westbury, Yeovil and Weymouth. At that time there was no interlocking between points and signals, and considerable vigilance was necessary on the part of all concerned. The fixed signals of the time were very basic, and at most places consisted of just two signals for each direction of travel – the 'stop' signal immediately at the approach to a station or junction, and the 'auxiliary' some distance to the rear of it. There were no 'starting' signals, permission for a train to proceed into the section ahead being given by written train order and a handsignal from the policeman.

If there was a choice of routes, the route set at the points was not indicated by the signal, drivers having to take it on trust that the road was properly set. To assist them to check this, indicators were provided at each set of facing points showing the direction for which they were set. Most signals on the WS&W were of the disc and crossbar pattern which were revolved by means of a handle on the post. This gave the policeman plenty of walking, particularly when crossing two trains, but it did have the advantage of ensuring that he checked his points before clearing the signal. No train was allowed to enter a station or foul a junction unless the 'stop' signal was turned to show 'clear', and in this respect it can be considered the forerunner of the modern 'home', but the 'auxiliary', whilst in some ways being similar to the later 'distant', had a somewhat different application. To start with, it was not sited at the full braking distance for an approaching train, as no method of signal repeating then existed and the signal had to be visible from the station. On curved sections of track this gave rise to some very lofty structures! A clear 'auxiliary' only indicated that the 'stop' signal was also at clear and that the train could therefore enter the station. The written train order was still required before it could proceed into the next single line section.

A driver, with regard to the primitive braking system of the day consisting of tender brakes only on the engine plus the guards handbrake, needed to have the speed of his train strictly under control when approaching anywhere with signals. If he found the 'auxiliary' at 'clear' he could accelerate enough to take it into the station, but if the 'auxiliary' exhibited 'stop' he was required to do so as expeditiously as possible, bringing his train to a stand within that signal's protection and not moving forward until called on by the clearance of the 'stop' signal or verbal instructions from the policeman. By means of the telegraph, trains were signalled forward from station to station but not 'Blocked Back' – in other words, there was no 'Out of Section' message. The working was permissive, a train being authorised to enter a section with a caution note after a prescribed period of time or under full 'clear' signals if a longer time had elapsed since the previous train. It sounds a somewhat lax way to run traffic over long sections of single line, and it says much for the vigilance of the staff that accidents were few. No doubt safety was largely attainable because of the light level of traffic and the fact that the staff were not generally under pressure.

In 1859, the section from Yeovil to Evershot was doubled, the most steeply graded part from Yetminster to Evershot being governed by the same special instructions that existed between Weymouth and Bincombe. The single line crossing stations at that time were: Frome, Witham, Bruton, Castle Cary, Sparkford and Maiden Newton. By virtue of being on the double track sections, Dorchester, Evershot, Yetminster, Yeovil, Westbury and all points north, could of course accommodate two trains, but the stations at Grimstone, and Marston (renamed Marston Magna 1895) had but single platforms and could not be used for crossing trains. It would seem that the telegraph operators of the WS&W were not skilled enough to take full advantage of the double needle instruments, for in 1863 the GWR decided to replace them with the single needle variety which was much simpler to use. This was done over the next two years, (the Board of Trade report on the Bruton accident of 1865 indicates that the single needle instrument was in operation at that time). One advantage was that two sets of wires became surplus and could be used for other purposes. A circuit giving direct communication between the principal stations was therefore provided. The single needle telegraph gave good service for several years, but by about 1870 the Evershot and Bincombe inclines had been fitted with disc block telegraph. Although not as versatile as the single needle instruments – only certain specified messages regarding the state of the line could be sent – this system was found to be very efficient for the running of traffic, and by 1872 the following sections had been fitted with the disc block:

Bathampton to Bradford-on-Avon.
Westbury to Salisbury (throughout).
Frome to Yeovil. •
Evershot to Dorchester.

The method of working remained permissive, a second train being allowed into the section after a suitable lapse of time. The state of signalling on the WS&W in 1873 can be summarised as follows:

PERMISSIVE DISC BLOCK TELEGRAPH
Bathampton to Bradford-on-Avon.
Westbury to Salisbury (throughout).
Frome to Yeovil.
Evershot to Dorchester.

SINGLE NEEDLE TELEGRAPH
Thingley Jcn to Westbury (throughout).
Bradford-on-Avon to Bradford Junction.
Westbury to Frome.
Yeovil to Yetminster.
Dorchester to Bincombe Tunnel.
Frome to Radstock.

DISC BLOCK TELEGRAPH WITH SPECIAL INSTRUCTIONS
Yetminster to Evershot.
Bincombe Tunnel to Weymouth.

By December the following year, permissive block working was giving way to 'absolute block', a Board of Trade return for that month indicating that the WS&W was then being worked by this safer method except for the sections Thingley Junction to Westbury, Bradford-on-Avon to Bradford Junction, and Dorchester to Bincombe Tunnel (all double line), where it was stated to be in course of installation. Conversion of the Dorchester–Bincombe section was completed early in 1874, and at the same time the long Weymouth–Bincombe section was divided by an intermediate block post at Upwey.

Along with the introduction of 'absolute block' came the signal box, in which all the point and signal levers for each location were concentrated in an interlocked frame. This brought about a change in the role of policemen, who were now relieved of their more general duties to devote all their time to the signalling of trains. This in turn made it necessary to employ additional staff at most stations, but railways were then in their prime and could readily afford the extra costs. The idea of concentrating levers was not entirely new, even on the remote WS&W a 'covered stage' containing such an arrangement having been erected at Weymouth in 1865 to control the junction with the new branch line to Portland. This crude equipment was

short lived, being replaced the following year by a proper signal box containing a Chambers' patent locking frame, and also in 1866 a 'kind of observatory' containing levers was provided at Dorchester Junction. However, the bulk of the system remained unlocked until after 1874, in which year the GWR authorised new signal work for the entire WS&W line. All the equipment was manufactured in the Companys' own works at Reading, and installation had been completed by the end of 1877. The signal boxes provided at this time were:

Bathampton Branch – Limpley Stoke, Freshford, Avoncliff Siding*, Bradford-on-Avon, Bradford Crossing* (later known as Greenland Mill Crossing).

Main Line – Thingley Jcn, Dunch Lane Crossing*, Melksham, Holt Jcn, Bradford Jcn, Trowbridge No. 1, Trowbridge No. 2, Yarnbrook, Westbury No. 1, Westbury No. 2, Westbury No. 3, Frome No. 1, Frome No. 2, Frome No. 3, Witham, Bruton, Castle Cary, Sparkford, Marston Magna, Yeovil No. 1, Yeovil No. 2, Clifton Maybank*, Yetminster, Evershot, Maiden Newton No. 1, Maiden Newton No. 2, Grimstone, Dorchester, Dorchester Jcn, Bincombe Tunnel, Portland Jcn, Weymouth Station, (Upwey signal box 1874 was retained).

Salisbury Line – Warminster No. 1, Warminster No. 2, Heytesbury, Wylye, Wishford, Wilton, Salisbury.

Locations marked * were not designated as block posts, and although they had signals, were only manned as required. Clifton Maybank could only be used during the hours of daylight, so presumably the signals were not fitted with lamps! In connection with these new signal boxes, semaphore signals were introduced, at first mostly as starting signals with the old disc and crossbars being retained as 'homes'. It was to be about another ten years before the semaphore became universal throughout the line. The old single needle telegraph and the disc block instruments were also gradually phased out, to be replaced by the Electric Train Staff on the single lines and Spagnoletti's Absolute Block instruments over the double sections.

Somewhat surprisingly, the GWR were not very enthusiastic about the Electric Train Staff, claiming that it would interfere with the ready working of traffic and cause heavy delays, and continued to control the single lines by the disc block. The Board of Trade carried out an inspection of the WS&W lines in 1877 – no doubt upon completion of the new signal boxes, and pressed for use of the Electric Train Staff, but the GWR refused to accept the recommendation. Even a threat by the Board of Trade to withdraw sanction for the operation of a passenger service over the lines failed to persuade them, and there were several heated exchanges between the Board and the railway company. The GWR General Manager's report of March 1880 indicates that the Board of Trade had become tired of the argument and left the Company to carry on as they thought fit – a blow to bureaucracy, perhaps, but also an example of the degree to which large and powerful companies were free to continue with unsafe working practices despite official ruling to the contrary. However, the same report also reveals that the Board of Trade had rattled the Company sufficiently to persuade them to conduct trials with the

Electric Staff, and it had apparently proved "fairly satisfactory" with only occasional instances of significant delay. At that time, Electric Staff working had been introduced over the sections between Frome and Yeovil, Evershot and Dorchester, Bathampton and Bradford-on-Avon, and on the Radstock branch, the GWR deciding to retain it after the 'trial' period but not to extend its use. In fact, of the single line sections of the WS&W this only left the line between Warminster and Salisbury to be worked by the old method.

In 1884 the platforms at Weymouth station were lengthened and a new engine shed laid out, and this brought about several signalling alterations. Portland Junction box was abolished, and a new 'Weymouth Junction Signal Box' provided in the fork between the main line and the branch, about six chains south of the old box. Weymouth Station box was not renewed, but the whole structure was jacked up and moved five chains northwards to make way for the longer platforms.

The following year, the signal engineer was busy with the doubling of the Bathampton–Bradford-on-Avon section, but his services were called upon at the Dorset end of the line when the Abbotsbury Railway wished to make a new junction at Upwey. Upwey Junction signal box (22 levers) was provided, partly at the expense of the Abbotsbury company some 38 chains south of the old Upwey box, and came into use on 9th November 1885. It would seem that the old box was retained, although probably switched out of circuit, until the new junction station was opened in 1886, for the instruction issued to staff giving notice of the change in station arrangements on 19th April that year, states rather quaintly that on the same date the "...existing Upwey signal box will be thrown into disuse".

In 1895 the North curve was opened at Bradford Junction making it into a triangle, and two new signal boxes – Bradford West Junction (on the Bathampton line) and Bradford North Junction (on the Thingley line) both with 21 levers, were opened on 10th March that year. The original Bradford Junction box then became Bradford South Junction. Doubling of a section of the Salisbury line between Wilton and Salisbury with alterations to the track layout at the latter took place in 1896. The year 1896 also brought alterations in Dorset. An engine siding was provided between the up and down running lines at the north end of Bincombe Tunnel and a new 13 lever box replaced the original structure. This new facility greatly assisted with the disposal of bank engines, as trains were becoming heavier and demand for rear end assistance up the incline from Weymouth was increasing. A few months later a much larger signal box was erected in the fork at Dorchester Junction, second-hand parts from Maesteg being utilised for this work. A 37-lever frame was provided, this having enough spare capacity to allow for the provision of exchange sidings a few years later.

Much of the signal work carried out at the turn of the century was centred on the Salisbury line, upon which military traffic was increasing, and the section between Westbury and Castle Cary, which was being improved as part of the GWR's new route to the West. On the Salisbury line, Codford became a fully signalled crossing loop in 1898, and the following year the section between that station and Heytesbury was

doubled. The Codford–Wylye section was doubled in January 1900, followed in October that year by Warminster to Heytesbury. The steeply inclined section from Westbury to Warminster had been doubled way back in 1875, but the block section was still a long one made worse by the slow climb. From 10th December 1900 it was divided by a new signal box at Upton Scudamore, complete with short engine siding and crossover road, and this allowed bank engines to run loose at the rear of freight trains and return light to Westbury from that point rather than having to couple to the train and run through to Warminster. Also during that year the layout at Salisbury had again been rearranged and a new signal box with 95 levers opened to control it.

Meanwhile, Westbury station had been enlarged and remodelled in 1899/1900, and three new signal boxes – North, Middle and South had replaced the originals. Warminster lost its two signal boxes in 1904, a new box of 37 levers to control the whole station being opened on 19th June that year. The old box at Castle Cary was too small to control the junction and additional signalling brought about by the new line to Taunton, and it was replaced on 11th April 1905 by a new one with 55 levers. With the opening of the new cut-off line from Castle Cary, the following boxes were provided at the stations of Keinton Mandeville (opened 1st July 1905), Charlton Mackerell (opened 1st July 1905), Somerton (opened February 1906) and Langport East (opened February 1906), Long Sutton and Pitney was added as a halt on 1st October 1907, but was converted into a station with a goods depot on 6th April 1908 with a 21-lever signal box being provided from the same date. Further down the line a new junction was provided for the Durston to Yeovil branch with a new box, Curry Rivel Junction, being opened in 1905. The traffic likely to present itself on the new main line to the West made it desirable to shorten some of the longer block sections, a box being provided at Fairwood Crossing (between Westbury and Frome) on 1st July 1900 and another at Woodlands (between Frome and Witham) on 31st July 1905. It was soon found that many of the heavy freight trains which ran between Taunton and Reading or Acton Yard required the services of a bank engine in the up direction from Castle Cary to the summit, about $1\frac{1}{2}$ miles south of Witham, and a new 14-lever signal box known as Brewham was opened at that point on 20th March 1907. The box had the same layout as Upton Scudamore, and served exactly the same purpose.

In 1910 major work centred on Limpley Stoke, about halfway between Bathampton and Bradford-on-Avon, where the new layout was being enlarged to receive coal traffic from the Camerton line. Two new boxes (North with 44 levers and South with 32) replaced the original box of 1877 vintage. The heavy traffic of World War One stretched the Salisbury line to breaking point, so to relieve congestion two goods running loops were provided between Codford and a new signal box at Sherrington which opened on 30th December 1914. Military branches were also constructed from Heytesbury to Sutton Veny Camp and from Codford to Codford Camp. Apart from a few additional sidings there were few other changes on the WS&W lines until the return of peace. At the end of the War the state of signalling throughout the area can best be summarised by the following table:

An old postcard view of Castle Cary looking east, circa 1910. The line curving to the right leads to Yeovil and Weymouth, and the then new cut off line to Langport and Taunton, opened in 1906, swings away to the left. The signal box standing in the middle distance was built in connection with the new junction and replaced an earlier box which stood on the 'down' platform. Unfortunately the new box was to be destroyed by enemy action in the Second World War. Freight wagons crowd the back siding to the left of the goods shed, and cattle wagons stand in the dock siding at the 'up' platform, and an interesting bracket signal stands outside the signal box. Wording on the bottom of the postcard reads: "G.W.R. Station Castle Cary, and Creech Hill – The Cornish express runs through this station at the rate of about 60 miles an hour."

Norman Kibby Collection

Name of box	Year	No. of Levers
Thingley to Westbury		
Thingley Junction	1903	27
Melksham	1903	43
Holt Junction	1877*	44
Bradford Jcn North	1895	21 new frame 1910
Bradford Jcn South	1909	29
Trowbridge	1896	55
Yarnbrook	1877*	4
Westbury North	1899	82

Bathampton to Bradford Junction		
Limpley Stoke North	1910	44
Limpley Stoke South	1910	32
Freshford	1903	34 new frame 1910
Bradford on Avon	1877*	30 new frame 1914
Bradford West Junction	1895	21

Westbury to Salisbury		
Westbury Middle	1899	47
Westbury South	1899	74 new frame 1914
Upton Scudamore	1900	17
Warminster	1904	37
Heytesbury	1877*	34
Codford	1895	34 new frame c1914
Sherrington	1914	14
Wylye	1877*	?
Wishford	1895	23
Wilton	1895	27
Salisbury	1900	95

No. 6999 *Capel Dewi Hall* casts a cloud of smoke and steam whilst passing Brewham signal box at 11.15am with the 9.05am Minehead–Paddington on 2nd July 1955. The short siding used by the banking engines when awaiting a clear path back to Castle Cary can be seen to the right.

R. C. Riley

Weymouth Line

Fairwood Crossing	1911	6	replaced earlier box
Frome North	1877*	29	
Frome Middle	1877*	23	
Frome South	1877*	?	
Woodlands	1905	9	
Witham	1896	50	
Brewham	1907	14	
Bruton	1877*	25	new frame 1909
Castle Cary	1905	55	
Sparkford	1877*	23	frame relocked 1918
Marston Magna	1877*	22	
Yeovil Pen Mill North	1877*	25	
Yeovil Pen Mill South	1877*	26	
Clifton Maybank Junct.	1896	21	
Yetminster	1877*	27	
Evershot	1913	23	
Maiden Newton	c1896	30	
Grimstone & Frampton	1903	20	
Dorchester Station	1908	29	
Dorchester Junction	1896	37	
Bincombe Tunnel	1896	13	
Upwey Junction	1885	22	
Weymouth Junction	1884	43	
Weymouth Station	1877*	45	extended and re-located 1884

Note: Boxes shown as 1877* date from the general introduction of locking from 1874 to 1877.

From this list it will be seen that as the line emerged from wartime conditions the signalling was quite up to date with comparatively few boxes older than twenty years, and that the GWR had not only upgraded their signalling to cope with increasing traffic but also carried out a routine programme of renewals. Over the following years changes were slight, perhaps the only interesting items being the provision of a new signal box at Maiden Newton in 1921 and the closure of Sherrington signal box with abolition of the goods roads thence to Codford on 21st February 1923. However, by the 1930s the railways were feeling the need for economy, and one of the best ways of making staff reductions was the amalgamation of signal boxes. The perfection of the track circuit together with such inventions as the electric point machine, allied to the fact that the Ministry of Transport had approved the raising of the maximum distance for mechanically worked points from 200 to 350 yards, made it possible to control quite large layouts from one big box rather than two or three smaller ones, and several schemes of this nature were implemented. Two of these were carried out in 1933, one at Frome and the other at Bradford Junction. The latter involved the opening of one box of 45 levers to control the whole triangular junction, this being brought into use on 2nd May that year, the three old boxes being closed at the same time. The Frome scheme which came into service on 17th September, provided a new 'Frome South' box (73 levers) to take over the work previously done by the old Frome South and Middle boxes. Frome West box on the Radstock branch was reduced to ground frame status, but the original North box was retained.

In 1937, Yeovil Pen Mill received a new box with 65 levers to replace the old North and South boxes, this work commencing on 14th February and being completed on the 21st. In June that year the Clifton Maybank branch was closed and Clifton Maybank Junction box followed on 1st November, the block section becoming Yeovil Pen Mill–Yetminster.

Other new signal boxes of this period were brought about by the Westbury and Frome cut-off lines and the general increase in holiday and excursion traffic then taking place, particularly that to the West Country. In connection with the former, four new junction boxes (Heywood Road, Fairwood, Clink Road and Blatchbridge) came into use in 1932/3, the box at Fairwood Crossing being abolished at the same time. By the following year some of the sections were proving too long to pass the stream of holiday trains

The GWR Type 11 Yeovil Pen Mill signal box pictured here on 17th February 1968, was opened on 14th February 1937 and replaced two former boxes. Box size 38ft 2in x 12ft 2in, elevated 8ft. The box was equipped with a VT 5 – Bar Frame, 65 levers, 4in centres, Spagnoletti block on main lines, and electric key token to Yeovil Town. A closing switch was provided (removed 1968) plus an illuminated diagram.

C. L. Caddy

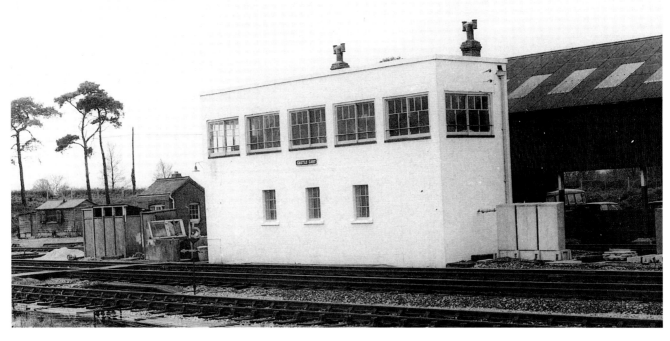

Castle Cary signal box pictured here on 26th April 1970 was the first wartime ARP box to appear on the WS&W system, replacing the earlier signal box which received a direct hit in the air raid of 3rd September 1942.

C. L. Caddy

without delay, and break section boxes were provided at Wyke (between Castle Cary and Bruton) on 28th June and at Pinkwood (between Brewham and Bruton) on 4th July 1934. Any further modernisation was brought to an abrupt halt by the outbreak of the Second World War, but once it became apparent that it was going to be a protracted conflict, several new signal boxes were built to control military stores depots, and additional sidings were installed at a number of places. At Alford Halt on the Castle Cary–Taunton line, a 22-lever signal box was opened on 15th September 1940. This box, situated alongside the 'up' main line controlled a crossover between the 'up' and 'down' lines and the connection into the ammunition depot at Dimmer Camp. Access into the depot was gained from the 'down' main.

However, the first wartime box to appear on the WS&W system replaced an earlier box destroyed by enemy action. Castle Cary received a direct hit on 3rd September 1942, and a temporary 22-lever box was provided to control the basic layout until the new permanent structure with a frame of 85 levers opened on 27th October the same year. The opportunity was taken to enlarge the track layout to include long goods loops – valuable assets in view of the heavy freight traffic passing at the time, hence the need for more levers in the box. An East Chord was constructed at Westbury to allow through running from the direction of Reading towards Trowbridge and vice versa, thus furnishing a useful emergency route. The eastern end of the chord line was controlled by Heywood Road Junction signal box, which already existed to work the junction between the original Stert Valley line and the Westbury avoiding line, but the northern end required a completely new box known as Hawkeridge. This also controlled access to a marshalling yard for Government stores traffic and was a 38-lever box opened on 14th July 1942. It was unusual for the time by being constructed in the traditional style, rather than the brick and concrete ARP structures being erected elswhere. The layout at Somerton on the Castle Cary–Taunton section was enlarged by the addition of long up and down loops brought into use during

June/July 1943, each capable of holding 86 wagons plus locomotive and brake van.

There had already been considerable activity at the extreme northern end of the line with the opening of a depot and signal box at Beanacre (between Lacock and Melksham) in January 1939, and this was soon joined by a very large Government establishment in the neighbourhood of Thingley junction. A large layout of sidings appeared at the junction itself, together with a large signal box known as Thingley West situated slightly further towards Bath on the main line. A double track curve ran from this latter box to Lacock, where there were more extensive sidings and a new 67-lever box which opened on 15th February 1943. This curve, which provided through running from the Melksham line towards Bath, was not signalled for passenger traffic and was intended to facilitate the exchange of Government stores rather than provide an emergency diversionary route. A couple of months later, on 27th May, the two goods loops between Codford and Sherrington (on the Salisbury line) were reinstated, a new 25-lever box being opened at the latter location. The following year, additional sidings were put in at Beechgrove Depot on the Salisbury side of Warminster station and a 28-lever signal box was opened there on 11th April 1944.

On the Weymouth section there were fewer developments. A supply depot had sprung up in the flat fields around Marston Magna in 1940, and on 16th December that year, the layout was altered to provide a long reception loop with a facing connection in the down line. A siding at Beer Hackett serving a government buffer store, and operated by a ground frame released from Yetminster signal box, was brought into use on 30th September 1942. A new connection between the Southern Railway Yeovil Town branch and the WS&W line, together with a 33-lever box named Yeovil South Junction was opened on 13th October 1943 (see History chapter), but only about half of the frame was ever used because the second part of the junction, which would have given through running from Weymouth towards Yeovil Town, was not provided. Finally, in May 1944, some government

Daisies bloom on the railway embankment on a beautiful summer's day in the wartime England of 1942. In this view looking towards Trowbridge, Hawkeridge signal box and loop are under construction. Newly erected signals stand with white crosses on the arms indicating to the engine crews that they are not yet in use. Workmen are busy on the Westbury–Trowbridge lines in the foreground, whilst the new Hawkeridge loop (east chord) can be seen behind the signal box. This important loop line, connecting the Trowbridge–Westbury line with the Westbury–Newbury line, avoiding the need for locomotive reversal at Westbury is still in use today. Hawkeridge signal box also controlled the connections to the War Department sidings which were situated alongside the 'up' Trowbridge line past the bridge in the background.

National Railway Museum

sidings were provided at Sparkford, a new ground frame being installed to control the points.

The end of World War II witnessed the signalling of the WS&W lines at its peak, and several of the facilities provided to cater for wartime traffic remained intact well into BR days, although in many cases they were virtually disused after the early 1950s. Woodlands box was closed in 1953, but it was to be towards the end of the decade that the greatest alterations took place. By then, the line south of Castle Cary, and from Dilton Marsh Halt to Salisbury, had passed into the hands of the Southern Region. The prospect of this transfer had caused the Western Region engineers to postpone a lot of signal renewals which had become due, and in consequence the SR rail-built upper quadrant began to appear in former GWR territory from about 1955. In some cases only the fittings were worn, and upper quadrant arms were attached to the original square wooden signal posts. The ground disc signals were also renewed as required, with the Westinghouse pattern favoured by the Southern. However, there was never any wholesale installation of Southern equipment, and at most places there was an interesting mixture of types. The block instruments remained WR until the end of the double line below Castle Cary.

On 14th April 1957, the Southern Region opened a new signal box at Weymouth to replace the (by then) very ramshackle ex-GWR boxes. This new box had a 116-lever Westinghouse A3 frame and two illuminated diagrams, the frame being laid out for two men. It was double manned on early and late turns, with one signalman on nights. Some new signals were provided, but many of the old GWR structures were connected to the new box and WR 1947 type block instruments were provided. Several improvements, intended as part of a total reconstruction of Weymouth station, were made to the track layout, but in the event no further work was done until electrification.

The following year, the goods lines between Codford and Sherrington were again removed and Sherrington box abolished, but the lines remained remarkably intact until the era of Dr Beeching. Beeching's policy was to close many of the small stations and withdraw stopping trains, plus the shedding of freight traffic except for bulk train loads. As this began to take effect, the frequency of trains became such that many lines could be singled and those that remained double could be worked with longer block sections. Furthermore, as most stations lost their goods facilities the sidings could be removed, and it was no longer necessary to retain signal boxes to control them. The 1960s were, therefore, the years of mass box closures and layout simplifications, the latter leaving many of the boxes which did survive with more spare levers than working ones! As an example of the sort of economy practised around this time, Dorchester West goods yard was closed on 6th September 1965, all freight for the town being handled at the South station. This in turn allowed the pointwork to be removed, and in consequence the West station box was closed on 15th March 1968. That the box lasted for over two years after freight closure, was due to acceptance difficulties at Dorchester Junction, where the signals were not out far enough to make full 'Line Clear' to Maiden Newton permissible with a Southern train crossing the junction.

Three photographs of the Castle Cary backing signal showing the different routes that could be offered. Note how the junction between the Taunton and Weymouth lines has been simplified with the singling of the line to Yeovil from Castle Cary. More alterations were to follow with the abolition of the signal box.

Left: Displaying the route 'TAUNT'N ('down' main) 9th April 1982.

Middle: Displaying the route GOODS SHED, 9th April 1982.

Right: Displaying the route WEY– (Weymouth 'down' main), October 1984.　　　　　　　　*M. Marshall*

In July 1959, the goods curve at Thingley Junction, which had seen little use since the war, was finally abandoned and Thingley West box closed, although the large layout at Lacock remained intact until 1964. This northern section was the first to be reduced to single track, the whole line between Thingley Junction and Bradford Junction becoming one key token section on 26th February 1967. (Holt Junction box had closed with the Devizes branch in 1966.) The token machine at the North end of the line was housed in a hut on Chippenham platform, the whole area being by then under the control of Swindon panel box. An intermediate instrument was provided at Melksham so that freight trains could be 'shut in' when required.

The Weymouth section south of Castle Cary was singled in three stages in 1968, Castle Cary to Yeovil Pen Mill being dealt with on 12th May. This was followed on the 26th of that month by Yeovil Pen Mill–Maiden Newton, together with the connecting spur to Yeovil Junction which then formed a parallel line from the site of Yeovil South Junction to the south end of Pen Mill station. This allowed South Junction box to be abolished. All these sections were controlled by conventional key tokens, but the final section, from Maiden Newton to Dorchester Junction, which was carried out on 9th June, employed the 'Tokenless Block' system similar to that installed on the Salisbury to Exeter line. Two tracks were retained from the north end of Dorchester station through to Weymouth, the connection to the single line being worked from Dorchester Junction by means of motor points.

The Bathampton–Westbury–Salisbury route was destined to remain double, this now taking the main flow of traffic. There were signalling economies, of course, all the intermediate boxes between Westbury and Salisbury except Warminster, Codford and Wylye

being closed in the 1960s. This was perhaps not the big reduction in facilities that it seems, for Heytesbury and Wishford had been permanently switched out for some years. On the Bathampton line, the box at Bradford-on-Avon closed in 1966, the block sections then being Bradford Junction–Limpley Stoke–Bathampton, but the following year, track circuit block supervised from Bristol Panel took over. The signal boxes at Upwey and Broadwey (formerly Upwey Junction) and Bincombe Tunnel were closed on 1st March 1970, track circuit block with automatic colour light signals being introduced between Dorchester Junction and Weymouth. No train describers were provided, description being by bell only.

Later that year at Frome, on 19th August, another short section of the line was reduced to single track. Frome South box was closed and a new 34-lever frame was installed in the old North box. A facing junction was made at Frome North enabling trains from Westbury to run direct onto the Radstock branch instead of having to reverse into a siding in order to cross the up and down main lines and enter the branch as before. The line between Frome North and Blatchbridge Junction was singled using tokenless block instruments, and ground frames were provided to control access to several sidings in the Frome station area.

Westbury was the next place to receive attention. There had already been some rationalisation of the layout with the closure of the Middle box on 5th May 1968, but on 16th September 1978, the South box was abolished and control of that part of the layout was transferred to a miniature panel in the old North box which then became simply Westbury. The 99-lever mechanical frame was shortened by one lever but was retained to control the northern end of the station. On

Westbury station can be seen in the distance in this view of the south end of the layout taken in 1974. The gantry signals as viewed from the rear, read from right to left: goods loop with display case, 'down' Salisbury (lowered), 'down' Salisbury to 'down' main (with fixed distant), 'down' main to 'down' Salisbury, 'down' main and distant. With the goods shed in the distance, empty stone wagons stand on the right awaiting their next trip to one of the Mendip quarries, whilst their loaded brethren stand in the 'up' sidings to the left.

Adrian Vaughan Collection

The interior of Westbury North signal box in 1974, showing the 99-lever frame with VT 5 Bar locking. The box was originally supplied with an 82-lever frame and the larger frame was installed in 1949. The coal-burning stove standing on the right would give the box a rosy glow on chilly winter nights as signal boxes were inclined to be a bit draughty to say the least, with the wind whistling up through the frame from the locking room below. This box was fortunate in having electric light with a spare paraffin lamp hanging above in case of a power failure. The signalman is using the telephone, whilst his reporting ledgers into which every train and engine movement are registered, lie on top of the desk this side of the stove.

John Morris

3rd June of the following year, the mini panel was extended to control Warminster, the box there then being closed. By the end of the decade the trend was firmly towards panel boxes, the old mechanical signalling being doomed to virtual extinction over the next ten years. On 28th August 1981 a panel was opened at Salisbury, its area of control being extended to eliminate the boxes at Wylye (19th April) and Codford (22nd June) the following year. The entire line between Westbury and Salisbury was then controlled by track circuit block.

A somewhat bigger scheme was carried out at Westbury during 1984, a panel box being opened at the North end of the station over the weekend 11th–14th May. At first this only controlled the immediate area of Westbury and allowed the closure of signal boxes at Hawkeridge, Heywood Road Junction, Westbury (former North box), and Fairwood Junction, but on 6th October, Frome North, together with the junctions at Clink Road and Blatchbridge were taken into its control. On 26th November, Witham box was closed and the signalling there brought under the control of Westbury, and finally Castle Cary, where the layout was substantially altered, was transferred to Westbury Panel on the weekend 1st–4th February 1985. The method of working the single line thence to Yeovil was altered from key token to track circuit block at the same time.

All this modernisation left just one mechanical signal box, complete with semaphore signals, north of Yeovil, this was Bradford Junction, the signalman there was in the most unusual position of fringing with three different panel boxes – Bristol, Swindon and Westbury, with track circuit block in all directions. Bradford Junction box survived because of uncertainty over the retention of the North curve, which proved very useful for occasional diversions during engineering work around Box Tunnel but was otherwise unused. In the end it was decided that the elimination of the loco hauled train by widespread use of HSTs and 'Sprinters' would remove the hardship of reversing, and the box and the North curve eventually closed on 17th March 1990 when a greatly simplified layout was placed under the control of Westbury Panel.

Meanwhile the Southern Region was busy rationalising their end of the system. The signal box at Dorchester South, which had been reduced to ground frame status in March 1970, was reopened as a panel on 1st June 1985, this taking control of Dorchester Junction on 5th July of the following year. The layout at Weymouth was greatly simplified and the station rebuilt over the next two years in readiness for electrification of the Bournemouth–Weymouth service, and

The platform starter at the Weymouth end of the 'up' platform at Yeovil Pen Mill pictured in 1991. The stencil is displaying Mn (main) as the route is set for the Weymouth line.

Norman Kibby

on 19th September 1987 Weymouth box was closed and control of the terminus transferred to Dorchester Panel. This left just two mechanical signal boxes on the whole of the WS&W system, Maiden Newton and Yeovil Pen Mill. The former did not last much longer, being closed in May 1988 when the loop was fitted with spring points and point indicators and converted into a remote crossing place. Yeovil Pen Mill, however, remains in use for the present, an island of semaphore signals in a sea of colour lights. The route from Castle Cary to Dorchester West is 'low priority' when it comes to investment, and Pen Mill box could well remain in service way into the 21st century.

Locomotives used on the Wilts, Somerset & Weymouth

Broad Gauge Locomotives

Westbury

The Wilts, Somerset & Weymouth engine shed at Westbury was situated on the 'up' side of the line just south of the station. Opened in September 1848 the shed was used for engines working on the line to Chippenham and ballast engines working on extension construction for the WS&W. *Sagittarius,* a member of the 'Leo' class, was used for the opening of the line from Westbury to Warminster on 9th September 1851. However the GWR had shown no interest in keeping a permanent pool of motive power at Westbury, and the shed ceased to have a regular allocation of engines after the locomotive depot at Frome was opened in March 1854. For some time after the opening of Frome shed there was an occasional goods or ballast engine stationed at Westbury, and *Thunderer,* one of the 'Caesar' class 0-6-0 goods engines built at Swindon under '3rd Lot Goods' in July 1851, is recorded as being there in July 1862, and was used in the construction of the East Somerset branch to Wells. Westbury was closed c1862/3 and ceased to be used by the locomotive department until the wheel turned full circle and the modern shed was opened there in February 1915.

Frome

In March 1854, a wooden single-road engine shed was opened at Frome. This shed was situated a short distance to the west of the station and became the main WS&W locomotive depot in the area for locomotives working on the construction of the line to Weymouth and the mineral line to Radstock.

Broad Gauge Allocation March 1854

Argo. 'Fury' class, 0-6-0 goods engine. Originally built as 'Premier' class after the first engine, *Premier,* emerged from the works in February 1846. Designed by Daniel Gooch and one of a class of twelve. This was the first class of 0-6-0 engines constructed at Swindon under '1st Lot Goods' although not entirely Swindon built as the boilers were supplied by outside contractors. *Argo* was built in July 1846, and had inside sandwich frames, wheels 5ft and cylinders 16in x 24in. The average weight complete with tender was 26 ton 15 cwt. Boilers had dome shaped fireboxes (not identical) and these engines were the last to be built for the broad gauge with haycock fireboxes and were the basic design for the numerous series of goods engines to follow. *Argo* ceased work in March 1866 and was withdrawn from stock in July 1870. Tender engines incorporating 'Premier' and 'Hercules' classes were amalgamated into the 'Fury' class.

Eclipse. 'Wolf' class, 2-2-2 saddle tank. Originally built as 'Sun' class. One of a class of 21 locomotives designed by Gooch and built as 2-2-2 tender engines between April 1840 and January 1842 by three different manufacturers. *Eclipse,* builder's No. 294, was built by R. & W. Hawthorn and Co., Newcastle, and delivered in August 1840. The locomotive had 14in x 18in cylinders when built, 6ft driving wheels and 3ft 6in carrying wheels. The wheelbase of 6ft 10in + 6ft 10in was 6in longer than the 'Fire Fly' class, of which the 'Sun' class were smaller editions. Boiler pressure 50lb (increased later). Lacking in adhesive weight, all of the class were altered to 2-2-2 saddle tanks with 15in x 18in cylinders, most of them in 1849/50. *Eclipse* ceased work in June 1864 and was withdrawn from stock in July 1870. c1865 the 'Sun' class together with six 'Stars', three 'Fire Fly' class, and six unclassified engines were amalgamated into the 'Wolf' class.

Stromboli. 'Leo' class. One of a class of 18 locomotives designed by Gooch and originally built as 2-4-0 tender engines between January 1841 and July 1842 by three different manufacturers. *Stromboli,* builder's No. 36 built by Fenton, Murray & Jackson, Leeds, was delivered to the GWR in April 1841. The engines were the GWR's first goods locomotives and were built with outside frames and a wheelbase 6ft 4in+ 6ft 5in, 5ft coupled wheels and 3ft 6in leading wheels, cylinders 15in x 18in, boilers with domed firebox casings, and a 50lb boiler pressure. To increase the adhesive weight, all of the class were altered to 2-4-0 saddle tanks with frames lengthened at the rear. The engine ceased work in July 1870, the average mileage for the class was about 400,000 miles. *Stromboli,* in company with other members of the class, *Aries, Cancer, Capricornus, Dromedary, Libra, Pisces, Scorpio,* and *Taurus* worked on the South Devon Railway from 1846, during the period when the line was worked by GWR locomotives. *Pisces* and *Pegasus* ('Fire Fly' class) hauled the opening passenger train from Newton (later Newton Abbot) up over Dainton bank to Totnes on 20th July 1847, and *Pisces* driven by Daniel Gooch, and *Capricornus* driven by M. C. Rea, worked the opening train to Laira Green (a temporary station just east of Plymouth) on 5th May 1848. *Taurus* hauled the opening train to Torquay on 18th December 1848. Most of the GWR locomotives had returned to the parent company from the South Devon Railway by the summer of 1852 with the exception of *Cancer* which was still recorded as being in Devon two years later.

Virgo. 'Leo' class. As above except – built by Rothwell & Co, Bolton. Builder's No. 71, delivered December 1841, and ceased work December 1870.

Morning Star. Built as 'Star' class. One of a class of twelve 2-2-2 tender locomotives designed and built by Robert Stephenson & Co. *Morning Star,* in company with the first of the class *North Star,* was built for the 5ft 6in gauge New Orleans Railway, USA. However, due to financial problems with the New Orleans, the two engines were regauged and sold to the GWR. *North Star* became the first engine on the company's books and the most reliable of the early locomotives. *North Star* was delivered by barge to Maidenhead on 28th November 1837, which was nearly six months before the railway reached the town, and on 31st May

1838 hauled the first GWR passenger train – a directors' special, four days before the opening of the line. *Morning Star*, builder's No. 149, was not despatched from Newcastle until December 1838, and was accepted by the GWR in January 1839. Total cost of engine and tender with some spare parts was £2,825 2s 6d. The locomotive was supplied with its original 6ft 6in driving wheels (all other members of the class had 7ft driving wheels), and 4ft carrying wheels, slotted outside sandwich frames, a wheelbase of 6ft 1in + 6ft 5in, cylinders 16in x 16in, boilers with round top raised firebox casing (*North Star and Morning Star* only) the other members of the class having dome shaped casings. The locomotives proved themselves to be very reliable and efficient, and resulted in a class of twelve engines being built by Robert Stephenson & Co. for the GWR, six of which were rebuilt as 4-2-2 saddle tanks. *Morning Star* is cited in one account as being rebuilt as a 4-2-2 saddle tank in lieu of *North Star*, whilst official records give it as being cut up as a tender engine in November 1869, the engine being withdrawn in July 1870. All of the class gave sterling service varying from 23 to 33 years. It is a well known fact that the GWR placed some of their oldest locomotives to work on the Wilts Somerset & Weymouth in its early years, and a glance at the Frome allocation of 1854 shows us that the oldest engine was *Morning Star* dating from 1839, with *Eclipse* (1840), *Stromboli* and *Virgo* (1841), and the Gooch 0-6-0 goods engine *Argo* being relatively new as it dated from 1846.

With their engine shed just 30 miles away at Frome, the GWR had no need for a shed at Yeovil. However, in 1856, the Company required a temporary building at Yeovil to house their engines whilst working on the extension of the line and also awaiting completion of their shed at Weymouth. The GWR obtained a lease on a piece of land belonging to the Bristol & Exeter company, the two-road shed being opened in September 1856, and when the shed at Weymouth was opened in 1857, the GWR then gave up the shed at Pen Mill to the B&E. The Bristol & Exeter then closed their shed at Hendford on the western outskirts of Yeovil and moved their engines to Pen Mill. The wheel again turned full circle when the GWR regained the shed at Yeovil Pen Mill after absorbing the Bristol & Exeter in 1876. The shed was later extended to three roads by the addition of a 102ft x 20ft side extension in 1877, which in later years was used as a repair shop. Some days before the final section of the WS&W from Yeovil to Weymouth was opened on 20th January 1857, a Gooch 0-6-0 Standard Goods engine of the 'Caesar' class, *Iris* (built at Swindon, March 1854) hauled the train, conveying Brunel and other company officers on the customary inspection tour of the main line.

Weymouth
Broad Gauge Allocation March 1857
Antelope. 'Wolf' class, originally built as 'Sun' class. One of a class of 21 locomotives designed by Gooch. Built by Sharp, Roberts & Co., Manchester in May 1841, builder's No. 122, but not actually delivered to the GWR until August 1841. Pending the completion of the Clegg and Samuda atmospheric system on the South Devon Railway, the line from Exeter to Teignmouth was opened for passenger traffic on 30th May 1846 with locomotives hired from the GWR, and *Antelope* hauled the opening train from Teignmouth to

Newton (later Newton Abbot) on 30th December 1846. *Antelope* ceased work in July 1870. Although built as 2-2-2 tender engines, the 'Sun' class were rebuilt as 2-2-2 saddle tanks with 15in x 18in cylinders, most of them in 1849/50.

Aurora. 'Wolf' class, originally built as 'Sun' class by R. & W. Hawthorn & Co., Newcastle builder's No. 318. Delivered to the GWR in December 1840. The locomotive, in company with *Comet*, and *Hesperus*, was fitted with 15in x 18in cylinders, whilst all other members of the class had cylinders of 14in x 18in, (when converted to saddle tanks they were all fitted with 15in x 18in cylinders), and in common with other members of the class had 6ft driving and 3ft 6in carrying wheels. *Aurora* ceased work in December 1866 and was withdrawn from stock in July 1870.

Creese. 'Wolf' class, originally built as 'Sun' class by Stothert & Slaughter, Bristol and delivered to the GWR in January 1842. The locomotive ceased work in March 1866 and was withdrawn from stock in July 1870.

Meridian. 'Wolf' class, originally built as 'Sun' class by R. & W. Hawthorn & Co., Newcastle, builder's No. 293, and delivered to the GWR in August 1840. *Meridian* ceased work in December 1870.

Stiletto. 'Wolf' class, originally built as 'Sun' class by Stothert & Slaughter, Bristol and delivered to the GWR in December 1841. *Stiletto* ceased work in July 1870.

Sun. 'Wolf' class, originally built as 'Sun' class by R. & W. Hawthorn & Co., builder's No. 291 and delivered to the GWR in April 1840; rebuilt at Swindon, July 1863 with a boiler of 120lb pressure. *Sun* ceased work in June 1873.

Sunbeam. 'Wolf' class, originally built as 'Sun' class by R. & W. Hawthorn & Co., Newcastle, builder's No. 292, and delivered to the GWR in May 1840. *Sunbeam* ceased work in July 1870.

Wolf. 'Wolf' class, originally built as 'Sun' class by Sharp, Roberts & Co., Manchester, builder's No. 129, and delivered to the GWR in July 1841, rebuilt at Swindon, April 1859 with a boiler of 120lb pressure. *Wolf* ceased work in June 1873 when it was put into use as a stationary boiler until being cut up in January 1882.

Yataghan. 'Wolf' class, originally built as 'Sun' class by Stothert & Slaughter, Bristol. Delivered to the GWR in August 1841. *Yataghan* ceased work in June 1871.

Fire King. 'Priam' class, originally built as 'Fire Fly' class. One of a class of 62, 2-2-2 tender engines, designed by Gooch and built between March 1840 and December 1842 by seven different manufacturers. *Fire King* was built by Jones, Turner & Evans, Newton-le-Willows, builder's No. 22. Delivered to the GWR in May 1840, the locomotive was built with outside slotted sandwich frames, and four inside stays with additional bearings for the driving axle, 7ft driving and 4ft carrying wheels. *Fire King* was altered into a 2-2-2 saddle tank with 6ft driving wheels by 1849, further alteration taking place at Swindon in January 1861 when the engine (as well as 17 other members of the class) was fitted with a domeless boiler with round top raised firebox casings, and lengthened frames. *Fire King* ceased work in June 1875.

Druid. 'Caesar' class, one of a class of eight 0-6-0 tender engines built at Swindon under '3rd Lot Goods', the locomotives had 5ft wheels, cylinders 16in x 24in (later altered to 17in x 24in). Boiler pressure 120lb. Weight 32 ton 9½ cwt (with tender). *Druid* was built in February 1852, ceased work in March 1879, and was withdrawn from stock in December 1879.

Nero. 'Caesar' class. Gooch Standard Goods, one of a class of 102 locomotives built at Swindon in seven lots, of which *Nero* was built at Swindon in January 1855 with 40 other engines as part of '6th Lot Goods'. The locomotive ceased work in November 1877.

Pallas. 'Caesar' class. Gooch Standard Goods. *Pallas* was built at Swindon in May 1856 to '6th Lot Goods'. The locomotive ceased work February 1879.

Sphinx. 'Caesar' class. Gooch Standard Goods, built at Swindon in September 1854 to '6th Lot Goods'. The locomotive ceased work in December 1873.

Otho. 'Victoria' class, one of a class of 18 2-4-0 tender engines built at Swindon in two lots; '5th Lot Passenger' (8) and '6th Lot Passenger' (10). *Otho* was built in November 1856 as part of the '5th Lot Passenger' group. The locomotive was involved in the opening day at Weymouth hauling the 8.30am departure on 20th January, 1857. The engine ceased work in December 1880.

The locomotive allocation at Weymouth as shown above in March 1857, comprised a mixture of the old and not so old, with some members of the 'Sun' class, although altered to tank engines in 1849/50, were 17 years old by the time the line from Yeovil to Weymouth had opened. The oldest locomotives were, *Aurora*, *Meridian*, *Sun* and *Sunbeam* all dating from 1840, with *Antelope*, *Stiletto*, *Wolf* and *Yataghan* dating from 1841, and *Creese* dating from 1842. The other locomotives allocated to Weymouth at the time were much newer engines, with *Druid* (1852), *Sphinx* (1854), *Nero* (1855), *Pallas* and *Otho* (1856) being only a year old when recorded at Weymouth in 1857.

The locomotive *Sun* is the engine that Daniel Gooch refused to accept from the builders, R. & W. Hawthorn, Newcastle and in a letter dated 4th April 1840 to the builders stated the following. "I cannot pass the engine in her present state, she not being in conformity with our drawings and specifications and thereby totally defeating our main object in furnishing drawings and templates, viz, to get our engines so that one part of any engine will fit another"... With the unsatisfactory and unreliable service record of the early locomotives Daniel Gooch had been authorised by the directors of the GWR to prepare drawings for future locomotives, and with his chief draughtsman, T. R. Crampton, he based his designs on the most efficient of his locomotives, namely *North Star*, built by R. Stephenson & Co. Between March 1840 and December 1842, the GWR took delivery of 105 six-wheeled tender engines of four classes, built by nine different makers, the Great Western being the first railway company to adopt standardisation on such a scale, and this practice set by Daniel Gooch was to be the norm for the GWR throughout its life.

The following 'Victoria' class 2-4-0 tender locomotives, and one member of the 'Caesar' class are recorded as being at Weymouth in July 1862:

Alexander. Built at Swindon in November 1856 to '5th Lot Passenger', the locomotive ceased work in March 1878, and was then sold to the Avon Colliery.

Leopold. Built at Swindon in September 1856 to '5th Lot Passenger', the locomotive ceased work in January 1877.

Otho. As described above in March 1857 list.

Victor Emanuel. Built at Swindon in October 1856 to '5th Lot Passenger' the locomotive ceased work in June 1878, and was then sold to the Avon Colliery.

Victoria. Built at Swindon in August 1856 to '5th Lot Passenger', the locomotive ceased work in January 1879. On 26th August 1862 *Victoria* hauling a late evening 'down' train due in at Weymouth at 10pm, was in trouble whilst descending Upwey bank and consequently ran through the station and stop blocks, crossed King Street and stopped just short of the Somerset Hotel.

Sirius. 'Caesar' class, 0-6-0 tender goods engine, built at Swindon in June 1861 to '9th Lot Goods', the locomotive ceased work in December 1880.

Bridport
Broad Gauge Allocation 1857 and 1862
The locally promoted Bridport Railway opened a 9 mile 21 chain broad gauge line from Maiden Newton to Bridport on 12th November 1857, the branch being worked by the GWR from the outset and was later leased to the GWR and absorbed in 1901.

Hesiod. A 4-4-0 bogie saddle tank, built by R. & W. Hawthorn & Co., Newcastle, in March 1855. Builder's No. 886, it was used on the branch in November 1857. The locomotive had inside sandwich frames, the main frames extending only from the front of the driving wheels to the back buffer beam. With cylinders of 17in x 24in, the engine had 3ft 6in bogie wheels and 5ft 9in coupled wheels. The four-wheel bogie swivelled in a ball and socket joint, the weight being taken from a double gusset riveted to the boiler barrel and steam chest, and transmitted to the axle boxes by inverted springs, one on each side of the engine. The saddle tank had a water capacity of 930 gallons. *Hesiod* ceased work in February 1872. *Theocritus*, another member of the class, builder's No. 883, and built by R. & W. Hawthorn in December 1854 is also recorded as having worked on the branch for most of its life, the locomotive ceasing work in December 1873, and was sold to the Staveley Iron & Coal Company in February 1874.

In 1862, two 2-4-0 tank engines of the 'Leo' class were based on the branch:

Aries. Built by Rothwell & Co. Bolton, builder's No. 66, delivered to the GWR in June 1841, it ceased work in June 1871.

Virgo, (previously based at Frome) also built by Rothwell, builder's No. 71, delivered to the GWR in December 1841. *Virgo* ceased work in December 1871.

Brindley, a 2-4-0 tender engine of the 'Victoria' class is also recorded as being on the branch, although tender engines were not used to that extent as the line was mainly worked by saddle tanks.

Chippenham
Broad Gauge Allocation 1857 and 1862
The allocation at Chippenham on 25th April 1857 prior to the opening of the shed in 1858 is recorded as being two 0-6-0 goods engines of the 'Caesar' class built at Swindon to '6th lot goods' – *Pallas* dating from May 1856, and *Thames* built in February 1854. Two locomotives are recorded as being at Chippenham in 1862 – *Abdul Medjid*, a 2-4-0 tender engine of the 'Victoria' class. Built at Swindon in October 1856, the locomotive ceased work in December 1877, and withdrawn from stock in December 1878. The other was *Nero* an 0-6-0 goods engine of the 'Caesar' class, built at Swindon in January 1855 to '6th Lot Goods', which ceased work in November 1877.

Devizes
Broad Gauge Allocation 1857 and 1862
The engine shed at Devizes was opened from April 1857, although the line was not opened for passenger traffic until 1st July of the same year. *Dreadnought*, an 0-6-0 goods engine of the 'Fury' class, originally built as 'Premier' class at Swindon in October 1846, is recorded as being at Devizes for the opening of the line. *Tityos*, an 0-6-0 tender engine of the 'Hercules' class (later 'Fury' class) built by Nasmyth, Gaskell & Co., builder's No. 46 and delivered to the GWR in October 1842, is recorded as failing on Caen Hill bank in July 1858 whilst working a Trowbridge to Devizes train, leaving the passengers to continue their journey by foot.

Nemesis, an 0-6-0 goods tender engine of the 'Caesar' class (former 'Caliph' class), was in trouble at Devizes in November 1862 when it became derailed whilst shunting, and effectively blocking the 'engine house' which contained two other engines. Two locomotives of the 'Fire Fly' class are also recorded as being at Devizes in 1862, including *Fire Fly*, a 2-2-2 tender engine, builder's No. 18, built by Jones, Turner & Evans, Newton-le-Willows and delivered to the GWR in March 1840. This locomotive ceased work November 1870 and was withdrawn from stock in July 1870. *Fire Fly* was driven by Daniel Gooch on 17th March 1840 hauling a directors' train of three vehicles from Paddington to Reading, a distance of 36 miles in 45 minutes.

Jupiter. A 2-2-2 tender engine, builder's No. 11, built by R. B. Longridge & Co., Bedlington in April 1841 the locomotive ceasing work in July 1867 and was withdrawn from stock in July 1870.

Shepton Mallet
Temporary Shed November 1858
The East Somerset Railway Company opened a 9-mile long single broad gauge line to Shepton Mallet from Witham on the WS&W Weymouth branch on 9th November 1858, an intermediate station at Cranmore

was also opened on the ESR branch with another station being added at Wanstrow in 1860. The line was worked by the GWR and absorbed in 1874. With the extension of the East Somerset branch to Wells a temporary engine shed was opened at Shepton Mallet in November 1858 for the use of locomotives working on the ESR extension. The shed housed *Thunderer*, an 0-6-0 tender engine of the 'Caesar' class built at Swindon under '3rd Lot Goods' in July 1851 with inside sandwich frames, 5ft wheels, cylinders 16in (later 17in) x 24in. The weight of engine and tender was 32 ton 9$\frac{1}{2}$cwt, and boiler pressure 120lb. The other engine based at Shepton Mallet was *Homer*, a 4-4-0 bogie saddle tank, builder's No. 876, built in August 1854 by R. & W. Hawthorn, Newcastle. The temporary shed at Shepton Mallet was closed in March 1862.

Wells
Broad Gauge Allocation 1862 and 1872
With the opening of the East Somerset line to Wells on 1st March 1862, an engine shed was erected by the company to the east of their station and two 4-4-0 bogie saddle tanks built by R. & W. Hawthorn, Newcastle, are recorded as being there. *Virgil*, builder's No. 877, built in September 1854, was at Wells in March 1862. *Virgil* ceased work in December 1873, and was sold to Dobson, Brown & Adams in July 1874. *Seneca*, another member of the same class, builder's No. 881 built in November 1854 was based at Wells by July 1862. *Seneca* ceased work in March 1872.

Salisbury
Broad Gauge Allocation 1856
Two locomotives of the 'Sun' class. *Javelin*, built by Stothert & Slaughter, Bristol and delivered to the GWR in July 1841, and *Sunbeam*, built by R. & W. Hawthorn & Co., Newcastle, builder's No. 292 delivered to the GWR in May 1840 are both recorded as being at Salisbury upon the opening of the remaining section of the branch from Warminster on 30th June, 1856. *Javelin* is known to have been allocated to Cheltenham in 1849.

Many other broad gauge locomotives were frequent visitors to the Wilts, Somerset & Weymouth line including the 'Victoria' class 2-4-0 tender engines with their 6ft 6in driving wheels which were designed for lighter routes such as this. Members of the class seen on the line, included, *Oscar*, *Napoleon* and *Abdul Medjid*. Engines of the 'Fire Fly' class including *Mentor*, *Arrow* and *Lethe* were used on the line although they were reported as not taking too kindly to the Evershot and Upwey banks. *Comet* of the 'Sun' class, and *Tityos* and *Nemesis* are reported as working on the line.

There was a cascading effect as older engines were withdrawn and replaced by more modern motive power. The 'Hawthorn' class of Joseph Armstrong began to replace the 'Victoria' class, the handsome 'Waverley' class with their 7ft coupled wheels and named after the heroes and novels of Sir Walter Scott, appeared at times and what splendid names they carried: *Ivanhoe*, *Rob Roy*, *Lalla Rookh* and *Coeur de Lyon*, to name a but a few of the class. They were the only class of 4-4-0 tender engines to run on the broad gauge. The magnificent 4-2-2 'Alma' class with their 8ft driving wheels including, *Swallow*, *Amazon*, *Balaclava*, and the *Lord of the Isles* were seen on the Weymouth line.

The Vale of Neath Railway was taken over by the GWR in February 1865 and 25 locomotives (19 being broad gauge) were added to the Great Western stock list in December 1866. After the South Wales line was converted in 1872 some of the Vale of Neath 0-6-0 saddle tanks were put to work on the Weymouth line, however, they did not last long as the GWR was pressing ahead with the conversion of its broad gauge empire.

In February 1874 the decision was made by the GWR to convert the Wilts, Somerset & Weymouth and the Berks & Hants to the standard gauge. The WS&W was converted to standard gauge by 25th June 1874 and the last survivors of the Vale of Neath Railway were sent to Newton Abbot and there they ended their days employed on banking duties up over Rattery and Dainton banks. *Europa*, another member of the 'Caesar' class built at Swindon in March 1853 to '5th Lot Goods' worked on the WS&W. The locomotive was the only one of its class to be rebuilt at Swindon when it was fitted with a new boiler in June 1869. After conversion of the WS&W in 1874 *Europa* was sent to Plymouth and was the last broad gauge engine to leave Plymouth for Swindon at about 4am on Saturday, 21st May 1892. This locomotive was the last of her class and survived until the end of the broad gauge.

Standard Gauge Locomotives

With the gauge conversion of the Wilts, Somerset & Weymouth it was now the turn of the standard gauge locomotives to perform on the route previously used by their broad gauge forebears. The Armstrong, inside framed 2-4-0 tender engines of the 481 class were amongst the first engines to be used on the Weymouth services. After a short period of use the engines were relocated to secondary duties between Bristol and Salisbury, and the Berks & Hants. Nos 56, 717, 719, 720 and 724, were 2-4-0 tender engines of the 717 class and were based at Weymouth for nearly twenty years. Other classes of locomotives included the 2-2-2 'Sir Daniel' or 378 class, Dean's 2-4-0 2201 class, and

Armstrong's 0-6-0 Standard Goods. The 'Barnum' or 3206 class, the last class of GWR locomotives to be built with outside sandwich frames, arrived on the line in the late 1880s. In the early 1890s the 2-4-0 tender engines of the 3232 class had largely replaced the earlier 2201 class. The 0-6-0 Dean Goods was now to be seen on the line and in the last few years of the nineteenth century, William Dean's 4-4-0 'Duke' or 3252 class appeared, working on most of the faster trains. In the early years of the twentieth century the 4-4-0 'Bulldogs' appeared and monopolised the Weymouth services by replacing the 'Dukes'. William Dean's final freight design, namely the double framed 'Aberdares' worked the main through goods traffic.

Steam railmotors were introduced on various routes including Westbury–Castle Cary, Westbury–Patney & Chirton, Westbury–Warminster, Trowbridge–Devizes, Weymouth–Dorchester, and Weymouth–Abbotsbury. In turn these were mainly displaced by auto trailers and 0-4-2 tanks of the 517 class and over the years many and various tank engines of the pannier and Prairie types were seen on branch and local services. As locomotive production increased and more and improved classes were introduced, thus bringing a cascading effect to the improvement of services on the secondary lines, the 4-4-0 'Counties' known as 'Churchward's rough riders', and the famous 'City' class appeared, of which No. 3710 *City of Bath* was involved in the tragic collision at Yeovil Pen Mill on 8th August 1913.

Churchward's versatile 4300 class 2-6-0 Moguls (known to the Weymouth crews as the 'big engines') became common users of the line during the 1920s. With the 'Saint' class being allocated to Reading, Westbury and Weymouth sheds in 1926 many examples of this class were seen working the Weymouth express trains as they replaced the 4-4-0 'Counties' on this duty. The free running and popular 'Star' class were also used during the 1920s, and with 13 of the class becoming allocated to Bristol in 1932, from c1935 they mainly replaced the earlier 'Saints'. As soon as their numbers increased during the late 1920s

With Clink Junction signal box and the line into Frome in the distance, No. 5067 *St Fagans Castle*, hauling a light load of six carriages, races down the Frome avoiding line in 1937. This is the third part of the 3.30pm from Paddington, running to Taunton at least, and thence to Ilfracombe and Minehead if required. Reporting number 197 was the third part to Taunton of the 3.30pm Paddington–Penzance on 1.8.36, but by 5.8.39 it was a relief, run as required from Paddington to Minehead and Ilfracombe, to the 3.25pm 'down' Kingswear. This was itself a relief to the 3.30pm 'down'. The GWR was amazingly well organised to be able to turn out a train like this at short notice, and then run it as far as was necessary to cater for the passengers involved, and who made it worthwhile to do so.

Adrian Vaughan Collection

and early 1930s, members of the 'Hall' and 'Castle' classes appeared. Many of the GWR passenger classes were used on the line except for the 'Kings' which were banned from using the route from Castle Cary to Weymouth.

The AEC built diesel railcars came to the line in 1936 with Nos 10, 11 and 12 being used on services from Bristol to Salisbury, and Bristol to Weymouth. At that time the diesel timings on the Weymouth line were the fastest in the country. The GWR built railcars were in use on the line from the early part of the war, including from time to time the twin sets. From the post war years until the appearance of the dmus in 1959, the single GWR diesel railcars based at Weymouth worked certain Bristol trains, and local services to Yeovil.

The cascading of locomotives continued with the 'Aberdares' being replaced by the 28xx 2-8-0s on heavy goods traffic. Traffic after the Second World War was still in the hands of 'Castles', 'Halls', 'Manors', Moguls, and by this time the Hawksworth 'County' class 4-6-0s had appeared. This powerful class of locomotive gave sterling service whilst transversing the undulating route up over Evershot and Brewham banks. BR Standard class 4-6-0 locomotives of the 5MT and 4MT variants, and "Black Fives" were also used on the line, although the latter were mainly confined to goods trains, but they were also used on passenger trains through the busy summer season. WD 2-8-0s appeared now and again on freight workings from Bristol. Regular diesel multiple unit workings started on 6th April 1959 forming three down and up services interspersed with the normal steam services.

The first regular diesel locomotive workings occurred on 16th September, 1961, with the 10.10am Sundays only service from Bristol to Weymouth, and 15.25 return from Weymouth being worked by a 'Hymek' diesel hydraulic. It was not long before the 'Hymeks' started to appear on various freight and parcels workings. With the withdrawal of steam locomotives, the services were worked by dmus, Class 52 'Westerns', and 'Hymeks'. The very last steam workings over the Weymouth–Westbury line occurred on Sunday 9th July 1967 when three special tomato trains were worked from Weymouth. The three locomotives, each hauling their respective trains were, Nos 34052 *Lord Dowding*, 34095 *Brentor*, and Class 5MT 73092. Services today are worked mostly by two-car 'Sprinters' with Class 37 and 47 diesels appearing during the summer months on excursion traffic. Class 33s and 50s have also been recorded on the line.

Sheds and Allocations
Westbury
Westbury locomotive shed, built to the G. J. Churchward standard straight road pattern, opened in February 1915 and was built in brick with a slate roof. The main running shed 210ft x 66ft, comprised four roads in the usual pattern of two roads per roof span with raised timber louvred vents placed centrally along each ridge. Shed roads were capable of holding three tender engines or six tank engines. Attached to, and to the right of the running shed as viewed from the front, was a single-road lifting shop measuring 84ft x 40ft. Offices attached to the main building were provided, the dimensions being 125ft x 15ft. A 45,000 gallon water tank formed the roof of the 30ft x 32ft brick built coaling stage, while a brick built boiler house stood in

front of the lifting shop housing a stationary boiler, which supplied steam for the machinery in the repair shop and for the hot water boiler washing out plant. A sand furnace was also provided, this standing a little distance in front of the boiler house.

A 65ft diameter over-girder turntable was situated at the rear of the shed and four water columns were provided. The gas lighting for the shed and shed yard was later altered to electric. The shed occupied a spacious layout compared with the cramped conditions at the nearby Trowbridge establishment, with a fan of five storage sidings to the left of the shed for stabling engines, plus a siding situated to the rear of the coaling stage for stabling coal wagons. A siding for ash wagons was positioned alongside the disposal and coaling line. The depot was constructed to hold some 70 locomotives and was built to allow future extension.

During the Second World War ash shelters were built over the ash and coaling roads at all sheds to hide the glow of firebox clinker from enemy aircraft. The shelters were built of brick and corrugated iron sheeting 30ft wide and 100ft long. Westbury shed closed to steam in September 1965.

GWR shed code WES, numerical code 172.

BR shed codes, 1949–1963 82D, 1963–1965 83C.

A diesel refuelling and maintenance depot situated on the site of the former ambulance sidings up side of the main line near the station, was opened on 15th June 1959, initially for the new dmus. A shelter with inspection pit for the locomotives and an office with mess and staff rooms were provided. Diesel allocations for June 1964 included 0-6-0 shunters: Nos D3511, D3998, D4019, D4021 and D4023. Over the years the depot has had locomotives representing most of the main diesel classes based there, mainly for the heavy limestone traffic from the local quarries at Whatley and Merehead. The diesel depot and office closed on 1st March 1993, the site being cleared in the December of that year.

Allocations 1922
3252 class. 4-4-0 No. 3254 *Cornubia*.
3300 class. 4-4-0 Nos 3340 *Camel*, 3356 *Sir Stafford*, 3432, 3439 *Weston super Mare*, 3448 *Kingfisher*.
3700 class. 4-4-0 Nos 3712 *City of Bristol*, 3716 *City of London*.
3800 class. 4-4-0 Nos 3806 *County Kildare*, 3815 *County of Hants*, 3832 *County of Wilts*.
'Atbara' class. 4-4-0 No. 4128 *Maine*.
2800 class. 2-8-0 Nos 2850, 2863.
4300 class. 2-6-0 Nos 4348, 4365, 6396.
2301 class. (Dean Goods). 0-6-0 Nos 2337, 2450, 2468, 2517, 2565, 2566.
2361 class. 0-6-0 No. 2380
3232 class. 2-4-0 No. 3235.
3206 ('Barnum') class. 2-4-0 Nos 3212, 3213, 3219, 3221.
1076 class. 0-6-0ST Nos 739, 1624.
1854 class. 0-6-0PT No. 1856.
1661 class. 0-6-0PT No. 1663.
2721 class. 0-6-0PT No. 2735.
3901 Class. 2-6-2T Nos 3908, 3910.

Twenty 2301 class Dean Goods were withdrawn and converted to 2-6-2 tanks during 1907/10. No 3908 (previously Dean Goods No. 2497) was converted in November 1907, and No. 3910 (previously No. 2500) was converted in February 1908.

The new locomotive shed at Westbury in 1915 with a lone 2221 class 'County' 4-4-2 tank engine standing on the ash pit. The shed and coaling stage are so new, and the yard so tidy that you can almost smell the fresh new paint! Loco coal wagon No. 9071 stands inside the coaling stage in readiness for the next locomotive. Two gas lamps are attached to the coaling stage, and five gas lamp standards adorn the shed yard.

National Railway Museum

The interior of the new Westbury shed in 1915, looking fresh and clean with its gleaming paintwork and clean windows.

National Railway Museum

Two locomotives, Nos 6 and 10, under the heading 'CR Engines' are recorded as being on loan in 1922 to the GWR and stationed at Westbury. No. 10 had been returned to the government in March 1922, and No. 6 being returned in March 1923, and it is believed that the two engines were 4-4-0 tanks Class 1 of the Caledonian Railway but further research is continuing into this subject.

Allocations 1934
3252 class. 4-4-0 No. 3283 *Comet*.
3300 class. 4-4-0 Nos 3316 (former *St Columb*), 3343 *Camelot*, 3354 (former *Restormel*), 3384 (former *Swindon*), 3389 (former *Taunton*), 3421.
2900 class. 4-6-0 Nos 2933 *Bibury Court*, 2977 *Robertson*.

4900 class. 4-6-0 Nos 4932 *Hatherton Hall*, 4964 *Rodwell Hall*, 4982 *Acton Hall*.
4300 class. 2-6-0 Nos 4314, 4315, 4326, 4349, 4365, 4368, 6341, 6382, 6384, 7302.
2301 class. (Dean Goods) 0-6-0 Nos 2394, 2435, 2518, 2529, 2566, 2639.
2361 class. 0-6-0 No. 2364.
4575 class. 2-6-2T Nos 5511, 5546, 5556, 5570.
5600 class. 0-6-2T Nos 5689, 6690.
850 class. 0-6-0PT No. 1915.
1076 class. 0-6-0PT No. 1644.
1813 class. 0-6-0PT No. 1816.
2721 class. 0-6-0PT Nos 2779, 2780.
5400 class. 0-6-0PT No. 5419.
5700 class. 0-6-0PT Nos 5718, 6712, 7711, 7726, 7727, 7730, 7749, 8722, 8744.
4800 class. 0-4-2T No. 4829.

43xx Mogul 2-6-0 No. 6353 stands alongside 4-6-0 No. 4956 *Plowden Hall* at Westbury shed on 2nd June 1963.　　　*C. L. Caddy*

During the Second World War locomotives from various companies were on loan to the GWR and the following were allocated to Westbury:

LMS 2F 0-6-0. Nos 3023 (10/39), 3048 (12/39), 3096 (1/40), 3517 (10/39), 3526 (12/39), 3543 (11/39), 3603 (12/39), 3689 (11/39). No 3090 went to Westbury at a later date, and only Nos 3048 and 3096 stayed at Westbury throughout the war, the other locomotives were allocated to other depots on the GWR including 3023 which went to Weymouth. All of the LMS 2F engines had left the GWR by November 1945.

USA 2-8-0. Nos 2422 (8/43), 2434 (8/43). These were later allocated to Swindon and all of the class had left the GWR by September/October 1944.

WD 2-8-0 No. 7412 (9/44–12/44)

Allocations 1947
1000 class. 4-6-0 No. 1027 *County of Stafford*.
2900 class. 4-6-0 Nos 2928 *Saint Sebastian*, 2941 *Easton Court*, 2946 *Langford Court*.

4000 class. 4-6-0 No. 4028 (originally named *King John* when built in September 1909, but upon the introduction of the 'King' class the locomotive was renamed *The Roumanian Monarch* in July 1927, this nameplate being removed in November 1940, and apart from the suffix, 'Star Class' painted on the splashers the locomotive then remained nameless until withdrawal in November 1951). Nos 4038 *Queen Berengaria*, 4045 *Prince John*.
4900 class. (Hall) 4-6-0 Nos 4926 *Fairleigh Hall*, 4927 *Farnborough Hall*, 4963 *Rignal Hall*, 5900 *Hinderton Hall*,
5924 *Dinton Hall*, 5925 *Eastcote Hall*, 5961 *Toynbee Hall*, 5971 *Merevale Hall*, 5974 *Wallsworth Hall*, 5985 *Mostyn Hall*.
6959 class. (Modified Hall) 4-6-0 6966 *Witchingham Hall*.
6800 class. 4-6-0 6804 *Brockington Grange*, 6845 *Paviland Grange*, 6966 *Morfa Grange*.
3300 class. 4-4-0 Nos 3363 *Alfred Baldwin*, 3364 *Frank Bibby*, 3438 (former *Launceston*).

A shed yard scene at Westbury on 19th August 1951, with 43xx Mogul 2-6-0 No. 7309 (note number still on bufferbeam) and Dean Goods No. 2444 standing behind. No. 2444 hauled the last goods train over the Limpley Stoke–Camerton branch to and from Monkton Combe on 14th February 1951, the locomotive being crewed by Driver Webb and Fireman Knighton from Westbury shed.

Hugh Ballantyne

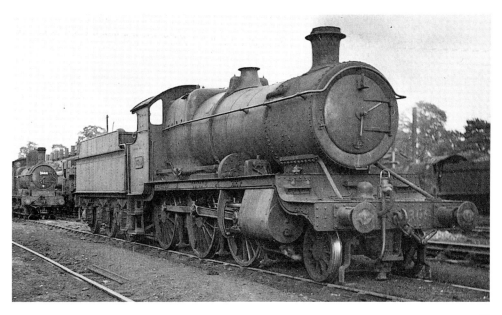

Westbury shed on 5th May 1963. A lone diesel shunter lurks amongst the steam stock at this busy shed, a mineral wagon stands filled with clinker and smokebox ash and more empty wagons stand on the coaling ramp.

C. L. Caddy

Two members of the 'Grange' class. Nos 6875 *Hindford Grange* and 6819 *Highnam Grange*, stand in the smoky atmosphere outside Westbury shed on 19th August 1951.

Hugh Ballantyne

Dean Goods 0-6-0 No. 2534 stands outside Westbury shed on 19th August 1951. No. 2534, dating from July 1897, received a boiler change in August 1915 when it was fitted with a B4 boiler. The locomotive was superheated in September 1925, and withdrawn in January 1953.

Hugh Ballantyne

2800/2884 Class. 2-8-0 Nos 2803, 2818, 3842, 3849, 3850, 3863.
3000 class. (ROD) 2-8-0 Nos 3014, 3019, 3032, 3032.
4300 class. 2-6-0 Nos 4365, 4377, 5306, 5311, 5326, 6314, 6351, 6365, 6368, 6369, 6375, 6399, 7300, 7302, 7309.
2301 class. (Dean Goods) 0-6-0 No. 2445.
4500 class. 2-6-2T Nos 4508, 4520, 4573.
4575 class. 2-6-2T Nos 5508, 5509, 5554.
5600 class. 0-6-2T Nos 5689, 6690, 6699.
2000 class. 0-6-0PT No. 2053.
5700 class. 0-6-0PT Nos 3696, 5757, 5771, 5781, 5785, 7727, 7784, 9612.

5400 class. 0-6-0PT Nos 5402, 5419, 5422, 5423.
Total 71 Locomotives.

Allocations 1950
1000 class. 4-6-0 No. 1027 *County of Stafford.*
4000 class. 4-6-0 Nos 4028, 4038 *Queen Berengaria,* 4045 *Prince John.*
6800 class. 4-6-0 Nos 6804 *Brockington Grange,* 6845 *Paviland Grange.*
4900 class. 4-6-0 Nos 4926 *Fairleigh Hall,* 4927 *Farnborough Hall,* 4963 *Rignal Hall,* 5900 *Hinderton Hall,* 5924 *Dinton Hall,* 5925 *Eastcote Hall,* 5961

A closer view of Westbury locomotive shed on 12th July 1964. Smoke stained, broken windows, and nearing the end of its days, it is a far cry from when new in 1915.

Barry Eagles

Prairie tank No. 4591 stands under the coaling stage at Westbury in company with 0-6-0 pannier tank No. 3739 amongst the mounds of clinker and smokebox ash on 12th July 1964.

Barry Eagles

The new diesel fuelling and stabling point at Westbury, seen here on 9th April 1959, at first used by the new dmus and later by diesel locomotives. The depot officially opened on 15th June 1959 and closed on 1st March 1993 being demolished, along with fuelling equipment and staff amenity block, in December 1993.

National Railway Museum

Toynbee Hall, 5971 *Merevale Hall*, 5974 *Wallsworth Hall*, 5985 *Mostyn Hall*, 6935 *Browsholme Hall*, 6955 *Lydcott Hall*.
6959 class. 4-6-0 (Modified Hall) Nos 6966 *Witchingham Hall*, 6978 *Haroldstone Hall*, 6982 *Melmerby Hall*, 6991 *Acton Burnell Hall*.
4300 class. 2-6-0 Nos 4377, 5306, 5326, 5385, 6314, 6365, 6368, 6369, 6375, 6399, 7300, 7302, 7309.
WD 2-8-0. Nos 90343, 90360, 90701.
5600 class. Nos 0-6-2T 5689, 6690, 6699.
4500 class. 2-6-2T Nos 4508, 4510, 4572, 4573.
4575 class. 2-6-2T Nos 5508, 5509, 5554.
2000 class. 0-6-0PT Nos 2023, 2053.
5400 class. 0-6-0PT Nos 5402, 5403, 5406, 5419, 5422, 5423.
5700 class. 0-6-0PT Nos 3696, 3735, 3758, 4636, 4647, 5718, 5757, 5771, 5781, 5785, 7727, 7784, 8744, 9612, 9615, 9628, 9762.
Total 75 locomotives.

Allocations 1959
4900 class. 4-6-0 Nos 4917 *Crosswood Hall*, 4933 *Himley Hall*, 4945 *Milligan Hall*, 5945 *Leckhampton Hall*, 5963 *Wimpole Hall*, 5974 *Wallsworth Hall*, 5975 *Winslow Hall*, 6945 *Glasfryn Hall*, 6955 *Lydcott Hall*.
6959 class. (Modified Hall) 4-6-0 Nos 6994 *Baggrave Hall*, 7909 *Heveningham Hall*, 7917 *North Aston Hall*, 7924 *Thornycroft Hall*.
2800/1884 class. 2-8-0 Nos 2811, 3819.
4300 class. 2-6-0 Nos 5358, 6320, 6358, 7300, 7302.
2200 class. 0-6-0 2268.
5600 class. 0-6-2T Nos 5689, 6625.
4500 class. 2-6-2T Nos 4536, 4555, 4567.
4575 class. 2-6-2T Nos 5508, 5526, 5542, 5554.
5400 class. 0-6-0PT Nos 5414, 5416, 5423.
5700 class. 0-6-0PT Nos 3614, 3629, 3696, 3735, 4607, 4636, 4647, 5757, 5771, 7727, 7748, 7784, 8744, 9612, 9615, 9628, 9668, 9762.
6400 class. No. 6408.
9400 class. No. 8482.
Total 53 locomotives.

A new shed code, 83C (the former shed code for Exeter, 1949–1963) was allotted to Westbury from September 1963. The depot stock had shrunk to a total of eight tank engines in 1965.

Allocations 1965
5700 class. 0-6-0PT Nos 3669, 3735, 4607, 4636, 4673, 4697, 9605, 9790.

Westbury steam depot closed in September 1965 with all steam locomotives withdrawn.

Frome
The single-road, timber built former broad gauge locomotive shed measuring 60ft x 20ft was situated west of the station and lay on the up side of the station layout behind the goods shed. A brick built office adjoined the building. A sand drier was to be found inside the shed and there was an inspection pit and a water column outside the shed. There was also a coal siding with an inspection pit which was used for fire dropping and ash pan raking. Engines were also stabled on the Malt house sidings, much to the annoyance of the shunters who had to move the dead (out of steam) engines out of the way prior to making a shunt either for the Malt house or cattle pen sidings. Other buildings in the area included a mess hut, and enginemens' and shunters' cabins. With the introduction of steam railmotors on the GWR in the early 1900s two of these were allocated to Frome from 1905 to 1928 working services from Westbury to Castle Cary and Taunton, Westbury to Chippenham, and Westbury to Warminster. Westbury shed from 1922 to 1925 also worked the same services with steam railmotors in conjunction with the Frome crews. When the steam railmotors were eventually withdrawn their place was taken by auto fitted tanks and driving trailers. The shed crews also worked the local shunting duties, passenger and goods trains over the North Somerset and Cheddar Valley lines in conjunction with Bristol crews, and various duties in the Frome area including

Frome shed in October 1949 with 4500 Class 2-6-2T No. 4572. On the right is the old broad gauge goods shed.

John Edgington courtesy of Roger Griffiths

Class 56 No. 56041 with a 'not to be moved' board stands at Westbury depot on 28th December 1991 with sister locomotives, Nos 56043 and 56001 *Whatley* in the distance.

Peter Nicholson

The impressive bulk of Class 60 No. 60041 *High Willhays*, seen here at the Westbury stabling point on 28th December 1991.

Peter Nicholson

Driver Russell and Fireman Millett pose for posterity in front of 'Barnum' 2-4-0 No. 3211 which is standing off the end of the 'up' platform at Frome in the 1920s. No. 3211 was built in May 1889 and was one of a successful class designed by William Dean for express passenger work, and which were the last type of locomotive designed by the GWR with outside sandwich frames. They were nicknamed the 'Barnums' as they were used at one time to convey the American type rolling stock for Barnum & Bailey's Circus and Menagerie on their tour of the country. When newly built the engines worked trains from Swindon to Gloucester and South Wales, and were used on the Weymouth line. From 1900 to 1922 most of the class were allocated to Oxford, Bristol, Swindon, and Westbury. No. 3211 was in Swindon Works in 1921, and based at Trowbridge shed in 1922, but by this time the class had been reduced to local and branch line work. The 'Barnums' in the Bristol Division, except for Nos 3208, 3212 and 3215, were sent to the Northern Division of the GWR in the 1920s. No. 3211 ended her days at Croes Newydd shed and was withdrawn in November 1934.

Courtesy of Mrs G. Russell. G.W. Quartley Collection

goods trains to Sparkford. Frome would be home to engines from other sheds including Bristol before returning on their respective duties. Shed staff at least during BR days included two fitters, eight loco crews, nine shedmen used for fire dropping and coaling, and three chargehands. The depot became a sub shed to Westbury with engines being supplied from the parent shed. Frome shed was closed in September 1963.

Allocations 1922
517 class. 0-4-2T No. 215
'Metro' class. 2-4-0T No. 986
633 class. 0-6-0T No. 638
1854 class. 0-6-0PT No. 1791
1076 class. 0-6-0PT Nos 1135, 1180, 1228, 1598.
1813 class. 0-6-0PT Nos 1814, 1817.
2721 class. 0-6-0PT No. 2769.
Steam Railmotor. Nos 56, 57.

Allocations 1934
655 class. 0-6-0PT No. 2705.
2721 class. 0-6-0PT No. 2799
4500 class. 2-6-2T Nos 4536, 4566.
4575 class. 2-6-2T Nos 5514, 5563.
5400 class. 0-6-0PT Nos 5402, 5403.
5700 class. 0-6-0PT No. 8745.

Allocations 1947
5700 Class. 0-6-0PT Nos 3731, 3735, 3758, 4636, 5718, 8744, 8745, 9762.
2000 Class. No. 2023.
5400 Class. Nos 5403, 5406.

Up until the closure of Frome shed a varied assortment of pannier tank engines were allocated from the parent shed at Westbury over the years, together with 2-6-2 tanks for the branch passenger services.

Yeovil Pen Mill
The former broad gauge shed occupied a site in the vee of land created by the Weymouth main line and the single track branch to the joint station at Yeovil Town. Originally constructed as a two-road shed 105ft x 40ft, an additional single-road shed 102ft x 20ft was added in 1877 and in later years was used as a repair shop. It remained virtually as built until closure on 9th January 1959. The depot comprised the three-road timber built shed, a 30ft x 22ft coaling platform with a timber lean to, providing protection for the coalmen unloading the coal wagons. A 33,000 gallon water tank formed the roof of the coal stage, while a small 44ft 8in turntable used for turning tank engines, and small tender engines was located to the rear of the shed near the Yeovil Town branch. The turntable was equipped in 1928 with extension bars known to the enginemen as 'skis', and a 22XX 0-6-0 tender engine or a small Mogul could be turned with difficulty using the extension bars, and was known to many enginemen visiting the shed to turn as, 'that pig of a table'. Two breakdown vans and a snow plough were allocated to the depot. In 1909 the shed had 14 locomotives with 17 locomotive crews plus fitters, coalmen, firedroppers and shed staff.

GWR shed code YEO, numerical code 192.
BR shed codes 82E 1949–1958, 71H 1958–1959.

With all of the steam stock and staff being despatched to the nearby Yeovil Town shed the previous January, the former broad gauge timber built shed at Yeovil Pen Mill was now host to a two-car dmu in 1959. The advanced starting signal in the foreground for the branch to Yeovil Town station is lowered, and in the distance a Bulleid Pacific heads tender first towards Yeovil Junction from the Town station.

John Day

Fred Martin, with whom I have shared many a footplate when the Pen Mill men were moved to our shed at Yeovil Town, started his footplate career as an engine cleaner at Pen Mill in 1937. There were six cleaners employed at the shed, two per shift 6am–2pm, 2pm–10pm, 10pm–6am, and all of the engines were oiled down and cleaned to perfection. Fred was 17 years of age when he started at the shed and therefore could only work the day shift until he was 18. One of the night cleaners had to cycle around the town calling the footplatemen out on early turns to make sure that they got to work. This was from 2.15am to 6am, when the breakdown gang was called out at night or in the early hours of the morning. The cleaners went out in the breakdown vans to assist the gang, for which they were paid an extra shilling (5p) in their wages. When the cleaners had accomplished 52 spare firing turns they were rewarded with an overcoat.

Fred recalls that the depot consisted of ten engines plus two spare locomotives, and they were used on double or treble shifts for banking duties at Evershot and Castle Cary, passenger and freight work on the Taunton branch. Also, shunting at Hendford goods yard and Pen Mill, with various trip workings along the Westbury–Weymouth line, local goods from Castle Cary to Durston, and at one time, a passenger working to Bristol. Pannier tanks were used for banking and local goods work, and the Prairie tanks for the branch passenger work.

One interesting passenger service worked by Pen Mill crews was that from Taunton to Trowbridge via Curry Rivel junction and the branch to Yeovil Pen Mill. The train was booked to a 2-6-2 tank, leaving Pen Mill with the 11.39am to Taunton. Upon arrival at Taunton at 12.36pm the engine was taken to the shed,

and later in the same day departed from the station with the 4.25pm to Yeovil. After arriving at Pen Mill at 5.45pm, the train then formed the 5.56pm to Trowbridge arriving at 7.14pm.

When Fred was firing during the Second World War he remembers working on troop trains, tank trains, ammunition trains, and ambulance trains to the military hospital at Norton Fitzwarren. There was an occurence during the war that upset many local footplate crews and that was when RAF Spitfire pilots used to practise strafing attacks on trains. "Very often you were looking forward out of the side of the cab, when you observed two streaks and a spinner coming towards you. It put a nasty taste in your mouth for the moment, but glad to say, a few weeks later, a main line driver who had also been upset by the Spitfire pilots, stopped his train at Curry Rivel Junction signal box to complain to the signalman and the practice was soon stopped."

Allocations 1922
3300 class. 4-4-0 No. 3392 *New Zealand.*
3521 class. 4-4-0 No. 3552. Built as a broad gauge 0-4-2 convertible saddle tank in December 1888, converted to 0-4-4 side tank October 1890, and to the standard gauge August 1892, rebuilt as a 4-4-0 tender engine in October 1900, and withdrawn from service in November 1929.
Metro class. 2-4-0T No. 626.
1076 class. 0-6-0PT Nos 1242, 1626, 1646.
1076 class. 0-6-0ST Nos 1177, 1232, 1250, 1589.
    Converted to pannier tanks (1177, 6/1924), (1232, 3/1923), (1250, 11/1925), (1589, 9/1922).
3571 class. 0-4-2T No. 3576.
Steam railmotor. No. 53.
Steam railmotor. No. 89.

49

A wintry scene at Yeovil Pen Mill in 1960 with the cattle pens in the foreground, and the locomotive shed and coaling stage in the distance, lying between the Weymouth main line and the branch to Yeovil Town.

Allocations 1934
1076 class. 0-6-0PT Nos 1166, 1179, 1180, 1598, 1620, 1624.
1501 class. 0-6-0PT No. 1525.
1854 class. 0-6-0PT No. 1860.
4575 class. 2-6-2T Nos 5548, 5554.

Allocations 1947. As at June 15th
4500 class. 2-6-2T No. 4572.
4575 class. 2-6-2T Nos 5529, 5565.
5700 class. 0-6-0PT Nos 3671, 3733, 4689, 5767, 9601, 9615, 9771.
1854 class. 0-6-0PT No. 1767.

Allocations 1950
4575 class. 2-6-2T Nos 5529, 5565.
5700 class. 0-6-0PT Nos 3671, 3733, 4689, 5767, 8745, 9601, 9732, 9771.

Final Locomotive Allocations 1959
4575 class. 2-6-2T Nos 5548, 5563.
5700 class. 0-6-0PT Nos 3671, 3733, 4656, 8745, 9732, 9764.

Upon the closure of the shed on 5th January 1959, the engines and staff were transferred to the Southern Region shed at Yeovil Town.

Bridport
The former broad gauge single-road shed was built of stone under a slate roof and measuring 60ft x 22ft, dated from 1857. This former sub shed of Weymouth closed in 1959 with the last two engines, Nos 4507 and 4562, departing for Weymouth on 15th June of that year.

Allocations 1921
2021 class. 0-6-0PT Nos 2113, 2119.

Allocations 1934
1076 class. 0-6-0PT Nos 1239, 1289.

Weymouth
The first WS&W locomotive shed was situated near the station and opened in January 1857. The two-road building was timber built with a slate roof. A 35ft diameter turntable with mixed gauge track was shared with the two-road LSWR shed which faced the GWR depot at the far end of the layout. With the cramped layout of the original shed it was found that more locomotive room was needed, with the continued growth of traffic, especially to the Channel Islands. A new locomotive shed was built to the north of the station alongside the down main line. The four-road straight shed built to the Dean pattern was opened in June 1885, being constructed of brick with a northlight slated and glazed roof. The dimensions were: shed 180ft x 62ft, lifting shop (with 20-ton crane) 90ft x 22ft, boiler house 90ft x 15ft, offices 100ft x 20ft, sand furnace 20ft x 15ft, turntable 49ft 9in diameter, and a flat type coal stage was sited in front of the repair shop. New engine departure and arrival lines were also laid and brought into use at the same time as the new shed. The new depot occupied a spacious layout with room for future extension compared with the original shed.

By 1920 the turntable had been equipped with extension bars to turn the larger engines which were now appearing, and in 1925 it was removed and replaced by a 65ft diameter turntable which was situated towards the end of the shed yard. More improvements came in 1930 when the original coaling stage was replaced by a ramp approach version and located on the other side of the shed yard. The new brick built coaling stage measured 30ft x 32ft. Other improvements at the same time included altering the roof from the original northlight pattern to a single pitched slate style and replacing the 20-ton crane in the lifting shop with a 35-ton version. The original two-road LSWR shed closed in January 1939 as the site occupied by the depot was required for station improvements. Engines then used the GWR locomotive depot.

With the ending of steam Weymouth locomotive shed closed on 9th July 1967, although the depot

Class 3MT 2-6-2T No. 82030 takes the single line route to Yeovil Town from Yeovil Pen Mill station with a train for Taunton via Durston on 28th March 1964. The steam emitting from the front end is nothing unusual for this type of engine, and I must admit, as a footplateman, the Standard classes as a whole were not my favourite type of engine to work on. Note the trackless coaling stage to the right, still in good condition after the engine shed had closed five years earlier in 1959.

Gerald T. Robinson

remained as a signing on point until October 1970. The turntable spurs were removed in 1968 and all loco sidings were taken out of use on 27th November 1970.

GWR shed code WEY. Numerical Code 162.
BR codes 82F 1949–1958, 71G 1958–1963,
  70G 1963–1967.

Allocations 1922
3300 class. 4-4-0 Nos 3373 *Sir William Henry*, 3401
  Vancouver, 3411 *Stanley Baldwin*, 3421, 3426, 3428,
  3431, 3449 *Nightingale*, 3451 *Pelican*.
2600 class. ('Aberdare') 2-6-0 No. 2600.
4300 class. 2-6-0 Nos 4314, 5357, 6328.
2301 class. (Dean Goods) 0-6-0 Nos 2330, 2353.
2021 class. 0-6-0T Nos 2059 (saddle tank), 2119
  (pannier tank).
727 class. 0-6-0PT No. 751.
517 class. 0-4-2T Nos 546, 549, 561, 1430.
0-6-0ST No. 1337 *Hook Norton*, ex-Hook Norton
  Ironstone Partnership Ltd.
0-6-0T Nos 1376, 1377, former Bristol & Exeter Railway.

Allocations 1934
3300 class. 4-4-0 Nos 3330 *Orion*, 3345 *Smeaton*, 3432.
4900 class. 4-6-0 Nos 4923 *Evenley Hall*, 4929 *Goytrey
  Hall*, 4947 *Nanhoran Hall*, 4992 *Crosby Hall*, 5919
  Worsley Hall.
4300 class. 2-6-0 Nos 4370, 5367, 6307, 6344, 6397, 7309,
  8320, 8391.
1076 class. 0-6-0PT Nos 1281, 1566.

1813 class. 0-6-0PT Nos 1831, 1841.
0-6-0ST No. 1331 ex-Whitland & Cardigan Railway.
0-6-0ST Nos 2194 *Kidwelly*, 2195 *Cwm Mawr*, ex-Burry
  Port & Gwendraeth Valley Railway.
517 class. 0-4-2T Nos 219, 833, 1163, 1465.

Allocations 1947
2900 class. 4-6-0 Nos 2912 *Saint Ambrose*, 2955
  Tortworth Court.
4900 class. 4-6-0 Nos 4988 *Bulwell Hall*, 5968 *Cory
  Hall*, 5969 *Honington Hall*, 6945 *Glasfryn Hall*.
2800 class. 2-8-0 No. 2817.
4300 class. 2-6-0 Nos 5305, 5314, 5328, 5337, 5338, 5340,
  5359, 5384.
4500 class. 2-6-2T No. 4527.
1366 class. 0-6-0PT Nos 1367, 1368, 1370.
655 class. 0-6-0PT No. 1789.
7400 class. 0-6-0PT No. 7408.
5700 class. 0-6-0PT No. 9642.
1400 class. 0-4-2T Nos 1403, 1454, 1467.

Allocations 1950
2900 class. 4-6-0 No. 2912 *Saint Ambrose*.
4073 class. 4-6-0 No. 4080 *Powderham Castle*.
4900 class. 4-6-0 Nos 4930 *Hagley Hall*, 4988 *Bulwell
  Hall*, 5968 *Cory Hall*, 5978 *Bodinnick Hall*, 6902
  Butlers Hall, 6912 *Helmster Hall*, 6945 *Glasfryn Hall*.
6959 class. ('Modified Hall') 4-6-0 Nos 6988 *Swithland
  Hall*, 6993 *Arthog Hall*.
4300 class. 2-6-0 Nos 5305, 5314, 5328, 5337, 5338, 5359,
  5384.

The Dean pattern straight road shed at Weymouth photographed on 28th September 1921. 0-6-0ST No. 1337 *Hook Norton* stands in front of the lifting shop, the building attached to the left of which is the boiler house, and the brick building with the tall chimney to the right of the shed is the sand furnace. In front of this is standing Loco coal wagon No. 9348. The shed occupied a lower site than the main lines which can be seen to the left.

With the 83B (Taunton) shed-plate on the smokebox door 2-6-2 Prairie tank No. 4143 stands on the ash pit at Weymouth shed on 24th June 1962, after working a Taunton–Weymouth excursion via Langport West and the old Bristol & Exeter branch to Yeovil Pen Mill. Two rebuilt Bulleid Pacifics stand in the background.

C. L. Caddy

An overall view of Weymouth locomotive shed on 25th March 1962. Steam locomotives share the depot with a dmu, a diesel shunter and a 'Hymek'. Shed staff are clearing the ash pit, empty and full coal wagons abound in the sidings to the right, and box vans stand on the Jersey sidings to the left of the main lines

C. L. Caddy

Weymouth shed lies in the savage grip of winter on 29th December 1963. A handful of locomotives stand on the ash pit awaiting their turn for fire cleaning and coaling, and the ramped approach to the coaling stage can be seen to the right.

C. L. Caddy

4500 class. 2-6-2T Nos 4507, 4520, 4527, 4562.
1366 class. 0-6-0PT Nos 1367, 1368, 1370.
655 class. 0-6-0PT No. 1789.
7400 class. 0-6-0PT No. 7408.
5700 class. 0-6-0PT No. 9642.
1400 class. 0-4-2T No. 1453, 1454, 1467.

Allocations 1959
4900 class. 4-6-0 No. 6914 *Langton Hall.*
5MT class. 4-6-0 Nos 73017, 73018, 73020, 73022, 73029.
4300 class. 2-6-0 Nos 5384, 6344, 7303.
5101 class. 2-6-2T Nos 4133, 4166.
4500 class. 2-6-2T Nos 4507, 4166.
1366 class. 0-6-0PT Nos 1367, 1368, 1370.
5700 class. 0-6-0PT Nos 3737, 4624, 4689, 5784, 7780,
    7782, 8799, 9620.
1400 class. 0-4-2T Nos 1453, 1474.

Allocations 1965
'Merchant Navy' class. 4-6-0 Nos:
35005 *Canadian Pacific*, 35007 *Aberdeen Commonwealth*,
35012 *United States Lines*, 35014 *Nederland Line*, 35016
    Elders Fyffes,
35017 *Belgian Marine*, 35019 *French Line CGT*, 35022
    Holland-America Line, 35026 *Lamport & Holt Line*,
    35028 *Clan Line*, 35029 *Ellerman Lines,*
35030 *Elder-Dempster Lines.*
5MT class. 4-6-0 Nos 73002, 73018, 73020, 73042, 73080
    Merlin, 73083 *Pendragon.*
2MT class. 2-6-2T Nos 41261, 41284, 41298, 41305, 41324.

Locomotives used on the Weymouth Harbour Tramway

The tramway was unique in the fact that for many years, locomotives from various railway companies absorbed by the GWR were used on the line. Some of the locomotives were a regular sight over the years, whilst others were used for a short time as replacements for locomotives under repair.

The first known locomotive used on the tramway was a 2-4-0 side tank No. 2. This engine, originally named *King* was built by the Avonside Engine Co. (builder's No. 804) in 1871 for the broad gauge Torbay & Brixham Railway which was worked and staffed by the South Devon Railway. However, due to financial problems the Torquay & Brixham could not afford to pay for *King* and the locomotive was taken over by the South Devon. Upon amalgamation of the South Devon by the GWR in 1876, *King* received the number 2171. The locomotive was converted to the standard gauge in March 1878 and re-numbered 2, used for the construction of the Bodmin Road–Bodmin line the locomotive was withdrawn from service in March 1907 and sold to the Bute Works Supply Co. No. 2 was last recorded as being in use at the premises of the Anglo American Oil Co. at Purfleet in 1921.

Two former Bristol & Exeter 0-6-0 side tanks, Nos 1376 and 1377, were active on the quay by 1886, and arrived in Weymouth soon after rebuilding by the GWR in 1881. The two engines were built in Bristol by the B&E for the Culm Valley Railway (not opened until 1876). No. 114 (GWR No. 1376) was built in

No. 6870 *Bodicote Grange*, in immaculate condition, shares the coaling and ash pit line with a rebuilt Bulleid Pacific at Weymouth shed on 22nd June 1963. The heaps of clinker and smokebox ash in the foreground are a reminder that the romance of railways is just a myth; ask any former footplateman about 'squaring' up an engine in the middle of the night with the rain beating down and the wind whistling through the cab. Note the two tubs of coal on the coaling stage standing ready to be unloaded into the tender of No. 6870.

C. L. Caddy

With the main lines in the background 'Hymek' No. D7021 stands at Weymouth shed on 10th June 1964.

John Scrace

September 1874, and No. 115 (GWR No. 1377) was built in December 1875. Both engines were rebuilt by the GWR in 1881, and No. 1377 had a further rebuild in 1915 being fitted with a new boiler. They were used at Weymouth until the late 1920s, No. 1377 being withdrawn from service in January 1927, while No. 1376 was sent to Oswestry and ended its days on the Tanat Valley line.

During 1903–1906, and for a short time in 1908, an ex-West Cornwall Railway 0-4-0 saddle tank, No. 1391 *Fox*, was in use on the line. This locomotive was built by the Avonside Engine Company in 1872 (builder's No. 913). Upon the West Cornwall being taken over by the GWR in 1876, *Fox* became GWR No. 1391, and

was rebuilt at Swindon in January 1897. Sold in July 1912 to the Gloucester, Carriage & Wagon Company, No. 1391 was finally sold for scrap to Cashmore's of Newport in 1948. It is worth noting that no other standard gauge West Cornwall locomotive survived from the year 1881.

Hook Norton, No. 1337, an 0-6-0 saddle tank was used from 1904 until 1907 and between 1914 and 1926. It was built by Manning, Wardle & Co. in November 1889 (builder's No. 1127) for the Hook Norton Ironstone Partnership Ltd and was obtained in July 1904 from the aforesaid owner's liquidators by the GWR. The locomotive was sold in September 1907 to the Fishguard & Rosslare Railways & Harbours Co.

Weymouth shed on 29th July 1967 with lines of condemned locomotives, many of which, including the rebuilt Bulleid Pacifics, have many years of working life left in them, await removal to the scrapyards. Weymouth, in company with the former steam shed at Salisbury, was to be host to the gathering of locomotives at the end of Southern steam.

S. C. Nash

Hook Norton was returned to GWR stock in October 1913 and was withdrawn and cut up in January 1926.

1926 witnessed the arrival of two of the most remembered locomotives used on the tramway, Nos 2194 *Kidwelly* and 2195 *Cwm Mawr*. The two 0-6-0 saddle tanks were originally owned by the Burry Port & Gwendraeth Valley Railway (absorbed by the GWR 1st July 1922). Both locomotives were built by the Avonside Engine Co. Bristol. *Kidwelly*, former BPVG No. 4 dated from 1903 (builder's No. 1463) and *Cwm Mawr*, former BPVG No. 5 dated from 1905 (builder's No. 1491). Both engines remained at Weymouth until 1939/40. *Cwm Mawr* was withdrawn in March 1939, but was reinstated without its nameplates in December 1939 to the Bristol Division, usually working at Swindon it had a brief return to Weymouth in 1945 and was finally withdrawn in January 1953. *Kidwelly* left Weymouth in 1940 and after a brief spell at Cardiff Cathays spent its remaining years at Taunton until withdrawal in February 1953.

0-6-0 saddle tank No. 1331, ex-Whitland & Cardigan Railway (taken over by the GWR on 1st September 1886), was in use on the tramway from 1928 until 1935. No. 1331 (former Whitland & Cardigan No. 3 built by Fox Walker in 1877, builder's No. 340) was numbered 1387 after the takeover by the GWR and was withdrawn from stock in June 1902 after serving at various depots including Pontypool and Gloucester. It was then transferred to the Signal Department at Reading remaining there until 1925. No. 1387 was returned to stock and taken into Swindon works as No. 1331 in February 1926, and after rebuilding, the locomotive was returned to service in November 1927. After service at Weymouth the locomotive was based at Swindon and Oswestry until final withdrawal in January 1950 and cut up in March of that year. Another ex-Whitland & Cardigan 0-6-0 saddle tank, No. 1386 (former Whitland & Cardigan No. 2) was also used for a time on the line.

0-6-0 saddle tank No. 679 (former Alexandra Docks & Railways No. 18 built by Peckett in 1890, builder's No. 465) was recorded as being used for a few months at Weymouth, No. 679 was withdrawn from service in September 1929 and sold a few months later. After being used by various private owners, its last years were spent at Trimsaran Colliery and the locomotive was out of use by September 1953.

0-6-0 saddle tank No. 1397, ex-Cornwall Minerals Railway (former CMR No. 6 *Newquay*, built by Sharp Stewart in 1873, builder's No. 2355) was based at Swindon from 1928 onwards and withdrawn from service November 1933.

1366 class 0-6-0 pannier tank No. 1367 became the first GWR purpose built locomotive for docks and restricted areas to be allocated to the tramway when it arrived in April 1935 and stayed until 1962. No. 1371 of the same class arrived in March 1939 and by 1947 Nos 1368 and 1370 had been allocated to Weymouth, and over the years the entire class were used on the tramway during various periods. When one of the 1366 class was under repair it was replaced by one of the 1361 0-6-0 saddle tank class, and Nos 1363 and 1361 were used at various times as replacement engines on the tramway. With the rebuilding of the quay wall during 1950–1 it was found that the 1366 class were too heavy for the line, and although the locomotives only weighed 35 tons the problem was that the weight was spread over a short, 11ft wheelbase compared with the 45 tons of the larger pannier tank engines which was carried on a 14ft 8in wheelbase. For six months from March 1953 locomotives of the 7400 pannier tank class, Nos 7415, 7418, and 7421 worked the line, and then the 1366 class were again allowed on the tramway. Soon after this the 5700 and 8750 class panniers were allowed to use the line. On 23rd June 1962, Nos 1367 and 1369, the last two 1366 class tanks left Weymouth and were despatched for the Wenford Bridge branch in Cornwall, leaving the tramway to be operated by the larger panniers and diesel shunters, of which No. D2292 was used for trials in 1961. The last ex-GWR locomotive worked the boat train along the tramway on 24th December 1963. However, this was not to be the end of steam on the line for in April 1964 an Ivatt Class 2P 2-6-2 tank No. 41261 appeared on the tramway. Weighing 63 tons they were the heaviest locomotives to work on the line but as the weight was spread over five axles it cleared the engine for working over the route, and the class was used for several more trips during the summer of 1964. No. 41298 appeared working a special train on 3rd July 1966. With the decline of steam, diesel power now reigned supreme and diesel shunters Nos D2082, D2292, D2398, 2179 and 15231 were regular users and, like the steam locomotives, were all equipped with the obligatory warning bell. On 13th February 1973, a Class 33 diesel, No. 6533, fitted with an electric bell and amber flashing beacon hauling a TC push-pull set was tested on the tramway. This class, with a weight of 78 tons, was the heaviest ever locomotive allowed on the quay line at the time, and they replaced the 240hp diesels on the boat trains. Nos 33106, 33112, 33137, 33116, and 33029, are recorded as being used on the tramway, and the push-pull fitted 33s were the normal users of the line but on 16th July 1967 an unfitted member of the class, No. 33204, was in use on a boat train along the tramway. The heaviest diesel locomotives, the Class 37s, appeared working special trains on the tramway in 1993.

Working the Westbury to Weymouth Line

George Pryer now recalls his steam days at Weymouth:

"I soon discovered upon joining the staff of British Railways in 1959 that it was by no means romantic. However, steam engines made an everlasting impression and gave me a life-long love of railways. As an engine cleaner at Weymouth shed (very quickly passed out for firemans' duties) the steam locomotive soon emerged in its true colours. Yet it was this very unpredictability that called for skill and judgement on the part of the crews, and elevated the enginemen's calling above the common place. And there was something about those giant machines, each one individually built by craftsmen with top quality materials, that inspired respect even when they were giving trouble. The most common problem was shortage of steam.

On one occasion I was booked to work the 2.13pm Weymouth–Swindon parcels as far as Westbury. This was often a well loaded train as not only did it convey parcels traffic but also any coaching stock going to Swindon works for overhaul. The driver and I prepared our own engine, a 'Hall', and got her steaming nicely. We were looking forward to a good run when the foreman fitter, who just happened to walk by on his way to another job, stopped in his tracks beside our engine, peered over the frame, then came up and asked us if we intended taking it out. The reply being affirmative, he said we couldn't use that engine because he had spotted a cracked leaf spring, so we had to rush over to the running foreman to see what else he could offer us. We ended up with a '73' Standard which had only just come in off a Waterloo service. The fire was dirty and the ashpan full, and I had great difficulty in raising the steam pressure even with the engine stationary. This was obviously not going to be an enjoyable trip, our last hope being that there would be no carriages for the works today and the train would therefore be light. This hope soon vanished when we dropped into platform 6 and found that we could just get in clear of the signal, and the load turned out to be equal to eight bogie vans – just under the maximum for an unassisted engine.

Somehow we cleared Bincombe Tunnel with steam dangerously low and the water bobbing about in the bottom nut of the gauge glass, and with much poking about of the fire I managed to recover the situation a little as we freewheeled down into Dorchester. At Maiden Newton things did not look good, and we eventually ground to a stand close to Evershot's up distant, the steam pressure then being so low that there was not enough to maintain the vacuum to keep the brakes off. For a full 20 minutes we stood there poking the fire, and eventually we had enough steam and water to make further progress. The long downhill run from Evershot to Yeovil allowed a bit more recovery, and whilst we managed to keep going for the remainder of the trip, it was necessary for my driver to nurse the engine all the way and speed was well below normal. We arrived at Westbury about 50 minutes late, hot, filthy, and exhausted, and dreaming of diesels with nice clean cabs!

The majority of work allocated to junior 'passed cleaners' was of a more humble nature. Of course there were a lot of shunt engine turns at Weymouth and the 'Dorchester Pilot', an engine which spent all day shunting the yards at the West and South stations and working transfer trips between the two. Perhaps the most interesting job that I had on a fairly regular basis was the afternoon 'Bridport Goods'. This involved travelling 'Pass' to Yeovil Pen Mill and walking over into the yard to relieve a pannier tank. After about 30 minutes shunting we set off with the pick up goods, pausing briefly at Yetminster and Evershot to set down any wagons consigned to those stations. Actually the Evershot stop could be quite lengthy, as it was often necessary to recess the train in the long siding behind the down platform for a passenger train to overtake. On arrival at Maiden Newton we reversed what was left of our train into the down siding by the signal box and ran light engine to Bridport, where there was much shunting to be done before departing with the evening freight which ran through to Weymouth with only one stop at Maiden Newton to put off 'Up line' traffic.

Perhaps the hardest turns were the 'Bankers', involving as they did a lot of heavy work for the engine and therefore a well maintained head of steam. On average one made about five trips 'up the bank' in the course of a turn, but on summer Saturdays it was a continuous process. Indeed, very often the signalman at Upwey would cross us over onto the rear of an up train because we had insufficient time to run to Weymouth before our services were required again. Most trains were capable of struggling out that far unassisted, the really steep part of the bank starting at the northern end of Upwey station. Not only was this duty hard physically, it could also be extremely uncomfortable. It was usually the older classes of engines with open backed cabs that appeared on banking jobs, and this involved running back from Bincombe Tunnel to Weymouth with the grit and coal dust from the tender being blown all over the crew with considerable force. It was like standing in a sand blaster! Added to this there could be rain, snow, or even hail blowing into the footplate. The tunnel would be full of smoke and steam, and often we were obliged to cover our mouth and nose with dampened handkerchiefs in order to breathe at all.

During the Autumn of 1960 the turntable at Weymouth was out of action for several weeks to allow it to be repaired, with all of the engines going to Yeovil Junction to use the turntable there. Usually three or four engines were coupled together to save pathways, the route being Yeovil Pen Mill, Yeovil Town, Yeovil Junction. This was another uncomfortable job because it involved almost the whole round trip tender first, and unless one was lucky enough to be on the leading engine, one was the recipient of the smuts and coal dust of the other locos as well as your own.

By 1961, firing turns for we juniors were becoming few and far between as a result of the introduction of dmus on some local services, and as I had no wish to spend several years cleaning engines in the shed I sought a transfer to the Traffic Department, and was given a general purpose relief job. My district was designated as being Easton to Sparkford, and

No. 1023 *County of Oxford* heads northwards out of Weymouth with the Weymouth Town–Westbury parcels on 27th June 1962.

C. L. Caddy

Dorchester to Bournemouth Central and branches, although in fact I never worked north of Yeovil, or east of Poole."

Working the Excursions from Yeovil to Weymouth
Excursion trains were run from Pen Mill to Weymouth on a frequent basis during the summer months and were very popular at weekends and on bank holidays. The excursions had to fit in with the normal services to Weymouth plus other excursion traffic from places far and wide, travelling through Yeovil Pen Mill to reach Weymouth. After the closure of Pen Mill shed in 1959 it became the responsibility of Yeovil Town shed to supply the motive power.

The normal engines used were the 2-6-0 U class of which the Town shed had several of the best. They were a superb type of engine to work on, and in the case of more than one excursion starting from Pen Mill, as in the case of bank holiday weekends, engines would be 'borrowed' from other sheds that happened to be stabled at the Town for the weekend, before working back to their various depots on the following Monday. I have known ex-GWR 2-6-0 Moguls, Collett 22xx 0-6-0 tender engines, and Bulleid Pacifics to be used. In fact Pen Mill would have so many engines hanging about before leaving with their respective trains, that some engines were stabled in the Pen Mill locomotive shed yard which, although having being closed the previous January, was still extant. I must point out that this happened only during the very busy bank holiday workings like Whitsun or August. Coaching stock was also a problem. Some empty stock trains were run from Westbury or Taunton a few days before, and at times the Taunton branch stock was combined with other sets, or spare Southern stock from Yeovil Town.

I well remember being booked on duty one particular Sunday to work a Weymouth excursion. Our engine was Southern U class No. 31790, one of a class that I, in common with my footplate comrades at the Town shed had worked on many times and she was well known for her steaming and pulling qualities. The shed as always on a summer Sunday was packed with engines, and not all of them would be used this day as they were awaiting their next turn of duty early the next morning on

the Southern main line. All types of Southern motive power from sheds far and wide would be simmering away or awaiting the attentions of the firelighter; Bulleid Pacifics, S15s, King Arthurs', S15s, T9s, "Black Motors" (700 class), U class Moguls, and ex-GWR pannier and Prairie tank engines. On this Sunday morning the weather was bright and already getting hot with the promise of a lovely summer's day ahead as my mate and I climbed aboard No. 31790. My driver was a Southern Passed Fireman well known for his excellent driving qualities. We put our kit away in the lockers on the tender and started to prepare the engine. My mate climbed down from the engine with the oil feeder to oil the straps and rods, and I levelled out the fire across the firebox with the long handled pricker with just a touch of the steam blower to stop the fumes and smoke drifting back into the cab. The damper was opened and whilst the fire was burning through I collected the oil cans and climbed down from the footplate and walked through the shed to the stores and refilled the cans.

On my return to our engine I left the can with the oil for the rods and straps on the ground with the driver, whilst I climbed aboard with the can containing the lubricator oil and the small can of paraffin for the headlamps. Now it was time to start making the fire up. The U class engines liked a large fire under the door sloping down to the brick arch and the best lumps of coal from the tender were cracked with the coal pick and shovelled into the firebox. The fire started to roar and throb as it was made up, smoke and flames danced in the firebox, and smoke from our chimney drifted across the loco yard. The engine slowly came to life in the way that only a steam engine can. The water was bobbing up and down in the gauge glasses and the needle on the steam pressure gauge was starting to climb towards the red line. After I had judged that there was enough coal in the firebox for the time being, it was time for the footplate to be brushed clean, the lubricator filled and sight glasses cleaned. The injector was turned on to fill the boiler and the footplate and coal on the tender were washed down with the pep pipe, making sure that my mate wasn't in the vicinity of the hot spray.

Now the headlamps were cleaned and refilled with paraffin and I made sure that we had our supply of detonators, red flags and spare gauge glass tubes. Then came the outside checks and I climbed down from the footplate with the spanner and tightened the smokebox clips, checked the sandboxes and refilled them, a head-lamp was placed on the tender and a tail lamp on the front buffer as we would be travelling tender first to Pen Mill. The driver and I climbed aboard our engine and whilst he filled the oil boxes I wiped the pipes and gauges with an oil filled rusty. (Rusty was the nickname given to the woven cloths supplied by the Southern Region which were far superior to the cotton waste supplied to the Western Region crews.) My driver put his cans away and wiped his hands with a clean rusty and lit his pipe whilst he opened the large and small ejectors to test the vacuum brake. The twin needles in the gauge climbed to the regulation 21 inches of vacuum, and with a large hiss he lowered the brake handle in order for me to unscrew the tender brake. The reverser was spun into forward gear, the vacuum brake handle was lifted and the regulator was opened and we moved forward to the water column with a massive roar of steam from our open cylinder cocks. After topping up the tender from the water column we had about ten minutes to spare to have a wash in the drivers' cabin and make a can of tea. Other engines were being prepared, either for the Southern main line, banking engines for Evershot and other excursions and so crews would be entering and leaving the cabin constantly. I poured out two steaming cups of tea as my mate and I sat in the drivers' cabin. He puffed on his pipe whilst reading a Sunday paper of which there were many scattered around on the tables. There was always a daily or a Sunday paper in the drivers' cabins by courtesy of the early morning paper trains. I rolled a cigarette and chatted with my mates in the time honoured fashion of footplate crews as all shed cabins were debating chambers on all subjects under the sun, and I have many happy memories of my former comrades at Yeovil. The footplate society was a closed one, rather akin to a Masonic brotherhood as the foot-plate crews were the 'elite' of the railway. I know that other railway workers were also a vital part of the system; signalmen, guards, shunters and fitters, etc. But as a young fireman I must admit, that I enjoyed being part of this elite society and I am as proud today as I was then to have been a fireman and shared a footplate in times good and bad with many fine comrades, many of whom, alas are no longer with us.

Anyway, our engine is ready, standing outside the cabin with her safety valves lifting, and our passengers are gathering at Pen Mill for a day at the seaside. It is now time to leave the locomotive yard so we make our way from the cabin and climb aboard our engine. The cab is hot with the fire burning through bright and red, the footplate is spick and span with its washed down floor and wiped over pipes and gauges and the engine has the aroma of hot oil and steam. The shed starting signal arm is lowered and the tender brake is unscrewed, the vacuum brake is blown off and with a blast on the whistle we pull out of the loco yard. The shed signal slams to 'danger' behind us as we stop just past the twin ground signals, points move behind us and the left hand 'dummy' clangs over. My mate has already spun the reverser over, and with a touch on the regulator, we reverse over the points and crossings and cross on to the ex-GWR branch line. As we near the Town signal box I cross over to my mate's side of the engine. (The U and N class engines were right hand

drive, i.e. with the driver and his controls to the right hand side of the footplate, compared with the majority of Southern and ex-LSWR engines which were left hand driven. The former GWR classes were right hand driven and as all fireman were expected to fire towards the driver, you had to fire either left or right hand according to which type of engine you were working on.) The signalman is leaning out of one of the box windows with the hoop containing the single-line token. This is collected and checked by reading the inscription on the token; Yeovil Town/Yeovil Pen Mill. I hang up the hoop on one of the coat hooks inside the cab and we travel through the GWR platform at the Town station, and over on the Southern platform, the branch auto train with its M7 Drummond 0-4-4 tank engine awaits the next trip to Yeovil Junction. The crew is sitting on one of the platform seats by the engine having a breath of fresh air as the morning hots up. We clank through the station, the lower quadrant starting signal arm is clear with the fixed distant for Pen Mill on the same post, we whistle for the barrow crossing (making a few passengers standing on the platform 'jump') and bustle under the foot and road bridges and take the single line for Pen Mill.

It only takes a few minutes to reach the ex-GWR station and the tall outer home signal looms into view with its arm lowered. We coast past the signal and pass the abandoned GWR engine shed standing to our right, the inner home signal is also clear and we pass under the A30 roadbridge and come to a stand just inside the up platform. The shunter collects the token and walks over to the auxiliary token apparatus housed in a small hut on the down platform. This was worked in conjunction with the signal box at the far end of the down platform. The signal arm was lowered and 'Down Main' is shown in the destination box, we pull forward over the crossings and stand on the down main, the dummy clangs over and we reverse into the down goods yard and back on to our coaches. Whilst the shunter is coupling up I take the chance to remove our tail lamp and walk to the front of our engine and place our headlamps, one over each buffer, or a 'twin lamper' in footplate language. We would be booked to run to Weymouth non stop, while other excursions from Yeovil would stop at various stations en route.

There is a shout from the shunter, "try the brake, driver". My mate opens up the ejectors and the twin needles move in the duplex gauge to the regulation 21 inches and held, the guard appears and takes the driver's name and the engine number for his journal "nine on driver, do you want a banker?" For a minute I thought the driver was going to have a shouting match with the guard, but he just glares down at him and replies, "no thanks". He turned to me and said, "bloody Western men, they can't go anywhere without a banker." His reaction was just what I would expect as we Southern men were not used to bankers on the Southern main line between Salisbury and Exeter as we had to soldier on without them on severe climbs such as the Sherborne, Semley, Chard and Honiton banks. Even double heading was a rare occurrence and the only place to find bankers on our main line was the steep ascent between Exeter St Davids and Exeter Central stations.

I glance across to the down platform which is begin-ning to fill up with passengers with more climbing across the footbridge. Excursion trains were always happy trains to me with loads of people and children full of expectancy for the day ahead at Weymouth, more so if the weather was good. The shunter walks over to the telephone to contact the signalman, a few minutes later the yard exit dummy clangs over and my driver opens the regulator and we pull forward with a gentle cough from our exhaust with our long train of coaches following on behind. We pull past the cattle dock and over the river bridge, and I keep an eye on the shunter who is standing under the roadbridge. As soon as the last coach has passed the points he holds both arms straight in the air, I shout out to my mate to stop and he applies the brake and spins the reverser into reverse, I turn the injector on to top up the boiler as the pressure is high on the red mark, the shunter is now waving us back, and we gently run back to the down platform. My mate closes the regulator as our engine glides back like a well oiled sewing machine, every rod and piston working in unison and not a breath of steam from the cylinders, a perfect engine. As we run under the roadbridge my mate applies the brake and stops the engine at the end of the platform. Our passengers move forward to board the train, carriage doors open and slam shut as they embark. On our engine everything is ready, the steam pressure is on the red line, the fire is red hot and burning through, and the engine is throbbing away. The reverser is in full forward gear ready to go, the starting and South junction distant signals are lowered clearing the way ahead. Just as we are about to depart there is a shout from the ticket collector by the booking hall on the up platform asking us to hang on, and the last few passengers run across the footbridge and dive into the train, slamming the carriage doors behind them. A long sharp blast on the guard's whistle and a wave of his green flag gives us the right away.

My mate opens the regulator and our engine moves forward with a loud bark from the chimney. It is muffled for a few seconds as we pull under the A30 road bridge, the reverser is wound back as we rumble over the bridge carrying the main line over the River Yeo. I close the firedoors and glance back at our long train of coaches trundling on behind. We round the curve at South junction and gather speed as the track straightens out through the small forest of signals. The engine is now well into her stride as we thunder under the bridge carrying the Southern main line above us, the cab starts swaying with the momentum, I open the firedoors and put a few rounds of coal around the firebox, not too much as there is enough fire for the moment, I do not want to black the fire in, especially with Evershot not far away. We run past Thornford Bridge Halt, heading towards Yetminster, our engine is pounding away not missing a beat.

We are now looking out for Yetminster distant signal, will it be 'on' or 'off'? We pound on, and there is the distant signal in the 'off' position. The regulator is opened as wide as it will go, the station appears ahead with a banker waiting in the siding, and with a loud scream on the whistle we hammer through and attack the bank. The engine slows but not too much. I start to lay the fire whilst my mate concentrates on the road ahead, steam and smoke from our chimney shoots skywards, the engine is well known as a good 'un' and this day she is at her best. We storm past Chetnole Halt with our exhaust beating out a loud machine gun staccato from the chimney, the harder my mate works the engine, the better she steams, I attend to the requirements of the firebox, left back corner, right back corner and under the firedoor with a check now and then that there isn't too much fire building up under the brick arch. Injector on to keep the boiler topped up with a quick spray with the pep pipe over the coal on the tender. The engine is pounding higher and higher up the bank, every part of her is alive with the exhaust beat rising to a crescendo, the steam pressure and vacuum gauge needles quivering in their brass cases with the massive forces at work. To be on a footplate of a steam locomotive when she is working hard is a sensation never to be forgotten.

Class U 2-6-0 No. 31626 from Yeovil Town shed and crewed by Yeovil footplatemen, heads the 10.30am Yeovil Pen Mill–Weymouth past Yeovil South Junction on 23rd August 1959. This photograph shows the varied stock that was put together to form the Yeovil–Weymouth excursion trains.

S. C. Nash

We are now reaching the summit and are moving slower as we reach the steepest part of the bank, my mate gives her another nick on the reverser as we storm onwards, up ahead is the right hand curve which leads into the cutting. As we round the curve the Evershot distant signal arm is in the 'clear' position, our exhaust echoes around the cutting as we approach the mouth of the dark tunnel. A long blast from our whistle echoes around and around the cutting as we enter the tunnel, our pounding exhaust beat against the tunnel mouth showering red hot sparks down onto the cab roof and the first carriage, steam and smoke is billowing everywhere, making breathing difficult. We pound on out of the tunnel with our exhaust beat softening. I turn the injector on as it will be downhill to Maiden Newton, all signals are clear ahead of us as Evershot station appears, and we gather speed as we run past the platforms and signal box. As we thunder past the Evershot advanced starter my mate eases the regulator and winds the reverser back, whilst I put the firing shovel away for the time being as it is downhill to Maiden Newton. I take a breather from the exertions of working up from Yetminster, with time to roll a cigarette and my mate puffs away on his pipe. We are now running down the bank at a fair pace with our string of coaches pushing us on. As I turn the injector off, the safety valves lift with a tremendous roar with the amount of fire in the firebox. We sweep around the curves and our coupling rods are just a blur. Up on the swaying footplate, coal spills onto the floor from the shovelling plate on the tender and clouds of coal dust fly everywhere. Time to turn the injector on to keep the boiler topped up and give the tender a good soaking with the pep pipe to lay the dust. A plume of steam appears ahead of us and an up train with a 'Hall' on the front comes barking up the bank.

The track starts to level out as my driver turns the blower on to stop a blow back and shuts the regulator in one movement as we near Maiden Newton down distant signal. He applies a touch of brake just in case the signal is at 'caution' and we can feel the brakes coming on the train as the coaches start to drag. The distant signal is 'clear' as we approach and the brakes come off, we pick up our heels again as we are still running down the bank. We run past the outer home signal and the Bridport branch line swings in to our right. I lift my hand to the whistle cord and give a long warning blast on the whistle to warn of our approach as the main line curves to the left under an overbridge and then straightens out through the station. We hammer through the platforms with our long train of coaches swaying behind us. The Bridport branch bay to our right is empty as the branch train has left for Bridport following the departure of the up train which passed us up the bank. Signals slam to danger behind us as we thunder past Maiden Newton's advanced starter leaving a trail of steam and smoke in our wake.

We pound along with the footplate of 31790 swaying from side to side. I tend to the fire which by now has levelled out over the firebox due to our fast descent from Evershot. I slide open the firedoors and the heat from the firebox beats against my sweating brow making the sweat intermingle with the coal dust as I turn and scoop up a shovel full of coal from the shovelling plate on the tender and place it in the firebox as the fire dances with the beat from our exhaust. The coal is soon swallowed up amidst the flames as the fire

is built up under the door, and then concentrating on the left and right hand back corners of the firebox, and when the requirements of the firebox are met for the moment it is time for a breather and a chat with my mate. He is busy refilling his old pipe and at the same time keeping an eye on the road ahead. I am dying for a drink but there is no relief for my thirst until we reach Weymouth. Some of the older drivers used to bring a bottle of cold tea with them but I always liked it hot, a glance in my tea can gives me no joy as the remnants are swimming in the bottom of the can with tea leaves, so I have a roll-up instead and have a smoke whilst soaking the coal in the tender with the pep pipe to keep the dust down. Coal dust is so fine it reaches everywhere, and no matter how many times the tender was hosed down, the dust was always in your throat, eyes, nose and ears and to cough and clear your throat would leave a black deposit on the floor, and if you sneezed a large black lump of coal dust would be left on your handkerchief. Even today, many years have passed since I have left the footplate, I can still taste coal dust.

I turn the injector off as we steam along under a perfect blue sky. There is a roar and a rattle alongside as another up train passes us. Our engine is steaming well as I tend to the fire, keeping the firebox full and topping up the boiler with the injector. The dark portal of Frampton Tunnel looms ahead and with whistle screaming we plunge into the dank gloom. Our exhaust booms against the tunnel roof, steam and smoke billow around the cab as we thunder through the tunnel, a faint glimmer of daylight appears ahead and we rattle out into the sunshine still hammering along. I just top up the fire now as the firebox is crammed full and although we are cracking on, the engine is in mid gear with the regulator half open as most of the Southern engines were extremely free running engines, and the worst of the journey like the climb to Evershot is now over. We pass Grimstone and Frampton and rattle along like a good un. We are still steaming well with our engine swaying and rocking along the main line. We pass Bradford Peverell and Stratton Halt, and soon Dorchester West down distant signal appears at 'caution' as we pace the road traffic to our left, coaches and cars speed along but with Dorchester then being a notorious bottleneck for road traffic we will be in Weymouth long before them. A long whistle for the Dorchester West down distant signal and then another blast on the whistle as we enter Poundbury Tunnel. The regulator is closed and the brake is applied as we slow for adverse signals, the outer and inner home signals are clear as we near the station but the station starter is at 'danger' and we come to a stand at the end of the platform. The injector is on to keep the boiler topped up and also to stop the safety valves from lifting and causing a nuisance whilst standing at the platform.

Signal arms are lowered and we pull forward with a bark from the chimney, we lurch over the points at Dorchester junction with the main line from Bournemouth coming in from the left. We gather speed as the engine gets into its stride. Up ahead of us Bincombe down distant is clear as we approach the tunnel with the line dipping down the bank. We enter the cutting and to our right stands Bincombe signal box with a banker in the middle siding waiting to return to Weymouth. With a long blast on the whistle we run into the dark 814-yard long north tunnel, gathering speed as we start to run down the bank. The tunnel is

Bulleid Pacific No. 34066 *Spitfire* has arrived from Yeovil Junction with the 8.55am Sherborne–Weymouth Sunday school excursion, formed mainly of Eastern Region stock, and uses the crossover at Yeovil South Junction to pass from the Junction–Yeovil Town branch to the 'up' Weymouth line into Yeovil Pen Mill for reversal.

S. P. J. A. Derek

No. 34066 *Spitfire,* after running around its train at Yeovil Pen Mill, heads for Weymouth along the 'down' main line and passes the signal box at Yeovil South Junction with the 8.55am Sherborne–Weymouth Sunday school excursion. The GWR Type 13 signal box can be seen in the background; opened 13th October 1943, and closed on 26th May 1968 it is of interest for the fact that it was provided with two closing switches. This enabled the signalman to work the GWR lines and leave the Southern lines switched out, or vice-versa, or both lines switched in. Standard GWR Block was used on the main lines, and Preece 1–Wire Block on SR lines.

S. P. J. A. Derek

full of smoke and steam not only from our engine, but from trains that have struggled up the bank from Weymouth and it is a welcome relief when we exit from the tunnel and then pass through the short 48-yard south tunnel that carries the line under the main Dorchester to Weymouth road. We then cross the main road again with traffic starting to queue below us as they enter the outskirts of Weymouth. There will be no firing from now on as our destination is not far

away, the injector is on to keep the boiler up as we head down hill and it's time to tidy the footplate up with a quick spray from the pep pipe to keep the dust down. An up train with a Bulleid Pacific on the front and a banker at the rear hammers towards us on the up line heading for Bournemouth and Waterloo. We pass Upwey & Broadwey station with the former branch to Abbotsbury at this time reduced to a siding to our right. As we clear Upwey heading for Weymouth and my mate is now easing the engine, Radipole Halt appears and we start slowing as there are adverse signals ahead. We enter the environs of Weymouth and pass the large engine shed which stands to our left, packed full of hissing engines with steam and smoke billowing everywhere. To our right lines of box vans used for the fruit and vegetable produce from the Channel Islands which, in those days, was almost exclusivly handled by the railway, stand on the Jersey sidings.

Weymouth, being one of the premier resorts in the west would be packed, with coaches stabled everywhere, trains waiting to depart, and pilot engines and bankers fussing about. We lurch over the maze of points heading for the station and its vast layout of sidings. We pass the signal box standing to our left and the regulator is closed as we drift in towards platform 4. I look out for the shunter as he will give us the tip, if we either had to uncouple or leave the coaches on, in order to back out into the carriage sidings. As we pass him he lifts his arms and crosses his wrists, which means 'uncouple at the platform'. We clank along the platform and my mate starts to brake until we come to a stand with a large hiss from the brake ejector, near the buffer stop at the end of the platform. The carriage doors burst open and our happy hordes stream along the platform to the exit. I climb down from the footplate and ease myself between our engine and the leading coach, the vacuum pipes are unclipped and parted, and as the coupling is tight, I shout out to my mate to 'ease up'. As the engine is reversed the buffers are compressed and I unscrew the coupling and lift it off the coach hook and secure it on its carrying hook on our tender. Now to walk to the front of the engine and take off one of our headlamps, leaving the other one to act as a tail lamp.

The platform, which a few minutes before, was packed with a happy throng is now deserted except for the station staff who are busy slamming the carriage doors. A slight lurch of the carriages means that the station pilot has buffered up to the far end of the train, a whistle from the pilot and an answering hand signal from the Station Inspector and our coaches are pulled away, leaving us standing alone at the platform. We reverse slowly along the platform and stop at the far end watching our coaches cross the tracks to the carriage sidings, the signals clear for us and we trundle off along the engine line to the shed and stop our engine on the disposal pits. As the shed is an ex-GWR one and has its own firedroppers, unlike the Southern sheds where the fireman cleans out the clinker from the firebox if he had time or 'square up' the engine as it was called, I screw the tender brake on. We gather our kit together and head for the cabin for a wash, make a welcome can of tea and relax with mother's sandwiches. The shed would be packed full with engines of all types including ex-GWR and Southern classes plus BR Standards and a sprinkling of ex LMS locomotives. The whole area would be alive with activity as engines would be in the process of preparation or disposal, safety valves would be roaring away with the smell of smoke and steam everywhere with lines of engines waiting on the ash pits by the large coal stage with glowing piles of red hot clinker in the pit and alongside the track. Behind the coal stage are the six sidings used to stable the loco coal trucks, and the shed pilot engine would be kept busy removing empty coal wagons from the coal stage and replacing them with full wagons for the ever growing queue of engines waiting to replenish their tenders. As Weymouth was a terminus the turntable would be busy turning engines for their next trip. Between the turntable and the shed there are seven sidings which are used to stable engines, the shed itself having four roads one of which was used for heavy repairs with a hoist at the far end between the shed and the buffer stops. Inspection pits were located on three of the shed roads and on one of the stabling sidings nearest the shed. The drivers' cabin was located to the far side of the shed near one of the sidings. As this was located near the main line, trains would be rattling in, and departing trains would be barking away heading for Bincombe with a banker pushing away at the rear. On some excursion turns the crews would book off at Weymouth, leaving them to while away the hours before going back with the return trip in the evening, but on this trip we would be returning home on the cushions, with a relief crew coming down later on to work the train home.

Working the Excursions Back to Yeovil

Working the return excursions to Yeovil involved riding down to Weymouth on the cushions on a normal service train, and upon reaching our destination we would hitch a lift to the shed on the engine that brought us down. We would never know what engine awaited us until we reported to the shed office. On one occasion we had No 34013 *Okehampton*, a rebuilt Bulleid Pacific, awaiting us on one of the shed preparation roads. 90 tons of solid muscle with a tractive effort of 27,715lb and driving wheels of 6ft 2in diameter, and a boiler pressure of 250lb per square inch. A superb class of engine on which we Southern crews earned our bread and butter day in day out through the vagaries of the English weather, and at times the worst of working conditions. After booking on at the shed office we would head for our engine. Preparing a large Bulleid with its deep firebox involved opening the tender doors and dragging the largest lumps of coal down onto the footplate and piling them into the firebox, keeping the back corners of the box crammed full with a touch on the blower to bring the fire up.

It was important to leave Weymouth with a hot bright fire in order to have a crack at the bank which extended almost from the end of the platforms to the far end of Bincombe Tunnel. Once the fire was made up and burning through it was time to clean up the footplate by brushing up the coal dust and hosing down with the pep pipe. Bulleid Pacifics had a tender sprinkler system which worked when the injectors were turned on, and by this time my mate had finished oiling the engine. I climbed down from the engine to place the tail lamp on the front bufferbeam and also to check that the smokebox door was tight and fill the sand boxes with clean dry sand from the hopper in the shed. Filling sand boxes on Bulleid Pacifics was no joke as you walked along the greasy engine framing, hanging onto the boiler handrail with one hand and holding a heavy shute of sand in the other. The original Bulleids were the worst as you had to stand on a ladder resting against the streamlined boiler casing and balance yourself whilst tipping a shute of sand into the sand boxes. After checking the water level in the tender I rejoined my mate on the footplate.

The heat on the enclosed footplate would be building up as the fire burnt through and the steam pressure was rising high on the pressure gauge. The engine

A superb engine in immaculate condition. No. 34057 *Biggin Hill* having left Yeovil South Junction heads towards Weymouth on 6th September 1964 with the 10.25am Yeovil Pen Mill–Weymouth. I fired this locomotive many times, and like the majority of her class, she was a superb engine. The Yeovil Town–Yeovil Junction branch can be seen in the background rising towards the junction.

Gerald T. Robinson

would be gurgling and throbbing with the smell of hot oil and steam as my mate filled the oil boxes and then put the oil cans away, the vacuum brake was tested and the steam sanders are turned on to check that the sand pipes were clear. The sanding gear is vital to a steam locomotive, especially on the climb from Weymouth up to and through Bincombe Tunnel. If the sand pipes were blocked, which was a common occurrence, it was the fitter's job to clear them, using a long length of wire through the pipe to clear the obstruction.

Time for a quick cup of tea from the ever-warm can on the shelf over the firedoors and then it is time to leave the shed as my mate checks his pocket watch. I unscrew the tender brake, my mate opens the vacuum ejector and winds the reverser into reverse gear. With a glance over both sides of the cab to check that no other engines are moving in our vicinity and a blast on the whistle, the regulator is opened and we reverse out of the shed yard with steam billowing out from the open cylinder cocks. The massive bulk of our engine moves slowly towards the engine departure line, and we trundle along and stop at the signal. I climb down and use the telephone attached to the signal to contact the signalman, '7.30 Yeovil, engine ready'. Back comes the signalman's reply, 'platform 6'. The signal clears as I

return to the footplate and we run along clanking over the points and enter platform 6, easing gently against our coaches which have been placed there by the carriage shunter. I climb down and place the heavy coupling over the coach hook and screw it tight and then clip the vacuum pipes together and return to the front of the engine and place the twin headlamps over each buffer for our non stop run to Yeovil.

On the footplate everything is ready. The fire is red hot and burning through nicely, the vacuum ejector is open to test the brake on our train, dampers are open with a touch on the blower to stop the smoke drifting and I turn on the injector to stop the safety valves lifting. The residents of Ranelagh Road which adjoined platform 6 were known to complain about smoke and steam and I always tried to keep the natives happy, although at times it would be a job keeping an engine quiet. Our guard wanders along and takes the driver's name and engine number for his journal and gives us the load. The coach doors are opened as our tired, suntanned trippers wandered along the platform with all of the trappings of a day out at the sea side; buckets and spades, beach balls, candy floss and sleeping children being carried by their parents. Engine spotters take our number and ask about our destination, and as the coach doors are slammed shut by the station staff the latecomers come running along the platform and dive aboard the train. The starting signal is 'off', and there is always an air of expectancy on the footplate as the departure time approaches and the adrenalin starts flowing.

A long shrill blast on the guard's whistle echoes along the platform, and with a blast on our whistle, the regulator is opened and we move forward out from the platform, slowly at first and then gathering speed over the points and crossings. As platform 6 is on the arrival side of the station we have to cross over all the tracks to reach the up main. I close the firedoors as the massive blast from our exhaust beats down on the fire, a glance behind us shows our train of coaches snaking along over the crossings. We are now on the up main and up ahead of us all signals are clear as my mate opens the regulator wider and the huge locomotive gets into her stride with a quiet beat from the chimney. As we pass the siding where the banking engines lurk I cross over to my mate's side of the engine, and the banking engine driver gives me a sign with the fist of one hand pushed against the open palm of his other hand. This means, 'do we want a banker?'. I answer with a thumbs down, 'no we don't. A thumbs up from the driver and we are past him and on our way.

We pass the end of Jersey sidings heading for Radipole with the footplate rocking and swaying as my mate opens the regulator wider and winds the reverser back. Smoke and steam billow back over the coaches as we wind our way past Radipole Halt. A down train passes us, slowing for the terminus as we cough along. Time for a glance in the massive firebox, and as I open the firedoors the heat hits me with a white hot blast, the knack with the Bulleids was to keep the deep back corners of the firebox full, fire them this way and you would have no problems. The problem being that the firebox was so deep that it would tax even the strongest fireman on a long run. I tend to the fire shovelling the coal from the tender plate into the firebox. The normal rule of thumb for firing was the maxim of 'little and often', but in the case of the Bulleid Pacifics, if the engine was being worked hard, it was the case of 'a lot and often'. As we pass Upwey junction under clear signals we are now well into the bank and my mate has the regulator wide open with our engine chopping off the beats in rapid time. Higher and higher we climb with the engine gobbling coal like a good 'un' and our exhaust beat chattering away, throwing steam skywards. On the footplate the heat is unbearable as I tend to the requirements of the firebox and keeping the boiler topped up with the injector and spraying down the footplate with the pep pipe to keep the dust down.

There is a rattle alongside us as a banking engine runs back to Weymouth having assisted an up train to climb the bank. We are slowing as we attack the steepest part of the bank, and ahead of us is the first and shortest of the two tunnels. The driver gives the reverser another notch as we blast through. Bincombe 'up' distant signal is clear, and in front of us is the gaping dark tunnel mouth of Bincombe Tunnel itself. Smoke and steam billow out from the passage of a previous train. By now we have slowed right down but the engine is still ploughing on with the quiet beat of a well tuned Bulleid, and a blast on the whistle we enter the tunnel. Our quiet exhaust beat now becomes violent within the confines of the tunnel, red hot

clinker showers down from the tunnel roof, bouncing down onto our cab and the first coach. As I had turned the steam generator on before leaving Weymouth, the cab is now lit up by electric lights behind the water gauges and other vital points of the footplate. Conditions in any tunnel were unbearable, but, Bincombe was one of the worst, clouds of steam and smoke would be billowing around the cab making breathing difficult. Slowly we climb through the tunnel, the steam sanders are turned on for the engine to keep her feet. To slip to a standstill here would be fatal and the Bulleids were well known in this capacity. The noise in the tunnel would be so bad that it would be difficult to know if we were moving at all or just slipping, so the best thing to do is to lean out of the driver's side of the cab and touch the tunnel wall with the firing shovel.

At last, daylight appears and we burst out into the fresh air. Time for a lean out of the cab to refresh our lungs as we pass the bankers' siding and Bincombe signal box with the signalman leaning out waving us on with a cheery smile. As we top the bank we gather speed with a vengeance as my mate winds the reverser back and eases the regulator as we race towards Dorchester junction. Road traffic homeward bound from Weymouth is starting to queue away to our left on the outskirts of Dorchester. Dorchester junction up distant is 'off' as we approach the junction, with the left hand signal on the gantry ushering us straight on to the ex-GWR route, whilst the Southern main line to Bournemouth and Waterloo curves away to our right. All signals are clear as we burst under Weymouth Avenue bridge and storm through Dorchester West. The footplate bangs and rocks as we thunder through the station with whistle screaming and scattering paper and debris in our wake. Signals rise to danger as we pass, and bells are ringing in signal boxes along the line as we are accepted from box to box. Another blast on the whistle and we pass through Poundbury Tunnel. The engine is speeding along with the cab rolling and rocking and the needles in the brass bound gauges bouncing with the momentum. The demands on the fire have eased, but this no time for slackness as the fire has to be kept up and the needs of the boiler attended to, but there is still time to roll a cigarette and a glance at my mate shows me that he is stuffing his old pipe with 'baccy' whilst keeping an eye on the road ahead. We are thundering along as only the superb Bulleid Pacifics can with our train of coaches following on behind. The rumble of the coach bogies rises to a roar as we hammer over and under bridges.

Bradford Peverell and Stratton Halt flash by, and under clear signals we hammer through Grimstone and Frampton, another blast on the whistle and we pass through Frampton Tunnel. The engine is chopping off the exhaust beats in fine style as I tend to the fire and the boiler. Maiden Newton up distant is clear as we pass the outer home signal at speed whistling our approach. We gallop through the station with the branch to Bridport curving away to our left. We tackle the bank in fine style. The climb to Evershot northwards is nowhere as steep as the climb from Yetminster. The regulator is opened wider as we tackle the ascent, Evershot up distant appears ahead showing 'clear' as we approach the top of the bank. The station appears ahead and we swoop through, the regulator is eased as we run through Evershot Tunnel and start the run down the bank. The firebox is full with enough fire to last us until Yeovil, and as I have to clean the fire out at the Town shed I don't want to arrive at the shed with a full box. We rattle down the bank and with a blast on the whistle we storm through Yetminster. The regulator is opened wider as we head towards our destination, and all too soon the bridge carrying the Southern main line over the Weymouth line appears ahead with Yeovil junction standing over to our left. We pass under the bridge, and Yeovil South junction fixed distant appears in front of us. The regulator is eased for the final lap of our journey as we enter the outskirts of South junction. The SR branch runs down from our left and the track becomes quadruple as the small forest of signals appears ahead of us. We have a clear road and we pass South junction box with the SR branch curving away to our left towards the Town station. The regulator has now been closed as we drift around the right hand curve with Pen Mill outer and inner home signals clear, and with a loud hiss from the ejector the driver starts applying the brake as we slow right down and pass under the A30 roadbridge, clanking along the up platform until we come to a stand at the far end of the platform by the signal box. We have enough fire in the box to take us to the Town station and the injector is on to keep the engine quiet.

The carriage doors burst open and our passengers disembark and head for the exit in a solid mass. When the coaches have emptied the doors are slammed shut by the station staff, and there is a shout from the shunter for us to pull forward in order to clear the points behind us so that we may run around the train. We pull slowly forward and stop, the shunter climbs down between the tender and the first coach, and after he has uncoupled our train we pull forward past the signal box on the up main and stop just clear of the ground signal. The points change and the dummy clanged over. We reverse on to the down main and rattle along the down platform and under the A30 roadbridge. We come to a stand and when the road is clear we pull forward on to the rear of our train and buffer up with a gentle clunk, the shunter couples up the coaches, gives us the tablet for the single line to Yeovil Town. The signal arm is dropped and my mate turns the reverser into full reverse gear, opens the regulator and we start our short journey to the Town station. There is enough fire in the box, so it's time for a roll-up and a sit down for five minutes. We roll into the Town station and surrender the tablet to the signalman, the shunter uncouples us and we run around, couple up again and push the coaches to the carriage siding at Nine Springs (up over heaven), and after stabling the coaches we drift back to the shed bringing the shunter back on the footplate with us.

After refilling our tender at the water column, we clank down to the pit on number one road to clean the fire, the ash pan is unclipped with the iron bar and the already hot cab becomes a furnace as I rock the firebars and drop the red hot clinker out of the firebox which cascades into the ash pit sending clouds of choking dust up through the cab floor. When both sides of the firebox are cleared of clinker it is time to leave enough fire one side of the firebox to keep the engine in steam for its duty the next day, the ashpans are clipped back, and armed with the firing shovel and handbrush I open the smokebox door and shovel out the fine smokebox ash. After this chore the door is shut and clipped and any ash lingering on the front of the engine is brushed off. Back on the footplate I turn

on the injector to top the boiler up and wash down the footplate, turn the injector off, gather my kit from the engine locker and climb down from our engine with my mate who has been examining her for any defects of which there was none. We walk away from our engine now standing quiet, and gurgling away to itself, a vast difference to an hour before when we came storming up through Ridgeway to Bincombe Tunnel. We leave the engine standing on the No 1 shed road waiting to be coaled, and walk past the lines of engines standing quietly with a gentle hissing sound, and smoke drifting lazily from their chimneys casting a gentle haze over the shed yard. With that wonderful smell of hot oil and steam, it is time for a quick wash and a cup of tea in the drivers' cabin and home to mother's for supper after a day out to the seaside with a difference.

The Evershot Bankers

The Evershot bank starts almost at the end of the down platform at Yetminster station and climbs for $5^1/_2$ miles at a ruling gradient of 1 in 51, and in the days of steam most trains needed assistance to ascend the bank. Banking engines had always been supplied by Pen Mill shed, and when the shed closed in 1959 the engines and staff were transferred to our shed at Yeovil Town and I, in common with my Southern Region comrades from the Town shed, found ourselves at times rostered to banking duties, especially during the busy summer season. The Pen Mill station pilot was also used for banking duties during the weekdays, and the engine used to stay at the station until the last evening down passenger train had departed. If the down evening goods was not running or did not need a banker the engine departed for the shed at Yeovil Town.

Returning empty Per Pot box vans (when running) to Weymouth also usually needed a banker at night. These trains came down the Southern main line via Yeovil Junction and Yeovil Town and across the branch to Pen Mill. In the late 1950s many people still took their holiday by train, the busy Weymouth main line was no exception and during the peak season many extra trains were run and the brunt of the traffic occurred at weekends. The trains would arrive from London, South Wales, the North and the Midlands and all of the trains were usually packed with passengers, and by the time they had reached Yetminster the engine crews would be grateful for a push up the bank. When Yeovil Town had to find the extra engines and crews for the banking rosters, this also had to fit in with the extra duties called for on the busy Southern main line. Just how the shed coped at the busy weekends in the summer is still a mystery to me. All types of engines could be found banking; pannier and Prairie tanks, U class tender engines and, on one weekend even the spare M7 Drummond tank was used as a banker. In fact there would be so many down trains on some summer weekends that they would be waiting at Pen Mill and Marston Magna for a preceding train to clear Yetminster while there would be another one in the section between Castle Cary and Sparkford.

Well, the scene is now set, as we travel back through the years to a Saturday on a glorious summer's morning as I report for duty at the Town shed. After putting my old bike in the cycle shed and with my grub bag slung over my shoulder I walk past the engine cleaners' cabin in which I had spent many happy days as an engine cleaner. The engine shed and coaling crane is to my left, the air is heavy with the smell of smoke and steam as engines are being prepared or disposed. Safety valves are lifting and whistles are blowing as engines prepare to leave. Clinker and smokebox ash lie everywhere as I make my way to the shed office which is situated at the far end of the shed yard. I climb the stairs and book on. The two booking clerks are busy filling in large sheets of paper, booking on crews for Sunday and the following week. Telephones are ringing continually in the busy office. I collect my tea can from the locker room and have a word with my driver who has just arrived. I would like to point out that the Town shed was a happy place to work in. The majority of the crews were good mates, but, like any place of work there were a few 'grumblers' but by and large I have never worked since with a band of men like them. My mate and I enter the drivers' cabin which was a low building attached to the shed office. There would be a greeting and a bit of banter from the crews already in the cabin, some of whom would be on their way home. Others would be waiting to leave the shed or had just come on duty. I glance at the ever boiling kettle and remind myself to make a can of tea before we leave the shed. My driver and I walk down to the shed and find our engine standing over the inspection pit on number two road. It is a pannier tank, No. 9764. We climb aboard and stow our kit away in the small lockers.

We have to prepare our engine and a quick glance in the firebox shows me that the fire is banked up under the firedoor and the steam gauge is indicating about 120lb of steam, with about half a glass of water showing in the boiler gauge. The driver fills his oil feeder and climbs down to start oiling the webs and straps underneath the engine whilst I collect the oil and paraffin cans and make my way to the stores which is situated in the shed itself. The stores has the aroma of warm oil from the large tanks which are kept warm by gas rings to make the heavy lubricating oil more supple. The storeman fills the oil cans and the paraffin can and enters the engine number and amount of oil taken in the store register. I walk back to our engine, the shed is full of noise with fitters hammering away and water gushing from boilers as they are washed out.

I leave a full can of oil on the engine framing for my mate to refill his oil feeder whilst I climb aboard the engine with the can of lubricating oil and the small can of paraffin. It is now time to make up the fire, and after opening the dampers and turning on the steam blower to stop the fumes from coming back into the cab I ease the fire forward with the long handled pricker and spread the glowing mass all over the firebars. After putting the pricker away in its slot at the rear of the cab I open the bunker flap and start to make up the fire with the best lumps of coal under the firedoor and back corners. The panniers liked a saucer shaped fire to make them steam well and the fire starts to roar as it is made up and the heat in the enclosed cab makes streams of sweat intermingled with coal dust run down my face. After putting enough coal on for the moment and leaving the fire to burn through I shut the bunker flap and sweep the cab floor with the hand brush which is usually kept in the bucket on the fireman's side of the engine. As the steam pressure in the gauge rises I turn on the injector to put water into the boiler to keep the engine quiet. The pep pipe was used to spray down the cab floor and wash the dust of the boiler backplate and the cab fills with steam as the hot water from the pep pipe hits the hot pipes and gauges. After spraying

the coal in the bunker, as we will be travelling bunker first to Pen Mill, the injector is turned off.

I fill the lubricator for my mate and before putting the oil can away a drop of oil is put on a rusty and applied to the pipes and gauges to tidy the footplate up. The pipes start to shine with the effects of the oil. After checking that we have our safety equipment aboard, i.e. detonators, red and green flags, and spare tube for the gauge glass I climb down from the footplate and fill and clean the headlamps. I place a lamp on the front of the engine for our tail lamp, but a head lamp is not needed as we will be travelling in company with a Prairie tank and we will be the tail engine en route to Pen Mill. My mate has finished oiling underneath the engine and is now oiling the coupling rods whilst puffing away on a Woodbine. He is wearing his old oiling coat as did most drivers when they had to climb underneath an engine to oil up. It was not the most delightful of jobs, being in the pits and climbing over hot clinker and they usually had at least a foot of water or more to trap the unwary. This is a nice sunny morning but you can imagine oiling underneath an engine with the flickering light of a duck lamp in the early hours of the morning with the rain pouring down. After checking that the sand boxes are full, the smokebox door is tightly closed, and a climb into the pit to check that the ash pan is clear, we are nearly ready. My mate is now on the footplate as I climb aboard. He has taken off his old coat and is rubbing his hands on a rusty to wipe off the oil. He is a Southern man like myself, and the Saturday banking jobs are well liked as it might be a long day with the chance of overtime if we are lucky, although banking duties involve working the engine very hard for short spaces of time.

The fire is throbbing away and the cab is like an oven as my driver applies the steam brake for me to unwind the hand brake. He then gives a blast on the whistle, and with a glance out from the cab to make sure that no other engines are moving near us, he puts the reverser into full forward gear and opens the regulator. Steam issues with a roar from the open cylinder cocks as we puff slowly towards the water column which is one of two situated near the drivers' cabin. After stopping at the right spot we both climb down, my driver goes and pulls the water column arm around by its long chain whilst I climb onto the top of the pannier tanks and unclip and open the filler caps with a clang. I reach out for the chain and pull the column towards me and thrust the heavy leather bag into the tank. My mate turns the water on and the bag starts to move with the force of the water pressure. You have to judge the water just right, and it is important to shout to the driver to shut off the column when the water is about a foot from the top of the tanks. By the time he turns it off the tanks would be full and more than once I have seen tanks overflow with the water bag thrusting itself out of the top with the pressure, leaving a soaking wet driver and fireman. Anyway, no such trouble today as I pull the bag out, clang shut and clip the tank lids.

We pull up to allow the other engine, a Prairie tank to take water. We take the opportunity to have a wash in the cabin and make a can of tea, and return to our engine just as the Prairie is easing up to it. The driver takes our tea can aboard as I couple the engines together, and as we have a few minutes to spare the other crew go and make their tea and soon climb aboard their engine. The shed starting signal is off as my mate looks at his watch, takes time to light another

Woodbine whilst I roll my own brand of 'weed', and with a blast on the whistle, which is answered by the Prairie tank, our engines move forward and out of the shed yards puffing away up towards the ground signal. The shed signal clangs to danger as we pass and we come to a stand past the ground signal and the engine is put into reverse gear, points move and the ground signal clangs into the 'off' position and we drift towards the signal box and the single line to Pen Mill. The lead engine takes the single line token and we drift through the station towards Pen Mill, passing the Drummond M7 tank engine on the Town/Junction shuttle which was standing on the Southern platform to our right. The regulator is kept partly open as the leading engine does the pulling and uses the brake. We drift along the short stretch to Pen Mill. The outer and inner home signals are clear as we approach, and the old GWR shed abandoned the previous January appears with the Weymouth main line swinging in from the right. We stop at the Weymouth end of the 'up' platform, but there is no need to go right to the end to the signal box as the auxiliary token instrument, housed in a small hut on the down platform, can be used to surrender the single-line token. We are now the lead engine and as my driver puts the engine into full forward gear the starting signal is lowered with the indicator box showing 'Down Main'. We give a blast on the whistle and open the regulator as we pull forward over the points and head on to the 'down' main line.

Up ahead of us the double Sykes banner repeater for Yeovil South Junction shows 'clear' in the left hand aspect. The repeater was necessary as the South Junction outer home and crossover signals were situated on a curve and the repeater gave advance warning of which ever position the signals were in. We gather speed as we rumble over the bridge carrying us over the River Yeo, with the footplate clanging and banging and the needle on the steam pressure gauge quivering as it hangs on the 180lb mark – more than enough steam for the moment. The firehole doors are rattling with the beat of our exhaust on the fire and every part of the engine is alive as we head past South Junction signal box. The track now becomes quadruple as we run alongside the double-track branch that links Yeovil Town and Yeovil Junction. I notice that South Junction box is switched in, which means that a busy weekend is looming with excursions coming up from Exeter Central on the Southern main line and travelling to Weymouth via the South Junction connection and Pen Mill. I glance at the engine behind us as the exhaust steam from both engines beats down. My mate shouts out "what about the tea my boy?". He's standing there with a grin on his face holding up his tea cup. I lift the tea can from the tray above the firedoors where it has been keeping warm and pour out two steaming cups of tea. There is a long blast on a whistle from our right hand side as the Town/Junction branch tank bustles along pushing its two coaches on its way to the Junction with the Westinghouse pump on its smokebox panting away, pumping up the air pressure for the driver's controls in the auto coach. Our driver pulls our whistle cord and lifts his cup to the fireman on the branch tank as if to drink his health. The fireman gives a cheery wave as the Southern branch curves and rises to our right and the push-pull train continues on its way. We pass under the Southern main line and head towards Yetminster. A plume of steam appears ahead of us and an 'up' train from Weymouth headed by a gleaming 'Hall' carrying the twin headlamps of an express thunders past us, but she will soon have to start slowing down for the severe curve on the up platform line at Pen Mill.

We pass Thornford Bridge Halt and all too soon the Yetminster distant signal looms ahead standing at 'caution'. We run under clear signals and my mate shuts the regulator and applies the steam brake as we

Class U 2-6-0 No. 31790 and 5700 class 0-6-0 pannier tank No. 3733, both from Yeovil Town shed, are pictured at Yeovil South Junction en-route from Yeovil Pen Mill to Yetminster for banking duties on 23rd August 1959. I worked on both these locomotives during my footplate days, but as a Southern fireman, it will come as no surprise to inform you that the U class No. 31790 was one of my favourite engines.

S. C. Nash

'Heading for the bank' 2-6-0 No. 31637 and pannier tank 0-6-0 No. 3671, fresh off Yeovil Town shed, travel on the 'down' Weymouth main line between Yeovil South Junction and Thornford Bridge Halt en-route for Yetminster to perform banking duties on Evershot bank.

John Day

pass the signal box and stop at the platform. Ahead of us the platform starter stands at danger and the bank can be seen, starting almost under the road bridge. The points change and the ground signal clangs over behind us and we reverse into the down refuge bankers' siding, run just past the signal box and stop. I screw the hand brake on and my mate puts the reverser into mid gear, our engine gurgles away to itself as I turn the injector on to keep the engine quiet, and a quick glance into the firebox to check that everything is all right shows me that the fire is bright and hot and just right for the bank. After giving the floor and coal bunker a quick swill down with the pep pipe, the injector is turned off, the engines are uncoupled and while my mate walks up to the signal box to chat to the signal-man and find out what trains are about. I climb down and join the other crew, who by this time, have also climbed down from their engine to have a breath of air while they have the chance. Soon the pipes and roll ups are lit up and a bit of leg pulling takes place. As I recall my former footplate days, such memories of those sunny days (and the rainy ones) on the bankers' siding all that time ago are remembered with fondness, and more than make up for the bad times on the steam engine of which there were quite a few, as all former footplatemen know.

My mate arrives from the signal box puffing away on his Woodbine, "theres a Brummie on his way from Pen Mill and he wants a push" he says. ('Brummie' a down train from Birmingham Snow Hill.) At that moment the down inner home signal arm drops with a clang, and we climb aboard our engine, the fire is just right and the steam pressure is on the mark with about three parts of a glass of water bobbing up and down in the gauge glass as we await the down train. A long faint blast on a whistle behind us indicates that the 'Brummie' has arrived and is whistling her approach. A few minutes later there is a rumble and a roar as the train runs in with a travel stained 'Castle' on the front, a thumbs up from the fireman and as I glance into the

cab of the 'Castle' I see that the pressure gauge is well up on the red line. This means a good trip up the bank as they are doing well for steam. Coach after coach rumbles by, each one full to the brim with heads hanging out of the windows looking out over the Dorset countryside. Eventually the last coach squeals by with its tail lamp on the rear. The down train eventually stops at the platform, but the train is so long that the engine has passed the down starter and is standing just under the road bridge on the bank itself. The points change, the siding exit signal lowers and we chug out of the siding leaving the other engine behind and buffer up to the train. We don't couple up and we keep our engine tight up against the buffers of the coach. We won't move until the train engine is ready, so we are waiting, poised and ready for the whistle call, and here it comes, a long 'cock a doodle call' on the 'Castle's' whistle which echoes down from the front. This is repeated three times, my mate's hand lifts to our whistle chain and our answer in the same fashion resounds around the station in the tradition of the banker's reply. This is where the banking crew have to be on the ball, for as soon as the lead engine hears our second call he will open his regulator. My driver has the regulator open as we slowly move forward.

I close the firedoors and our engine coughs hard as the massive weight takes to the bank. We blast under the road bridge and the firedoors rattle with each huge blast on the fire, I slide open the firedoors and the glare from the fire is blinding as I pull up the firing flap by its chain across the firehole and then open up the bunker flap. In with the shovel, down with the firing flap and in with the coal, back corners first and all the time keeping the fire saucer shaped. The regulator is opened wider and our exhaust shoots high in the air as we hit into the bank. We have only just started climbing the bank, but the cab is like a furnace and sweat mingles with the coal dust, there is no time to gaze out over the cab side as I tend to the fire, firing flap down, in with the coal, firing flap up, shovel into the bunker, turn flick the firing flap chain, in with the coal, a quick squint in the firebox using the coal shovel to deflect the flames to see that the fire is how it should be. The regulator is wide open as we give all the assistance we can to the engine up front. My mate eases the reverser further forward and our engine barks louder throwing out clouds of steam and smoke even higher than before, every inch of the pannier is straining and shuddering as our entire tractive effort is brought into the fray. We are doing well for steam, and as the water starts to drop in the gauge glass it's time to turn on the injector and spray the bunker and floor with the pep pipe. The twin doors on the bunker are open to let as much air into the cab as possible as conditions are akin to a furnace. The injector is turned off when there is about three quarters of a glass in the gauge, we thunder past Chetnole Halt as I feed our hungry fire, shovel into the coal bunker, turn and flick the firing flap chain, in with the coal to where it is needed, shut the flap, and turn to the coal bunker for another shovel full of coal and into the firebox. We are storming up the bank in fine style. I have enough coal in the firebox for the moment as I cross over to my driver's side of the footplate, he grins and lights up another Woodbine, "he's a good un up front" he says, as I lean over the side of the cab for a breath of fresh air. Our engine is throwing out clouds of steam and smoke, the noise of the exhaust is deafening, and up ahead the 'Castle' is also throwing out steam and smoke high up into the air.

We are now approaching the top of the bank and the steepest point and our reverser is dropped into full forward gear for the final effort. We round the right hand curve and up ahead is the cutting leading into the gaping dark tunnel mouth. Evershot distant signal is showing 'clear', just past the signal is the catch point which is there to derail any run-away train and prevent it from going away down the bank. The thunder of our exhaust echoes around the cutting. I stop firing as we have enough fire in the box and the steam pressure is spot on, a faint whistle is heard from the 'Castle' as she enters the tunnel and steam issues from the tunnel mouth which grows larger as we approach. As we blast into the tunnel red hot cinders rain down from the tunnel roof, conditions are unbearable as steam and smoke from the train engine are mixed with our own. The tunnel walls reflect the lights from the carriage windows and the fierce glare from our firebox. There is a whistle and a roar to our right and an up train hammers through the tunnel. The carriage lights of the train flash past, and then they are gone. Up ahead, daylight appears and our exhaust beat softens as we leave the tunnel and into the welcoming fresh air. We pound up the last few yards of the bank, I turn on the injector to top up the boiler. Ahead of us is the overbridge, which is at the summit of our climb. Evershot station comes into view and all signals are clear for the Weymouth bound train. My mate closes the regulator for the first time since leaving Yetminster, the train accelerates away from us and there is a double toot from the 'Castle's' whistle as a 'thank you' for the push up the bank and then the train runs out of sight, hammering down the bank to Maiden Newton and onwards to Weymouth.

We coast along and stop at the end of the down platform as the platform starter is thrown to 'danger' in front of us. The signal arm drops and we pull forward

Class U 2-6-0 No. 31614 working tender first, and crewed by Yeovil Town shed footplatemen, gives rear end assistance on Evershot bank to a Cheltenham–Weymouth excursion on 14th August 1960.

S. C. Nash

of the crossover, the ground signal clears and we chug over the points and run alongside the up platform and stop at the water column which is situated at the far end of the platform. I give the coal in the bunker a good soaking with the pep pipe before turning the injector off to stop the coal dust flying as we will be travelling bunker first down the bank. I grab my tea can, tip the tea grouts out and climb down onto the platform. The water tank at Evershot was fed from a natural spring and even on the hottest day the water was ice cold and the purest water that I have ever tasted. My mate turns on the water and I hold my tea can under the bag I tip the first can-full over my head to cool myself down and wash the sweat and coal dust off. The second can of water is drunk in one go; what refreshing 'nectar'.

After filling the water tanks on the engine, we get the road and run through the tunnel and down the bank to Yetminster, we let the engine run quietly down the bank, but no matter how much a fireman damps down the bunker, coal dust swirls around the cab getting into eyes, nose and throat. As we approach Chetnole, a plume of approaching steam announces another train attacking the bank with a straining 'Hall' on the front with her exhaust barking high in the sky and another plume of steam from our mates on the Prairie tank pushing hard at the rear. We coast into Yetminster and stop at the up platform, and we cross over on to the down line and reverse into the down refuge siding, and as we coast to a halt I screw down the hand brake and turn on the injector to keep the engine quiet. Out come the 'grub' bags and time for a bite to eat before the next trip up the bank. All too soon the down signal arm drops with a clang and another train comes whistling in, and once again we chug out of the siding and place our engine against the rear of the waiting train. There is a bout of whistling and the heavy bark of straining engines can be heard for some time coughing up the bank. And so the day went on until the traffic dropped off and the remaining trains to come could be handled by the Pen Mill pilot engine and then we would be released to return to Yeovil Town shed. Upon arrival at the shed we would top up the water tanks, clean the clinker from the firebox, the ash from the smokebox and rake out the ashpan. Most drivers would rake the ashpan whilst the fireman cleaned the fire, the engine would then be left for coaling and the shed turning crew would then put the engine away for its next duty, and we would head for home.

But banking was not only done on nice summer days. Day in, day out, through daylight and darkness, sunshine and showers, fog, frost and snow the bankers were on duty. Some rough trips up the bank could be had if the engine up front wasn't doing too well for steam and I well remember banking a down goods from Pen Mill one day. I was booked on the station pilot with a Southern U class 2-6-0 and after a bout of shunting in the down goods yard we had stopped for a bite to eat. We had been informed that a down goods from Bristol was approaching and they were in need of a banker. Eventually it arrived with a Stanier "Black Five" on the front. Leaking steam from every pipe and joint the engine groaned to a halt by the water column on the down platform, and it looked a real old camel. Judging by the hiss of the blower from its chimney the engine was rather the worse for steam. Usually the Stanier "Black Fives" had a good reputation for steaming, but, as was the case in steam days, no two engines

of any class were the same for steaming and riding qualities. After taking water and dropping off and picking up a few wagons in the down yard the goods train was ready to leave. By this time we were at the rear of the train already coupled to the brake van. Up on our engine we were ready; I had levelled the fire with the pricker, the firebox was red hot, steam pressure was climbing and the footplate was washed down and the coal in the tender had a good soaking for good measure. The deep note of the "Black Five"'s Stanier hooter rang out from the front of the goods train, and our reply echoed around the station. We started pushing as soon as the brake van started to move, slowly at first and then gathering speed as we passed under the A30 road bridge. We approached Yeovil South Junction and up ahead of us the long train of wagons rumbled around the curve and past the junction. By now we were gathering speed as we passed under the Southern main line. My mate had not as yet given our engine full regulator, and this would happen when the Yetminster distant signal was seen to be clear. A black exhaust from the "Black Five" indicated that the fireman was attending to his fire, and on our footplate the steam pressure was up with a box full of red hot fire.

Yetminster down distant signal hove into view with its signal arm lowered, my mate opened the regulator wider for the climb ahead. We sailed through Yetminster and our speed decreased as we hit into the bank, our engine was barking away like a good 'un' as I tended to the needs of the firebox, shovelling in coal were it was needed, working the injectors to keep the boiler topped up and at the same time washing down the footplate and the coal in the tender to keep the dust down. Up ahead the "Black Five" was throwing clouds of exhaust steam high in the air but she was not doing too well as our speed dropped to a crawl and by now we were about half way up the bank. We were now working on a full regulator and about three quarter cut off and if we had any chance to get this train all the way up the bank we had to give all we had in the way of assistance. The reverser was spun into full forward gear, and the response from our chimney was dramatic, with an ear splitting bark our exhaust shot high into the air, the beat on the fire was tremendous and the heat from the firebox when I opened the firedoors took the breath from my lungs. It was shovel and shovel as we slowly moved the massive weight to the summit. Evershot distant signal was clear as we approached the tunnel mouth, our exhaust beat echoed back from the cutting, we entered the tunnel which was full of smoke and steam from the train engine. We were still on full regulator and the red hot cinders showered down from the tunnel roof onto our cab, daylight appeared ahead and we entered into the welcome sunlight. The regulator was closed as we topped the bank, our safety valves lifted with a tremendous roar as the train engine started braking and we came to a stand in the station. The guard climbed down from his van and uncoupled our engine The "Black Five" took a short time for a 'blow up' then pulled slowly away and down the bank to Maiden Newton, whilst we crossed over to the up main. We then took water at the column and when the road was clear we set off for Pen Mill for which we were allowed 22 minutes to complete the journey. At times, when Evershot signal box was not open, the bankers would travel from Pen Mill to Maiden Newton coupled to the rear of the train they were banking and then cross over and return to Pen Mill for another bout of shunting and await another trip up over Evershot.

Coming a Cropper on the Evershot Bank

Most footplatemen, even the best, have come a cropper on all banks including Evershot, and I was no exception. Every time footplate crews started their turn of duty, rough trips or engine failures could and would happen at any time with the shortest of notice. A goods train bound for Weymouth used to terminate at Pen Mill on Saturdays, and the crew from Westbury shed, after stabling their train in the 'down' sidings would bring the engine over to the Town shed and leave it there and return home on the cushions. Yeovil men would come on duty the following Monday morning, prepare the engine and work the train to Weymouth. I was booked on this duty one morning, and after booking on at 4 o'clock in the morning with Driver Don Willcocks we ambled from the drivers' cabin and walked down through the shed yard towards our engine which was standing on the number one road just outside the shed. The lighting in the shed yard was rather poor (the shed lighting was worse) and as we approached our engine I was quite unprepared for the unfamilair shape that appeared in front of us, for standing there, with its long Swindon boiler and copper capped chimney was No. 6804 *Brockington Grange*.

We climbed aboard and stowed our kit away. This was a class of engine that I had not fired on before and after examining the footplate controls we started to prepare the engine. My mate lit a duck lamp, gathered the oil cans and oil feeder and climbed down from the footplate to start oiling around the straps and rods. As the 'Grange' had been lit up the previous day (Sunday) she was low on steam with the gauge showing about 80lb of steam pressure, but she had a nice lump of fire under the firedoor. The blower was turned on, and after spreading the fire around the firebox with the pricker and after opening the dampers I started to make up the fire. The best lumps of coal were selected and fed into the box, the coal started to crackle and spit as the fire took hold and the locomotive began to come to life as the steam pressure started to rise.

After making up the fire I left it to burn through and filled and lit the headlamps and the gauge lamp which was placed on its bracket next to the gauge glass which was showing half a glass of water. On with the injector and turn on the pep pipe to wash down the footplate and the coal on the tender. I then climbed down with two headlamps, placing a white light on the tender bracket and a red light on the front bufferbeam, checked the smokebox door was tight and filled the sand boxes. By this time the driver had finished oiling and I rejoined him on the footplate. After topping the tender up at the water column we left the engine to simmer away, looking rather out of place amongst the Southern locomotives in the yard. We entered the drivers' cabin to make a can of tea, and as this was a busy time in the morning with crews arriving and departing it would be quite full with plenty of chat and banter as we sat on the wooden trestles enjoying a cup of tea amongst the cigarette and pipe smoke. My mate looked at his watch and indicated that it was time to go, we picked up our cups and tea can and left the cabin and climbed aboard No. 6804. The fire was burning through just right, the steam pressure was climbing to the red line on the pressure gauge and things looked to be all right as we left the shed yard and pulled up

over the crossover points and reversed back to the signal box. After collecting the token for the branch to Pen Mill we ran gently through the darkened platforms with the steady beat from our copper capped chimney echoing through the station. It only took a few minutes to reach Pen Mill and with all signals clear we entered the station and stopped just inside the up platform. I climbed 'down', entered the token hut on the down platform and put the token in the instrument and used the telephone to talk to the signalman. 'Light engine off branch', the signalman replied and I twisted the token and it dropped and locked into the token instrument, thus clearing the branch, the signal arm dropped showing 'down main' in the destination blind and we pulled forward on to the down main and stopped just past the ground signals. These then cleared and we reversed into the down goods yard, a white light from the shunter's lamp guided us on to our train, the lamp turned to green as we neared and then to red as we buffered up to the leading vehicle. The guard took the driver's name and our engine number for his journal, gave us the load which was under the limit required for a banker, the shunter telephoned the signalman to inform him that we were ready, and a few minutes later the yard exit ground signal clanged over.

With a blast on the whistle the regulator was eased open and we pulled out of the yard and on to the down main. I closed the firedoors and as we pulled slowly towards South Junction our exhaust beat grew louder with the splendid crackle and bark that distinguished the ex-GWR main line engines from any other class of locomotive. I exchanged lamp signals with the guard and we were on our way, coughing slowly around the South Junction curve with the darkened signal box to our right. As the box was switched out, all signals were clear as we gathered speed with our train of wagons bumping and banging along behind us. I opened the firedoors and the cab lit up with a brilliant white light from the mass of fire in the box, I tended to the needs of the firebox, being careful not to put too much in the box, just keeping the back of the box full. The footplate was rock steady which impressed me as some of our Southern engines used to roll about when the bit was between their teeth. The first rays of dawn were breaking as we approached Yetminster, the GWR ATC bell rang in the cab as we approached the distant signal which was in the 'off' position. This was expected as Yetminster box was switched out. The engine was given full regulator and we swooped through the station and started to climb the bank.

Our speed dropped as the bank took its toll, the engine was barking away, sending a torrent of noise over the sleeping countryside. Sparks flew skywards from the chimney as I fed the hungry furnace, thrusting the shovel into the tender. I turned and yanked the chain attached to the firing flap, placed the coal into the box where it was needed, pulled up the chain and shut the firing flap, turned and scooped another shovelful of coal from the tender into the box, and so it went on as we wove our way up the bank. It was always the way on the footplate, when you thought that you were doing well, as often as not, things would go wrong. The engine was not steaming too well and at the same time the exhaust injector on my side of the footplate started to play up for some reason. I just could not get it to work properly. It had been working all right up to now, the water was dropping in the gauge glass and I turned off my injector and used the injector on the driver's side of the footplate. By this time the steam pressure had started to drop alarmingly and, my mate could not afford to nurse the engine as we were approaching the summit with the tunnel not far away. The pressure was still falling and we came to a stand with about 120lb of steam and with the water in the bottom nut of the gauge glass. The only thing to do was to wait until the engine rallied round. I gave the fire a good poke with the long handled dart, and with a box full of red hot fire, to give the engine her due, the pressure started to rise quite quickly. It was not long before we had plenty of steam, the question now, was, would we pull away without assistance, as Yetminster and Evershot signal boxes were switched out and would not open for another hour or so and it would be a long walk to Maiden Newton to summon help.

By this time we had half a glass of water and enough steam to move. My mate gave her full gear and opened the regulator with a blast on the whistle to warn the guard that we were on our way. The engine gave an almighty bark from the chimney and we started to move, slowly, so slowly at first, and then starting to pull like a good 'un', and with not a trace of a slip we eased our way up the bank. The pressure held and to my relief the injector on my side of the footplate started to work. Evershot distant was clear and the ATC bell rang and with not much further to go, the massive blast from our exhaust echoed around the cutting as we approached and entered the tunnel. The noise was ear shattering in the confines of the tunnel and smoke and steam billowed around the cab, but the engine was still going strong as we left the tunnel and topped the bank. Our exhaust beat grew softer as the regulator was eased and the reverser wound back. Our pace quickened as we ran through the station and past the signal box which was switched out and would open not long after we had passed. We started to run down the bank cautiously and began to brake as the ATC siren sounded in the cab as we approached the Maiden Newton distant signal standing at caution. This was expected as we were booked to stop there to drop off

and pick up wagons. After dropping off wagons at Dorchester West we arrived at Weymouth without further incident, and after putting our train away in the sidings, we took the engine to shed, and left it on the ash pit. After a wash and a cup of tea and breakfast in the enginemens' cabin we left Weymouth and headed for home on the cushions.

On one memorable day I was booked on to work a track panel train from the civil engineers yard at Yeovil Junction to Weymouth with one of the Yeovil U class. I well remember arriving at Pen Mill with our massive train of track to find not one but two bankers waiting for us at the station and they were both Yeovil based Maunsell 2-6-0s. The noise from three sets of whistles calling to each other and three separate exhausts barking away as we left Pen Mill was spectacular. We had one banker coupled to us on the front and one at the rear, and the sight of three Maunsell 2-6-0s hammering up over Evershot was a sight never to be forgotten. I often wonder if any train spotters ever photographed this rare event, but I don't remember seeing any cameras on our journey.

Nowadays of course, diesels take Evershot bank in their stride without a banker. Long gone are the days when bouts of frantic whistling heralded another train taking the banker at Yetminster and straining engines barking up the bank to the summit at Evershot with sweating firemen shovelling coal into white hot fireboxes, hoping that they can make it to the top of the bank, especially if they had a rough engine, and were down the pan for steam.

Working the Yeovil to Westbury Freight and a Rough Return Trip

Like all footplatemen I have had my share of rough trips. They could come at any time without warning, with any type of engine and were part and parcel of the job. The following event happened to me one night when working a freight train from Westbury to Yeovil. My driver, Fred Martin, and I booked on at Yeovil Town depot one summer's evening to work the 8.22pm

Class U 2-6-0 No. 31794 stands on the No. 2 shed road inside Yeovil Town shed on 10th July 1956 *R. C. Riley*

Hendford goods yard to Westbury freight. We collected our kit from the locker room and after having a bit of banter with our mates in the drivers' cabin we walked over to our engine which was standing on one of the preparation roads in the depot.

We climbed aboard our engine which was one of the Southern U class 2-6-0 tender engines, No. 31632. She was already prepared for us with a nice bright fire burning away in the firebox, and after stowing our kit away we checked the engine. The fireman's duties included turning the steam feed on for the lubricator which was positioned on his side of the footplate, and after checking that the oil was dripping correctly through the sight feeds, my attention was now turned to checking that our safety gear of detonators, red flags, spare gauge glass tube was intact, the sand boxes were full, and the water level in the tender was all right. It was time to light the headlamps and gauge lamp as it would be dark by the time we arrived at Westbury. Meanwhile, Fred was opening the large and small vacuum ejectors to test the brake and was putting the trimmings in the brass oil boxes. When we were ready to leave, the tender brake was unscrewed, the vacuum brake was showing the 21 inches in its brass bound gauge, and with a glimpse over the cab side to see that the shed starting signal was 'off', Fred opened the regulator and with a sharp blast on the whistle, we rumbled slowly out of the shed yard and passed under the 'stars lane' footbridge. The shed starting signal slammed to 'danger' behind us as we coasted to a halt with the front of our engine standing clear of the twin ground signals. Fred wound the reverser into forward gear as the points moved in front of us and the left hand 'dummy' cleared. We ran forward over the crossovers and stopped in front of the signal box and my mate wound the reverser into reverse gear whilst I accepted the single-line staff from the signalman.

We now set off for Hendford Yard running tender first, the journey taking about five minutes and all too soon the Hendford fixed distant loomed ahead. With a blast on the whistle as we neared Ninesprings crossing we rattled into Hendford. Upon arrival we surrendered the staff to the Hendford signalman and pulled forward into the goods yard where the shunter coupled us onto our train. I climbed down from the footplate whilst the guard gave Fred the load, and placed the headlamps in the correct position, climbed back aboard and we were ready to leave. The normal procedure was to push our train out of the goods yard on to the branch and after collecting the single-line staff from the signalman we would set sail from Hendford for the short stretch to Yeovil Town. The Hendford advanced starter was clear, with the fixed distant for Yeovil Town sharing the

Fred Martin as I will always remember him, seen here looking down from the cab of Prairie tank No. 5565 at Yeovil Pen Mill in the late 1940s. Fred was my driver when we had a rough trip, whilst returning from Westbury one night with a Hendford Yard freight. No. 5565 was built to Lot 253 in January 1929 and withdrawn in September 1960.

Fred Martin

same post. The firing shovel would not be touched at this stage as there was an ample fire in the firebox which was burning through just nicely.

The steady beat from our exhaust echoed around the brick-lined cutting as we chugged under the Hendford Hill road bridge, and with a warning blast on the whistle we passed over the Ninesprings crossing with our long train of freight wagons of all shapes and sizes rumbling and banging behind us. Alongside to our right we passed the long ranks of green Southern coaches stabled on the long siding which ran beside the single track branch between Yeovil Town and Hendford. To all Yeovil crews this was known as "Up over Heaven". We rounded the curve and passed under the Adderwell Lane overbridge with just a breath of steam on the regulator as the Town station outer home signal loomed ahead in the 'off' position. The station appeared in the distance with the inner home signal clear, and I stood ready to exchange tokens with the signalman who was leaning out of one

Class N 2-6-0 No. 31842 arrives at Yeovil Town from Hendford with a civil engineers train on 24th September 1961.

John Day

of the Town signal box windows. With a quick movement the Hendford section staff was exchanged for the hoop containing the Pen Mill tablet, the platform starter was clear, it sharing the same post as the Pen Mill fixed distant.

With more steam on the regulator we rumbled through the Town station with a roar from the wheels and the clanking of buffers of our freight wagons echoed around the station. We passed under the road and footbridges at the end of the platform and headed along the single track branch to Pen Mill with the double track Yeovil Town–Yeovil Junction branch curving away to our right. We took it easy along the short stretch to Pen Mill, and as we approached I turned the injector on to top the boiler up and keep the engine quiet as we had more than enough steam for the moment. Fred started braking as we neared the outer home signal which was 'off', more brake was used now as we eased around the curve, approaching the inner home cautiously with the up main line from Weymouth swinging in to our right. The signal was spotted from my side of the cab, and as it was 'off' I shouted out to my mate "okay the board". He let the engine run and we lurched onto the main line banging over the crossings under the A30 road bridge and took the curving up line through the station with our engine clanking away as we travelled the length of the up platform. Ahead of us the platform starter was 'off' with the signalman leaning out of the signal box window to receive the single-line token. The token was accepted by the signalman as we passed the box, my mate worked the brake into our train and we came to a stand with a clanking of buffers which resounded along the whole length of our train, just before the top crossover which gave us access to the far end of the down goods yard via the down main. The shunter was standing by the side of the down main leaning on his shunter's pole waiting to cut out the first wagons. He came across and uncoupled our train about six wagons back from the engine, and after giving us the tip to pull up, we moved forward with the small raft of wagons hanging on our tail and leaving the rest of our train standing on the up main. The points were switched over behind us and the ground signal clanked over, we reversed back over the down main under the shunter's guidance and rolled back into the goods yard. As we had a right hand driven engine this meant that the shunter was on my mate's side of the engine, so this gave me the chance to pull a bit of coal forward on the tender and swill the footplate and tender down before turning off the injector as we had enough water in the boiler for our present needs. The driver braked as we came up against a raft of wagons in the goods yard with a clang and a bump, and after the shunter had coupled up and given us the tip to pull forward, the reverser was spun into full forward gear and we coughed out of the goods yard over the down main and onto the up main. The reverser was spun into reverse gear and when the road was clear we set back onto our train under the guidance of the shunter. After we were coupled up to our train again, the guard gave us the load and walked back to the brake van. The reverser was spun into full forward gear again, the footplate was throbbing away with the heat of the roaring fire, the steam pressure was high on the brass gauge, and the vacuum gauge was showing the regulation 21 inches of vacuum. Everything on the footplate was ready, with the water in the boiler gauges dancing up and down,

the gauge lamps were already in place and lit, up ahead of us the advance starter cleared and we were ready to depart. It was now time for a 'smoke' as my mate gave a shrill blast on the whistle to alert the guard far behind us. The regulator was opened slowly then shut and opened again, the engine shuddered as it took the weight of the train and we pulled forward slowly, with a massive bark from the chimney. I shut the firedoors as the blast from our exhaust beat stirred up the fire, and crossed to my mate's side of the engine to exchange hand signals with the guard to verify that our train was complete. After doing this I resumed my position on my side of the engine, and we were now gathering speed. The reverser was wound back and the regulator opened further as we passed the advance starter which clanged back to 'danger' behind us. The engine started rocking and swaying as our speed increased as we rolled along the main line.

I glanced back over our tender at our long train of wagons bumping and rolling along behind us, box vans, petrol tanks, empty coal wagons, flat wagons carrying army lorries from the RASC depot at Houndstone, and other flat wagons carrying large packing cases from the Royal Naval air station at Yeovilton, all pushing and banging along. The dying rays of the sun were reflected in our white exhaust beating down behind us as we travelled through the lush Somerset countryside. The engine was steaming well as I tended to the fire, the demands on the engine were not heavy at this point in our journey as the road to Castle Cary was quite an easy one. The distant signal for Marston Magna loomed ahead in the 'off' position and soon the outer and inner home signals hove into view, and with a blast on the whistle we passed through the station with its distinctive tall signal box on the up platform. Our engine was clanking away like a good 'un', with the footplate swaying from side to side, just a flick of coal was needed here and there to fill any holes in the firebed with the injector being used to keep the boiler topped up. A spray around the footplate and tender with the pep pipe to keep the dust down as we trundled along in the section between Marston and Sparkford and then I noticed that the water in the gauge glasses was turning to a murky colour suggesting that the boiler was overdue for a washout.

I did not take much notice of this at the time, and in any case, we could not do much about it. Ahead of us the Sparkford distant signal was standing at 'caution', but this was expected as we were booked to shunt here. My mate shut the regulator and pulled the whistle cord, the long shriek from our whistle echoing around the countryside. The outer home was 'off' as we approached cautiously and with the driver braking hard, we passed the dairy to our left with its rail siding holding milk tanks standing ready for their next journey. The station lights twinkled ahead as we rumbled under the A303 road bridge and stopped at the end of the platform. There was a rattle and a rumble to our right as the last evening down passenger train to Weymouth ran in and stopped. The glow from the carriage windows reflected against our engine and freight wagons, while up on our footplate the injector was on to try to keep the engine quiet, but it was not an easy task as the fire was red hot, and we would need all the steam we could muster for Brewham bank onwards from Castle Cary. However, I am thinking too far ahead, and for the moment let us concentrate on Sparkford. With a sharp blast from the exhaust the down train pulled away, the glow from the carriage windows moving faster until the train with its red tail lamp was out of sight. The signalman in his box could be seen moving and banging levers and the down line signals slammed back to danger, showing twinkling red aspects in the gathering gloom. The guard came along the platform with the shunter, who had his lamp in one hand and shunting pole in the other, walked in front of our engine and down the side of the train, the glow from his lamp reflecting against the wagons as he looked at the labels for his cut. There was a loud clang as a coupling was released, a shout to pull up, and a white light from the shunter prompted my mate to pull forward with a few wagons in tow. We came to a halt, and the driver wound the reverser back, the ground signal turned to green and we reversed slowly into the up goods yard. The shunter was now on my side of the engine, his white light swinging across guiding us back. I kept my mate informed of the shunter's signals, the light turned to green, which meant go steady. We eased slowly along the siding, then came a red light, we stopped as we clanged up against a raft of wagons, there was a clank as the wagons were coupled. The shunter's white light waved us away, the ground signal from the siding was 'off', and we pulled away onto the main line. After the points had been reset we backed down to our train and coupled up again, the guard gave us the load, and up ahead of us, green lights were showing us a clear road to Castle Cary. We pulled forward slowly with a crisp bark from our exhaust, and after exchanging lamp signals with the guard, it was time to put a few rounds of coal around the firebox. Keeping the back corners and under the firedoor packed full, we were travelling along in fine style – we had plenty of steam and all I had to do was to tend to the needs of the boiler.

My mate was whistling away to himself as he kept an eye on the road ahead, with one hand on the regulator and the other not too far away from the vacuum brake. All too soon the dim yellow glow of the Castle Cary distant signal glowed out of the darkness, the regulator was closed and my mate started braking, the weight of our train pushing against the engine as the brakes took their hold. The outer home signal was 'on' as we approached, the red shade of the semaphore grew larger and brighter as we approached and we stopped at the signal with a clanking of buffers from our wagons. I opened the firedoor and the cab was lit up with the fiery glow from the firebox, the fire throbbed away with just a touch on the blower to stop the smoke and flames from blowing back into the cab. The injector was singing away as I sprayed down the footplate with the pep pipe, Fred and I rolled our own cigarettes and had a 'puff' whilst waiting for the board to clear.

We were usually stopped at this signal on this trip as we had to wait for a West of England train to clear the junction. The Taunton line lay over to our left and a rattling noise announced a fast moving train as it approached the junction. A few minutes later, with a clang so characteristic of the GWR lower quadrants, our signal arm was lowered displaying a green light. I turned off the injector as Fred opened the regulator and we slowly moved forward. The inner home signal was clear as we rattled and clanged over the points and crossovers of the junction. The lights of the signal box and the station glowed out of the darkness as we trundled past and stopped at the end of the platform. After

dropping off and picking up a few more wagons, we were now ready for our run to Westbury, and apart from being stopped by signals we were not booked to pick up or drop off wagons at any other stations en route. We would usually take water at Castle Cary if we had a tank engine, but it was not necessary as our tender locomotive had ample water for our journey.

The road ahead was clear as green signal lamps beckoned to us out of the darkness I had taken the chance to make a can of tea, and Fred and I had enjoyed two steaming cups of 'brew' so we were now ready to assault Brewham bank. With a toot on the whistle to alert the guard we pulled forward, slowly at first, and as the engine took the weight of the train, the regulator was opened wide and the reverser was wound back. The firedoors were closed to stop the cold air being drawn into the firebox, and lamp signals were exchanged with the guard. As we passed the advanced starter the locomotive was barking away and pulling well, and as we climbed higher into the bank, so the reverser was wound forward a nick at a time. The blast on the fire was tremendous as sparks flew high into the sky and bounced on the roofs of the vans behind the tender. We stormed under the bridge which carried the Somerset & Dorset line over the ex-GWR main line, (only once in my firing career did I ever pass under this bridge at the same time as an S&D train was in the act of passing over). This did not happen on this trip, but on the time that it did, there was a flurry of whistle pulling from both crews as we approached the bridge, the S&D train as I remember was heading north, anyway, back to our journey, the footplate was vibrating with power as I fed coal into the firebox. Every time that I opened the firedoors, the sky was lit up with a fiery glow and the heat was tremendous, the engine was steaming well, although I had the feeling that the engine was not doing as well as she should, and the water in the gauge glasses was now very dark.

Bruton distant showed a green aspect ahead of us in the darkness, and we stormed through the darkened station and there is a slight easing of the bank through Bruton, but this is only a short respite as the steepest part of the bank lay ahead. We were now working flat out with full regulator, higher and higher up the bank we climbed. I kept toiling at the fire, feeding the back corners, closing the firedoors, opening the firedoors and feeding under the door, with a few shovelsful down the sides and front. Not too much down the front though as the oscillation of running down through Witham would push a lot of fire down the front anyway. As the Brewham distant signal showed a clear aspect ahead of us we were almost at walking pace as the weight of our train took its toll. We were now at the summit, and as we passed Brewham signal box, the regulator was eased and the reverser wound back as the weight of our train would push us onwards towards Witham. All signals were clear at Witham as we rushed past the signal box standing to our right with the shadowy figure of the signalman moving levers and throwing signals to 'danger' behind us. We swung and banged and lurched over the points, red signal lamps gleamed out of the darkness on the East Somerset branch away to our left, we rattled through the station and out of the section heading towards Blatchbridge Junction. The engine was still steaming adequately but I had the old fireman's feeling that things were not quite right, but at that time I had no inkling of the drama that was to befall us on the return journey.

As we approached Blatchbridge Junction the left hand distant signal was 'off', indicating that we were to be routed on to the Frome line. We rattled over the junction points and lurched to the left, heading up the old main line instead of going up the avoiding line. All signals were clear as we steamed along, the station appeared in front of us as we ran past the small engine shed standing to our left. We passed through the station with the glare from our firebox reflecting against the overall roof and the loud rumbling of fast moving wagon wheels echoed around the deserted station. Lights gleamed from the South box windows as we passed through, with the signalman standing against his levers ready to put the boards to danger behind us. We started to climb as we passed the North box with all signals clear ahead of us, and the train started to drag as we approached Clink Road Junction. Our engine was straining hard throwing out a loud crackling exhaust beat as I fed the firebox whilst Fred gave her more regulator and wound the reverser forward. More rounds into the firebox as we rejoined the main line at the junction, and passed Clink Road Junction signal box to our left. There would now be enough fire in the box to last us to Westbury as it was a downhill run all the way, so it was on with the injector to keep the boiler topped up and another spray down of the footplate with the pep pipe. As we topped the climb and passed under the Clink road bridge the straining beats of our exhaust eased as we started to run downhill. The regulator was eased and the reverser wound back as we gathered speed. It was now time to turn off the injector and to have a sit down and keep a look out ahead whilst puffing on a roll-up. There was a glow from another firebox as a down freight headed by a 28xx 'Long Tom' heading west approached us, climbing hard dragging a long train of freight wagons in its wake. We ran steadily with our long train swaying and rumbling behind us, and with all signals clear Fairwood Junction loomed up out of the darkness and we swung to our left heading for Westbury. We now eased down into Westbury and braking all the time as we passed signal after signal under the yellow caution aspects. We were routed on to the up goods line as we rattled and swayed over the maze of points and crossings with the wheel flanges of our wagons squealing in protest.

Eventually we came to a stand at the end of the goods line opposite the far end of the up platform and with a clanking of buffers from our train, my mate turned off the brake ejectors. Apart from the singing of the injector which I had turned on to knock back the steam pressure to stop the safety valves from lifting, and the gentle hiss of the blower on the fire, the engine was now quiet. The firedoors were open and the whole cab was lit up with a golden glow from the firebox with the fire spitting and crackling away. There was a gentle push from our train which meant that the up goods pilot engine had buffered up to our brake van, and a few minutes later there was a loud clang of a coupling being dropped as the shunter uncoupled our train and with a quiet rumble it was pulled away by the pilot engine leaving us standing alone.

I climbed down from the footplate and placed a headlamp on our tender and converted one of our headlamps to a tail lamp by turning the red shade. This is where we became the bain of the Westbury signalmen. When tank engines were used on the Hendford to Westbury goods they had no need to use the turntable, but it became a different story when the

tender engines were put on the job and it was quite a complicated movement to route us from the up goods line to the shed which was at the Salisbury end of the station.

Westbury in those days at that time of night would be full of goods trains arriving and departing, with shunting engines fussing about marshalling and remarshalling trains and banking engines whistling and pushing trains up to Warminster on the Salisbury line. Westbury was then, as it is still, a major railway junction with routes converging from Taunton and the West, Weymouth, Paddington via the Newbury line, Salisbury, Swindon via Bradford Junction, and traffic from South Wales via Bristol. There is also a passing loop between Heywood Road and Fairwood Junction for traffic to and from Paddington not requiring to stop at Westbury, and an avoiding line between Hawkeridge and Heywood Road Junctions for traffic from Bristol to gain access to the Newbury line without the need for reversal at Westbury. Anyway back to our engine, we had moved out of the goods line and after signalling movements involving all three of the Westbury signal boxes we at last ran into the engine shed yard which was packed full of engines of the ex-GWR type and our Southern engine stuck out like a sore thumb as we pulled onto the turntable. After balancing the engine Fred and I pushed her round until she was facing the way home. We pulled off the table and took water. I took the opportunity to pull the best of our coal forward on the tender, but we had no need to recoal at the shed as we had enough for the return journey. However, I recalled the story of a Yeovil driver on the same trip who did pull up at the Westbury coal stage with one of our U class, and was told in no uncertain terms to clear off as he had a 'foreign' engine. After a lot of arguing and shouting on both sides, the engine was eventually coaled.

Fred climbed down with the oil feeder to oil up the straps and rods and I built up the fire for our return journey, after this I made a can of tea and when we were ready and the road was clear we pulled over to the goods lines and coupled onto our train for the return trip. Now was the chance to have a cup of tea and a bite to eat and our guard would also have a cup of tea with us on the footplate while he gave us the load.

I well remember on this occasion, a Westbury fireman climbing aboard and asking us for a lift to Frome. This was agreed and he commented that he had not been on a Southern U class before. Well this was my chance to show what a Southern fireman and engine was made of. The down Hendford goods was always a full load and a very heavy train comprising of petrol, coal, fertiliser, timber and van traffic. The yard signal cleared for us and we pulled away across the maze of tracks with our train hanging on behind us. I exchanged lamp signals with the guard and Fred opened the regulator wider and wound the reverser back as the signals cleared away in front of us on the main line. Our engine barked louder and louder as we took the weight of the train. I started firing, the fire was a red hot mass pounding away with the beat of our exhaust and the steam pressure was high on the gauge. By this time we had cleared Fairwood Junction and our engine was pounding up the bank towards Clink Junction and up until now we had been doing all right for steam when all of a sudden, our loud bark turned into a woolly muffle as our engine started to prime. With water flying everywhere from our chimney my mate shut the regulator and opened it again but the engine still kept on priming. I put the injector on as the water was going down fast in the boiler gauge glasses. The steam pressure crept back and our train was starting to drag as we lost speed. How we made it to Clink Junction that night I still do not know, as it was poke and blow all the way as we lost steam and water but the engine hung on (just) and I was glad to see Clink Junction distant signal appear out of the darkness at the top of the bank. The right hand signal on the gantry was 'off' and we swung to the right over the junction and headed into Frome with about 140lb of steam and the water bobbing in the bottom nut of the gauge glass and our long train banging and clanking behind us.

We eased cautiously past Frome north signal box with the distant signal on, and Frome South box distant signal was showing 'caution' as we approached, which was not surprising as we had lost so much time coming from Westbury. We neared a signal showing a red shade and came to a stand, the signal came 'off' and we pulled forward slowly. Up ahead of us there was a bracket signal with the left hand down yard signal in the 'off' position and we swung left and ran behind the signal box and the station buildings and stopped in the goods yard. Our passenger climbed down from the footplate and wished us luck, and I got the feeling that he was not too impressed with our engine! Whilst I tried to retrieve our depleted water and steam supplies, Fred went up to the signal box to explain our situation and at the same time collect the key to Frome engine shed and get the blowdown key. I use the word key, but in fact it was a long metal handle with a socket at one end which was placed over the protective nut at the lower end of the boiler on the fireman's side of the engine. The knack was not to turn the nut too far, but far enough. It could be a dangerous operation if it went wrong as there is a lot of force in a locomotive boiler. We used the key to blow the scale and muck from out of the boiler and we were surrounded by a massive cloud of steam which roared out of the boiler like thunder, the noise echoing around the station like a jet engine. We turned off the blowdown key and Fred returned it to the engine shed, I climbed back aboard to find the water showing about a quarter of a glass in the gauges, and it was still mucky but not as bad as it had been. As I tended to the fire the pressure was rising and we eventually had about three parts of a boiler full of water showing in the gauge glasses. This was just about right as I did not want too much water in the boiler in case the engine primed again.

After waiting for a fast down goods to clear Frome, the road was pulled off for us and we eased out of the goods yard. The Frome signalman had told us not to hang about and we were to be looped into Witham in order to allow the down paper train to pass. We approached Blatchbridge Junction – so far so good, and pulled on to the main line with our long train of freight wagons banging along behind us. Fred opened the regulator wider and we sailed along the down main line and cleared the Blatchbridge down main advanced starting signal. I fired to the requirements of the engine and we were doing fine as we approached the automatic colour light section situated between Blatchbridge and Witham. The green lights glowed ahead of us in the darkness, we passed the first signal and then it happened. The engine primed her guts out and nearly emptied the boiler. My mate shut the regulator and opened it but the same process started all over again. I put the injector on to stop dropping the lead plug and we came to a halt on the main line with hardly any steam or water in the boiler. Now we were in a right pickle, stuck on the West of England main line with the paper train not far away. Fred climbed down from the footplate and called the Witham signalman from the telephone attached to the colour light signal whilst I walked back with a tin of detonators to meet the guard who, by this time, was walking along the track. After a quick chat he went back to protect the rear of the train with the detonators in compliance with the rules. As I climbed aboard the engine, Fred informed me that he had telephoned the Witham signalman with the result that the paper train, which by that time, was stopped by signals at Frome would push us as far as Witham. I walked back to the guard's van and informed him what was happening. After a short while in the distance the faint glow of the paper train's headlights grew stronger and the rails started quivering as she approached.

The detonators which had been put down by our guard exploded as the 'Warship' diesel locomotive rumbled up to the rear of the train. I climbed up into the warm cab and explained to the driver that the Witham signalman had the road set into the goods loop. I set off on the long walk back to our engine and by this time we had about 140lb of steam with half a glass of water. I waved a lamp to the guard to indicate that we were ready, and we started to move forward with the diesel pushing at the rear. We rumbled along the main line with my mate giving the engine a touch of regulator to give what assistance we could to the diesel. The yellow glow of the Witham distant signal appeared ahead of us in the darkness, we gave a long blast on the whistle as we approached; well at least we had enough steam for a good whistle call! We entered Witham station under clear signals, passed the box and entered the down goods loop, the diesel reversed out and tooted up as he passed us on the continuation of his journey to Exeter.

I uncoupled the train and placed a red tail lamp on our tender and with the guard on the footplate we set off light engine to Yeovil. We rolled down the bank to Castle Cary and branched left on to the Weymouth line. Just before Sparkford the engine primed again but not for long, and I was very glad to see the yellow glow of the Yeovil Pen Mill distant signal appear ahead of us. We picked up the token for the Yeovil Town branch from the signal box and dropped the guard off on the platform, and upon arrival at the Town locomotive shed, two very weary and fed up footplatemen climbed down from their engine and headed towards the drivers' cabin. While Fred made out his report I made a welcome can of tea. No. 31632 went in for boiler washout the next day, and a few days later I had her on a fitted van train to Exeter and she ran like a sewing machine without a hint of trouble. That particular rough trip stands out in my memory as it was one of the few times that I have been glad to see a diesel! The train of wagons we had left at Witham was collected by the early turn Hendford shunting engine and taken direct to the goods yard.

Westbury–Weymouth Freight – 1954 Winter Working Timetable

The Weymouth line had a considerable freight working in its heyday, and locomotives of all types, 28xx 2-8-0s,

Moguls, 'Halls', grimy WDs, "Black Fives", and the Standard engines, would bark their way up Brewham and Evershot banks with a banker pushing away at the rear. Some goods trains would travel from loop to loop in order to let passenger trains have precendence, and footplatemen on engines that would be having trouble in steaming would be glad of the respite allowed whilst running down the various dips in the route in order to bring the pressure gauge up to a better working pressure. All footplatemen have stopped for a 'blow up' more than once in their careers much to the displeasure of signalmen who would be waiting for a late running freight train to clear their section. An engine low on water would creep along a station platform with the steam blower hard on and stop at the water column with a clanking of buffers from its long freight train in tow. Fuming signalmen standing over their levers would have no choice but to wait whilst the footplatemen would fill their tender and with a blast on the whistle the engine would slowly move forward with a loud bark on the exhaust and roll off into the night with its long train of freight wagons gathering speed until they were out of the section. The signalman would then slam his levers in the frame putting the advance signals to 'danger' to protect the train.

Weymouth Line Freight. Winter 1954.
Down Line
3.15am, (MX) Westbury–Weymouth (1.20pm ex-Bristol.)
4.20am, light engine, Castle Cary–Yeovil Pen Mill. arr 4.40am. (release of night banker.)
10.40pm, (MX) Paddington–Weymouth. arr 8.05am.
3.15am, (MX) Westbury–Weymouth. arr 6.47am.
4.00am, (MO) Westbury–Weymouth (continuation of 10.40pm ex Paddington Saturday). arr Weymouth 7.58am.
5.10am, (MOQ) Bristol East Depot–Weymouth. arr 1.27pm.
5.20am, Westbury–Wells. arr Witham 6.11am.
5.50am, (MO) Rogerstone–Weymouth loco coal. arr 4.00pm.
6.00am, Yeovil Pen Mill–Hendford Goods Yard.
6.25am, (MX) Loco coal Westbury–Yeovil Junction. arr Pen Mill 8.50am.
6.30am, Transfer freight Yeovil Pen Mill–Yeovil Junction. arr 6.55am.
8.10am, light engine SR Yeovil Pen Mill–Yeovil Town.
8.10am, (SX) Westbury–Sparkford, stops at Brewham signal box 9.06am–9.07am to pick up water cans, runs to Marston Magna if required.
8.30am, (Q) Dorchester West–Dorchester Junction, WR Transfer.
8.40am, (MX) Bristol East Depot–Weymouth. arr 4.00pm.
9.20am, Castle Cary–Durston.
9.30am, Yeovil Pen Mill–Langport West.
10.40am, (Q) Westbury–Weymouth. arr 2.12pm.
11.45am, Severn Tunnel Junction–Weymouth. arr 10.34pm.
11.49am, Upwey–Weymouth.
11.57am, (MX) Yeovil Pen Mill–Yeovil Junction transfer freight.
12.25pm, (SX) light engine Yeovil Pen Mill–Hendford.
12.55pm, (SX) Yeovil Pen Mill–Weymouth, arr 4.50pm.
1.20pm, Swindon–Weymouth. arr 9.27pm.

4.30pm, (SX) light engine Castle Cary–Yeovil Pen Mill. arr 4.50pm.
5.50pm, (SX) EBV Westbury–Frome Mineral Loop. (after working 4.00pm Radstock.)
6.35pm, (SO) Bristol East Depot–Weymouth.
6.50pm, (SO) Westbury–Castle Cary.
7.40pm, (SX) Westbury–Frome Mineral Loop.
8.45pm, Yeovil Pen Mill–Yeovil Junction.
9.00pm, (SX) Westbury–Yeovil Pen Mill. arr 11.17pm.

Weymouth Line Freight. Winter 1954
Upline
1.50am, (MX) Weymouth–Avonmouth Docks.
3.00am light engine, Yeovil Pen Mill–Castle Cary. arr 3.25am.
4.30am, (MXQ) Weymouth–Avonmouth Empties.
5.55am, light engine, Yeovil Town–Yeovil Pen Mill. arr 6.00am.
6.45am, Weymouth–Cardiff empties.
7.25am, Yeovil Junction–Yeovil Pen Mill, arr 7.50am.
7.40am, light engine, Yeovil Pen Mill–Castle Cary, arr 9.12am. Shunts at Sparkford, arr 7.55am.
9.37am, (SX) Weymouth–Yeovil Pen Mill. arr 11.57am. Shunts at Evershot and Yetminster.
10.10am, (SO) EBV Wells–Frome Mineral Loop. arr 11.42am.
11.00am, (SX) Weymouth–Upwey.
11.10am, (Q) Wells–Witham. arr 1.17pm.
11.30am, (SO) light engine, Hendford–Yeovil Pen Mill. arr 11.35am.
11.45am, (SX) Sparkford–Westbury. Starts from Marston Magna if required, stops at Brewham signal box 12.32pm–12.33pm to set down water cans.
11.55am, (SO) Frome Mineral Loop–Westbury. arr 12.10pm.
12.05pm, (SX) light engine Hendford–Yeovil Pen Mill.
12.35pm, Yeovil Junction–Yeovil Pen Mill. arr 1.13pm.
12.45pm, (SO) Radstock–Westbury. arr Frome Mineral Loop 1.49pm.
1.30pm, Durston–Castle Cary. arr 4.00pm.
1.48pm, Weymouth–Rogerstone Empties.
3.15pm, (SX) Langport West–Yeovil Pen Mill. arr 5.10pm.
3.35pm, (SO) light engine Hendford–Yeovil Pen Mill. arr 3.45pm.
4.00pm, (SX) Radstock–Westbury. arr Frome Mineral Loop 4.44pm. dep 5.06pm.
4.25pm, (SX) Wells–Westbury. arr 7.38pm.
4.45pm, (SX) Cheddar–Witham.
4.50pm, (SX) Mells Road–Westbury. arr 6.08pm.
5.30pm, (SO) Wookey–Witham.
6.20pm, (SX) Hendford–Westbury. arr 8.14pm.
7.00pm, (SX) Hendford–Yeovil Pen Mill. arr 7.10pm.
7.55pm, Weymouth–Bristol.
9.30pm, light engine, Yeovil Pen Mill–Castle Cary. arr 9.50pm. (banker).
9.32pm, Yeovil Junction–Yeovil Pen Mill. arr 9.52pm.
10.30pm, (SO) Weymouth–Bristol East Depot.

Freight traffic today (1994) is non-existent on the Castle Cary–Weymouth line. When the above timetable was operating, every station however small, had sidings serving the local coal traders, etc. with tank engines arriving daily on local pick up goods to shunt the yard, and regular long distance freight trains calling at the larger stations to pick up and set down wagons.

The Route Described

Hawkeridge Junction Signal Box

109 miles 14 chains from Paddington (via Swindon)
95 miles 30 chains from Paddington (via Berks &
   Hants)
Opened 14th July 1942
Closed 11th/14th May 1984

The double-track Hawkeridge loop was one of a number of diversionary junctions and loops built during the Second World War. At the start of construction, a north ground frame and engineers siding located at the Berks & Hants end of the intended loop was brought into use on 16th January 1942 for work on the new curve. The important Hawkeridge loop (East Chord) connected the Trowbridge line with the Newbury line at Heywood Road West Junction and avoided the need for reversal at Westbury by trains travelling to and from either route. The new route also saved trains from using the steeply graded Devizes line. Hawkeridge Junction signal box, equipped with a 38-lever 5-Bar VT frame, opened with the loop on 14th July 1942, box size 23ft x 12ft x 8ft. The box situated alongside the down Trowbridge main line also controlled facing and trailing points to nearby War Department sidings located on the up side of the Trowbridge main line north of the signal box. The Hawkeridge loop was renamed Westbury East loop on 13th May 1984, and Heywood Road West Junction became Westbury East Loop Junction. Hawkeridge Junction signal box closed on 11th/14th May 1984. The connecting loop is still in use today and forms an important diversionary route.

Hawkeridge signal box, looking towards Trowbridge on 2nd March 1974, with the Westbury–Trowbridge lines in the foreground. The 38-lever signal box, measuring 23ft x 12ft x 8ft opened with the new loop on 14th July 1942, and closed on 11th May 1984.

Adrian Vaughan Collection

Hawkeridge Junction, looking towards Westbury with the East Chord line curving towards the left, as Class 5MT 4-6-0 No. 73020 with plenty of steam to spare, rumbles across the junction with the 11.05 (SO) Weymouth–Wolverhampton on 14th August 1965.

Hugh Ballantyne

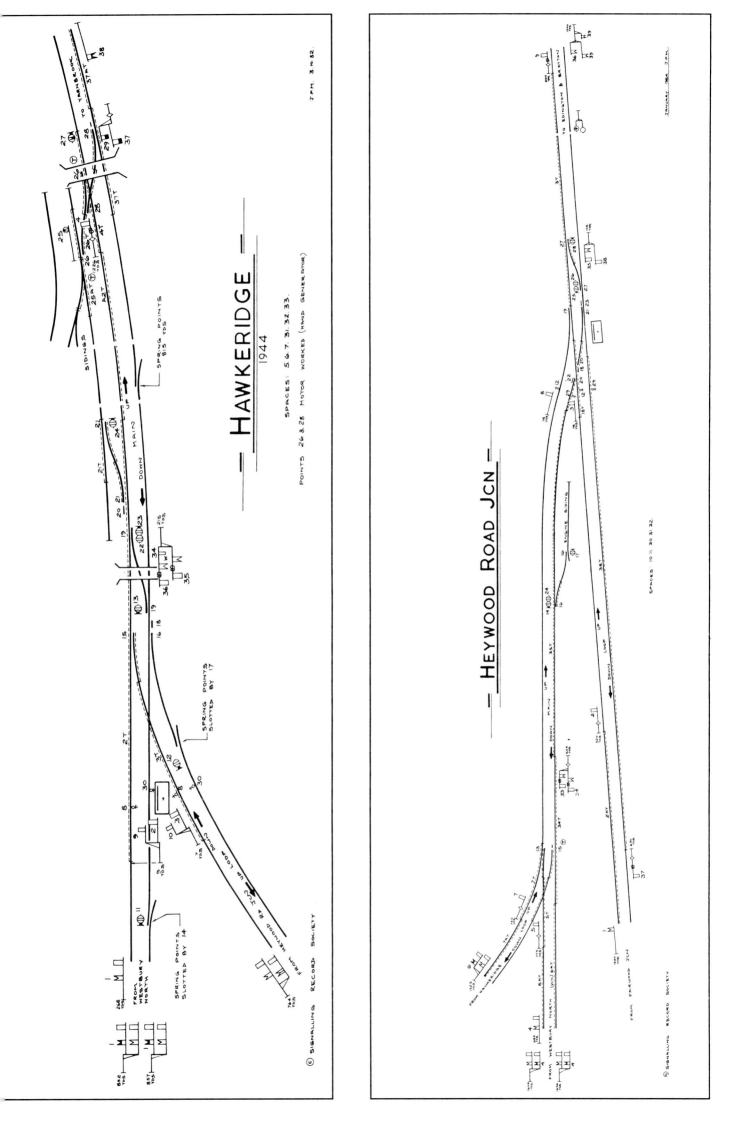

— HAWKERIDGE —

1944

SPACES: 5.6.7. 31. 32. 33.

POINTS 26 & 28 MOTOR WORKED (HAND GENERATOR)

© SIGNALLING RECORD SOCIETY

— HEYWOOD ROAD JCN —

SPACES 10.11. 30. 31. 32.

© SIGNALLING RECORD SOCIETY

No. 4932 *Hatherton Hall* approaches Hawkeridge Junction from Trowbridge with the 10.20am Cardiff–Bournemouth Relief on 15th June 1963. The weed covered loop leading to the wartime ammunition depot can be seen to the left of the 'up' Westbury–Trowbridge main line.

Gerald T. Robinson

Heywood Road Junction Signal Box
94 miles 45 chains from Paddington (via Berks & Hants)
Opened 1st January 1933
Closed 11th May 1984

The 39-lever 5-Bar VT frame signal box situated at the junction of the eastern end of the Westbury avoiding line and the Berks & Hants main line, opened on 1st January 1933. Box size 25ft x 12ft x 8ft. When the Hawkeridge loop opened on 14th July 1942, the double line junction with the Newbury main line, known as

Heywood Rd West Jcn, was controlled by the signalman at Heywood Rd Jcn box using hand generated electric motors. An engine siding used by the Westbury pilot engines awaiting collection of the coaches slipped from down express trains was situated on the down Westbury main line west of the box. This siding was taken out of use on 29th April 1963, and removed in December of the same year. The siding for the Westbury cement works situated east of the box off the up main line was brought into use 30/9–1/10 1962. The signal box closed on 11th May 1984.

Heywood Road Junction signal box on 4th May 1975. The box closed on 11th May 1984.

Adrian Vaughan Collection

The interior of Heywood Road Junction signal box on 4th May 1975 showing part of the 39-lever frame. The diagram above the instrument shelf shows the junctions with the Avoiding/Westbury lines, and the Hawkeridge loop (East Chord). The gas lamp and the highly polished floor were typical of many signal boxes.

Adrian Vaughan Collection

Heywood Road West Junction in 1974, looking towards Westbury showing the Hawkeridge Loop (East Chord) curving away towards the right. The Heywood Road Junction 'down' advanced starter and Westbury North box 'down' distant signal arms are 'off'. The signals on the right hand side of the bracket are the Heywood Road advanced starter for the Hawkeridge Loop with the Hawkeridge box fixed distant arm below.

Adrian Vaughan Collection

Westbury

109 miles 64 chains from Paddington
Thingley Jcn–Westbury opened 5th September 1848
Westbury–Frome opened 7th October 1850
Westbury–Warminster opened 9th September 1851
Warminster–Salisbury opened 11th June 1856 (mineral traffic)
Warminster–Salisbury opened 30th June 1856 (passenger traffic)
Bradford–Bathampton opened 2nd February 1857
Holt Junction–Devizes opened 1st July 1857
Westbury–Warminster line doubled May 1875
Bradford–Bathampton doubled 17th May 1885
Patney & Chirton–Westbury opened 29th July 1900 (goods traffic)
Patney & Chirton–Westbury opened 1st October 1900 (passenger traffic)
Westbury avoiding line opened 1st January 1933
Hawkeridge Loop opened 14th July 1942

After the inspection of the line by the Board of Trade on 26th August 1848, a special train hauled by the locomotive *Vulture* with Daniel Gooch and Isambard Kingdom Brunel on the footplate conveying the directors and other worthies, arrived at the temporary terminus at Westbury from Thingley on Saturday 2nd September. The train was met by an excited local population with flags waving and brass bands playing at Melksham and Trowbridge. At Trowbridge the town reverberated to the sound of cannons fired in salute from the iron foundry. Upon arrival at Westbury, the Mayor and the Chairman of the Board exchanged the usual congratulatory address and reply. The new line with intermediate stations at Melksham and Trowbridge was opened to public traffic on Tuesday 5th September 1848 to a temporary all-over roofed timber built terminus designed by Geddes. The locomotive of the first train from Chippenham to Westbury was decorated with laurel leaves in the customary fashion. There was a daily service of five trains each way and three on Sundays. With the completion in 1856/7 of the routes to Salisbury, Weymouth, the Devizes branch, and with the Avon Valley line between Bathampton and Bradford opening up a direct route to Bristol, Westbury was now developing into an important cross country junction.

Devizes was connected with Hungerford on 11th November 1862 giving passengers from Westbury a more reasonable route to Reading via Newbury. Doubling and upgrading of the Berks & Hants Extension line from Hungerford to Stert, and construction of a new 14½-mile double-track route from Stert to Westbury with a new station named Patney & Chirton Junction being constructed one mile east, where the new route forked away from the Devizes line and with intermediate stations at Lavington and Edington & Bratton, was started in 1897. This was the first chapter of the Great Western Railway's short route to the West which had been planned since 1848. The old overall roofed Westbury station was demolished and extensively rebuilt by 1899 with two 600ft island platforms connected by a subway and provided

Lower quadrant signals abound in this view of Westbury station in 1974, bulk grain wagons stand in Messrs Nitrovit's sidings to the left. Westbury North signal box is in the foreground, with a Class 52 'Western' diesel standing to the right. Cranes and building plant of all kinds occupy the former site of the Westbury Iron Works to the far right.

John Morris

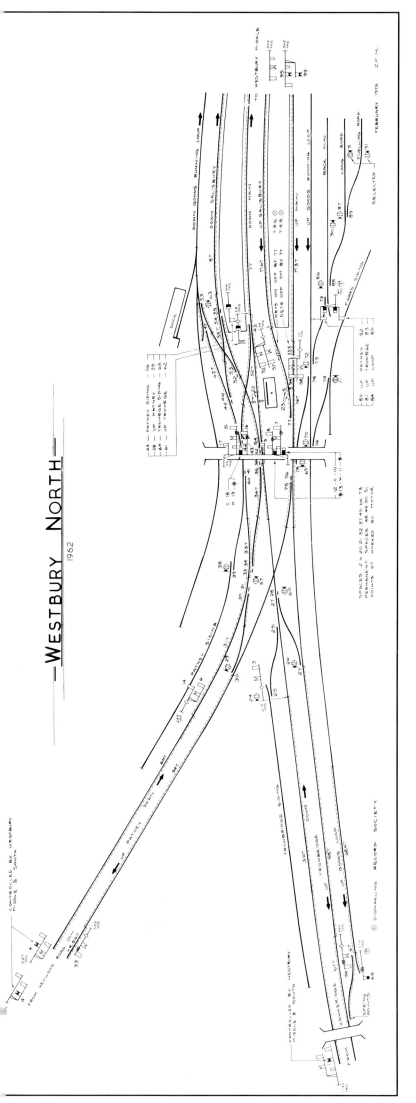

WESTBURY NORTH

1962

© SIGNALLING RECORD SOCIETY

A view of Westbury North Box interior taken on 1st April 1984. The station layout controlled by the box can be seen on the diagram above the signal levers. The floor is so highly polished you can almost see your face in it.

M. Marshall

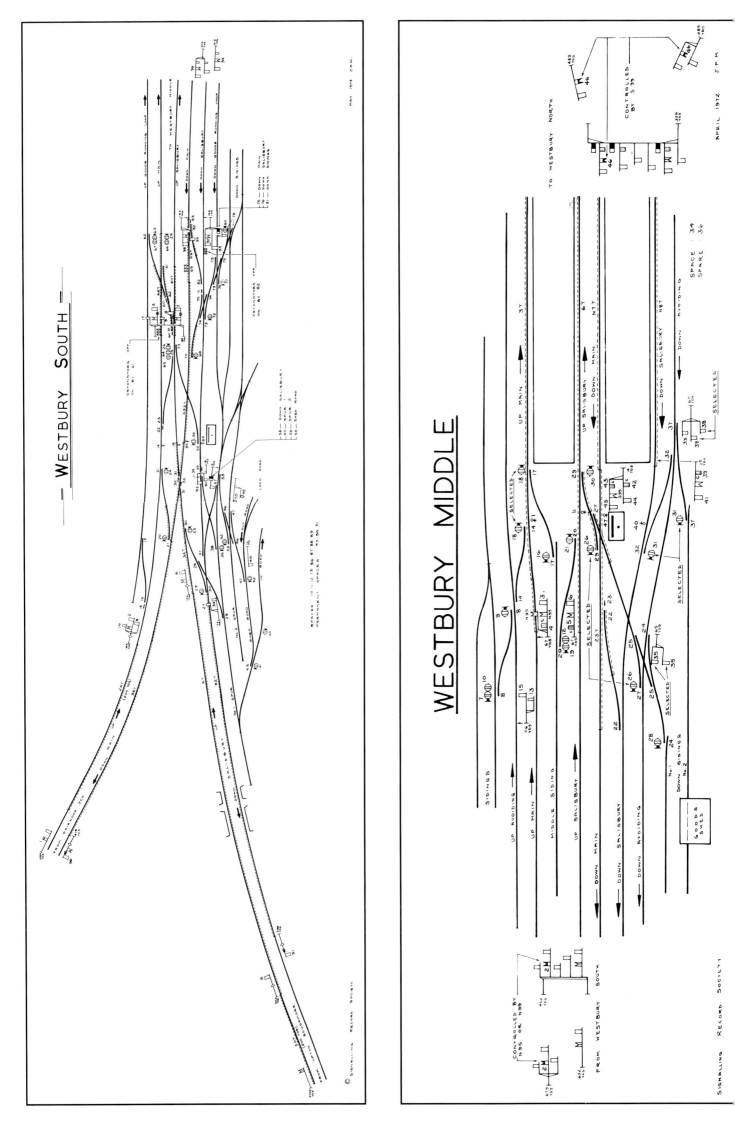

WESTBURY SOUTH

© SIGNALLING RECORD SOCIETY

WESTBURY MIDDLE

SIGNALLING RECORD SOCIETY

An end on shot of Westbury North signal box in 1974 with signalman Sid Fleming leaning out of the window posing for the camera. The left hand arms (looking from the rear) on the bracket signal in the background are the Westbury North starter, with Heywood Road Junction distant arm below for the Newbury line, and to the right, the North starter and Hawkeridge distant for the Trowbridge line. This impressive GWR box, measuring 50ft x 14ft x 9ft became the sole survivor in the station layout after the closure of Middle and South boxes, before succumbing itself to the demolition gang on 28th April 1984.

Adrian Vaughan Collection

Westbury Middle signal box, looking south to the goods shed in the middle distance, on a murky day in 1968, with the 'up' Salisbury line on the right, and the 'down' main to the left. Middle box, measuring 33ft x 13ft x 9ft and equipped with a 47-lever frame, closed on 5th May 1968 being the first of the three station layout boxes to be demolished.

Adrian Vaughan Collection

Westbury South signal box in 1974. The ground signal in the foreground is 'off' and the shunter leaning on his trusty shunting pole outside the shunters' cabin awaits the next move from a locomotive which is lurking out of camera shot. The 99-lever South box, measuring 38ft x 13ft x 11ft closed on 16th September 1978.

Adrian Vaughan Collection

with luggage lifts. An 83ft long goods shed with a 150ft loading platform plus extensive siding accommodation was provided for freight traffic. Three new signal boxes all opened in 1899; North, Middle and South, replaced the older No. 1 and 2 boxes. Westbury North box was situated off the end of the up platforms and was originally fitted with an 82-lever frame, which was subsequently altered to 99 levers with VT5 Bar locking in 1949. Box size 50ft x 14ft x 9ft. Westbury Middle was located off the end of the down platforms and had a 47-lever frame. Box size 33ft 6in x 13ft x 9ft, Westbury South box was situated where the Salisbury and Weymouth lines diverged and was equipped at first with a 57-lever frame, altered to 72 levers in 1914, and to 99 levers with VT5 Bar locking in 1953. Box size 38ft x 13ft x 11ft.

Quadruple tracks were laid between the South and North signal boxes namely; Up Weymouth, Up Salisbury, Down Weymouth, Down Salisbury, the goods lines, namely the Up Goods and Down Goods were laid alongside the Up Weymouth and Down Salisbury respectively. At Westbury South box the four main lines divided for Weymouth and Salisbury whilst at the northern end of the layout, under the control of the North box, the lines diverged left for Trowbridge and right for Newbury (known to all railwaymen over the years as the Patney). The 1,644ft down goods loop between North and South boxes was opened in 1907, and the longer up loop of 2,478ft was provided in 1915.

Goods traffic started using the Stert Valley line from 27th July 1900 and passenger traffic from 1st October. From 1st July 1901 three fast daily passenger trains were routed over the new line from Paddington to Weymouth via Newbury. The best of the services took 3 hours 40 minutes, this accelerated service being a vast difference to the old route via Swindon and Chippenham. The 9.35am Paddington–Weymouth using the new line slipped a coach at Patney which was worked to Devizes arriving two hours after leaving the

Capital. This service was withdrawn in 1910 and from July 1902 the 5pm Paddington–Weymouth slipped a coach at Savernake which formed a stopping train to Devizes. With the opening of the cut off line via Castle Cary and Cogload Junction in 1906, the importance of Westbury as a major cross country junction was established and many expresses were diverted over the new route to the West including the 'Cornish Riviera' which had previously run via Bristol. This train slipped coaches for Weymouth at Westbury and for a short time the slipped portion was known as the 'Weymouth Limited Express'. In 1910 the 8.30am Plymouth–Paddington slipped a coach at Westbury which was attached to the 12.24am all stations stopper to Swindon. A new engine shed was opened in 1915, again adding status to Westbury. Also in 1915, sidings situated alongside the down Trowbridge and down Patney lines north of the station were extended. As traffic increased over the years more siding and track alterations took place including the opening of the avoiding line on 1st January 1933 for the West of England expresses thus accelerating the timings by ten miles an hour. The down 'Cornish Riviera Express' was switched to the avoiding line route and slipped its Weymouth portion at Heywood Rd Junction. A short siding was laid off the down main line west of Heywood Rd box for the pilot engine to stand whilst awaiting the arrival of the down express. When the express had raced down the avoiding line, the slip portion was collected by the pilot engine and brought into the station and attached to a waiting Weymouth bound train. During the Second World War more siding accommodation was constructed. Ambulance train sidings were laid by 1940 near the up sidings and additional sidings were added to the up and down freight yards in October 1944, but by far the most important alteration took place when the Hawkeridge Loop was opened in 1942. This formed a triangular junction, the double-track line known as Westbury East Chord connected the Trowbridge line with the

With the starter off for the Trowbridge line, and the Hawkeridge distant arm at caution, No. 5043 *Earl of Mount Edgcumbe* pulls away past Westbury North signal box on 15th June 1963 with the 4.33pm Salisbury–Bristol. No. 6930 *Aldersey Hall* awaits the 'road' on the right with the 5.25pm Westbury–Swindon.

Gerald T. Robinson

North British Type 4 'Warship' No. D850 *Swift*, heading a westbound passenger train, ticks over at Westbury on 5th May 1963, whilst No. 6945 *Glasfryn Hall* rattles in on the 'up' Salisbury line with the 2.15pm Portsmouth–Cardiff passenger train. The roof of Westbury Middle signal box can be seen above the cab of the diesel. No. D850 was introduced to traffic in June 1961 and was allocated to 83D (Laira) and was cut up at Swindon in March 1972.

R. E. Toop

Berks & Hants, thus allowing trains travelling via Bristol and Reading to avoid reversal at Westbury.

The junction of the East Chord with the Berks & Hants line, known as Heywood Road West Junction, was controlled by Heywood Rd Junction signal box. The up siding lying alongside the up Trowbridge line north of the station was converted into an up loop on 16th August 1942. During the late 1940s and early 1950s the East Chord was used as part of a test course by Swindon Works for testing steam locomotives on performance trials. The circular route from Swindon to Swindon was via Reading, Newbury, Trowbridge and Thingley Junction.

Westbury was, and still is, an important cross country junction and during my firing days it was quite a sight on the approaches to the station as we eased down from Fairwood Junction to see the gantries of lower quadrant signals appear and the tracks fan out in front of our train. The double-track Salisbury line coming in from our right as we rattled over the switches and crossings,

The driver of 4-6-0 No. 5974 *Wallsworth Hall* on an 'up' train takes a breather whilst waiting for the road at Westbury on 4th June 1963. The signals are off for an adjacent train on the next platform which is routed via the Trowbridge line.

J. Miller

Westbury South, looking over the junction from the signal gantry in 1974. The Salisbury line curves away to the left and the West of England line diverges to the right. Westbury South box stands alongside the 'down' Salisbury line with tracks to the 'down' goods yard and former engine shed passing behind the box, the small building standing next to the signal box being the shunters' cabin. Plenty of freight traffic including coal and limestone can be seen in the 'up' goods yard to the right, and limestone traffic from Merehead and Whatley quarries still dominates the freight scene at Westbury today.

Adrian Vaughan Collection

freight yards packed full of wagons on the up and down sides of the layout, far over to the right drifting smoke and steam hung over the locomotive shed and yard, ex-GWR locomotives of all types including, 'Castles', 'Halls', 'Granges', "Long Tom" 2-8-0s, Moguls, pannier tanks fussing about in the sidings or working local services, "Black Fives", BR Standards, groaning WDs, and with the coming of the diesels, shiny new 'Hymeks', 'Warships', 'Westerns' and dmus intermingled with the steam traffic, locomotives needing water or being changed over, crews swopping footplates before heading to all points of the compass. The whistling of banking engines resounded over the station as they were kept busy assisting trains up over the Salisbury line to Upton Scudamore. Cross country services between Cardiff and Portsmouth Harbour arriving and departing via the Avon Valley and Salisbury lines, trains from Wolverhampton to Weymouth arriving via Thingley Junction and Bradford Junction, West of England trains arriving over the Berks & Hants, and from Taunton over the Castle Cary cut off lines, most of which hammered up and down the avoiding line. Local trains serving the web of local services which radiated from Westbury, to Frome, Devizes, Savernake, Warminster, Trowbridge, Chippenham, Calne, Bath and Bristol arrived and departed in a regular sequence. Goods traffic of all types intermingled with passenger traffic, coal trains from Aberdare heading for Salisbury or Weymouth steamed slowly along the Avon Valley, at times running from loop to loop to let faster trains overtake. Vacuum fitted freight trains, petrol trains, pick up goods from the local stations, mineral trains, wagon loads of Somerset coal from the Radstock branch, all passed through or stopped to shunt at Westbury. The following timings from the 1957 summer Saturday working timetable show the steam workings through Westbury or via the avoiding line at their zenith before the impact of dieselisation.

Westbury Departures and Arrivals
Summer Saturdays – Working Timetable 1957 – WR Bristol District.

Down Trains. Passenger unless otherwise stated.
Pass Heywood Rd Jcn at 12.08am, and via avoiding line of the 10.12pm (FO) Paddington–Penzance.
Arr 12.14am. dep 12.17am of the 11.00pm (MX) Fish. Marston Sidings–Plymouth.
Pass Heywood Rd Jcn at 12.46am, and via avoiding line of the 10.50pm (FO) Paddington–Penzance.
Dep at 12.55am, (arrival 11.58pm previous night) of the 3.50pm Fish (FO) Milford Haven–Weymouth.
Arr 1.07am, of the 12.05am MX from Swindon.
Dep at 1.12am, of ECS to Frome after working 12.05am from Swindon (ECS working is SO).
Arr Heywood Rd Jcn 1.11am, to change engine crews, depart 1.16am via avoiding line of the 10.18pm (FO) parcels (previous night) Paddington–Plymouth.
Pass Heywood Rd Jcn at 2.06am (MX), via avoiding line of the 12.30am News and Parcels Paddington–Penzance.
Pass Heywood Rd Jcn at 2.25am, via avoiding line of the 12.35am SO Paddington–Penzance sleeper.
Arr 6.26am, of the 4.30am ex-Swindon Passenger and Parcels.
Dep of 6.28am to Castle Cary, arrive Castle Cary 7.07am and connects with the 7.13am Castle Cary–Weymouth. Then forms 8.10am Castle Cary–Taunton.
Arr 6.31am, dep 6.38am of the 5.05am (SO) (Q) Marston Sidings–Newton Abbot Fish.
Arr 6.48am, dep 7.18am of the 5.25am Swindon–Salisbury.
Dep 6.50am, (SO), of the Milk Empties to Weymouth.
Arr 7.01am, dep 7.15am of the 5.45am Bristol–Weymouth.
Dep 7.10am, (MX), of LE to Frome to work 8.15am Frome–Paddington.
Arr 7.50am, dep 7.51am of Trowbridge–Bruton.
Arr 8.03am, dep 8.10am of the 6.00am Cardiff–Weymouth.
Dep 8.20am, light engine to Salisbury.
Arr at 8.33am, of the 6.58am ex-North Filton.
Arr 8.40am, dep 8.42 of the 7.55am Devizes–Warminster.
Pass Heywood Rd Jcn at 8.40am, via avoiding line of the 6.55am Paddington–Penzance.

No. 6972 *Beningbrough Hall* having left the station, now approaches Westbury South signal box on 15th June 1963 with the 5pm Bristol Temple Meads–Portsmouth.

Gerald T. Robinson

Pass Heywood Rd Jcn at 8.48am, via avoiding line of the 7.00am Paddington–Kingswear.

Arr 8.51am, dep 8.56am of the 7.49am Bristol–Portsmouth Harbour (13th July–17th August 1957 inclusive).

Arr 8.58am, dep 9.03am of the 8.05am Bristol–Weymouth.

Dep 9.00am, light engine to Salisbury.

Arr 9.05am, of the 8.20am ex-Chippenham. (passenger SO, railmotor SX).

Arr 9.20am, dep 9.29am of the 8.10am Bristol–Portsmouth Harbour.

Booked to pass Heywood Rd Jcn at 9.22am, via avoiding line of the 7.40am Paddington–Paignton.

Dep 9.27am, Westbury–Weymouth.

Arr 9.30am, of the 4.30am ex-Paddington–News and Milk Empties.

Pass Heywood Rd Jcn at 9.35am, via avoiding line of the 7.05am Paddington–Penzance (starts from Ealing Broadway 29th June–17th August inclusive).

Dep 9.47am to Wells and Bristol T.M. (via Witham and the East Somerset line to Wells, and then via the Cheddar Valley Line to Yatton and Bristol). (An interesting trip!)

Pass Westbury at 9.57am, of the 9.10am Bristol–Weymouth (until 7/9/57)

Pass Heywood Rd Jcn at 10.10am, via Westbury Avoiding line of the 8.10am Paddington–Paignton.

Dep 10.30am, light engine to Salisbury.

Arr Heywood Rd Jcn 10.18am, to change engine crews, dept 10.20am, of the 8.20am Paddington–Weymouth Quay, via avoiding line.

Pass Heywood Rd Jcn at 10.27am, via avoiding line of the 8.25am Paddington–Penzance.

Arr Heywood Rd Jcn 10.33am, to change engine crews, dep 10.35am of the 8.30am Paddington–Weymouth Quay, via avoiding line.

Arr 10.39am, dep 10.50am of the 8.30am Weston-super-Mare–Weymouth.

Pass Heywood Rd Jcn at 10.43am, via avoiding line of the 8.50am Paddington–Paignton.

Arr 10.59am, of the 10.37am from Patney and Chirton via Lavington.

Pass Westbury at 11.03am, of the 7.50am Birmingham Snow Hill–Weymouth until 7/9/57.

Pass Heywood Rd Jcn at 11.12am, via avoiding line of the 9.30am Paddington–Newquay.

Arr 11.12am, dep 11.17am of the 9.00am Cardiff–Portsmouth & Southsea (until 31/8/1957).

Pass Westbury at 11.18am, of the 8.00am Birmingham Snow Hill–Weymouth Town and Quay. Train routed to Westbury from Chippenham via Thingley Jcn. (until 7/9/1957).

dep 11.25am, light engine to Salisbury.

Arr 11.25am, dep 11.38am of the 9.35am Paddington–Minehead.

Pass Heywood Rd Jcn at 11.30am, via avoiding line of the 9.40am Paddington–Paignton.

Arr 11.32am, dep 11.44am of the 9.34am Reading General–Weymouth. Train routed to Westbury via Devizes

Arr 11.53am, dep 11.58am of the 10.50am Bristol–Portsmouth Harbour.

Arr 12.00noon, dep 12.06pm of the 9.28am Cardiff–New Milton (via Salisbury, Wimborne etc).

Pass Heywood Rd Jcn at 12.02pm, via avoiding line of the 10.20am Paddington–Kingswear.

Arr 12.08pm, dep 12.32pm of the 11.25am Chippenham–Weymouth.

Pass Heywood Road Jcn at 12.10pm, via avoiding line of the 10.30am Paddington–Penzance. 'Cornish Riviera Express'.

Arr 12.17pm, dep 12.23pm of the 10.08am Cardiff–Portsmouth and Southsea.

Pass Heywood Road Jcn at 12.20pm, via avoiding line of the 10.35am Paddington–Penzance.

Pass Heywood Rd Jcn at 12.28pm, via avoiding line of the 10.40am Paddington–Paignton.

arr 12.36pm, dep 12.43pm of the 10.30am Cardiff to Portsmouth & Southsea.

Pass Heywood Rd Jct at 12.44pm, via avoiding line of the 11.00am Paddington–Penzance.

Pass Heywood Rd Jct at 12.54pm, via avoiding line of the 11.05am Paddington–Penzance.

Pass Westbury at 1.02pm, of the 9.25am Wolverhampton–Paignton. Train routed to Westbury via Chippenham and Thingley Jct (29/6–7/9/57).

Arr 1.06pm, dep 1.11pm of the 9.20am Swansea–Bournemouth Central via Salisbury and Wimborne until 7/9/57.

Pass Heywood Rd Jct at 1.15pm, via avoiding line, of the 11.30am Paddington–Minehead.

Arr 1.37pm, of the 12.48pm from Patney and Chirton. via Devizes.

Pass Heywood Rd Jct at 1.43pm, via avoiding line of the 12.00noon Paddington–Kingswear. 'The Torbay Express'.

Arr 1.56pm, dep 2.03pm of the 12.45pm Bristol–Weymouth.

Pass Heywood Rd Jct at 2.00pm, via avoiding line of the 12.05pm Paddington–Plymouth.

Arr 2.27pm, of the 1.50pm Railmotor ex-Chippenham.

Arr 2.40pm, dep 2.47pm of the 12.30pm Paddington–Weymouth.

Dep 2.45pm, to Warminster.

Arr 2.50pm, dep 2.55pm of the 12.53 Cardiff–Portsmouth Harbour.

Arr 3.04pm, dep 3.08pm of the 1.00pm Cardiff–Brighton.

Pass Heywood Rd Jct at 3.14pm, via avoiding line of the 1.25pm Paddington–Kingswear.

Arr 3.14pm, dep 3.37pm of the 11.05am Wolverhampton–Weymouth, train routed to Westbury via Chippenham and Thingley Jct.

Arr 3.26pm, dep 3.31pm of the 1.35pm Paddington–Penzance. 'The Royal Duchy'.

Arr 3.41pm, of the 1.52pm ex Newbury via Devizes.

Dep 4.15pm Westbury–Weymouth.

Arr 4.17pm, dep 4.20pm of the 4.10pm Trowbridge–Warminster.

Arr 4.55pm, of the 4.15pm ex-Chippenham.

Pass Heywood Rd Jcn 5.03pm, via avoiding line of the 3.20pm Paddington–Kingswear.

Pass Heywood Rd Jcn at 5.11pm, via avoiding line of the 3.30pm (Slip) Paddington–Penzance. The slip portion collected from Heywood Rd Jcn at 5.18pm by station pilot, arrive Westbury 5.21pm and worked forward to Weymouth on 5.27pm Westbury–Weymouth.

Arr 5.17pm, dep 5.27pm of the 4.25pm Bristol–Weymouth.

Arr 5.31pm, dep 5.45pm of the 5.10pm Melksham–Taunton.

Arr 5.39pm, dep 5.46pm of the 4.32pm Bristol–Portsmouth & Southsea.

Arr 6.08pm, dep 6.15pm of the 5.02pm Bristol–Weymouth.

Arr 6.46pm, dep 6.53pm of the 4.25pm Cardiff–Portsmouth & Southsea.

Arr 6.55pm, of the 4.36pm ex-Newbury via Devizes.

Arr Heywood Rd Jcn 6.11pm, dept 6.16pm via the Westbury avoiding line of the 2.55pm Wood Lane–Plymouth milk empties.

Pass Heywood Rd Jcn 7.11pm, via avoiding line of the 5.30pm Paddington– Plymouth.

Arr 7.24pm, of the 6.45pm ex-Devizes.

Arr 8.06pm, of the 5.51pm Swindon milk empties, (conveyed passengers between Chippenham and Trowbridge, not advertised in timetable).

Arr 8.19pm, dep 8.36pm of the 7.10pm Bristol–Portsmouth Harbour.

Arr 8.24pm, dep 8.32pm of the 6.00pm Paddington–Weymouth.

Dep 8.50pm Passenger and milk empties to Weymouth.

Arr 9.00pm, of the 8.25pm ex-Chippenham.

Arr 10.02pm, dep 10.09pm of the 9.00pm Bristol–Salisbury.

Dep 10.15pm to Frome.

Arr 10.25pm, dep 10.36pm of the 7.45pm Kensington–Penzance Parcels.

Pass Heywood Rd Jcn 10.43pm, via Westbury East Chord of the 7.55pm Wood Lane–Whitland milk empties.

Arr 10.58pm, dep 11.10pm of the 9.00pm Paddington–Weymouth Quay. 'The Channel Islands Boat Express'. 13/7 to 17/8/1957.

Arr 11.03pm, of the 9.53pm ex Bristol.

Arr 11.58pm, of 10.40pm Lawrence Hill Fish. (10.45pm on 10/17/24/ August 1957).

Arr 12.08pm, dep 12.12pm of the 11.00pm Bristol–Warminster.

Slip Coach Working at Heywood Road Junction. 1958.

10.30am Paddington–Penzance. [SX] Double Ended Slip.

3.30pm Paddington–Penzance. Two Double Ended Slips. (Two-day working).

The 10.30am ex-Paddington ceased slip coach working at Heywood Rd Junction in September 1958, and the 3.30pm ex-Paddington slip service was withdrawn from January 1959.

Up Trains. Passenger unless otherwise stated.

Arr 12.28pm, dep 12.36pm of the 11.20pm (previous night) (MX) Taunton–Wolverhampton parcels (via Chippenham).

'Hymek' diesel hydraulic No. D7025 stands at Westbury on 2nd June 1963 with the 8.30am Cardiff General–Portsmouth. The 'Hymeks' suited the original colour scheme of BR Brunswick green, with a lime green band below the door level and white window surrounds. No. D7025, dating from March 1962 (builder's No. 7919) went new to Cardiff Cathays depot (88A). The locomotive's final depot was Bristol Bath Road (82A) before being withdrawn in January 1972 and cut up at Swindon in July of the same year after only ten years' service.

C. L. Caddy

Pass Fairwood Jcn at 1.54am, via avoiding line of the 6.20pm Penzance–Kensington Milk.

Pass Fairwood Jcn at 2.56am, via avoiding line of the 8.15pm (previous night) Penzance–Paddington.

Arr 3.35am, dep 3.36am of the 2.55am Salisbury–Bristol T.M. Mails and Passenger.

Pass Fairwood Jcn at 4.19am, via avoiding line of the 9.30pm (previous night) Penzance–Paddington.

Dep 5.50am, to Trowbridge.

Dep 6.00am, light engine to Trowbridge.

Dep 6.30am, light engine to Trowbridge. (To work 7.15am Trowbridge–Paddington via Devizes.)

Arr 6.44am, dep 6.47am of the 6.35am Frome–Bristol T.M. via Bradford-on-Avon.

Dep 7.00am, light engine to Trowbridge.

Dep 7.10am, Westbury–Reading General via Lavington.

Arr 7.15am, dep 7.18am of the 7.06am Frome–Chippenham.

Dep 7.35am, Westbury–Taunton via Bristol T.M. ('The Great Way Round').

Pass Fairwood Jcn at 7.47am, via avoiding line of the 3.50am Plymouth–Old Oak Common ECS.

Dep 8.00am, light engine to Trowbridge.

Arr 8.24am, dep 8.40am of the 8.15am Frome–Paddington via Lavington.

Arr 8.25am, dep 8.30am of the 7.44am Salisbury–Bristol T.M.

Dep 8.45am, Westbury–Swindon.

Arr 9.05am, of the 8.35 Bruton–Westbury.

Arr 9.14am, dep 9.15am of the 9.04am Warminster–Devizes.

Dep 9.27am, to Reading General via Lavington.

Arr 9.37am, dep 10.00am of the 7.17am Weymouth–Chippenham.

Arr 9.53am, dep 9.55am of the 8.15am Weymouth–Bristol T.M.

Arr 10.27am, dep 10.30am of the 7.00am Plymouth–Paddington.

Arr 10.50am, dep 10.59am of the 9.00am Weymouth–Paddington.

Arr 10.50am, dep 11.02am of the 8.03am Portsmouth & Southsea–Bristol.

Pass Fairwood Jcn 10.51am, via avoiding line of the 8.00am Kingswear–Paddington.

Pass Westbury at 10.59am, of the 9.25am Weymouth–Wolverhampton. Train routed from Westbury via Trowbridge–Chippenham.

Dep 11.10am, ECS to Trowbridge. To work 12.45pm Trowbridge–Weston-super-Mare, (Locking Rd).

Pass Fairwood Jcn 11.15am, via avoiding line of the 7.25am Plymouth–Paddington. (29/6–31/8 inclusive).

Arr 11.19am, dep 11.23am of the 9.00am Bournemouth Central–Cardiff (until 7/9/1957.)

Arr 11.25am, dep 11.30am, of the 10.00am Weymouth–Birmingham Moor Street. (Westbury first stop).

Arr 11.33am, dep 11.36am, of the 8.48am New Milton–Swansea.

Arr 11.34am, dep 11.42am, of the 8.30am Plymouth–Paddington.

Arr 11.52am, dep 11.57am, of the 9.00am Portsmouth Harbour–Cardiff.

Arr 12.00noon, dep 12.08pm, of the 9.33am Portsmouth & Southsea–Cardiff.

Arr 12.15pm, dep 12.25pm of the 10.20am Weymouth–Wolverhampton, train routed onwards via Trowbridge & Chippenham.

Pass Westbury at 12.21pm, of the 9.43am Paignton–Birmingham Moor St, train routed onwards via Trowbridge–Chippenham.

Pass Fairwood Jcn 12.26pm, via avoiding line of the 9.45am Churston–Paddington.

Pass Fairwood Jcn 12.39pm, via avoiding line of the 10.40am Minehead–Paddington.

Pass Fairwood Jcn 12.46pm, via avoiding line of the 10.35am Torquay–Paddington.

Arr 1.03pm, dep 1.08pm, of the 10.34am Portsmouth & Southsea–Cardiff.

Arr 1.11pm, dep 1.16pm, of the 11.12am Weymouth–Paddington via Lavington.

Arr 1.20pm, dep 1.25pm, of the 10.00am Brighton–Cardiff.

Arr 1.22pm, of the 11.50am ECS ex-Weymouth. (This was stock of the 9.27am Westbury–Weymouth.)

Pass Fairwood Jcn 1.38pm, via avoiding line of the 11.30am Torquay–Paddington.

Arr 1.42pm, dep 1.56pm, of the 11.15am Portsmouth & Southsea–Bristol. Pass Fairwood Jcn 1.51pm, via avoiding line of the 8.15am Perranporth–Paddington.

Pass Fairwood Jcn 2.01pm, via avoiding line of the 8.35am Falmouth–Paddington.

Arr 2.03pm, dep 2.08pm, of the 11.35am Portsmouth Harbour–Cardiff.

Pass Fairwood Jcn 2.12pm, of the 11.20am Kingswear–Paddington. 'The Torbay Express'.

Dep 2.15pm, Westbury–Swindon.

Arr 2.19pm, dep 2.26pm of the 11.00am Brighton–Cardiff.

Arr 2.22pm, of the 12.40pm Weymouth–Bristol T.M.

Pass Fairwood Jcn 2.27pm, via avoiding line of the 11.15am Plymouth–Paddington.

Pass Fairwood Jcn 2.36$\frac{1}{2}$pm, via avoiding line of the 12.18pm Newton Abbot–Paddington.

Pass Fairwood Jcn 2.47pm, via avoiding line of the 9.20am St Ives–Paddington.

Dep 2.50pm, Westbury–Trowbridge.

Arr 2.53pm, light engine from Salisbury.

Arr 3.03pm, dep 3.06pm, of the 1.35pm Weymouth–Cardiff.

Pass Fairwood Jcn 3.06pm, via avoiding line of the 10.00am Newquay–Paddington.

Arr 3.15pm, light engine from Salisbury.

Pass Fairwood Jcn 3.16pm, via avoiding line of the 8.20am Penzance–Paddington.

Dep 3.15pm, Rail Motor to Calne.

Arr 3.24pm, of the 3.12pm ex Warminster.

Pass Fairwood Jcn 3.30pm, via avoiding line of the 10.00am Penzance–Paddington. 'Cornish Riviera Express'.

Arr 3.37pm, dep 3.40pm of the 1.45pm Weymouth–Bristol T.M.

Dep 3.50pm, Westbury–Weston-super-Mare.

Pass Fairwood Jcn 4.04pm, via avoiding line of the 1.30pm Paignton–Paddington. (6th July to 31st August inclusive.)

Pass Fairwood Jcn 4.14pm, via avoiding line of the 1.55pm Torquay–Paddington.

Pass Fairwood Jcn 4.22pm, via avoiding line of the 2.15pm Minehead–Paddington.

Dep 4.25pm, Rail Motor to Melksham.

Dep 4.47pm, light engine to Heywood Rd Jcn. (To work slip portion into Westbury off the 3.30pm Paddington–Penzance.)

Arr 4.51pm, of the 2.32pm Weymouth–Westbury.

Arr 5.06pm, dep 5.18pm of the 2.33pm Portsmouth & Southsea–Bristol T.M.

Arr 5.06pm, dep 5.20pm of the 1.40pm Kingswear–Paddington.

Arr 5.15pm, of the 5.05pm ex-Warminster. (Empty rail motor conveying parcels traffic.)

Pass Fairwood Jcn 5.15pm, via avoiding line of the 2.45pm Paignton–Paddington.

Pass Fairwood Jcn 5.27pm, via avoiding line of the 12.30pm Newquay–Paddington.

Dep 5.30pm, Westbury–Swindon (via Chippenham).

Pass Fairwood Jcn 5.40pm, via avoiding line of the 3.45pm Weymouth Quay–Paddington.

Dep 5.42pm, Westbury–Devizes.

Arr 5.58pm, dep 6.07pm of the 4.14pm Weymouth–Paddington.

Arr 6.00pm, dep 6.22pm of the 3.27pm Portsmouth Harbour–Cardiff.

Arr 6.07pm, dep 6.12pm of the 4.18pm Weymouth–Cardiff (conveys TCs Weymouth Quay to Cardiff and Birmingham).

Dep 6.19pm, to Birmingham Snow Hill (attaches Birmingham Snow Hill portion off the 4.18pm Weymouth–Cardiff).

No. D1011 *Western Thunderer* sweeps into Westbury from the Patney line under an impressive array of lower quadrant signals in 1974. The signals left to right are: goods loop, 'down' Salisbury, 'down' Salisbury to 'down' main, 'down' main to goods loop, 'down' main to 'down' Salisbury, 'down' main and Westbury South distant. The small arms with horizontal red/white stripes were worked in conjunction with the 'stencil' boxes; a 'C' in the display box when the signal was lowered meant that the platform ahead was occupied, or 'W' for 'Warning', this referring to the section to Westbury South being clear but the line was blocked beyond the home signal there. The signals are easy to spot on a bright day like this, but put yourself in a footplateman's position, trying to look out for the dim lights of the calling on arms whilst creeping up in the dark of night with rain beating down and steam swirling from the engine.

Adrian Vaughan Collection

Arr 6.48pm, dep 7.01pm of the 4.15pm Taunton–Trowbridge. (Routed to Westbury via Langport West–Martock–Yeovil Pen Mill.)

Dep 6.52pm, Westbury–Swindon (via Chippenham).

Pass Fairwood Jcn 6.54½pm, via avoiding line of the 4.15pm Paignton–Paddington.

Pass Fairwood Jcn 7.03pm, via avoiding line of the 1.45pm Newquay–Paddington.

Pass Fairwood Jcn 7.17pm, via avoiding line of the 1.20pm Penzance–Paddington.

Pass Fairwood Jcn 7.35pm, via avoiding line of the 4.35pm Kingswear–Paddington.

Arr 8.15pm, of the 6.10pm Weymouth–Westbury.

Arr 8.20pm, dep 8.24pm of the 5.45pm Portsmouth & Southsea–Cardiff.

Dep 8.33pm, Westbury–Chippenham.

Arr 8.39pm, of the 7.00pm from Taunton (via Somerton and Castle Cary).

Arr 7.45pm, dep 8.45pm of the 6.15pm Yeovil–Cardiff Parcels.

Arr 9.10pm, dep 9.20pm of the 6.35pm Weymouth–Paddington milk via Trowbridge and Chippenham.

Arr 9.23pm, dep 9.35pm of the 7.30pm Weymouth–Bristol T.M.

Dep 9.25pm, Parcels vans to Trowbridge.

Arr 9.40pm, dep 9.58pm of the 12.20pm Penzance–Kensington milk.

Pass Fairwood Jcn 11.29pm, via avoiding line of the 3.40pm Penzance–Paddington perishables.

The handsome bracket signal in the foreground stands sentinel at the exit from the diesel depot and the 'up' goods lines at Westbury on 28th April 1974. Each arm could route enginemen three ways via the stencil in the display case, the various routes being: 'up' Trowbridge, 'up' Patney, 'up' goods. North box stands in the middle distance, and bulk grain wagons stand in Nitrovit's siding to the right.

Adrian Vaughan Collection

Weekday 1954 Winter Working Freight Timetable. WR Bristol District

Westbury Freight Trains. Down.

Arr Heywood Rd Jcn 1.15am, dept 1.20am, of the 8.40pm (SX) Paddington–Penzance, via avoiding line.

Arr 2.05am, dep 2.45am of the 10.00pm (MX) Avonmouth–Salisbury.

Pass Heywood Rd Jcn at 2.24am, via Westbury East Chord of the 11.20pm (MX) Old Oak Common–Bristol West Depot.

Arr Heywood Rd Jcn at 3.03am, dep 3.08am of the 11.20pm (SX) Paddington–Newton Abbot, via avoiding line.

Pass Heywood Rd Jcn at 3.19am, via Westbury East Chord of the 1.15am (MX) Reading–Bristol Temple Meads.

Arr 2.52am, dep 3.15am of the 1.20pm (MX) Bristol T.M.–Weymouth.

Arr 3.04am, dep 3.45am of the 7.45pm (MX) Bassaleg–Salisbury.

Arr 3.32am, dep 4.15am of the 1.20am (MO) Scours Lane–Tavistock Jcn.

Arr 3.52am, dep 4.35am of the 10.40pm (MX) Paddington–Weymouth.

Dep 4.00am (MO) to Weymouth, (continuation of 10.40pm ex Paddington Sat).

Arr 4.38am, dep 5.10am of the 1.25am (MO) Severn Tunnel Jcn–Salisbury.

Arr 4.41, dept 5.29 of the 10.00pm (MX) Banbury–Hackney.

Arr 5.15am, dep 6.10am of the 1.10am (MX) Severn Tunnel Jcn–Salisbury.

Dep 5.20am to Wells.

Arr 5.33am, dept 6.00am of the 1.20am (MX) Scours Lane–Tavistock Jcn.

Dep 6.25am, (MX) Loco coal to Yeovil Junction.

Arr 7.12am, of the 9.45pm (MX) from Oxley Sidings.

Arr 7.14am, dep 7.50am of the 5.10am (MO) Bristol East Depot–Weymouth.

Arr 7.17am, dep 7.55am of the 9.15pm (MX) Aberdare–Salisbury.

Dep 7.35, to Salisbury.

Arr 7.36am, dept 8.20am of the 2.20am (MO) Cardiff–Salisbury.

Dep 8.10am, (SX) to Sparkford, (collects water cans from Brewham Box).

Arr 8.12am, dept 9.00am of the 2.25am (MX) Radyr Jcn–Salisbury Loco Coal.

Arr 8.13am, of the 4.32am (MO) ex-Swindon.

Arr 9.29am, dept 10.15am of the 3.30am (MO) Cheltenham (High St)–Salisbury.

Arr 9.32am, of the 4.32am (MX) ex-Swindon.

Arr Heywood Rd Jcn 10.04am, dept 10.09am via avoiding line of the 6.30am (MO) Acton–Tavistock.

Arr 10.10am, dep 11.02am of the 8.40am (MX) Bristol East Depot–Weymouth.

Dep 10.40am (Q) to Weymouth.

Arr 11.09am, dep 11.40am of the 5.50am (MO) Rogerstone–Weymouth Loco Coal.

Arr 11.09am, dep 11.55am of the 6.45am (MX) Severn Tun Jcn–Salisbury.

Arr 11.58am, dep 12.55pm of the 5.45am (MO) Radyr Jcn–Salisbury.

Arr 1.44pm, of the 11.30am (SX) ex-Ludgershall.

Arr 1.49pm, dep 2.15pm of the 10.55am Bristol East Depot–Salisbury.

Dep 2.30pm (SX) to Heytesbury.

Arr 3.08pm, dep 3.40pm of the 8.15am Banbury to Tavistock Jcn.

Arr 3.45pm, dep 4.28pm of the 1.20pm Swindon–Weymouth.

Arr 4.32pm, of the 10.30am ex-Banbury.

Arr 4.45pm, dep 5.30pm of the 11.45am Severn Tunnel Jcn–Weymouth.

Dep 5.50pm (SX), EBV to Frome (Mineral Loop).

Arr 5.47pm, dep 6.10pm of the 4.00pm (SX) Q Avonmouth–Salisbury.

Arr Heywood Rd Jcn 6.29pm, dep 6.34pm of the 3.30pm (SX) Scours Lane–Hackney, via avoiding line.

Arr 6.33pm, dep 7.20pm of the 3.40pm Swindon–Newton Abbot.

Arr Heywood Rd Jcn 6.36pm, dep 6.41pm of the 3.30pm (SO) Scours Lane–Hackney, via avoiding line.

Arr 7.55pm (SX), 5.10pm ex-Devizes.

Dep 6.50pm (SO), to Castle Cary.

Arr 7.35pm (SO), 6.15pm ex-Melksham.

Dep 7.40pm (SX), to Frome (Mineral Loop).

Arr 8.40pm, dep 9.10pm of the 6.35pm (SO) Bristol East Depot–Weymouth.

Dep 9.00pm (SX) to Yeovil Pen Mill.

Arr 8.58pm, dep 9.20pm of the 4.10pm Severn Tunnel Jcn–Salisbury.

Arr 10.05pm, of the 8.50pm (SX) ex-Melksham.

Arr 10.45pm, dep 10.55pm of the 9.50pm (SX) Bristol East Depot–Salisbury.

Pass Hawkeridge Jcn at 11.22pm, of the 9.15pm (SX) Bristol TM–Acton, via Westbury East Chord.

Arr Heywood Rd Jcn 11.13pm, dep 11.18 of the 7.00pm (SO) Acton–Tavistock Jcn, via avoiding line.

Pass Heywood Rd Jcn at 11.09pm of the 8.55pm (SX) Paddington–Penzance, via avoiding line.

Pass Heywood Rd Jcn at 11.17pm, of the 8.05pm (SO) Paddington–Bristol, via Westbury East Chord.

Arr 11.45pm, of the 9.05pm (SO) ex-Swindon.

Pass Heywood Rd Jcn at 11.46pm, of the 8.05pm (SX) Paddington–Bristol, via Westbury East Chord.

Arr 11.50pm, of the 6.05pm (SO) ex-Didcot.

Arr 12.15am, of the 6.05pm (SX) ex-Didcot.

Arr 12.27am, of the 9.25pm (SX) ex-Swindon.

Arr 12.19am, dept 12.45am of the 11.15pm (SO) Bristol East Depot–Salisbury.

Westbury Freight Trains. Up.

Arr 12.34am, dep 1.14am of the 11.15pm (MX) Salisbury–Aberdare.

Dep 12.45am (MO) Westbury–Severn Tunnel Jcn.

Arr 12.55am, dep 2.10am of the 9.00pm (MX) Exeter–Crewe

Dep 1.20am (MO) Westbury–Oxley Sidings.

Pass Fairwood Jcn at 1.11am, of the 2.50pm (MX) Penzance–Paddington, via avoiding line.

Arr Hawkeridge Jcn 2.27am, dep 2.37am of the 11.20pm (MX) Old Oak Common–Bristol West Depot, via Westbury East Chord.

Arr 2.05am, dep 3.10am of the 12.45am (MX) Salisbury–Severn Tunnel Junction.

Dep 2.40am (MX) Westbury–Swindon.

Dep 3.20am (MX) Westbury–Acton.

Arr Hawkeridge Jcn 3.24am, dep 3.45am of the 1.15am (MX) Reading–Bristol T.M.

Arr 3.39am, dep 4.45am of the 2.26pm (MX) Tavistock Jcn–Swindon.

Dep 3.50am (MX) light engine to Freshford.

Arr 4.14am, dep 4.24am of the 3.10am (MX) Salisbury–Avonmouth empties.

Dep 4.30am (MX) Westbury–Oxley Sidings.

Arr 4.49am, dep 5.05am of the 3.30am (MX) Salisbury–Avonmouth.

Dep 5.05am (MO) to Avonmouth (continuation of 4.30am ex-Salisbury, Suns).

Arr 5.35am, dep 6.25am of the 11.0pm (MO) (Sundays) Tavistock Junc–Oxley Sidings.

Arr 5.42am, dep 6.25am of the 4.15am (MX) Taunton–Banbury Jcn.

Arr 6.34am, dep 7.05am of the 1.50am (MX) Weymouth–Avonmouth Dock.

Dep 7.15am (MSX) Westbury–Ludgershall. (arr Woodborough 8.53am).

Dep 7.15am (MO) Westbury–Ludgershall. (arr Woodborough 9.58am).

Arr 7.21am, dep 7.48am of the 5.00am (MO) Norton Fitzwarren–West Drayton.

Arr 7.35am, dep 7.45am of the 6.30am (MO) Salisbury–Bassaleg Empties.

Arr 7.35am, dep 7.45am of the 6.55am (MX) Codford–Rogerstone.

Arr 8.07am, dep 8.20am of the 4.30am (MX) Weymouth–Avonmouth Empties.

Arr 9.16am, dep 9.55am of the 1.55am Tavistock–Banbury Jcn.

Arr 10.09am, dep 10.39am of the 2.45am Tavistock Jcn–Acton.

Arr 11.29am, dep 12.15pm of the 6.45am Weymouth–Cardiff Empties.

Arr 12.10pm, of 10.10am (SO) ex-Wells, (engine & brakevan).

Dep 12.40pm (SX), Westbury–Bristol East Depot.

Pass Fairwood Jcn at 1.15am, of the 6.35am Tavistock Jcn–Hanwell Bridge.

Dep 1.30pm, Westbury–Swindon.

Arr 2.19pm, of the 11.45pm (SX) ex-Sparkford, starts from Marston Magna if required, stops to set down water cans at Brewham Box.

Arr 2.20pm, dep 2.45pm of the 1.45pm (MO) Codford–Rogerstone Empties.

Arr 3.00pm, of the 12.45pm (SO) ex-Radstock.

Arr 3.42pm, light engine 3.30pm (SO) ex-Warminster.

Arr 5.24pm, of the 4.00pm (SX) ex-Radstock.

Arr 6.08pm, of the 4.50pm (SX) ex-Mells Road.

Arr 6.17pm, dep 6.55pm of the 1.48pm Weymouth–Rogerstone Empties.

Arr 6.18pm, dep 6.32pm of the 4.30pm Salisbury–Severn Tunnel Jcn.

Arr 6.34pm, dep 6.55pm of the 2.30pm (SX) Southampton–South Wales.

Arr 7.24pm, dep 7.55pm of the 3.50pm (FSX) Southampton–South Wales.

Arr 7.38pm, of the 4.25pm (SX) ex-Wells.

Dep 8.05pm, (SX), Westbury to Hayes & Harlington.

Arr 8.14pm, (SX), of the 6.20pm ex-Hendford.

Arr 9.32pm, of the 6.00pm ex-Salisbury.

Dep 10.15pm, (SX) Empties to Penarth Curve North.

Arr 10.34pm, dep 10.55pm of the 6.40pm (SX) Southampton–South Wales.

Arr 10.52pm, dep 11.45pm of the 9.30pm (SX) Taunton–Acton.

Arr Hawkeridge Jcn 11.20pm, dep 11.30pm of the 8.05pm (SO) Paddington–Bristol T.M., via Westbury East Chord.

Arr Hawkeridge Jcn 11.49pm, dep 11.59pm of the 8.05pm (SX) Paddington–Bristol T.M., via Westbury East Chord.

Pass Fairwood Jcn 11.57pm, of the 8.00pm (SX) Newton Abbot–Acton, via avoiding line.

Arr 12.22am, dep 1.05am of the 7.55pm Weymouth–Bristol.

Arr 1.06am, dep 2.25am of the 2.26pm (SO) Tavistock Jcn–Swindon.

Westbury. Freight Trains. Sundays. Up.

Dep 1.40am to Swindon.

Pass Fairwood Jcn at 2.27am, of the 2.50pm (Sat) Penzance–Paddington via avoiding line.

Arr 2.05am, of the 12.45am Salisbury–Severn Tunnel Jcn, terminates at Westbury and re-starts 12.45am Monday.

Arr 2.59am, dep 3.50am of the 10.30pm (Sat) Weymouth–Bristol East Depot.

Arr 5.42am, dep 6.25am of the 4.15am Taunton–Oxley Sidings.

Arr 5.49am, dep 6.50am of the 4.30am Salisbury–Avonmouth. Terminates at Westbury if necessary, and re-starts 5.05am, (Monday).

Westbury. Freight Trains. Sundays. Down.

Arr 1.18am, dep 1.45am of the 7.45pm (Sat) Bassaleg–Salisbury.

Pass Heywood Rd Jcn 2.20am, of the 10.10pm (Sat) Paddington–Tavistock Jcn.

Pass Heywood Rd Jcn 2.53am, of the 10.00pm (Sat) Banbury–Hackney, arr at Castle Cary at 4.20am and stable, re-start 8.50am Monday.

Arr 3.36am, of the 10.40pm Paddington–Weymouth, stables at Westbury until 4.00am Monday.

Arr 4.50am, of the 6.25pm (Sat) ex-Oxley Sidings.

Westbury. Bank Engines
Authorised Hours. 1954.

Starting Time	Mon	Tues	Wed	Thurs	Fri	Sat	Sun	Total Hours
5.00am	19	24	24	24	24	24	6	145.0

Assists trains between Freshford and Upton Scudamore, as required.

2-8-0 No. 3814 rumbles past Hawkeridge Junction on 15th June 1963 with the 10.55am Severn Tunnel Junction–Weymouth freight. Note the superb GWR conical water tower standing alongside the East Chord line in the background.

Gerald T. Robinson

Westbury. Bank Engines Running Light.
Point to Point Times. 1954.

Warminster–Westbury.	11 minutes.
Upton Scudamore–Westbury.	8 minutes.
Brewham–Westbury ...	28 minutes.
Trowbridge–Westbury ...	9 minutes.
Westbury–Trowbridge ...	9 minutes.
Savernake (Low Level)–Westbury.	55 minutes.
Devizes–Holt Junction.	18 minutes
Thingley Jcn–Trowbridge.	25 minutes.
Trowbridge–Bradford-on-Avon.	8 minutes.

Westbury. Shunting Engines.
Authorised Hours. 1954.

Starting Time	Mon	Tues	Wed	Thurs	Fri	Sat	Sun	Total Hours
No. 1. 6am	18	24	24	24	24	24	6	144.0

Down Side Pilot: Also shunts in the up yard between 6am and 9am, Tuesdays to Fridays, and 6am to 2pm on Saturdays.

Starting Time	Mon	Tues	Wed	Thurs	Fri	Sat	Sun	Total Hours
No. 2. 9am	15	21	21	21	21	16	14	129.0

Up Side Pilot: Between 6am and 2pm Sundays, works on the up and down sides, and between 10am and 2pm, assists trains to Warminster if required.

Trowbridge. Shunting Engines.
Authorised Hours. 1954.

Starting Time	Mon	Tues	Wed	Thurs	Fri	Sat	Sun	Total Hours
5.30am	18½	24	24	24	24	24	2½	141.0

On weekdays also performs passenger shunting if necessary.

The vast Westbury cement works situated alongside the up Patney main line north of Heywood Road Junction was opened on 29th April 1963. A siding giving access to the depot was brought into use 30/9–1/10 1962. A private sidings agreement with APCM dates from 13th July 1966, and the siding is still open today. Westbury is now vastly altered from its steam days. Although the station buildings themselves remain rela-tively unchanged it is the trackwork and signalling that has seen massive changes. The Middle box was the first to go, being closed on 5th May 1968, South box followed on 16th September 1978, and from Sunday 17th September to 16th October 1978 the lines south of the station were out of use to enable the engineers to completely rebuild the track formations at the south and middle ends of the station in the first major rebuilding of the station since the 1899/1900 alter-ations.

North signal box now renamed Westbury was equipped with a small panel to work the layout to the former site of the South box. The station was closed completely from 7th April to 13th May 1984 for rebuilding of the layout to the north of the station, Westbury box was closed on 27th April 1984 and demolished on 14th May. The massive new Westbury power box situated north of the station alongside the down Patney main line was brought into use on 13th May 1984. Colour light signals now abound instead of the lower quadrants which graced the area.

The track layout today is very functional for modern working and a great improvement on the previous steam age formation and much of the new trackwork is laid for bidirectional working giving greater flexibility of operation. The cross country route between Bristol and Salisbury still sees a great variety of traffic, and the original line from Thingley Junction is still open but is now single line. West of England trains now formed by High Speed Trains from the Berks & Hants route still speed along the avoiding line with various services diverted to stop at Westbury, but by far the main growth in freight traffic has come from two major quarries, the Foster Yeoman Merehead Quarry on the East Somerset branch, and the ARC Whatley Quarry on the Radstock branch. The massive General Motors Class 59/0 and 59/1 locomotives privately owned by both companies and worked by BR drivers handle the bulk of the limestone traffic.

The former ambulance train sidings alongside the up yard were converted into a fuelling siding for the then new dmus in May 1959. This three-road siding which was extended in 1976 formed the present diesel re-fuelling and stabling point which closed on 1st March 1993.

The driver and guard of Class 45 No. 45004 *Royal Irish Fusilier* keep a wary eye to the rear whilst propelling their train of ARC wagons out on to the 'up' Trowbridge main line at Westbury north end on 24th June 1980. The stencil on the bracket signal above the locomotive reads 'Up T BDGE' (Up Trowbridge).

A. White

With the North signal box in the background, Class 37 No. 37208 rumbles through Westbury with a ballast train on 23rd February 1984.

John Day

Westbury Iron Works

PSA 11.6.1870 Westbury Iron Co. Ltd
PSA 13.4.1904 New Westbury Iron Co. Ltd
PSA 28.5.1906 New Westbury Iron Co. Ltd
PSA 26.1.1917 New Westbury Iron Co. Ltd
PSAT 26.8.1941.
PSA 3.9.43 A. E. Farr Ltd
        Bovis Ltd

A bed of iron ore upon which Westbury station is built extends for some 2½ miles long by a quarter of a mile wide from Heywood in the North, to Fairwood was discovered in 1855. The Westbury Iron Co. Ltd was formed on 24th July 1857 to excavate and smelt the local deposits. A blast furnace was erected north of and overlooking the station, and as all furnaces need coal it is not surprising that the shareholders also had interests in the local collieries, reached from the Frome to Radstock mineral line. Another shareholder was Rowland Brotherhood of the well known Chippenham firm of railway engineers and contractors. It is recorded that the first ore was quarried in 1856 with the furnace not put into blast until 1858. The importance of the nearby Somerset collieries to supply the required tonnages of coal for the demand of the Westbury Ironworks can be gauged by the fact that it

took one ton of coal and one ton of ore to make 8cwt of pig iron. A web of 2ft gauge tracks (loco worked after 1875) connected the Westbury workings with the ironworks, the engines being 0-6-0 saddle tanks from the various builders of Hudswell, Clarke & Rodgers, Leeds. Andrew Barclay, Kilmarnock, Peckett & Sons, Bristol and an 0-4-0 saddle tank from Bagnall Ltd, Stafford, which subsequently went to the Moorewood Colliery, Oakhill. The works had two broad gauge 0-4-0STs by Henry Hughes of Loughborough and with the GWR gauge conversion in 1874 they were converted to the standard gauge at Westbury in 1874. Standard gauge locomotives for the ironworks over the years comprised 0-4-0 and 0-6-0 saddle tanks from Peckett, Andrew Barclay, and Hudswell, Clarke.

A single road engine shed was situated in the works which also had a fan of standard gauge sidings serving the coke ovens and main works. In 1869, 100,000 tons of ore were raised, and although a production rate of 60,000 to 100,000 tons per annum was achieved, the fluctuations of the industry witnessed a rise and fall of the company's prospects, and the works was virtually shut down from 1901–02 and following the formation of a new company, production was restarted. But in 1908 the furnaces were shut down and a small amount of brown ore was raised annually for the gas purifying

Westbury in the summer of 1993. Class 60 No. 60059 *Samuel Plimsoll*, after arrival off the Trowbridge line has reversed and stabled its coal train bound for Westbury Cement Works into the siding. The locomotive then departed light engine via the Trowbridge line. Note the space in the foreground once occupied by the North signal box. The massive bulk of the present day Westbury panel box can be seen behind the bridge.

Chris Giles

market and despatched to London, Liverpool, Birmingham and Swansea. The First World War witnessed a resurgence in the quarrying operations for iron ore. Production came to a halt with the last ore quarrying taking place in 1923, the receivers were appointed until 1938, and the remaining locomotives were sold in February 1939. The private sidings agreement was terminated in 1941 with the company being dissolved in 1949. A private siding agreement dated 3.9.1943 was passed to A. E. Farr Ltd who occupied part of the site, and subsequently to Bovis Civil Engineering Ltd. Some 70 years after the last quarrying operation the landscape is still scarred by the old workings, many of which are now flooded and landscaped.

Fairwood Crossing Signal Box
111 miles 54 chains from Paddington
Opened (1) 1st July 1900. Closed 23rd February 1911
Opened (2) 23rd February 1911. Closed 1st January 1933

Fairwood Junction Signal Box
111 miles 16 chains from Paddington
Opened 1st January 1933
Closed 11th May 1984

In 1900 part of the GWR's main West of England main line was openend, namely the direct Stert Valley line from Patney and Chirton to Westbury. It was found

Fairwood Junction and signal box, looking towards Clink Junction on 21st March 1965. The signal for the line into Westbury has been lowered indicating that an 'up' train is due. The large water tanks standing by the 'down' main line in the distance were for the water troughs situated at that location and supplying both of the main lines.

C. L. Caddy

Fairwood Junction looking towards Westbury. The avoiding lines pass under the right hand arch of the bridge, and the lines to the station are to the left. The bridge has been a vantage point for photographers and engine spotters for many years.

John Morris

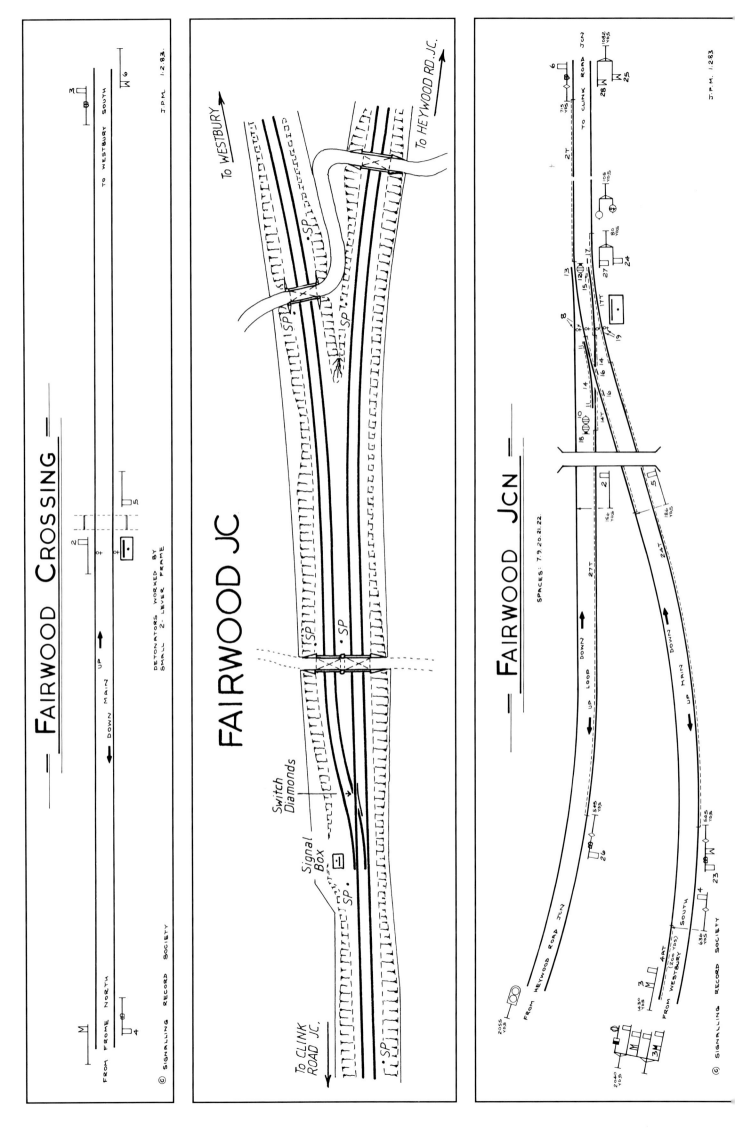

FAIRWOOD CROSSING

TO WESTBURY SOUTH

DOWN MAIN UP

FROM FROME NORTH

DETONATORS WORKED BY
SMALL 2-LEVER FRAME

© SIGNALLING RECORD SOCIETY

J.P.M. 1.2.83.

FAIRWOOD JC

To WESTBURY

TO HEYWOOD RD. JC.

To CLINK
ROAD JC.

Switch
Diamonds

Signal
Box

FAIRWOOD JCN

TO CLINK ROAD JCN

FROM HEYWOOD ROAD JCN

FROM WESTBURY SOUTH

UP LOOP DOWN

UP MAIN DOWN

SPACES: 7.9.20.21.22.

© SIGNALLING RECORD SOCIETY

J.P.M. 1.2.83.

The interior of Fairwood Junction box on 16th September 1974. The windows are open on a hot day, and signalman Sid Fleming takes a breath of fresh air as he awaits the passage of the next train. Conditions in a signal box on a warm day would be akin to a greenhouse with the vast area of glass abounding the box.

Adrian Vaughan Collection

4-6-0 No. 6934 *Beachamwell Hall*, heading the 12.05pm Paddington–Plymouth, takes water at Fairwood Troughs on 16th July 1955. The locomotive is nearing the end of the water trough, and the fireman at this moment is in the process of winding the handle in order to raise the scoop. Water troughs were a plumbers' dream as they had to refill within three minutes between trains, and in the busy summer season, trains would follow hard on the heels of each other on the West of England main line. The water tanks which supplied the troughs can be seen on the right, one water tank being used for each line. No. 6934 had been preceeded by No. 5028 *Llantilo Castle* on the 'down' 'Torbay Express' reaching Exeter ten minutes late at 3.55pm after a very good run.

R. E. Toop

4-6-0 No. 5925 *Eastcote Hall* in perfect condition, without a breath of steam from the cylinders or smoke from her chimney showing the engine to be in fine fettle, takes to the Westbury line at Fairwood Junction with an 'up' express on 2nd July 1955. *Eastcote Hall* was built in May 1933 and withdrawn in 1962.

R. E. Toop

On a glorious summer day No. 6913 *Levens Hall* speeds past Fairwood Junction and takes the Westbury avoiding line to Heywood Road Junction with the 9.45am Churston–Paddington on 2nd July 1955.

R. E. Toop

that with the expected increase in traffic, it was desirable to shorten some of the longer block sections, a box being provided at Fairwood Crossing between Westbury and Frome on 1st July 1900. Initially the new route was used to accelerate the Paddington to Weymouth service, and with the opening of the Castle Cary to Cogload line in 1906, many trains from London to the West used the route avoiding the congested lines at Bristol. The box was replaced on 23rd February 1911, by a new 6-lever box, (15ft x 10ft x 7ft). This second box was in turn abolished by the opening of the Westbury avoiding line when a new signal box, 'Fairwood Junction', was opened on 1st January 1933 controlling the junction between the Westbury and avoiding lines at the western end of the new route. The new box had a 28-lever frame with 5–bar vertical tappet interlocking, and was 22ft x 12ft x 8ft. No coaches were slipped here, as down express trains slipped their coaches at Heywood Road Junction situated at the Newbury end of the avoiding line. Fairwood signal box was closed on 11th May 1984 upon the opening of the new Westbury Power box.

No. 4087 *Cardigan Castle* storms towards Fairwood Junction from the Westbury station line with the 1.30pm Paddingto Penzance on 23rd April 1955. No. 4087 was built to Lot 232 in June 1925 and withdrawn in 1963. Note how the signals are positioned ease of sighting by the drivers of right hand driven GWR locomotives, the signal to the left is for the approaching train, and the signal the right is for the 'down' avoiding line, which is the track to the far right.

R. E. To

No. 5003 *Lulworth Castle* powers along the Westbury 'down' avoiding line heading for Fairwood Junction with the 'Torbay Express' on 22nd July 1956. The bridge in the background takes the Salisbury line over the avoiding line. The mounds on either side of the track bear witness to the once prolific iron ore workings in the area.

R. C. Riley

Fairwood Junction 29th September 1986. The signal box has been demolished, and the trees and water tanks have now gone, as Class 59/0 No. 59004 *Yeoman Challenger* takes the Westbury station line with a limestone train from Merehead Quarry. This superb locomotive, one of five owned by Foster Yeoman Ltd and crewed by BR drivers, was built by General Motors at La Grange, Illinois, USA.

John Day

Class 37/0 No. 37244 rumbles across Fairwood Junction with the 10.40am Radyr–Exmouth Junction coal train on 24th August 1989.

John Day

Clink Road Junction Signal Box
114 miles 39 chains from Paddington
Opened 2nd January 1933
Closed 7th October 1984

With the construction of the 2 mile 5 chain Frome avoiding line, two new boxes were provided at either end of the new route. Clink Road Junction signal box controlled the northern end of the layout where the new avoiding and the former WS&W main line into Frome converged. The new signal box was brought into use on 18th December 1932, but was switched out until the opening of the avoiding line on 2nd January 1933. The box was equipped with a 29-lever frame and 5-bar vertical interlocking. Box size was 22ft 2in x 12ft

2in x 8ft. The avoiding line was used by goods trains at first to settle the trackbed, but with the introduction of the 1933 summer timetable the new route was used by express trains. This further accelerated express train timings over the West of England main line compared with the old route through Frome with its curves and 35mph speed restriction. The up avoiding line was out of use from April to May 1977 due to a derailment at the junction involving an up limestone train from Frome, which involved all up workings having to pass through Frome station until the line was cleared. When normal working resumed the line into Frome from the junction had been singled for a distance of 9 chains before reverting to double track as far as North box. The box at Clink junction closed on 7th October 1984.

Clink Road Junction, looking west on 21st March 1965 with the permanent way gang working away on the track. The original WS&W main line into Frome curves to the right, and the 1933 avoiding line stretches away to Blatchbridge Junction on the left. The field behind the signal box is now a housing estate.

C. L. Caddy

Clink Road Junction signal box, looking east in 1973. The overbridge in the background carries the road to Clink (from which the box was named) over the railway. With the construction of new road works for the Frome Bypass, the bridge was demolished and replaced by a concrete version situated further east.

Adrian Vaughan Collection

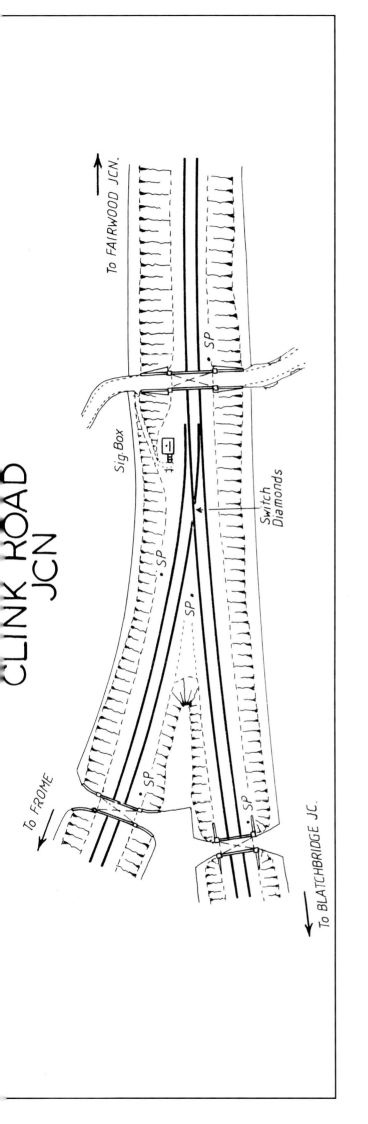

CLINK ROAD JCN

To FAIRWOOD JCN.

To FROME

Sig. Box

Switch Diamonds

To BLATCHBRIDGE JC.

SP · SP · SP · SP · SP

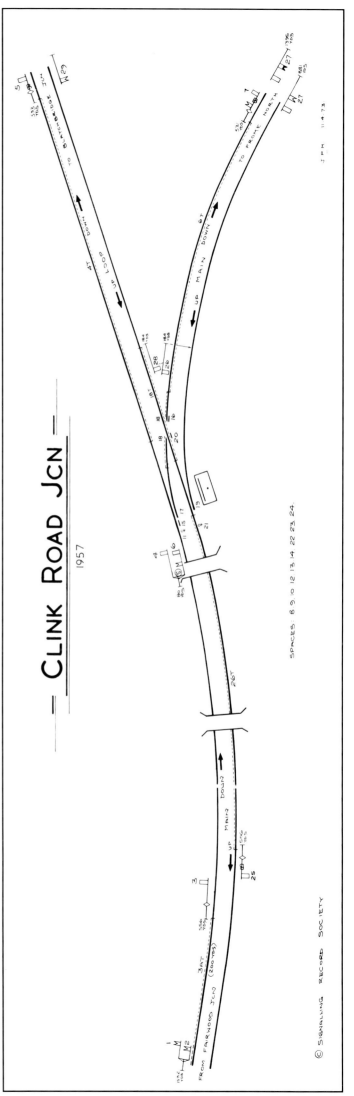

— CLINK ROAD JCN —

1957

To BLATCHBRIDGE JCN

UP LOOP 4T

UP MAIN DOWN 6T

To FROME NORTH

UP MAIN DOWN 26T

FROM FAIRWOOD JCN

UP MAIN DOWN 3AT (200 YDS)

SPACES: 8 9 10 12 13 14 22 23 24.

J.P.M. 11.4.73.

© SIGNALLING RECORD SOCIETY.

Smoke drifts lazily from the signal box chimney, and limestone dust scurries over the countryside on 3rd September 1979 as Nos 37070 and 37206 roar past Clink Road Junction box from the avoiding line en-route to Westbury with a limestone train from Merehead Quarry on the East Somerset branch. Note how the houses in the background are nearing the railway.

A. White

Class 47/0 No. 47121, hauling a limestone train from Whatley Quarry on 11th March 1983, utilises its full tractive power to drag its heavy train past Clink Road Junction box on the ascent out of Frome. The houses have now reached to the top of the embankment.

John Day

The signal box has now been demolished leaving a few bricks and other debris in this view of Clink Road Junction taken on 19th April 1985 as Class 31/1 No. 31250, using the simplified junction installed in 1977, takes the Frome line with a bitumen train destined for the Mobil depot at Frome station. Due to a derailment in May 1977, the throat of the line from the junction into Frome for a distance of nine chains was singled at that time and the junction was also altered then. Note the 100mph sign alongside the 'up' main line in the foreground.

John Day

Class 56 No. 56032 *Sir De Morgannwg/County of South Glamorgan* hauls a limestone train northwards on the 'up' main line between Frome and Westbury on 18th November 1988. The new Frome Bypass and its bridge are seen under construction in the background.

Peter Nicholson

Frome

115 miles 46 chains from Paddington
Westbury–Frome opened 7th October 1850
Mineral line to Radstock opened 14th November 1854
Frome–Yeovil Pen Mill opened 1st September 1856
Gauge conversion Thingley Junction–Frome.
    20th/22nd June 1874
Gauge conversion Frome–Dorchester. 18th/22nd June
    1874
Gauge conversion Frome–Radstock. 18th/26th June
    1874
Line doubled Frome–Witham 1875
Frome–Radstock opened for passenger traffic on 5th
    July 1875
Frome North box (previously No. 1) opened 1875.
    Closed 7th October 1984
Frome Middle box (previous No. 2) opened 1875.
    Closed 20th September 1933
Frome South box (previously No. 3) opened 1875.
    Closed 17th September 1933
Frome West box opened 1875 reduced to ground frame
    24th September 1933
Frome South box opened 17th September 1933,
    replacing previous Middle and South boxes
Last service passenger trains run on Radstock branch
    31st October 1959
Engine shed closed September 1963
West Curve closed 10th November 1963
Frome South box closed 19th August 1970
Main line singled North Box–Blatchbridge Junction
    19th August 1970

The Diary of Thomas Green

Through the diaries of Thomas Green born in Nottingham in 1801 and having settled in Frome by 1840 we can be transported back to the 19th century. However, before the coming of the railway the difficul-

ties of travelling on the stage coach are vividly described when Thomas Green set out from Nottingham in 1825 to visit his relatives in the West Country for the first time. Tuesday 1st June "Set off from Nottingham about 8 o'clock in the morning on the outside of the Birmingham coach and after a pleasant ride (with the exception of running over a little child at Sawley) arrived in Birmingham about 3. Dined at the Chickens Hotel and afterwards went to the Crescent and took tea with Mrs Wrightson. Started from Birmingham about 6 in the evening inside the Bristol Mail. Took tea at 10 in Gloucester and arrived Wednesday at Bristol about 6 in the morning". Wednesday 2nd June "After waiting in Bristol about 2 hours at the Bush Tavern near the Exchange took an outside place on one of the Bath coaches and after a beautiful ride between those 2 eminent cities got into Bath about 10 o'clock. Took my abode up at the White Hart Hotel opposite the Pump Rooms. Breakfasted about ¹/₂ past 10 and afterwards walked about Bath till 4 o'clock when I returned to dinner. After dinner went in company with a gentleman at the Hotel to Sydney Gardens. The weather being rainy no company was there although there was a band in attendance. Returned to rest about 9 o'clock without either tea or supper being too tired to stop for either". Thursday 3rd June: "Set off in the Exeter Subscription coach for Ilminster about 8 o'clock going thro' Wells where I saw the Cathedral. Got into Ilminster about 2 o'clock and dined at the Inn". (Before returning home. Thomas Green visited his aunt and cousins at Frome.) Another entry in the diary records a journey by stage and train from Frome to Manchester in 1840 when Thomas went to visit his sister who was seriously ill after childbirth. 14th November: "After an early dinner left by the Weymouth coach at ¹/₂ after 3 and got to Bath soon after 5. Left Bath by the Birmingham Mail at 6 thro'

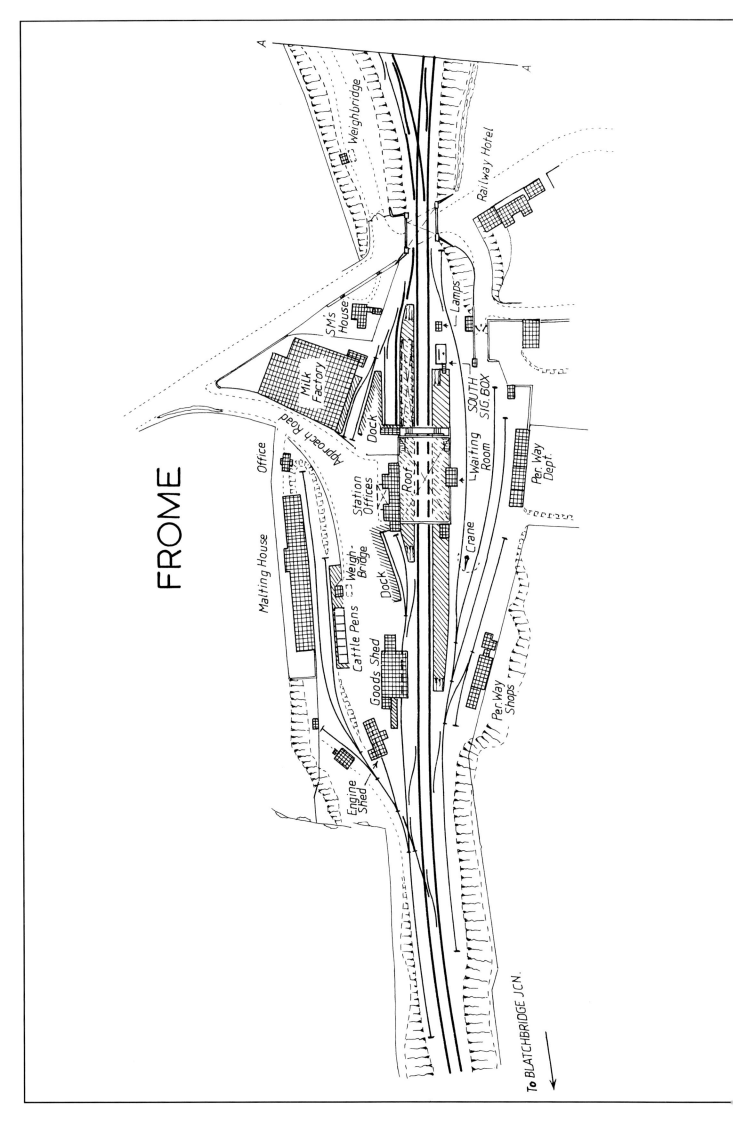

FROME

Weighbridge

Railway Hotel

SM's House

Lamps

Milk Factory

Dock

Office

Station Offices

Roof

SOUTH SIG. BOX

Approach Road

Waiting Room

Per. Way Dept.

Malting House

Weigh-Bridge

Crane

Cattle Pens

Dock

Goods Shed

Engine Shed

Per. Way Shops

To BLATCHBRIDGE JCN.

A — A

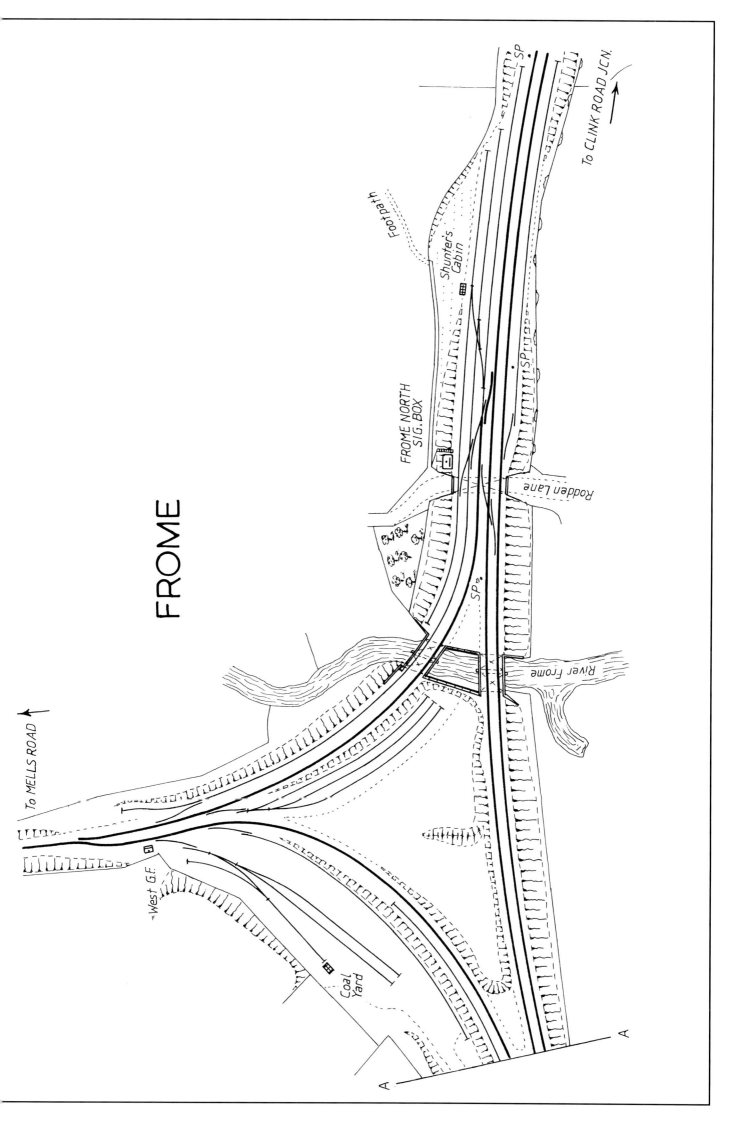

FROME

To MELLS ROAD

West G.F.

Coal Yard

River Frome

SP

Rodden Lane

FROME NORTH
SIG. BOX

Shunter's
Cabin

Footpath

SP

SP

To CLINK ROAD JCN.

A

A

Frome station, looking east on 27th October 1962, showing the beautiful Brunelian over-all roof which is still in situ today. A dmu is just leaving the 'up' platform heading for Westbury, and part of Frome South box can be seen at the end of the 'down' platform. The large building to the left of the station is the former Express Dairy Creamery in Station Road. The 'down' goods yard is located behind the fence to the right.

C. L. Caddy

Bristol (inside)." The following day: "arrived at Birmingham about ½ past 5 when I got some breakfast, and then proceeded by Railway to Manchester which I reached at ½ past 1." (Unfortunately his sister had died before his arrival.) The return journey to Frome commenced on 27th November: "Left Manchester by the Birmingham Railway at ½ past 10 and arrived in Birmingham at about 3 o'clock." Thomas Green dined at the station and after he had made some visits continued his journey onwards to Frome by stage coach: "Left Birmingham at eight o'clock by the Mail, from the Nelson inside and after a very cold journey arrived at Bath about eight o'clock next morning. At Droitwich we were enclosed in so dense fog while passing thro' the town that the coachman and guard were obliged to go to the horses heads and even then they missed the turn in the street and were of necessity of putting back then feeling our way thro' the right turn." He records the following day: "Arrived at Bath at 8 this morning when I took coffee at the White Lion and then proceeded by Pool coach to Frome."

Today's travel even by the basic service provided by the modern 'Sprinters' is luxury compared to travelling by stage coach! The coming of the railway is first mentioned in the diary for 3rd November 1846: "Henry Miller (local solicitor) came in and said he had obtained for John (John Sinkins, a local cloth manufacturer, who lived at Wallbridge House, the brother in law of Thomas Green), from the railway £1,800 for five acres altogether. Two days later the diary records that "John has sold four and three quarter acres of his land for £1,800 which only cost him £90 per acre". On 25th July 1847, Thomas Green notes that he "Walked to the railway making at Berkeley". John Sinkins must have sold more land to the railway for the entry in the diary for 17th March 1849 records "Called on Henry Miller who gave John a cheque for £3,342, the amount paid by the railway for his land eight acres, and one for the church £258 making £3,600 for nine acres". Four days later the diary notes: "Walked to Wallbridge where the railway works were commenced in John's fields this morning". August 5th 1850, "Went to new railway station in course of erection", and on 5th September 5th "Met Mr Barnes the contractor of the railway station". Three days later, Thomas Green, "Walked to railway at Clink where they were putting down the rails". By 25th September the railway station is "nearly complete". The great day finally arrived, when the rail-

way was opened between Westbury and Frome on 7th October 1850, the diary recalls: "Fine but blowing. Frome railway opened this morning at seven o'clock by special train to Oxford and 4 regular trains to Chippenham. Walked to station at 10 and saw the half past ten train go and busses and coaches to meet it come in and new coach from Yeovil thro' Bruton and Cary". Thomas Green first used the railway a week later when he "Left Frome by train from Wallbridge for the first time since the rail was opened at half past ten. Arrived at Paddington about three".

The Great Exhibition at Crystal Palace in 1851 is recalled in the diary for 7th July "Very fine and cool. Between three and four hundred persons went by special train from this town today up to the Great Exhibition to return on Saturday". The return trip from the exhibition is described, "Excursion train to exhibition returns this evening at 12: 350 from Frome". Thomas Green and his family travelled to view the exhibition later in the month. With the mineral line to Radstock being under construction the diary records: "Walked to Pilly Vale (now called Willow Vale) to see progress of Radstock Railway". The Radstock line actually cut through the end buildings of the present 17 Willow Vale, the GWR purchased the premises from James Wichkham of North End House in 1851 and demolished part of the building, the blocked windows and doorway remain to this day on the railway side of the building. It is interesting to note that the remaining part of the building was then sold in 1858 and renovated, being described in a conveyance of 1871 as "recently erected". An entry in the diary for 14th November 1854 reads "Radstock Railway opened this day". Another entry for the diary dated 22nd January 1877, reads: "Mr Gladstone at our rail station at 11 on his way from Longleat to Wells. Liberal deputation address presented by Le Gros (his brother-in-law Philip Le Gros). Called at Garston and saw the crowds return from the station."

With its vast overall roof constructed of timber rafters with wrought iron ties, and supported by wooden columns, Frome station is as impressive today as it must have been to the populace of the town on the opening day of 7th October 1850. It is interesting to note that although the design of the station, goods shed, and engine shed is attributed to J. B. Hannaford who was one of Brunel's 30 or more assistants by the Chief Civil Engineer's Official Register of Plans and

Frome station staff pose for the camera on the 'up' platform in a photograph taken circa 1920s. Back row left to right: Joe Eggleton, Gus Rydon, George Hobbs, Jack Russell, Eric Mortimer, Tom Harvey?, Jack Ketch, Harry Gillard. Sitting left to right Bert Eggleton, Reg Newcombe, Clerk?, Station Master?, Miss Mortimer, H. Townsend, Joby Mayor (Out Porter). The Maltsters building stands in the background.
G. W. Quartley Collection

Drawings, the earliest plan dated 29th October 1849, bears the name of T. R. (not J. R. or J. B.) Hannaford. And a plan for the goods shed is credited to C. Hellman. Frome is a typical Brunelian station bearing all the hallmarks of, and reflecting Brunel's original ideas. The work was supervised in the office of J. H. Bertram, one of Brunel's chief assistants. The whole complex of buildings at Frome was designed by men closely associated with Brunel to his basic plan and approved in his office. Bertram also designed the overall roof for Warminster station.

The station itself was built in the summer of 1850 in preparation for the opening of the line, although the earthworks between Westbury and Frome were built for a double line, initially a single line of track was laid. The contractors were Roach & Pilditch, with Barnes & Turner being responsible for laying the permanent way, the 35-yard long wooden viaduct spanning the River Frome on the approach to the station from the Westbury end was designed by R. P. Brereton who also designed most of the stations between Westbury and Salisbury, as well as those between between Frome and Maiden Newton. The wooden viaduct was replaced by a metal structure in 1880 at the same time as a similar viaduct spanning the River Frome on the Radstock branch. The Station Master's house dating from 1882 was built by John Vallis, a Frome builder with premises in King Street, for the cost of £260 with an extra room. Joseph Holbrook of Westbury is quoted as designing Frome signal box.

The first train out from Frome on the opening day was an excursion to Oxford at a cost of 3s 6d (17½p) and less than 100 passengers were carried. Daniel Gooch was on hand personally piloting trains for the occasion. Although the inhabitants were given a public holiday for the opening, there were no celebrations or bands playing as had been witnessed two years before with the opening from Thingley Junction to Westbury. A contemporary newspaper report of the day from *The Times* no less, throws a rather scathing light on the day: "Our reporter was dispatched to Frome to chronicle the usual rejoicings and public demonstrations which occur when a line first connects a town with railway communication. But our reporter returns with a blank note book. Frome is an exception to his experience of similar occasions. There was no enthusiam in the place to be recorded." (The reporter after referring to the celebrations at Westbury and Melksham now contin-

ues) – "But at Frome no officials welcomed the commencent of a mode of communication undoubtedly calculated to exercise considerable influence on the trade and commerce of the town. The bells of the parish church were silent, no flags were hoisted, no cannon discharged, the work people of the town who had been granted a holiday, had no other occupation than wandering to and from the station to watch the arrival and departure of the trains. The whole population, by their listlessness and apathy, seemed to exemplify the truth of the saying, A want of occupation is not rest, the mind that's vacant is a mind distressed."

Scathing words indeed from *The Times*, and the *Bath Chronicle* dated October 10th 1850 reports: "Opening of the line from Westbury to Frome – The line between Westbury and Frome, on the Wilts., Somerset, and Weymouth branch was opened on Monday. The distance between Westbury and Frome is six miles and twenty chains in length, and as yet only one set of rails has been laid down. Four trains run daily each way, and a considerable traffic is expected from the manufactories of Frome to the trunk line. No public demonstration took place on the occasion, with the exception of a dinner at the Crown Hotel, in the evening at which Henry Miller, and C. E. Olive, Esq., officiated as chairman and vice chairman."

At the dinner, of which, it seems that not all of the 50 tickets issued were used, there was some measure of dissatisfaction with the slowness of the railway on reaching the town, especially as Westbury station had opened two years previously, and this is reflected in the remarks at the dinner. The first engine to come to Frome was named *Wolf* and there was a dig at the GWR in the speech of John Sinkins, in which he mentions that: "They (the GWR) had been calling 'Wolf' for a long time with regard to the railway coming to Frome, but at last it had come."

With the opening of the line to Frome there was a daily service of four trains each way in operation. Upon the opening of the railway to Yeovil in September 1856 the service was increased to five each way daily plus two on Sundays. The mineral line from Frome to Radstock was opened on 14th November 1854 thus tapping the lucrative coal and limestone traffic from the local area. No passenger services operated between Frome and Radstock until 5th July 1875. The completion of the line to Weymouth opened on 20th January 1857 increased the service to six daily trains, the fastest down trains from Westbury to Weymouth, which omitted some of the stops, made the journey in two hours and eight minutes. From April of the same year, cheap excursions to Weymouth were put on by the GWR running from Bath, Bristol, and London.

The standard gauge Bristol & North Somerset Railway opened to Radstock on 3rd September 1873, this creating a break of gauge until the gauge conversion in 1874. From 5th July 1875, passenger trains to Radstock commenced from Frome via a new west curve giving access to the branch from the station, thus creating a triangular junction. The main line services in August 1877 comprised seven from Bath to Weymouth, and six Weymouth–Bath, plus two each way on Sundays. six each way between Chippenham and Weymouth, plus one each way on Sundays. All fast trains stopped at the main intermediate stations of Westbury, Frome, Yeovil and Dorchester. With the opening of the Stert Valley line from Patney to Westbury the Weymouth service was accelerated with a daily service of three fast passenger trains being intro-duced on 1st July 1901 between Paddington and Weymouth via Newbury.

The opening of the Castle Cary cut off line in 1906 brought a huge increase in West of England traffic through Frome and the station became a bottleneck with its speed restrictions and curvature of track, especially with the emerging growth of traffic after the First World War. This situation was eased with the opening of the avoiding line in 1933, thus allowing the main line express trains to travel at high speed unhindered by the slacks through Frome, plus the savings in coal consumption.

The station was served by three platforms: No. 1 (down trains), No. 2 (up trains) and the bay platform, No. 3 situated at the north end of the 'up' platform. Care had to be taken whilst shunting passenger vehicles into the bay platform, and vehicles over 70ft long and later diesel cars, were prohibited. After reversing into the bay, engine drivers were not to proceed forward until the guard had checked that the couplings were intact. The reason for this was due to the severe

Collett 0-6-0 No. 2213 stands alongside the 'down' platform at Frome with a Frome–Bristol train via Witham and Wells. Freight wagons and a 'B' set stand in the goods yard behind the platform fence. Note how the smoke from countless locomotives over the years has stained the overall roof.

H. B. Priestley

Class 5MT No. 73018 pulls out of Frome station and trundles past the goods shed with the 10.45am (SO) Wolver-hampton–Weymouth on 31st July 1965. Note the 30mph speed restriction near the goods shed for 'up' trains. A bogie parcels van stands in the 'down' yard to the right.

Hugh Ballantyne

curvature which sometimes caused the coupling links to rise over the drawbar hooks. The up bay extended beyond the overall roof with an attractive canopy of its own which also covered the Westbury end of the platform 2. Sidings connecting with the Express Dairy Creamery also ran off the bay line from which many railborne tank wagons conveyed milk to London. The north end of the up platform, which also served the bay line, was extended by 50ft in 1893, and there was a plan dated 22/11/1892, covering the platform, and signed James C. Inglis, Engineers Office, Paddington. Noted on it: "Exceeded the estimate and another design was made £5 5s 9d per square."

Passenger trains for Bristol via Radstock used the bay unless they were of the type prohibited. Trains for the branch also started from the up platform when occupancy allowed. It is interesting to note that passengers for Bristol could traverse three routes from Frome: via the Radstock branch, the East Somerset line via Witham and Wells, or the main line through Westbury and the Avon Valley. I well remember as a young boy whilst living in Frome entering the station with my father during the early 1950s to travel to Bristol via Radstock to visit my Uncle and Aunt, and standing on the up platform was our train which was one of the lovely ex-GWR AEC diesel railcars in chocolate and cream livery. It was purring away gently until the driver was given the right away and we glided from the station and down onto the branch.

The station was also unique in having an internal covered footbridge at the Westbury end and the station would echo to the sound of rushing feet over the wooden floorboards as passengers walked or ran to and from the down platform. Like all young boys I have run up over the footbridge and down on to the platform to catch the Weymouth train for a holiday by the seaside in the days when few people owned a car. The first thing to look out for was the lowering of the signal at the platform end announcing the arrival of the train. With a roar and a hissing of steam a dark green engine with its copper capped chimney and brass nameplate would run in with its long train of packed carriages and stop with a squeal of brakes. There would be a quick glimpse of a roaring fire and the driver and fireman before my parents ushered my brother and I with our suitcases into the train. One thing sticks in my mind from those far off days. My father was a former GWR shunter and he had taught us boys to look out for the headlamps on the engine; twin headlamps over each buffer meant a fast run to Weymouth, whilst one lamp on the chimney bracket meant stopping at every station. When the twin lamps were spotted, we would excitedly shout out, "it's a fast one." Between trains the station would be silent except for the occasional rumbling of an iron wheeled porter's trolley and the cooing of the pigeons from their nests in the station roof.

The main offices of the station were situated on the up platform, booking office, Station Master's office, waiting room, toilets, staff offices, first class waiting room, another waiting room, ladies' room, porters' room, lamp room, telegraph office and stores. On the down platform was another waiting room complete with its heavy leather furniture. On a cold Christmas Eve in 1949 in company with my parents and brother, I went to the station to catch a train to Yeovil as we were spending Christmas with our grandparents. Upon entering the waiting room on the down platform we were greeted by the sight of an enormous coal fire roaring away in the cast iron grate. We warmed ourselves by the welcome heat of the fire whilst the hissing gas lights spread a yellow glow around the room. A few minutes later there was a rumbling noise that grew louder making the glass in the waiting room windows rattle and our train rattled along the platform with the bright fierce glow from the firebox reflecting against the station roof. We left the waiting room to be greeted by coaches wreathed in steam and with the lights from the carriage windows reflecting along the platform.

Station staff during the 1940s/50s consisted of a Station Master, five porters, two yard foremen, eight guards, eight shunters, three booking clerks, and three signalmen (Frome South Box). Today the platform is manned by an early turn from Monday to Friday, plus a short late turn until 17.45pm on the same days. The station is unmanned from the end of the late turn on Saturdays to the early shift on Monday mornings, except for the summer service when there is a short Sunday manning to deal with the Weymouth traffic.

Frome Signal Boxes

Frome North (previously No. 1) opened 1875. Situated alongside the up main line near the junction with the goods line to Radstock controlling the eastern curve of the triangle (mineral loop junction) with the main line. With 29-levers, the box was open in 1945 from 5am until 10pm weekdays, and from 10.30am to 6.30pm on Sundays. Re-framed with a VT 34 lever frame ex-Marsh Junction in August 1970. Box closed 7th October 1984.

Frome Middle (previously No. 2) opened 1875. Situated alongside the down main line at the northern end of the rail overbridge near the junction with the passenger line to Radstock controlling the western curve of the triangle (Radstock branch junction) with the main line. 23 levers, closed 20th September 1933.

Frome South (previously No. 3) opened 1875. Situated near the entrance/exit points to the engine shed and coal yard at the Blatchbridge end of the station. Closed 17th September 1933.

Frome West situated at the point where the west and east curves of the triangle converged with the Radstock line, (Frome West Junction) reduced to ground frame 24th September 1933 when the Middle and South boxes closed.

Frome South opened on 17th September 1933, replaced the former Middle and South boxes. New South box situated at the northern end of the down platform. 73 levers, VT3 Bar. Reduced to 28 levers at closure. Box size 36ft x 11ft x 7ft 6in. Closed 19th August 1970.

With the growth in traffic over the years many alterations to the track layout took place and one of the first private siding agreements was granted to the Frome maltings:

E. Bailey & Son Ltd.
PSA 24.3.1891
PSA 7.9.1891
PSA 26.11.1962 to Samuel Thompson Ltd.
PSAT 24.3.1967

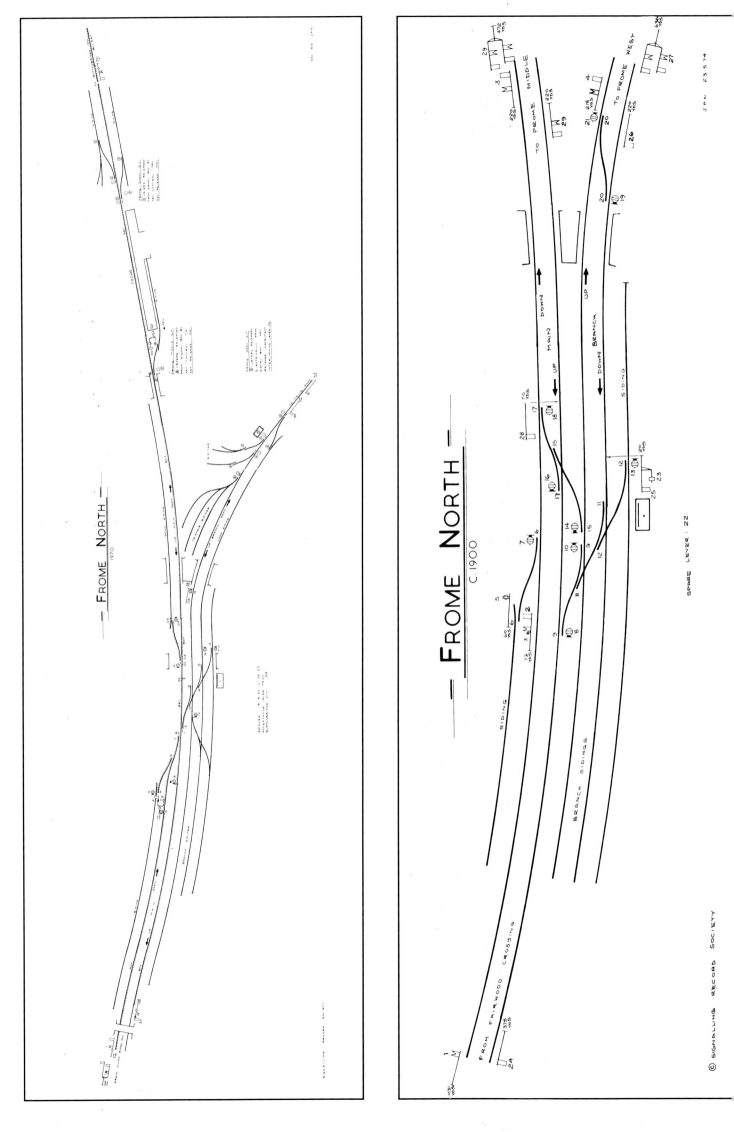

— FROME NORTH —
1970

— FROME NORTH —
C.1900

SPARE LEVER: 22.

© SIGNALLING RECORD SOCIETY

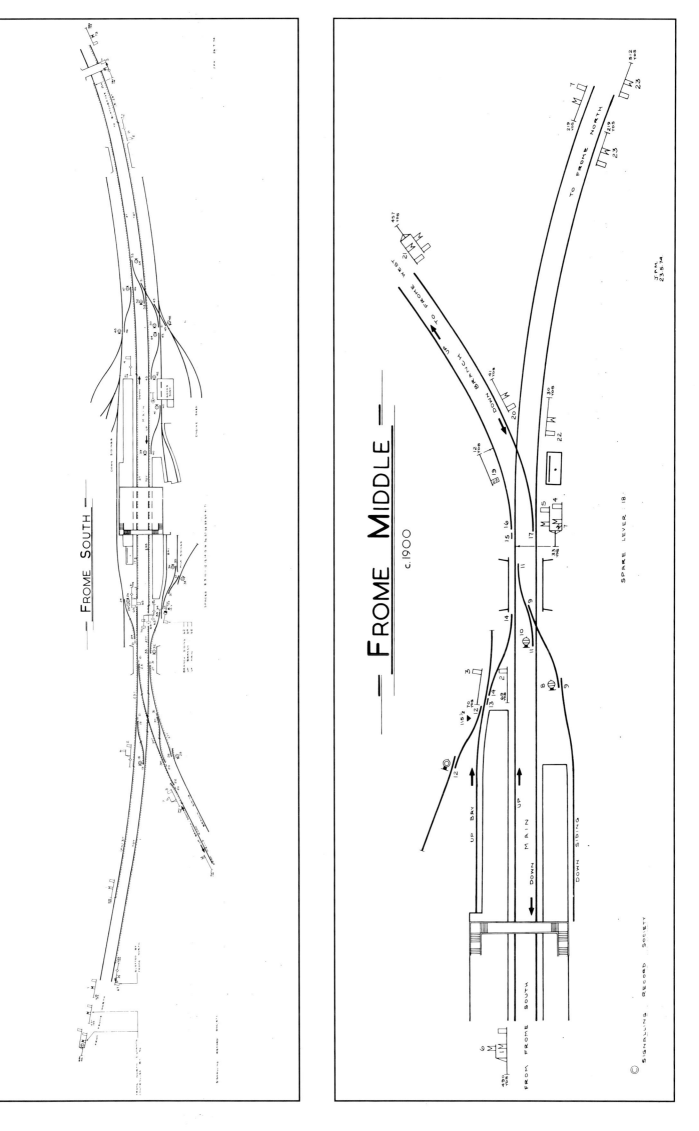

— FROME SOUTH —

— FROME MIDDLE —

c.1900

SPARE LEVER 18

© SIGNALLING RECORD SOCIETY

The 34-lever Frome North signal box pictured here on 21st March 1965, controlled the junction of the Radstock mineral branch with the main line. When the box was closed on 7th October 1984, the top portion was transported to the Didcot Railway Centre for restoration and has been restored to full working order, complete with its original name of Frome Mineral Junction. The ex-GWR signal box from Radstock has also been restored and can be seen working at Didcot.

C. L. Caddy

Frome North signal box, looking towards the station in 1973 showing the 'ladder' crossing in the foreground. Loaded limestone hoppers from Whatley Quarry on the Radstock branch stand in the background awaiting collection. The former Radstock branch swings to the right past the loaded hoppers in the distance, and the line to Frome station curves to the left.

Adrian Vaughan Collection

The interior of Frome North signal box in 1974 showing part of the 34-lever frame. Three lines of mineral wagons can be viewed from the end window bearing witness to the vast amount of quarry traffic dealt with at Whatley Quarry.

John Morris

A private sidings agreement was granted to E. Bailey & Son Ltd at the dates shown. The siding was situated behind the locomotive shed and adjoined the large malt house which dominated the station for many years. Many loads of malt barley conveyed in bulk grain wagons were delivered over the years. The private siding agreement was terminated on 24th March 1967 and the siding removed on 24th March 1969. A down relief siding was laid alongside the down main line at Mineral Loop Junction on 4th August 1902. A mileage siding was added to the layout controlled by the West box in 1916. In late 1920/early 1921 the down platform was extended, and the mileage siding controlled by West box enlarged to three sidings beside the West curve. Three sidings (coal wharf) were added to the inside of the triangle. (Bendles coal lorries used the wharf for many years, and their red painted lorries are well remembered from my younger days as they delivered their sacks of coal around the town.) The down relief siding at Mineral Loop Junction was extended, and also in 1921 a private siding agreement was granted to:

E. Cockey & Sons Ltd.
PSA 24.9.1921
PSAT 1964

The well known firm of Edward Cockey & Sons, makers of gas holders and standards, steam engines, boilers, pillars and iron roofs had a private siding agreement dating from 1921. The siding was situated near the West signal box adjacent to the west curve of the triangle and the agreement was terminated in 1964 with the track being removed 1963/64.

A milk siding was added to the up bay layout in late 1931, and a crossover was laid between the up and down main lines north of the Middle box on 6th November 1932. Alterations to the entrance/exit of the down goods yard at its Westbury end occurred on 13th November 1932. Saturday 31st October 1959 witnessed the last passenger trains from Frome to Bristol via Radstock when the 9.25pm to Bristol departed hauled by Nos 41203 and 9612. The west curve remained in situ until it was closed on 10th November 1963, and from 1963 the layout at Frome was gradually reduced. The engine shed closed in September 1963 with tracks

being removed from the building in 1966. The milk sidings were taken out of use on 15th June 1966 and removed three days later. The double track eastern curve of the former triangle was relegated to a single line on 11th August 1968 with the up branch converted to a siding and traffic now using the former down line to gain access to the Radstock branch.

The double track main line from North box through the station to Blatchbridge Junction was singled on 19th August 1970. Frome South box was abolished at the same time, and alterations were also made at Frome North to enable trains from Westbury to run direct onto the Radstock branch. Two ground frames; Middle, positioned to control the exit/entrance to the up bay, and South, located to control the points and crossovers near the goods shed were brought into use on 19th August 1970. The up bay was taken out of use 17th May 1971, and the Middle ground frame was removed at the same time. The former mileage sidings which lay alongside the former west curve were removed in December 1974. Two sidings inside the former triangle area were purchased in 1982 by Messrs Tarmac Ltd (no PSA) for the loading of limestone.

Mobil Oil Ltd.
PSA 1.9.1983

The firm had used the former down yard since the first week in January 1974. The sidings had been shortened the week commencing 5th July 1982 with all work completed, including the erection of compound fencing for security by 24th March 1983. Railborne bitumen tankers were unloaded into road transport for delivery to the local quarries. This traffic has now ceased.

Today, the site of the former North box is now known as North Junction and is signalled for bi-directional working over the up main. Up limestone trains approaching the junction from the Radstock branch can be routed direct on to the up main line or into the up loop alongside. Coming down from Clink Junction to Frome the line is at first single coming off the avoiding line then bifurcates into double: Down Frome, and Up Frome (by-directional), at North junction the single line to Whatley quarry and Radstock curves away to the right, whilst the single line to the station turns to the left.

Occupying the site of the former 'down' goods yard, bitumen wagons stand in the Mobil terminal at Frome on 12th April 1989. The bitumen was unloaded into road tankers and distributed to the local quarries for use in the tarmacadam process. The rear of the Brunelian station building can be seen in the background.

Peter Nicholson

Class 150/2 'Sprinter' No. 150282 stands under the all-over roof at the east end of Frome station on 10th November 1990. Note the box van in the bitumen terminal to the left, then used by Mobil as a store, but now preserved by the Somerset & Avon Railway at Radstock.

Peter Nicholson

During the 1970s the structure of the station was in such a bad condition that the overall roof had to be propped up, and with the massive costs involved in restoration, BR made suggestions about demolishing the building and replacing it with a bus stop type shelter. However, due to a public outcry, the importance and historic interest of the building was taken into account and since 1973 has been listed as Grade II in the Department of the Environment's List of Buildings of Special Architectural or Historic Interest in the Urban District of Frome. The description reads: "Circa 1850. Possibly designed by I. K. Brunel. All wood construction. Train shed covering both tracks. Aisled, with wooden posts and ceiling. Corrugated iron roof with full length glazed vent. Offices on up side. Single storey with 7 wooden casements, 2 and 3-lights. Original bracketed canopy over entrance. Hipped corrugated iron roof with red brick stacks. Largely unaltered example of a small station of the period, and probably the last through train shed of its type in use on the Western Region"...

The initial costs for restoration were estimated at £46,000, and work was suspended in 1980 when the costs rocketed to triple this figure with the finding of a number of structural faults. Work did continue and when completed brought the station back to its pristine glory. The September 1992–May 1993 timetable for Regional Railways regarding the Weymouth services shows a service of eight 'down' trains daily, plus three on Sundays, and nine up daily, plus three on Sundays. The good news for the station in the 1993 summer timetable was the return of InterCity services after an absence of many years with a return service to London on Saturdays with the 09.40 ex Paignton calling at 11.29am, and a return call by the 19.35 ex-Paddington–Plymouth. A new service on Sundays enables travellers from the station to return to London on the 12.42 from Penzance calling at Frome at 16.43.

Although compared to the 1957 summer timetable, todays services are very sparse.

Down Passenger Trains Booked to Stop at Frome. 1957 Summer Timetable.

Passenger except where stated.
Arr 1.22am (SO) of the 1.12am ECS from Westbury.
Arr 6.40am, dep 6.42 of the 4.30am Swindon–Taunton passenger and parcels.
Arr 7.00am, dep 7.10 (SO) of the 6.50am Westbury–Weymouth milk empties.
Arr 7.10am, (MO) ECS from Westbury (to work 8.15am Frome–Paddington).
Arr 7.20am (MX) LE from Westbury (to work 8.15am Frome–Paddington).
Arr 7.24am, dep 7.29 of the 5.45am Bristol–Weymouth.
Arr 8.07, from Bristol via Radstock West, dep 8.12am for Wells and Bristol via Witham and the East Somerset line.
Arr 9.05am, dep 9.07 (SX) of the 8.05am Bristol–Weymouth.
Arr 9.12am, dep 9.16 (SO) of the 8.05am Bristol–Weymouth.
Arr 9.36am, dep 9.38 of the 9.27am Westbury–Weymouth.
Arr 9.45am, dep 9.52 (SO) of the 7.05am Paddington–Penzance.
Arr 9.56am, dep 10.00 (SO) of the 9.47am Westbury–Wells and Bristol via Witham and the East Somerset line.
Arr 10.06, dep 10.09 (SO) of the 9.10am Bristol–Weymouth.
Arr 10.41am, dep 10.43 (SX) of the 8.30am Weston-super-Mare–Weymouth.
Arr 10.59am, dep 11.01 (SO) of the 8.30am Weston-super-Mare–Weymouth.
Arr 11.24am, via Radstock West of the 10.17am ex-Bristol, dep 11.49 for Witham.
Arr 11.54am, dep 11.57 (SO) of the 9.34am Reading General–Weymouth.
Arr 12.41pm, dep 12.43 (SO) of the 11.25am Chippenham–Weymouth.
Arr 12.51pm, dep 12.54 (SX) of the 11.45am Chippenham–Weymouth.*
Arr 2.12pm, dep 2.15 (SX) of the 12.43 Bristol–Weymouth.
Arr 2.38pm, of the 1.20pm Bristol T.M. via Radstock West.

The west end of Frome station as viewed from the disused 'down' platform on 15th August 1992. A two-car, Class 150/2 'Sprinter', No. 150280 formed of car Nos 52280 and 57280, stands at the platform with a Weymouth–Bristol service.

Chris Giles

Arr 2.53pm, dep 2.58 (SX) of the 12.30pm
Paddington–Weymouth.
Arr 2.56pm, dep 3.01 (SO) of the 12.30pm
Paddington–Weymouth.
Dep 3.17pm (SX) to Wells & Bristol via Witham and the East
Somerset line.
Dep 3.27pm (SO) to Wells & Bristol via Witham and the East
Somerset line.
Arr 3.37pm, dep 3.41 (SX) of the 11.05am
Wolverhampton–Weymouth.
Arr 3.46pm, dep 3.49 (SO) of the 11.05am
Wolverhampton–Weymouth.
Arr 4.00pm, from Bristol via Radstock West.
Arr 4.25pm, dep 4.27 of the 4.15pm Westbury–Weymouth.
Arr 5.36pm, dep 5.38 of the 4.25pm Bristol–Weymouth.*
Arr 5.54pm, dep 5.57 of the 5.10pm Melksham–Taunton.
Arr 6.17pm, dep 6.19 (SX) of the 5.02pm Bristol–Weymouth.
Arr 6.31pm, of the 5.20pm ex-Bristol via Radstock West, dep
6.40pm for Wells via Witham and the East Somerset line.
Arr 7.22pm, of the 6.15pm ex-Bristol via Radstock West.
Arr 8.41pm, dep 8.44 of the 6.00pm Paddington–Weymouth.
Arr 8.49pm, of the 7.45pm ex Bristol via Radstock West.
Dep 8.54pm (SO) ECS to Witham (empty stock from 7.45pm
ex Bristol, to work 9.20pm Witham–Wells).
Arr 9.00pm, dep 9.04 (FX) of the 8.50pm
Westbury–Weymouth, passenger and milk empties,
(passenger and milk empties to Yeovil PM, passenger from
Yeovil).
Arr 10.25pm of 10.15 Westbury.
Arr 10.53pm (WSX) of the 9.48 ex Bristol via Radstock
West.

* Conveys slip coach from Paddington collected from
Westbury.

*Up Trains Booked to Stop at Frome. 1957 Summer
Timetable.*
Passenger except where stated.
Dep 6.26am to Bristol via Radstock West.
Dep 6.35am to Bristol via Westbury.
Dep 7.06am to Chippenham.
Dep 7.37am to Bedminster via Radstock West.

Dep 8.15am to Paddington.
Arr 8.53am, dep 8.56 of the 8.35am Bruton–Westbury.
Arr 9.25am, dep 9.27 of the 7.17am Weymouth–Chippenham.
Arr 9.43am, dep 9.44 of the 8.15am Weymouth–Bristol.
Arr 9.54am of the 8.56am Wells.
Arr 10.38am, dep 10.41 of the 9.00am
Weymouth–Paddington.
Dep 10.50am to Bedminster via Radstock West.
Arr 12.00pm, dep 12.05 (SO) of the 10.20am
Weymouth–Wolverhampton.
Arr 12.09pm, dep 12.12 (SX) of the 10.33am
Weymouth–Wolverhampton.
Arr 12.52pm, (SO) of the 12.44pm ECS from Witham, (ex
11.12am Yatton–Witham, to work 1.10pm Frome–Bristol).
Dep 1.10pm to Bristol via Radstock West.
Arr 1.34pm, dep 1.39 (SX) of the 11.40am
Weymouth–Westbury.
Arr 2.07pm, dep 2.09 (SX) of the 12.35pm
Weymouth–Bristol.
Arr 3.19pm, dep 3.22 (SX) of the 1.40pm
Weymouth–Westbury.
Dep 4.00pm to Bristol via Radstock West.
Arr 4.40pm, dep 4.42 of the 2.32pm Weymouth–Westbury.
Arr 5.05pm (SO) of the 2.52pm ex-Yatton.
Arr 5.13pm (SX) of the 2.52pm ex-Yatton.
Arr 5.27pm, dep 5.33 of the 3.40pm Weymouth
Quay–Paddington.
Arr 5.44pm, dep 5.49 of the 4.14pm Weymouth–Paddington.
Dep 5.55pm to Bristol via Radstock West.
Dep 6.06pm to Bristol via Radstock West.
Arr 6.27pm of 5.00pm ex-Taunton.
Arr 6.37pm, dep 6.39 (SO) of the 4.15pm
Taunton–Trowbridge, (via Langport West and Yeovil Pen
Mill).
Arr 6.37pm, dep 6.39 (SX) of the 4.22pm
Taunton–Trowbridge, (via Langport West and Yeovil Pen
Mill).
Arr 7.49pm of the 6.13pm ex-Yatton.
Arr 8.04pm, dep 8.06 of the 6.10pm Weymouth–Westbury.
Arr 8.28pm, dep 8.30 of the 7.00pm Taunton–Westbury.
Arr 8.54pm, dep 9.00 of the 6.35pm Weymouth–Paddington
Milk.

Arr 9.11pm, dep 9.14 of the 7.30pm Weymouth–Bristol.
Arr 9.20pm, dep 9.30 of the 12.20pm Penzance–Kensington
  Milk.
Dep 9.20pm to Bristol via Radstock West.
Arr 10.03pm (SO) light engine ex 9.05pm Wells.

The best service between Frome and Bristol via Westbury and the Avon Valley route was accomplished in just over one hour. Stopping trains from Frome to Bristol via the North Somerset line, which being a more direct route and ten miles shorter, also made the journey in just over the hour. Frome station would be packed with passengers when the 3.40pm Weymouth Quay–Paddington, the 'Channel Islands Boat Express' arrived. The up 'Boat' was not booked to stop at Westbury, and the reason why the up train stopped at Frome is thus; passengers from Bristol to Jersey and Guernsey travelled on the 8.30am Weston-super-Mare–Weymouth as far as Westbury whereupon they connected with the down 'Boat' train. On their return journey, passengers for Bristol, etc. on their arrival at Frome, changed onto the 5.55pm Frome–Bristol via the North Somerset branch. This train would normally be formed of seven coaches during the busy summer season and running under express headlamps would only stop at Radstock West and Pensford.

Class 37/0 No. 37010 stands at Frome with a Cardiff–Weymouth train on 15th August 1992.   *Chris Giles*

'The Herald Angel' railtour (Hertfordshire Rail Tours/Network SouthEast) passes through Frome station on Saturday, 20th November 1993, formed of two 4TC sets, Nos 417 and 410, they were worked by Class 33/1 No. 33116. After a visit to Whatley Quarry the train, for which every ticket had been sold, went to the Foster Yeoman Quarry at Merehead and then to the East Somerset Railway at Cranmore.

Peter Nicholson

Locomotive workings on the North Somerset branch were shared between Frome and Bristol (Bath Road) crews. Ex-ROD 2-8-0 locomotives were used on the Radstock coal trains, 43xx Moguls were also used on branch coal and freight traffic. Excursion trains to Barry Island via the branch were very popular and well patronised and called at all the stations on the North Somerset branch and were hauled by a Westbury 43xx Mogul. On Bank Holidays the branch was used by excursions travelling to Weston-super-Mare, again hauled by a 43xx Mogul from Westbury. The branch may, one day, witness the return of the steam locomotive after many years with the creation of the Somerset & Avon Railway Association (SARA). The Association's objective is to re-open the Radstock–Frome line with steam hauled trains, although this may be difficult at the present time with ARC running stone trains from Whatley Quarry. But at least the track is still in place including the section from the junction with the Whatley Quarry branch at Hapsford and Radstock via Mells Road. The Association's headquarters are in the old GWR engine shed at Radstock where restoration is being carried out on their motive power and rolling stock. Also in the old engine shed you will find an exhibition on the Association and the history of the line.

Blatchbridge Junction Signal Box

116 miles 57 chains from Paddington
116 miles 42 chains (via direct line)
Opened 2nd January 1933
Closed 7th October 1984

Controlling the southern end of the avoiding line and the former WS&W main line into Frome, Blatchbridge Junction signal box was brought into use on 18th December 1932 but was switched out until 2nd January 1933 when the avoiding line was opened. The box was fitted with a 28-lever frame and 5-bar vertical tappet interlocking. Box size, 21ft x 11ft x 7ft 6in. A crossover located south of the box was added to the layout on 16th August 1953. The line into Frome from Blatchbridge Junction was singled on 19th August 1970. Blatchbridge Junction box closed on the same date as Clink Road Junction, 7th October 1984. The area then came under the control of Westbury Power box.

Woodlands Signal Box

118 miles 60 chains from Paddington
Opened 31st July 1905
Closed 16th August 1953

With the upgrading of the route to the West of England main line, new signal boxes were brought into use as 'break section' boxes to cope with the expected increase in traffic. Situated alongside the down main line in the then long section between Frome and Witham, this section was shortened by the opening of Blatchbridge Junction box in 1933. Woodlands signal box was opened on 31st July 1905, and a crossover between the up and down main lines was installed at the same time. The box was equipped with a 9-lever frame and was closed on 16th August 1953.

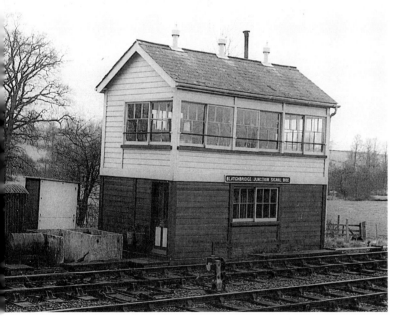

Blatchbridge Junction signal box on 21st March 1965, situated alongside the 'up' line, is in fairly good external condition compared with the state of the box before closure in 1984. The signalman's 'privy', coal bunker, and corrugated lamp hut stand neatly placed to the left of the box.

C. L. Caddy

The interior of Blatchbridge Junction box on 30th May 1982 showing the lever frame, instruments and the box diagram. The line into Frome can be seen curving to the left hand corner of the diagram. The water cans for the signalman's needs, stand behind the levers to the right.

M. Marshall

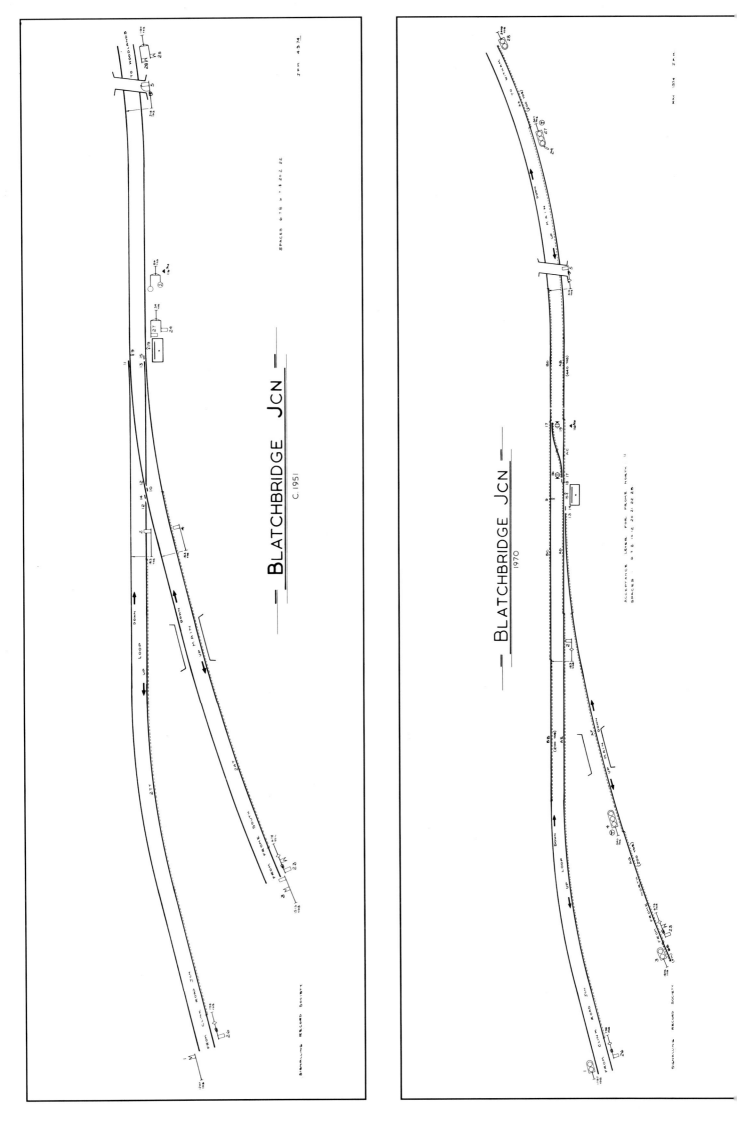

— BLATCHBRIDGE JCN —

C.1951

— BLATCHBRIDGE JCN —

1970

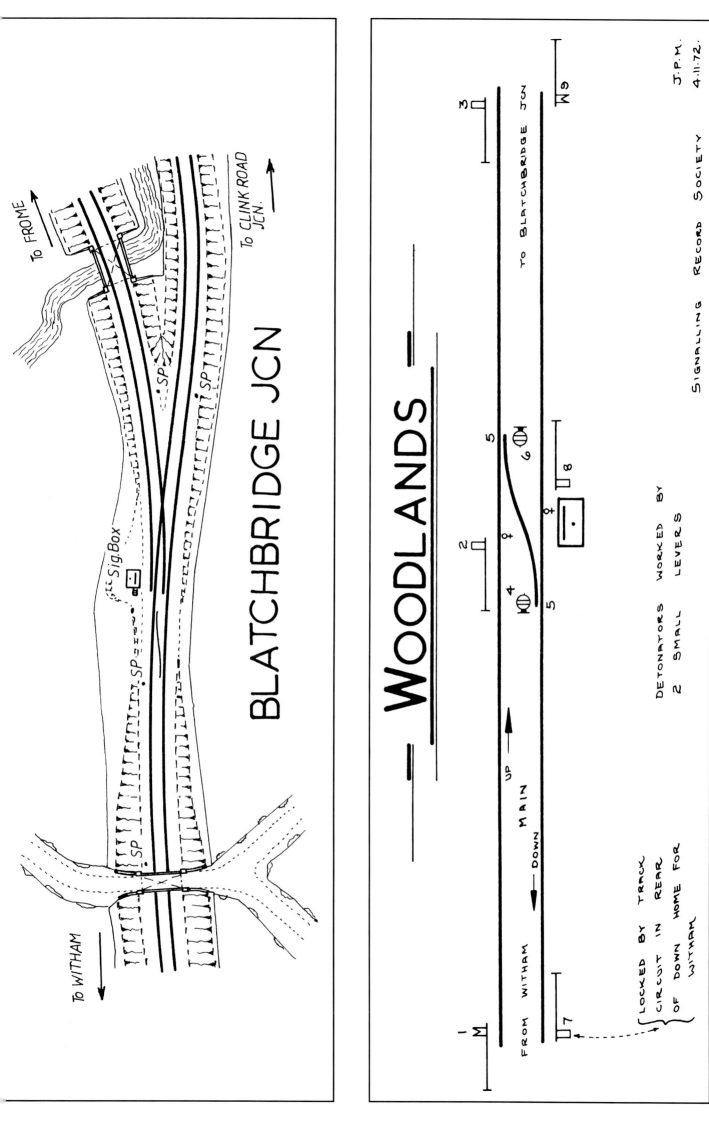

BLATCHBRIDGE JCN

To FROME

To CLINK ROAD JCN.

To WITHAM

SP

Sig.Box

WOODLANDS

FROM WITHAM

DOWN MAIN UP

TO BLATCHBRIDGE JCN

3

9 M

2

5

6

8

4

5

1 M

7

LOCKED BY TRACK
CIRCUIT IN REAR
OF DOWN HOME FOR
WITHAM

DETONATORS WORKED BY
2 SMALL LEVERS

J.P.M.
4.11.72.

SIGNALLING RECORD SOCIETY

Blatchbridge Junction, looking east in 1974. The Frome avoiding line lies straight ahead, and the line into Frome, which was singled on 19th August 1970, curves away to the left. Signalmen gained entrance to the box by parking their car in a lane to the right, and crossing the line via the footbridge to the right of the 'down' main line. Note the GWR pattern shunt disc signal for the main line crossover in the foreground. The signal in the background standing alongside the 'up' avoiding line is the home signal for the 'down' avoiding line, and is placed there for sighting purposes regarding the right hand driven GWR locomotives as they came around the curve in the distance.

John Morris

Witham

120 miles 63 chains from Paddington
Opened 1st September 1856
ESR branch opened to Shepton Mallet 9th November 1858
ESR branch extended to Wells 1st March 1862
Gauge conversion 18th/22nd June 1874
Signal box opened c1877, rebuilt 1896
Line doubled Frome–Witham 1875
Line doubled Witham–Castle Cary 1880
ESR branch closed to passenger traffic 9th September 1963
Closed 30th December 1963. (Goods)
Closed 3rd October 1966. (Passengers)
Signal box closed 26th November 1984

When originally opened on 1st September 1856 the station was a passing loop on the single track line to Yeovil before the opening to Weymouth in 1857. The track was doubled from Frome to Witham in 1875, as was Witham–Castle Cary in 1880. The station was rebuilt when the line was doubled. The station layout at Witham, five miles south west of Frome, consisted of two platforms with the main buildings including the slate hung Station Master's house situated on the up

platform. Branch services for the East Somerset branch to Wells and Yatton used the bay platform which was unique in having a wooden overall roof train shed with an extended canopy over part of the main up platform. The train shed in fact only covered one carriage and had been in situ since 1870 and survived intact until the early 1960s. The branch timetable for 10th September 1962–16th June 1963 shows a daily service of four trains between Yatton and Witham, plus two from Yatton to Wells, two services from Witham to Yatton (four on Saturdays), one from Witham to Wells, and two Wells–Yatton.

Yatton branch services (the branch was also known as the 'Strawberry line', due to the annual summer crop originating from the strawberry growers along the Cheddar Valley) would also start from Frome with Frome shed crews working the 'circuit' using the East and North Somerset branch lines on a circular journey. One of the regular workings was the 3.30 Frome–Yatton. The branch train, after connecting with the 12.30pm from Paddington arriving at Frome at 3pm, would depart for Witham, thence via the branch to Yatton and after arrival at Bristol Temple Meads would then form the 5.20pm to Frome via Radstock with an arrival at Frome of 6.30pm.

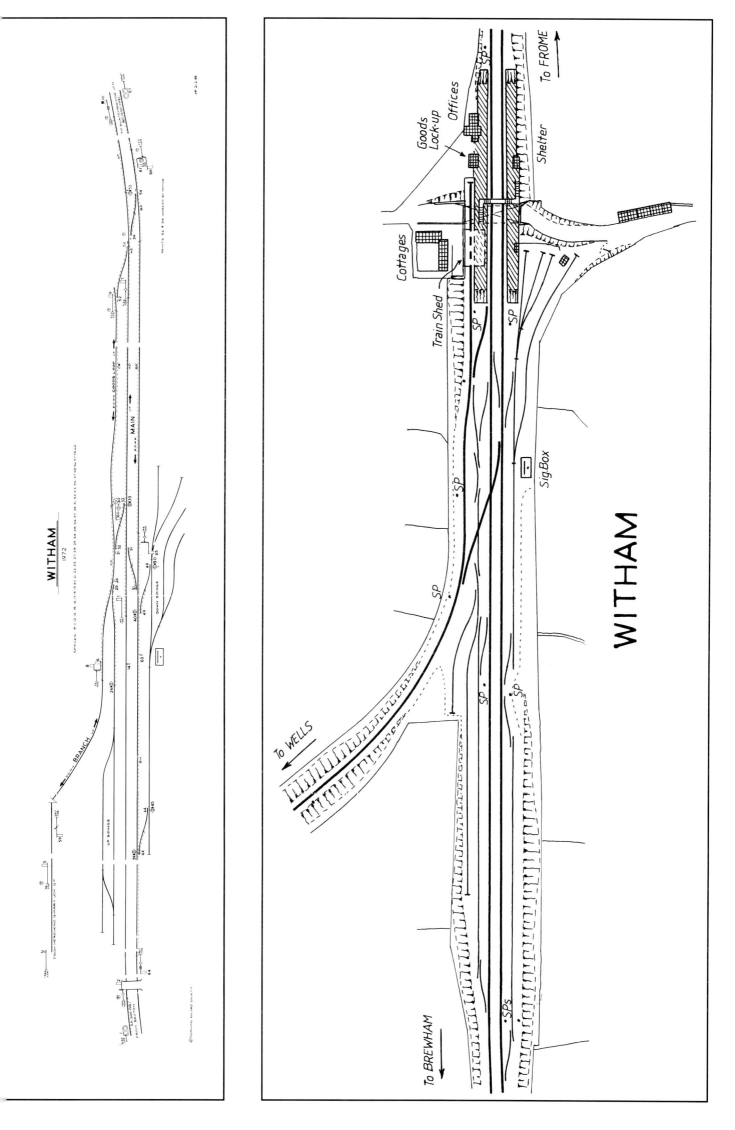

WITHAM
1972

WITHAM

To FROME

To WELLS

To BREWHAM

Goods Lock-up

Offices

Cottages

Train Shed

Shelter

SigBox

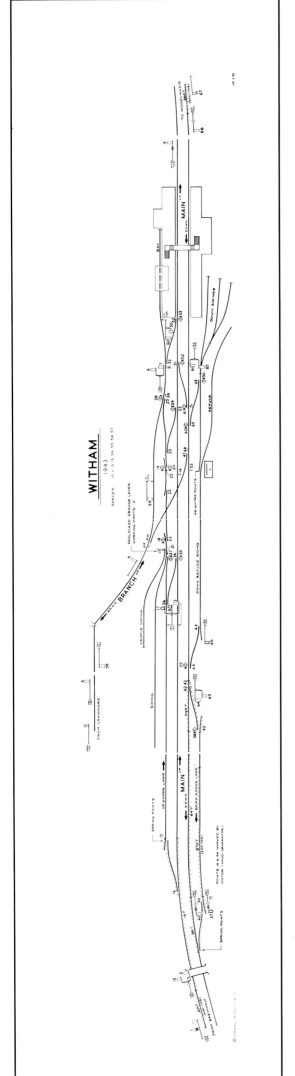

WITHAM

1943

SPACES 10·11·12·13·54·55·56·57

Witham, looking east on 27th October 1962. Although the branch bay overall roof and awning have been removed, one of the roof supports by the nameboard has been left in situ with a bracket on which to hang an oil lamp on dark nights.

C. L. Caddy

The bay platform at Witham used by passenger trains on the East Somerset branch, showing the timber overall roof and platform awning.

H. B. Priestley

Witham station, looking west in the 1960s. The stone built waiting shelter with its typical Brunelian chimney on the 'down' platform to the left, did not escape demolition when the station closed on 3rd October 1966. The overall roof on the branch bay had been removed by the time of this view. Note the attractive awning on the booking office/waiting room on the 'up' platform.

Lens of Sutton

No. 4924 *Eydon Hall* coasts into Witham with the 11.12am Weymouth–Paddington on 20th June 1959. No. 4924 was built in May 1929 to Lot 254, and withdrawn in 1963. Pannier tank No. 3773 stands in the branch bay with the 1.10pm Witham–Bristol. The fireman of the pannier strolls towards his engine, followed by his driver, the station staff and the branch train guard plus the porters' barrow complete the station scene. The large water tank in the background supplied the water columns for the branch trains.

R. E. Toop

East Somerset branch passenger services which had started running to Shepton Mallet on 9th November 1858 before the extension to Wells, were withdrawn on 9th September 1963 with the final passenger trains running on 7th September 0-6-0 No. 3218 worked the last eastbound train, the 2.45pm Yatton–Witham. At Witham a small stone built waiting room with a tall Brunelian type chimney stood on the down platform. No main line West of England trains stopped at Witham, this being left to Weymouth line trains and local passenger services. A 34ft 6in diameter turntable for turning tank engines was situated between the ESR branch and the up sidings, and was removed pre 1962. The track layout was vast. A fan of five sidings for local traffic ran to the rear of the down platform, plus sidings on the up side, and crossovers for trains to gain access to the branch from the 'up' and down main lines. Up and down loops were installed during

August 1943 thus increasing the layout further. The station was closed to passengers on 3rd October 1966 and demolished later, although destroyed would be the better word to use for the desecration of our railway history! The suffix 'Somerset' was added to the station nameboards from 9th June 1958 to distinguish the station from another with the same title in East Anglia.

The signal box dating from c1877 stood between the down sidings and the down main line. Originally equipped with 30 levers which increased to 47 levers with rebuilding in 1896, and in 1942 the frame was increased to 67 levers with VT5 Bar locking 4in centres. Box size, 30ft 9in x 10ft x 7ft. Major rationalisation of the trackwork took place with the loops taken out of use in May 1965. More track alterations took place in 1972 and the signal box was closed on 24th November 1984.

No. 7004 *Eastnor Castle* thunders through Witham with 'The Royal Duchy' 1.35pm Paddington–Penzance on 20th June 1959. No. 7004 was built in June 1946 to Lot 357, a double chimney was fitted in February 1958 and the engine was withdrawn in 1964.

R. E. Toop

Mineral traffic from the quarries along the East Somerset branch had always been considerable but it was nothing compared with the vast tonnages conveyed today along the branch from the giant Merehead quarry of Foster Yeoman and trains of 4,500 tons are regularly hauled by the General Motors Class 59/0 diesels. For lovers of steam locomotives, the station at Cranmore on the truncated branch line is a must for it is now home to the East Somerset Railway created by the renowned wildlife artist David Shepherd. The station has been restored, and a new locomotive shed has been erected to an authentic Victorian design. It is worthy to note that one of the last two surviving ex-GWR signal boxes in the area can be found at Cranmore in use as an art gallery. The only working ex-GWR signal box in the

North British built No. D604 *Cossack*, allocated to 83D (Plymouth Laira), growls through Witham with the 8.15am Perranporth–Paddington on 20th June 1959. No. D604 was introduced to traffic in January 1959 and withdrawn in December 1967. Lower quadrant bracket signals complete with finials, a water column complete with its 'fire devil', corrugated lamp huts, and the shunt ground signal between the main lines show how much is missing in the railway of today. 1959 was the year that the dmus were introduced on the Bristol–Weymouth services and the '6 car' stop sign at the end of the 'down' platform brings forth the writing on the wall for the steam locomotive.

R. E. Toop

With just a faint haze of exhaust fumes blowing into the hot summer air, North British built No. D601 *Ark Royal* speeds through Witham with the 11.05am Paddington–Penzance on 20th June 1959. The buildings on the 'up' platform are worthy of a glance, from the booking office complete with awning and bicycle, and the slate hung station master's house with a bicycle leaning against the porch, to the lamp hut and cast iron gents. On the 'down' platform a lonely parcel awaits collection by the next stopping train.

R. E. Toop

area still in situ is at Yeovil Pen Mill, of which more anon.

A Working Shift at Witham Signal Box

Former railway signalman Adrian Vaughan, well known for his books on railway signalling and GWR stations, has furnished details of a working shift (6am–2pm) that he worked at Witham box on 27th June 1975. After booking on at 6am and checking that everything was all right in the train register and having a welcome cup of tea, he was now ready for a busy morning's work. The sound of block bells resounded around the box as a down train was accepted from Blatchbridge Junction and passed on to Castle Cary box. The levers were then pulled for the first train of the shift, lower quadrant arms rattled down clearing the road for the 03.55 Salisbury

An interior view of Witham signal box showing part of the 67-lever, 5 Bar Vertical Tappet interlocking frame. Note the signalman's easy chair located between the levers.

Adrian Vaughan Collection

(SR)–Exeter (SR) ballast empties headed by No. 31110 which passed at 06.22. It is interesting to note that this train was routed to Exeter from Salisbury via Westbury, Yeovil Pen Mill, Yeovil Junction and the former L&SWR route to Exeter. As the train passed complete with its tail lamp, the signal levers were let back in the frame with a heavy thud and the lower quadrant signals slammed to 'danger' in the wake of the train.

The next down train, the 05.35 Bristol–Weymouth passed the box 33 minutes later, bang on time at 06.55 powered by No. 47097 hauling six coaches plus two GUVs. Two minutes later, at 06.57, No. 1067 *Western Druid* eased cautiously down the East Somerset branch with all signals clear and powered along the up main line towards Westbury with the Merehead–Merstham stone train formed of air braked 'Procors'. The 05.45 Weymouth–Bristol three-car dmu rattled through on

Witham signal box pictured here in 1974, controlled the junction between the main line and the branch to Wells and Yatton. The junction today, known as East Somerset Junction, is controlled by Westbury Panel box.

John Morris

A snowy scene at Witham on 27th March 1974 as a dmu forming a Weymouth–Bristol service, accelerates past the 'up' sidings, bitumen tanks dominate the sidings, and a Class 33 (fitted with SR multiple working equipment for use with SR emus, TC stock and Class 73s) stands coupled to more bitumen tanks in the siding to the right. The bitumen tanks were despatched to the depot at Cranmore station, situated on the former East Somerset branch.

Adrian Vaughan Collection

The station, and the signal box with its lower quadrant signals, have now vanished from the scene at Witham (now renamed East Somerset Junction) as No. 33004 travels through with the 16.20 Bristol–Weymouth on 19th April 1985.

John Day

Foster Yeoman Class 59/0 No. 59003 *Yeoman Highlander* enters the main line at East Somerset Junction (Witham) from the former East Somerset branch on 15th May 1991 and heads towards Westbury with a limestone train from Merehead Quarry. A redundant stop block lies discarded to the left, with nothing to 'stop'.

Peter Nicholson

time at 07.14. At 07.37, No. 47112 arrived with the Brentford–Merehead empty iron ore tipplers. This train was held on the down main for line clearance. No. 50049 *Defiance* then sped through on the up main at 07.39 on time with the 05.10 Plymouth–Paddington. At 07.44, another stone train arrived off the East Somerset branch and took the up main line to Westbury, this being the Merehead–Botley formed of air braked 'Procors' and hauled by No. 46014. The Brentford–Merehead empties which had been held on the down main awaiting the passage of the 05.10 ex-Plymouth and the Merehead–Botley, then departed along the branch at 07.45.

There was a brief respite for the signalman, but not for long, as at 08.20, the 05.45 Plymouth–Old Oak Common empty coaching stock sped through with No. 1011 *Western Thunderer* giving a toot on the horn whilst passing the box. The 07.20 Weymouth–Bristol three-car dmu, running one minute late, ran through at 08.58. No. 50028 *Tiger*, running two minutes early with the 05.05 Penzance–Paddington, came hard on the heels of the dmu at 09.07. Levers were then pulled for the branch as a Merehead–Westbury trip working (tipplers) arrived at 09.08 behind No. 47112. The train was put into the loop to await line clear and departed at 09.13. No. 46014 arrived at 09.09 with a Westbury–Merehead trip working (tipplers), the train was placed on the up main whilst the branch was cleared as the 07.30 ex-Paddington was running tight behind. The Westbury–Merehead departed along the branch at 09.16. No. 50002 *Superb*, running five minutes late with the 07.30 Paddington–Plymouth rushed through at 09.21. The 07.30 ex-Paddington, had been slowed by a distant signal check at Blatchbridge Junction and as a result had lost three minutes to Witham. No. 1055 *Western Advocate* ran through right on time at 09.45 with the 07.53 Paignton–Paddington. No. 50047 *Swiftsure* passed through on time at 09.56 with the 07.45 Kensington–St Austell car carrier. No. 1010 *Western Campaigner* whistled through at 10.27 running two minutes late with the 08.30 Paddington–Penzance. No. 46014 hauling air braked 'Procors' arrived from the branch with the Merehead–Fareham at 10.27 and ran off the branch direct to the up main and not via the loop. The Westbury–Cranmore bitumen tanks arrived at 10.40 behind No. 25158, which was put into the down sidings and departed along the branch at 11.01. No. 1057 *Western Chieftain* running five and a half minutes late with the 06.35 Penzance–Paddington passed the box at 11.00½. No. 1025 *Western Guardsman*, running two and a half minutes early, powered the 09.30 Paddington–Penzance through at 11.06½. *Western Guardsman* was on top form this day as it had passed Woodborough at 10.42, and Fairwood Junction at 10.54, (8 minutes early). The journey from Paddington to Fairwood Junction, a distance of 97 miles, had taken 84 minutes. The section from Witham to Castle Cary, a distance of 8¾ miles was made in 8½ minutes, one minute early. The 08.40 Old Oak Common–Plymouth empty coaching stock hauled by No. 1049 *Western Monarch* passed the box at 11.17. This train had used the Westbury avoiding line and followed the 09.05 Cardiff–Weymouth to Clink Junction, and then used the Frome avoiding line to overtake the Cardiff train which used the old line to run into Frome. The 09.05 Cardiff–Weymouth passed Witham at 11.27, running four minutes late hauled by

No. 47008 which was standing in for a three-car dmu. The next up train was the 10.05 Weymouth–Bristol running to time at 11.33 with No. 47097. This train was normally worked by a Class 31. The 09.55 Paignton–Paddington running two minutes early, passed through at 11.50 powered by No. 50020 *Revenge*.

No. 50050 *Fearless* headed the 10.30 Paddington–Penzance running through 1½ minutes early at 12.16½. The Brentford–Merehead arrived at 12.50 headed by a Class 47 and waited in the loop until 13.20 for the Cranmore tanks to clear the branch. The 11.30 Paddington–Penzance running a staggering eleven minutes early with No. 47129 screamed through at 12.52. This train was usually worked by either a Class 50 or 52, and had suffered no delays and picked up all 'recovery time'. Another up train, this time the 08.45 Penzance–Paddington running through at 12.54, two minutes late with No. 1022 *Western Sentinel*. An 11.45 Bristol–Yeovil parcels special headed by No. 31296 powered through at 12.59. No. 46014 arrived at 13.13 with the 12.20 Westbury–Merehead (tipplers, set 7683) terminated 38 wagons in the 'down' sidings. The ex-Cranmore bitumen tanks headed by No. 25158 arrived at the branch home signal at 13.11, reversed to the 'up' sidings at 13.17 and branch clear. And at 13.16 No. 47027 sped through Witham two minutes early hauling the 11.00 Plymouth–Paddington. A three-car dmu comprising the 12.08 Bristol–Weymouth rattled through at 13.31. The Westbury–Merehead trip waited at the down home signal from 13.37 until 13.45, ready to cross. Another three-car dmu, the 12.15pm Weymouth–Bristol, passed through at 13.39. No. 46014 departed ex-'down' siding at 13.40 light engine to Westbury. Followed at 13.44 by No. 25158 departing from the up siding and running light engine to Frome. No. 50048 *Dauntless* headed the 11.55 Paignton–Paddington through Witham at 13.56 running one minute early. (Although the Class 50s did not receive nameplates until 1978, I have included their names for interest.)

Adrian Vaughan, now relieved at 2 o'clock by his opposite number on the late shift, gathered his kit together and after sharing a cup of tea and having a chat with his fellow signalman headed home for a well earned dinner. This is a story of just one signal box out of many. Pulling heavy signal levers is no job for the unfit especially in a busy box. Nowadays there is no signal box or lower quadrant signals at Witham, no sounds of block bells or the slam of levers in the frame resounding from the open windows of the box followed by the rattle of the signal wires and the clatter of the signal arms. Main line trains still speed through today, and the branch is busy with the Merehead stone trains and the junction is known today as East Somerset Junction and is controlled by the Westbury Power box.

Brewham Signal Box
122 miles 46 chains from Paddington
Opened 20th March 1907
Signal box burnt down 24th July 1947
New box opened 17th August 1947
Engine siding taken out of use on 19th December 1963
Signal box closed 25th October 1996

Standing alongside the down main line at the top of the gruelling ascent from Castle Cary, Brewham signal box was a favourite haunt of photographers in the days of steam, expecially during the busy summer Saturdays. Every type of ex-GWR locomotive would be seen

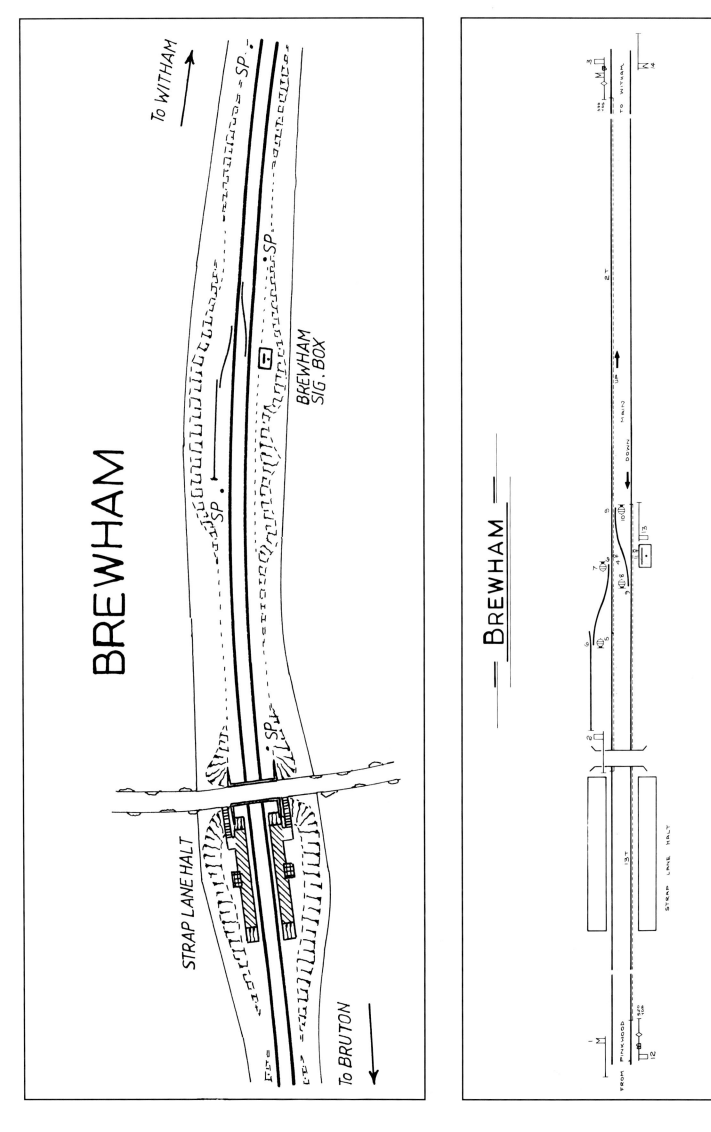

heading trains to and from the West of England, gleaming 'Kings' and 'Castles' would dominate the main express services intermingled with members of the 'Hall', 'Manor', 'Grange', 'County', and Mogul classes. As the up line lower quadrant signals would lower with a clang, the coughing bark of a straining engine would be heard in the distance. The sound of the pounding exhaust would grow louder with a plume of smoke and steam shooting skywards, camera shutters would click many times over as with a rear and perhaps a shriek on the whistle, the train with its pounding engine at its head would blast under the road bridge. With gathering speed it would run down the bank to Witham with the driver easing the reverser back, and the sweating fireman leaning over the side of the cab would be thankful for a breath of fresh air and a brief respite from his labours. Down trains would roar past the box and accelerate down the winding five miles descent to Castle Cary.

Brewham signal box was opened on 20th March 1907 and was equipped with nine levers, but this was increased to 14 in 1920. An engine siding for the use of the banking engines whilst awaiting a path back down the bank was situated alongside the up main line. There was also a crossover between the up and down lines to allow banking engines to gain the down line and return to Castle Cary after banking an up train. The box was destroyed by fire on 24th July 1947, and a new box, equipped with a second-hand 14-lever frame was re-opened on 17th August 1947. Box size 15ft 6in x 10ft x 7ft. Signalmen working the box at various times included: Norman Kibby, E. Kingdon and Ralph Bartlett. Norman Kibby recalls that when he was on early turn at the box he travelled on the empty stock from Yeovil. (Weymouth–Westbury) which in turn worked the 7.45am Westbury–Weymouth. This was one of the GWR AEC diesel railcars and stopped at the Yeovil Pen Mill home signal to pick up the railway workers that were waiting to travel to work. The railcar stopped at Strap Lane Halt in order for Norman to alight and walk the short distance to the halt. Point to point timings for bank engines running light were: Brewham–Castle Cary 14 minutes, Brewham–Westbury 28 minutes. The engine siding was taken out of use on 19th December 1963 and the number of levers reduced to nine. Box closed and crossover taken out of use on 25th October 1966.

'Castle' class No. 7017 *G. J. Churchward* storms past Brewham signal box at 11.04am on 2nd July 1955 with the second part of the 'down' 'Channel Islands Boat Express'. The first part had passed Brewham at 10.51am with No. 6923 *Croxteth Hall* at the head. The ground disc signal to the left controls the exit from the engine siding.

R. C. Riley

No. 7917 *North Aston Hall*, with a touch of steam issuing from the cylinder chest, approaches Brewham at 11.13am with the 8.30am Weston-super-Mare–Weymouth on 2nd July 1955.

R. C. Riley

No. 6902 *Butlers Hall* breasts the summit at Brewham on 9th July 1956 with the 4.05pm Weymouth–Paddington.　　　*R. C. Riley*

No. 7004 *Eastnor Castle* heads the 3.40pm Weymouth Quay–Paddington 'Channel Islands Boat Express' through Brewham at 5.18pm on 9th July 1956. The sharp ascent of Brewham bank can be gauged by the coaches at the rear of the train as they breast the summit.

R. C. Riley

No. 5978 *Bodinnick Hall* runs under the road bridge at Brewham with the 5.25pm Westbury–Weymouth on 9th July 1956. This train will be conveying coaches for Weymouth slipped from the 3.30pm ex-Paddington at Heywood Road Junction.

R. C. Riley

'King' class No. 6009 *King Charles II* with a fair bit of steam drifting from the cylinders, thunders under the road bridge at Brewham on 2nd July 1957 with the 8.30am Plymouth–Paddington. The ground disc signal to the far right, gives access to the engine siding.

R. C. Riley

No. 5006 *Tregenna Castle* heads the 8.50am Paddington–Paignton past Brewham on 2nd July 1955. No. 5006 was built to Lot 234 in June 1927 and was withdrawn in 1962. The ground signal between the main lines controlled the crossover enabling the banking engines to regain the 'down' main line in order to travel back to Castle Cary.

R. C. Riley

'King' class No. 6012 *King Edward VI* runs past Brewham signal box at 5.45pm with the 3.30pm Paddington–Penzance on 9th July 1956. The train has slipped its Weymouth portion at Heywood Road Junction and this portion will be attached to the 4.25pm Bristol–Weymouth at Westbury.

R. C. Riley

Sheephouse crossing on 21st March 1965. Located between Brewham and Bruton on the Brewham bank, the crossing was notorious for several close shaves between farm vehicles using the crossing and trains descending the bank at a fast rate, despite warning bells and other safeguards!

C. L. Caddy

Strap Lane Halt

122 miles 54 chains from Paddington
Opened 18th July 1932
Closed 6th October 1941
Re-opened 16th December 1946
Finally closed 5th June 1950

Strap Lane Halt opened on 18th July 1932 and was one of 14 halts and platforms constructed by the GWR in 1932. The halt was provided with two timber built platforms and was served mainly by the auto fitted trains on the Westbury–Taunton services. It was closed on 6th October 1951 re-opening on 16th December 1946, and finally closing on 5th June 1950.

Pinkwood Signal Box

Opened 4th July 1934
Closed 5th February 1940

Situated alongside the 'up' main line between Brewham and Bruton, Pinkwood signal box was a break section box, opened on 4th July 1934 with a six-lever frame. The box had a short life as it was taken out of use on 5th February 1940.

Bruton

126 miles 8 chains from Paddington
Opened 1st September 1856
Gauge conversion 18th/22nd June 1874
Signal Box opened May 1877
Line doubled Bruton–Castle Cary 1880
Closed to Goods Traffic 5th April 1965
Signal box closed 7th December 1983
Unstaffed Halt from 6th October 1969

Bruton station is situated on the eastern end of the ten mile long Brewham bank with gradients of 1 in 93 on the eastern end, and 1 in 98 westward. It was at first one of the crossing places on the then single track broad gauge line, the passing loop was rarely used with most trains using the up platform. The station was provided with up and down platforms having substantial stone buildings with small canopies. An accident at Bruton on 28th June 1865 highlighted the need for interlocking points and signals. Let us now look at Bruton in 1865 from the official report of the accident.

Bruton in 1865, nine years after its opening, and according to the report, was occasionally used as a passing place for up and down trains, although not intended to be so used when the line was built, and the down platform was seldom used. The down platform was situated alongside a siding which was entered by a pair of facing points placed a short distance to the north of the station platforms, and trains which entered this siding could only return to the main line by reversing back over the same points through which they had entered the siding, or by running ahead some 160 yards along the siding. It then had to be shunted back by another pair of points, south of the station platforms, which also presented facing points to a down train. There was also another siding lying west of the single line, passing through the goods shed, and terminating about 190 yards to the south of the facing points on the single line opposite to the up platform by which the siding was entered. The end of this siding was close to the turnpike road leading from Bruton to Wincanton, which crosses under the railway, the roadway being somewhere about 25ft below the level of the railway. Wooden buffers supported by props were placed at the south end of this siding, and a quantity of stone was also placed behind the buffers so as to increase the amount of resistance in the event of wagons or trucks being shunted too violently against them. Thus, there were three facing points against a down train, but no facing points against an up train.

On the evening in question, the 4.50pm down train from London, due at Bruton at 8.42pm arrived at 8.44pm. A carriage truck was taken off the train, and when the train had departed, the policeman on duty, James Andrews proceeded to put the truck into the siding (the up siding) lying west of the single line. He unlocked the padlock, opened the facing points opposite to the up platform and, assisted by the goods porter, put the truck out of the way, against the south end of the up platform. At that time there was a loaded flour truck standing under the goods shed and three empty timber trucks at the south end of the siding close against the buffers. The policeman, Andrews, who was then in sole charge of the station, according to his own statement, then went down to the gate at the entrance of the yard and locked it. Thence he returned to the office and telegraphed "line clear" to Witham Friary station 5½ miles north of Bruton for a ballast train to proceed. Then he received a telegraphic message from Castle Cary station three miles south of Bruton that the line was clear for the ballast train as far as that station. He then went and lit the down signal lamps and turned them to "all right" for the ballast train

Bruton, looking west on 27th October 1962 showing the picturesque station buildings. The main building containing the station offices stands upon the 'up' platform to the right. Nicely pruned bushes and carefully tended flower beds show the pride that the staff took in their station.

C. L. Caddy

— BRUTON —

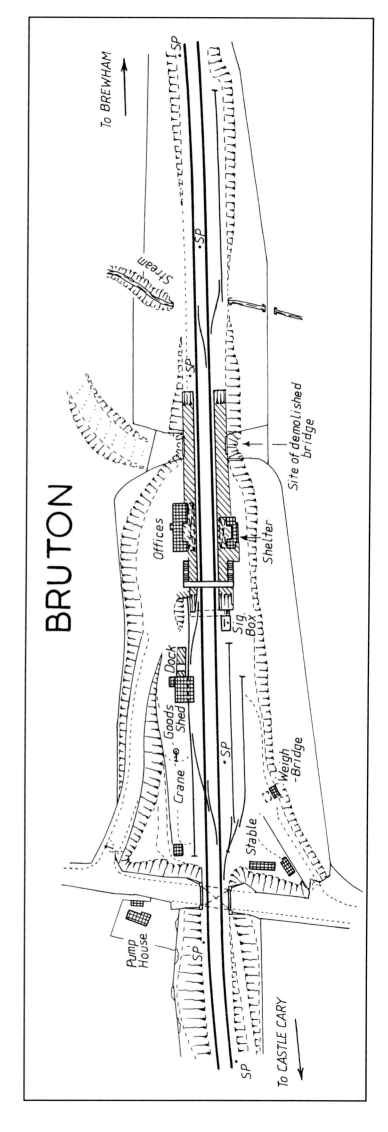

DETONATORS WORKED BY
SMALL 2-LEVER FRAME

© SIGNALLING RECORD SOCIETY

J.P.M. 7.7.76

GOODS SHED

DOWN SIDINGS

TO PINK WOOD

DOWN REFUGE SIDING

UP

DOWN MAIN

FROM WYKE

BRUTON

To BREWHAM

Stream

Site of demolished bridge

Offices

Goods Shed

Dock

Crane

Sig. Box

Shelter

Stable

Weigh-Bridge

Pump House

To CASTLE CARY

Looking east through Bruton station, showing the line rising towards Brewham. The station buildings complete with their attractive awnings are roughly of equal size which was unusual on stations constructed on the Westbury–Weymouth line. The ground shunt disc signal in the foreground controls the entrance to the goods shed.

Lens of Sutton

coming from the north to pass, thence he went and examined the facing points north of the platforms. Next he fetched the lamps for the up signals out of the lamp house, and examined the southmost pair of facing points, and then returned to the station building. (Although Andrews had examined the north and south points, he had, for some reason not examined the middle pair of points leading to the up siding. The scene is now set for disaster.)

At 9.55pm, Andrews received a telegraphic signal from Witham Friary station that the ballast train had left for Bruton. He then lit his hand lamp and stood on the up platform until the ballast train came into sight and showed a "white light" or "all right" signal towards it. The ballast train approached the up platform at 35 miles an hour, according to the policeman, or at 15 or 16 mph according to the under guard who was in a van at the tail of the train. When the train came to the facing middle points at the up platform it took the same course as the carriage truck had been pushed along, and passed into the siding lying west of the single line, first striking the truck loaded with flour standing under the goods shed with a crash. Someone on the engine having sounded the "brake" whistle just before doing so, thence the ballast train pushed the flour truck and the empty timber trucks against the buffers, sweeping everything before it, and it fell crashing down into the turnpike road below. The flour truck landed beyond the opposite wing wall of the under bridge, the engine falling against that wing wall and breaking it down, and then rolling over on to its right side. The tender was doubled up against the engine, nine of the loaded ballast wagons came off the rails and falling over the engine, tender, and timber trucks, filling up the space with a heap of ruins. Four trucks and a van of the ballast train remained above on the siding, and the sunken road was described by one of the witnesses as being full. The engine driver, Alfred White, and his fireman, Radford Bartlett were killed on the spot, but strange to say the head guard and the fitter, a one legged man, who were riding in the ballast truck next to the tender, lying down in the truck, escaped with their lives. The under guard and seven of the ballast men who were in the van at the tail of the train also escaped unhurt, with some of the ballast men who were inside the van being awakened from sleep some time after the accident had occurred! The engine was severely damaged and the tender almost destroyed, and the same may be said of the trucks which were precipitated into the road below the line. At the subsequent inquiry, Colonel Yolland presiding, made the following remarks which have been condensed from the original transcript:

"It points out as clearly as possible the absolute necessity of not depending solely on the recollection of a single man, and the expediency of contriving by mechanical means that in all cases no accident of this kind shall be possible without giving the drivers and firemen on engines a chance of providing for their own safety. Facing points on single lines cannot be avoided. On narrow-gauge lines they are usually self-acting and weighted so as to close of themselves when the lever handle is let go, and then stand right for the main line. On the broad-gauge system of railways self-acting points have always been objected to. I have always considered that this was a mistake; but recent improvements have enabled facing points to be made comparatively safe, by working them in connection with the station signals without actually connecting them together."

"I am glad to learn that the directors of the Great Western Railway Company have already determined that the signals at this station shall be so fitted that when they are turned to "all right" the facing points must previously have been set right for the main line on which the train is to travel. It would also be desirable to add distant signals at Bruton station and all other stations at present not furnished with them. I believe the advantage of having them is fully recognised by the officers of the Great Western Railway."

The accident at Bruton led to the introduction of a simple form of ground lock which prevented the signal wire being pulled unless the points were correctly set. The locks were mostly used on single lines, and were superseded when point and signal levers were concentrated in locking frames, to reappear later in an improved form as the additional safeguards called detectors. The policeman, Andrews, said to be a steady man, and attentive to his duty for which he had been employed for some 15 and 16 months was held responsible for the accident and sent for trial to Salisbury Assizes on the count of manslaughter. He was then found guilty and committed to Wells prison.

The small signal box situated off the down platform at the Castle Cary end was opened in May 1877. The box was re-framed to 25 levers with 4-stud interlocking in October 1909. Box size, 13ft x 11ft 6in. The box was

The signal box at Bruton standing off the end of the 'down' platform on 26th April 1970. Measuring 13ft x 11ft 6in, this was one of the smallest boxes on the line at the time of its closure in 1983.

C. L. Caddy

Bruton, looking west under the footbridge on 21st March 1965. The main line can be seen dipping away towards Castle Cary under the over-bridge in the distance. The signal box stands off the end of the 'down' platform and a solitary box van occupies the former broad gauge goods shed – the very goods shed through which the 'down' ballast train travelled to its doom on 28th June 1865.

C. L. Caddy

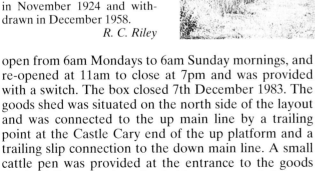

Prairic tank No 4572 has left Bruton station and now heads down the bank to the next stop at Castle Cary with the 5.44pm Westbury–Castle Cary local service on 9th July 1956. No. 4572 was built to Lot 226 in November 1924 and with-drawn in December 1958.

R. C. Riley

open from 6am Mondays to 6am Sunday mornings, and re-opened at 11am to close at 7pm and was provided with a switch. The box closed 7th December 1983. The goods shed was situated on the north side of the layout and was connected to the up main line by a trailing point at the Castle Cary end of the up platform and a trailing slip connection to the down main line. A small cattle pen was provided at the entrance to the goods shed, while a cast iron footbridge connected the two platforms. Sidings were also provided behind the signal box on the down side of the station. These sidings were revised c1912; the down refuge siding which was situated to the north of the down platform having been extended in September 1896 and further extended in October 1906 and was lifted in December 1963.

The track through the goods shed and its connection with the up main line was removed in 1965, the same year as the withdrawal of goods traffic. All sidings had been removed by 1965. As with all stations along the line, the staff took pride in their job with the hedges on

Bruton, looking west, as Class 47/0 No. 47297 propels an engineers ballast train plus a 'Shark' brake van slowly through the station on 10th January 1988, working from Castle Cary to engineering work north of Bruton. The goods shed has been replaced by a modern version, and note the four-aspect colour light signal standing on the 'down' platform, as well as the space off the platform end previously occupied by Bruton signal box.

Peter Nicholson

Bruton, looking east a few minutes later on 10th January 1988 as No. 47297 propels its engineers train along the 'up' line for an engineering working north of the station. The former WS&W station buildings have been demolished and replaced by bus stop basic shelters.

Peter Nicholson

the platforms being carefully clipped and the flowerbeds tended regularly. As with most of the WS&W stations no main line West of England trains stopped here as this was left to certain Weymouth line trains and local auto services. The station was down-rated to an unstaffed halt from 9th October 1969. During the days of steam, the platforms would quiver as train after train pounded through the station whilst climbing the bank, leaving a stream of steam and smoke hanging over the station with the distinctive GWR signals clattering to 'danger' after the passage of each train. The passing of a down West of England express train would be a sight not to be forgotten. The lowering of the down side signals would be followed by a momentary silence, then in the distance would come the faint sound of a whistle, the rails would start to quiver then a with a roar and a panting from the exhaust, a gleaming 'King' or 'Castle' with a long train

of coaches, would thunder through the station hammering down the bank towards Castle Cary. Nowadays, High Speed Trains thunder through the platforms and present day services stopping at Bruton are comprised of two-car 'Sprinters' on the Weymouth line service. The station buildings have been demolished and replaced by 'Bus stop' basic shelters.

Wyke Signal Box
128 miles from Paddington
Opened 28th June 1934
Closed 4th December 1955

Wyke signal box was another one of the break section boxes lying two miles west of Bruton and was sited alongside the down main line, just west of the Somerset & Dorset overbridge. The six-lever box was opened on 28th June 1934 and closed on 4th December 1955.

No. 5067 *St Fagans Castle*, with just a hint of smoke from her chimney, suggesting that the fireman is putting a few rounds of coal around the firebox for the climb to Brewham, approaches the S&D overbridge near Cole with the 11.00am Paignton–Paddington relief on 9th June 1962.

C. L. Caddy

No. 5003 *Lulworth Castle* approaches the local platelayers' hut and heads onto the bank near Cole with the 6.55am Penzance–Paddington weekday train in place of a diesel on Thursday, 15th July 1961. No. 5003 was built to Lot 234 in May 1927 and withdrawn in August 1962.

John Day

No. 7018 *Drysllwyn Castle* races under the S&D flyover near Cole with the 10.10am Paddington–Penzance pre-summer relief on 9th June 1962.

C. L. Caddy

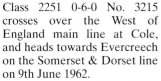

Class 2251 0-6-0 No. 3215 crosses over the West of England main line at Cole, and heads towards Evercreech on the Somerset & Dorset line on 9th June 1962.

C. L. Caddy

No. 6949 *Haberfield Hall* tackles Brewham bank at Cole on 2nd July 1955 with the 11.50am Weymouth–Westbury empty stock. No. 6949 was renumbered 3955 and converted to oil burning in May 1947, although this was a short lived scheme and the locomotive was re-converted and provided with its original number in April 1949.

R. C. Riley

No. 6008 *King James II* runs down the bank at Cole with the 'Cornish Riviera Express' on 2nd July 1955. The 'down' Castle Cary distant signal can be seen in the 'off' position at the rear of the train.

R. C. Riley

No. D1003 *Western Pioneer* streaks along the 'up' main line at Cole between Castle Cary and Bruton with the 7.30am Plymouth–Paddington on 8th September 1962. No. D1003 arrived twelve minutes late at Paddington, and returned later in the day with the 2.30pm Paddington–Penzance.

John Day

North British Type 4 B–B No. D842 *Royal Oak* powers the 'up' 'Mayflower' through the lush Somerset countryside between Castle Cary and Bruton on 16th June 1962. No. D842 was introduced to traffic in December 1960, and was cut up at Swindon in March 1972.

John Day

Castle Cary

129 miles 46 chains from Paddington
Opened 1st September 1856
Gauge conversion 18th/22nd June 1874
Line doubled Witham–Castle Cary 1880
Line doubled Castle Cary–Yeovil Pen Mill 1881
Signal box (1) opened May 1877, closed 11th April 1905
Signal box (2) opened 11th April 1905.
Signal box (2) destroyed by enemy action 3rd
   September 1942
Signal box (temporary) opened 5th September
   1942–27th October 1942
Signal box (3) opened 27th October 1942
Line opened Castle Cary–Cogload Junction 11th June
   1906 (Goods)
Line opened Castle Cary–Cogload Junction 2nd July
   1906 (Passenger)
Station closed to goods 3rd October 1966
Line singled Castle Cary–Yeovil Pen Mill 12th May 1968
Signal box closed 3rd February 1985

Castle Cary station, lying at the foot of the Brewham bank, was opened on 1st September 1856 and was initially provided with a passing loop on the then single broad gauge line. The pleasing stone built station buildings were built to the style of Brereton who was responsible for the design of most of the stations between Frome and Maiden Newton. The main buildings are grouped on the up platform, with a shelter on the down platform. After the gauge conversion in 1874 the line from Witham to Castle Cary was doubled in 1880 and to Yeovil in 1881. A signal box was opened in May 1877, and was situated on the Yeovil end of the down platform. In 1888 the shortest journey times between Paddington and Weymouth via Swindon were achieved in 4 hours and 45 minutes for first and second class travel only, with the best third class timings taking five hours. By 1900 this had been accelerated to 4 hours 15 minutes. In the summer of 1901 three new express services using the route from Newbury and the new Stert Valley line were put on to the Weymouth line and the best of these made the journey in 3 hours and 40 minutes. By 1912 the best service achieved the journey in 3 hours and 10 minutes.

With the opening of the new 'cut off' line in 1906, thus raising the status of Castle Cary to an important junction on the West of England main line, various improvements were made to the station and layout. The original signal box was found to be too small to work the new junction and was closed on 4th April 1905 and replaced on the same date by a new box situated nearer the junction, alongside the up main line. The new box was equipped with a 55-lever frame but it was destroyed by enemy action in 1942, of which more anon. Although with the opening of the new cut off line to Taunton, many main line express trains began to use the new route to the West and the line became busy with the growth in traffic, not one of the West of England trains stopped at any of the former WS&W stations. A steam railmotor service operating between Westbury and Taunton stopping at all stations began in 1906. The duties were worked by Frome and Taunton crews, and the steam rail motors were replaced in time by auto fitted rail motors. Westbury crews also worked the services from July 1922.

Water columns were to be found at the ends of the up and down platforms. The 10-ton crane, goods shed, and sidings serving the local traders, were situated behind the signal box. Vast amounts of coal were delivered by rail to the well known local firm of Snows who operated their coal delivery service from the goods yard, and the also equally well known firm of agricultural merchants, Messrs Bibby and Co. received large deliveries of cattle cake and feed delivered by the railway, and shipped onwards by lorry to the local farms. The railway lorries also operated a delivery service from the goods shed to the local farms and businesses. There was a refuge siding situated to the north of the down platform alongside the down main line, another

Castle Cary, looking east on 17th March 1962. The main buildings are grouped on the 'up' platform to the left. The backing signal standing to the left on the Weymouth end of the 'up' platform has a display case with a stencil which could route three ways (see page 32). Water columns were provided on both platforms, while the nameboard reads: 'Castle Cary junction for Somerton, Langport & Taunton'.

C. L. Caddy

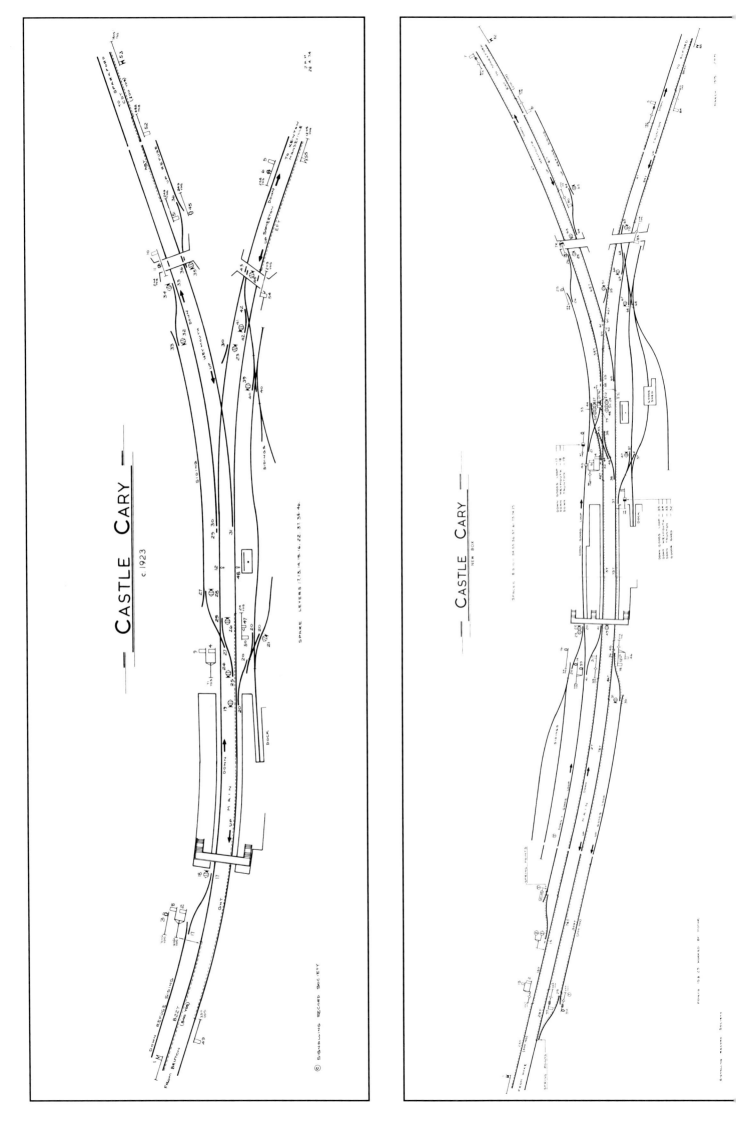

CASTLE CARY

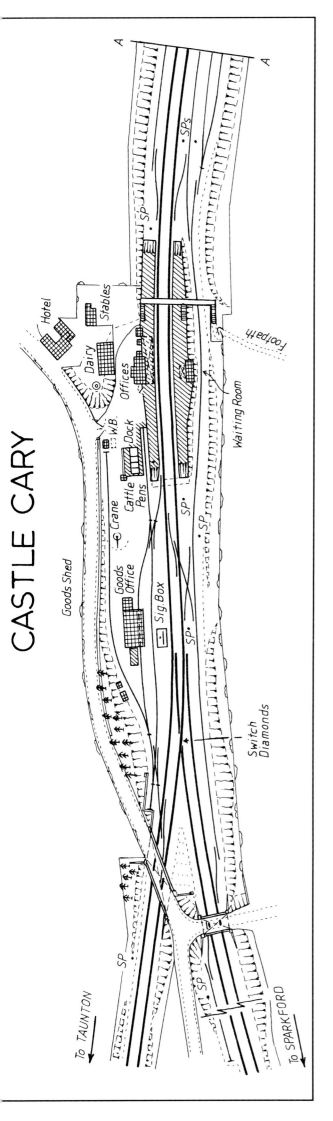

To TAUNTON

Goods Shed

Hotel

Stables

Dairy

Offices

W.B.

Crane

Dock

Cattle Pens

Goods Office

Sig. Box

Waiting Room

Footpath

Switch Diamonds

SP

SPs

SP

SP

SP

To SPARKFORD

A   A

A   A

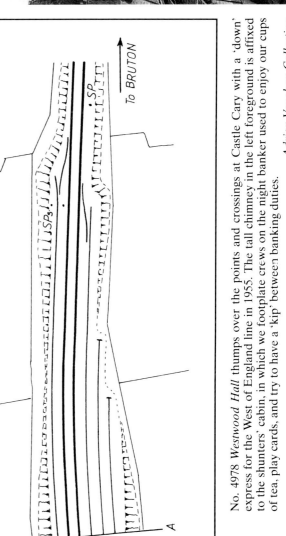

To BRUTON

SP

SPs

SP

A

A

No. 4978 *Westwood Hall* thumps over the points and crossings at Castle Cary with a 'down' express for the West of England line in 1955. The tall chimney in the left foreground is affixed to the shunters' cabin, in which we footplate crews on the night banker used to enjoy our cups of tea, play cards, and try to have a 'kip' between banking duties.

Adrian Vaughan Collection

The crew of pannier tank No. 8744 take a breather whilst standing on the 'down' refuge at Castle Cary on 22nd July 1958 before working their two coach 'B' set ('the tram') to Taunton on the all stations stopping service.

R. C. Riley

No. 6803 *Bucklebury Grange* minus nameplates, takes to the Weymouth line at Castle Cary on 3rd July 1965 with the 10.45 Wolverhampton–Weymouth. No. 6803 was withdrawn in September of the same year.

R. C. Riley

refuge siding south of the down platform alongside the down Weymouth line, and an up refuge siding alongside the up Weymouth line south of the road bridge. Other sidings and loops were installed in 1941 and 1943.

Footplate Memories of Castle Cary

The Durston Goods and The Cary Bankers

As well as the evening Hendford Goods to Westbury freight working, we also had two more duties working from Yeovil Town shed involving Castle Cary. For the Durston goods we booked on shed at 7.55am and after finding our engine which was already prepared, we would set off light engine for Castle Cary. This would be either a pannier or a 55xx Prairie tank. Upon arrival at Cary we would stop at the Yeovil end of the up platform, where the backing signal had a stencil which could show three routes. These were, Goods Shed, Taunton, or Wey. We would normally get the Taunton in which case we would reverse along the main line and stop just past the bridge and when the ground signal (or dummy as it is known) would show clear we would trundle forward into the goods yard and sort out the wagons that the shunter wanted moving. This would comprise shunting the empty coal wagons out of the way, and loaded ones into their place, and moving box vans into and out of the goods shed, plus forming our own train for the trip to Durston. It was not a hard

duty by any means as the goods yard was small. The junction would be a fascinating place especially during the summer months when the 'hard hitters' like the 'Kings' and 'Castles' were roaring through to and from the West plus the trains on the busy Weymouth line. All this plus the freight workings made Castle Cary a busy junction. The local Taunton to Castle Cary service known as the 'Tram' would appear, usually with a pannier or a large Prairie tank engine hauling a two-coach B set. The engine would run around and take water and would then stand out of the way whilst the crew had a bite to eat before returning to Taunton.

With the impact of the diesels it was that strange transition period on the Western Region that witnessed steam and the early 'Warships' and 'Western' diesels working side by side. It was fascinating seeing the various shades of paintwork that the 'Western' class used to appear in and I have seen all of the experimental colours whilst shunting at Cary; golden ochre, desert sand, maroon, brunswick green, they all appeared running through the junction with groups of inspectors, etc. in the cabs. The Sulzer prototype, *Lion* also appeared one day creating a small sensation in its all white livery. Whilst talking about the diesels I well remember when the stars of the day, the 'Beatles', were filming *A Hard Day's Night* aboard a train. The word got around the station that the special was belled off Bruton. My driver and I trooped up into the signal box to try to catch a glimpse of the 'fab four' as the train approached. We leant out of the box windows as the train sped through headed by a 'Western' diesel, but as most of the windows had the blinds drawn we drew a blank that day.

After we had completed our shunting duties, we would then form our train which would vary from a few wagons to a maximum of 15 or 20 plus the guard's brakevan depending on the day's traffic requirements. We would then set off down the West of England main line, shunting at all of the stations and yards. On one occasion we had a ballast wagon added to our train from Cary. The PW gang climbed aboard the brakevan and we had instructions to stop at Alford Halt. I well remember that it was a warm summer's day as we plodded along with our Prairie tank steaming away with our small train of wagons in tow. The Alford distant signal appeared ahead at caution and my mate shut off steam and we stopped at the designated spot for the unloading of the ballast. The gang climbed down from the brakevan complete with their lunchbags, shovels and picks. The chutes were opened on the ballast wagon, and as we moved slowly forward the ballast rattled down alongside the track until the wagon was emptied. The chutes were screwed shut and with a toot on the whistle we set off again on our journey. When we reached Somerton we would stay there for a while in order for some of the fast down trains to pass. Then, when our path was clear on the main line we would set off again, and when we arrived at Athelney we would traverse the single line to Durston which was situated on the Bristol–Taunton main line. This station was just as busy as Castle Cary with many fast trains passing through. After taking water and shunting the up and down yards we would set off on our return journey to Castle Cary with more wagons. Upon arrival we would leave our wagons in the up yard ready to be picked up by the evening Hendford–Westbury goods and then depart light engine to Yeovil, arriving at the Town shed about 5pm, book off and cycle home for tea.

Night Banking at Castle Cary

We used to book on at 7.55pm for this duty. The engine would be standing already prepared for us, the locomotives used on the banker at various times including: 2-6-2 Prairie tanks, Nos 4507, 5548 or 5563, and 0-6-0 pannier tanks Nos 3671, 3733, 8745 and 9764 amongst many others. This night we had Prairie No. 5548 and we set off for Castle Cary travelling light engine. Upon arrival there was no freight train standing in the up loop waiting for our services so we reversed into the up goods yard and stopped behind the shunters' cabin which stood next to the signal box. The boiler was filled up and the fire banked under the firedoors in order to keep the engine quiet. The night banking at Castle Cary varied, and sometimes we were kept busy most of the night, or at other times I have known the banker to be used only once. One could never guarantee what was going to turn up next. After banking the fire up and turning the injector off, my mate went up into the signal box to have a yarn with the signalman and find out what freight trains if any, needed banking. I was left with instructions to make a can of tea in the shunters' cabin and armed with my billy can, milk and tea, I climbed down from our engine, entered the cabin and made the tea from the boiling kettle. The cabin was the pinnacle of luxury compared to some I have known. The seats were from old carriages and cushions were spread along the length of the building, newspapers adorned the wooden table in the centre, and the cabin was warmed by the coal stove. I made the tea and had just poured it out when my mate came in and said, "there is one on the way, but he hasn't reached Somerton yet". The door opened and the shunter entered, took one look at my steaming 'billy can' and helped himself to a mug of tea. We were soon nattering away, as railwaymen do, my mate and I had our fags and were puffing away, whilst the shunter lit his old pipe, and the cabin was soon reeking of 'Old Holborn' and 'Dark Twist'. There was a rattle as the signal box windows were opened and the signalman shouted out "freight off Somerton, needs the banker". The windows rattled shut, and that was it, end of tea break.

Aboard 5548 I stirred the fire with the long handled pricker, and with just a touch on the blower the pressure gauge started to climb. The cab was lit with a bright orange glow as the fire sparked and crackled, and by the glow of the gauge lamp I could see the water bobbing up and down in the gauge glass. We were now ready for our first customer when there was a loud rumbling accompanied by the sound of escaping steam as a 28xx 2-8-0 'Long Tom' passed the box. The white hot glow of the firebox reflected against our engine, then wagon after wagon went by with buffers

Castle Cary signal box in 1974. This is the wartime (1942) replacement for the previous bomb damaged box. Measuring 42ft 10in x 12ft x 11ft it was built with local bricks from the nearby Evercreech brickworks.

John Morris

The interior of Castle Cary signal box in October 1984. As with all boxes it is neat and tidy; note the signalman's brushes standing in the middle of the frame. Originally equipped with an 85-lever frame, the number of levers had decreased by the time that this picture had been taken.

M. Marshall

Passengers waiting for their respective trains at Castle Cary, watch as 'Britannia' Pacific No. 70017 *Arrow* heads the 9.20am St Ives–Paddington through the station on 2nd July 1955.

R. C. Riley

clanking as the train braked. Finally, with its wheels squealing from the force of the guard's brake, the brakevan with its red lamps and a curl of smoke from the guard's fire appeared and stopped at the end of the platform. The dummy went to green at the far end of the yard and we reversed out under the bridge onto the up main, another dummy went to green ahead of us and we moved forward and buffered up to the waiting train. The guard appeared and took our number, and it was time to take our headlamp off in accordance with regulations. There was no need to couple up as Brewham box was still switched in, but when Brewham was switched out at 10pm we had to bank as far as Witham, and then we would have to couple up. The freight train we were banking would come to a stand at Witham in order for us to uncouple and return to Castle Cary. Way up ahead green signal lamps twinkled away in the darkness, "are you ready my boy?" my mate shouted out across the cab I nodded – we had plenty of steam. Although with certain tank engines, the engine up front had more steam than we could muster on certain nights.

The sound of our whistle, giving the banker's call, resounded around the empty platforms of the station, and far up ahead in the inky darkness came the answering call from the 'Long Tom'. We started to

move, slowly at first as the long train of freight wagons began to move, and I shut the firedoors to keep the cold air from blasting onto the fire. The driver gave the engine more regulator and at the same time eased the reverser back, and our engine shook as we took the weight of the train. The Prairies were prone to going down on their axleboxes when pulling away, but we were now moving at a faster pace with the wagon wheels rolling and banging away as we cleared the advanced starter which slammed to 'danger' in our wake. Up ahead the sky was lit up as the fireman of the 'Long Tom' tended his fire, then the glow was cut off as he closed his firedoors.

Now it was time to look into our firebox, and squinting my eyes at the fierce roaring glow, I dug the shovel into the bunker, pulled the firing flap down by its chain and thrust the shovelful of coal into the firebox under the door. Up with the flap, turn, then another shovelful, turn, down with the flap and into the back corners, until there was enough fire in the box for the moment. Sparks flew high into the sky as the regulator was opened wider, and the reverser went forward another notch. We slowed as the weight of the train went into the bank and my mate had his head hanging over the side listening to the beat of our engine. When he thought fit he gave the reverser another notch forward, the injector was turned on as the water in the gauge glass came down, and now was the chance to spray down the footplate and bunker as the coal dust swirled everywhere. We were holding our own for steam, although we did not have enough to lift the safety valves, but there was ample for the demands of the engine. Bruton distant signal appeared ahead in the clear position, and there was a brief respite through Bruton as the bank eased somewhat, but it did not last long as we hit the steepest part of the bank. Sparks were now flying higher and higher from our engine and the engine up front, and we were now at walking pace and pushing for all our worth. The engine up front was doing his best as well, with the glow of his firebox lighting up the way ahead. I kept the back corners of the firebox full as we climbed higher and higher and we were now at full regulator and the reverser was as forward as it would go. The engine was shuddering and shaking and the bark of the exhaust was almost enough to tear the chimney off. Brewham up distant appeared in the 'off' position, which was a good sign as the appearance of the signal meant that we were nearing the top of the bank.

With one last almighty push we topped the bank, my mate closed the regulator as we coasted under the overbridge and the orange glow from the Brewham signal box windows appeared to our right. The freight train was now gathering speed as it ran away into the night on its way to Westbury. We stopped just past the crossover and I left the injector singing away, climbed down and put the headlamp back onto the front buffer-beam. I put the red shade in as we would be running bunker first back to Castle Cary, and the red shade on our tail lamp on the bunker was now taken out and the lamp became our white headlamp. The dummy changed to green behind us and we moved over to the down road. The down main line signals were 'off' and we rattled down the bank to Castle Cary where, upon arrival we would replenish our water tanks. Providing there was not another up freight waiting for us in the up loop we would stable our engine in the goods yard again, shut the dampers, fill the boiler up to keep her quiet and await another train which required a banker.

During the few quiet spells during the night, my mate and I plus the shunter, would have a bit of a snooze in the warm cabin, and would be alerted that an up train was approaching and requiring the banker by the signalman dropping lumps of coal on the cabin roof. At certain times, an event used to occur which was part and parcel of the job. When an up goods was approaching Castle Cary, even if the crew needed a banker or not, the signalman would pull all up signals off. The reason for this being, that if an up train, with the crew confident enough with the engine, would like to have a run at the bank without stopping to pick up the banker, all well and good. The trouble being though, if we had been alerted to prepare for banking, we would climb aboard our engine, I would stir the fire up, and put a few rounds of coal around the firebox. So there we were on our engine waiting for the up goods, when all of a sudden, there would be a mighty roar, and the train that, 'so called' needed banking would tear past the signal box and roar through the station with the wagon wheels beating out a fast rhythm on the track heading for the bank as fast as the locomotive could go. That meant that our engine, now with a large fire burning away, would lift her safety valves, and this prevented any more 'snoozing' until the boiler level

dropped. The injector would then be turned on to knock back the boiler pressure.

Many years later, when I had left the railway service, I happened to meet a former driver from Taunton shed. Whilst talking about the old days, I mentioned the above story, and at this he started laughing. It appeared that Taunton men knew all about the banker crews at Castle Cary having a snooze, and after requesting a banker before leaving Taunton, they would fly through 'Cary going hell for leather, knowing full well that we would be standing ready for them! Another event that happened on a regular basis was the removal of wagons with 'hot boxes' from through freight trains. The train would come to a halt and we would shunt the train to remove the crippled wagon with its hot axlebox, I have seen axleboxes glowing red hot, and sometimes we would have to throw a bucket of water over the axlebox covers to stop the wagon catching fire. If the wagon was in the middle of the train as it often was, we had to perform quite a bit of shunting to split the train, and then shunt the wagon out of the way into one of the sidings and let the freight train continue its journey. After our night's efforts were over, we would set off light engine to Yeovil Town shed, leave the engine on the coal road, stroll across to the enginemens' cabin for a wash and brush up, a quick cup of tea, book off and head for home just as the cold light of dawn was streaking across the sky.

Banking Engines. Authorised Hours at Castle Cary. 1954 Winter Timetable

Engine No. 1. (Yeovil duty) Monday to Saturday, 6½ hours daily. Total of 33 hours per week. Ex-Yeovil Pen Mill shed 7.40am. Shunts at Sparkford 8am–9.00, thence to Castle Cary to shunt and bank as required. Return to Yeovil Pen Mill shed at 2.30pm.

Engine No 2. (Yeovil duty) Monday to Saturday, total of 56 hours, 15 minutes per week. Light ex-Yeovil Pen Mill at 9.30pm, calls at Sparkford to detach and berth empty milk tanks off 8.50pm Westbury Passenger. When engine required immediately at Castle Cary for banking purposes, Castle Cary signalman to advise Sparkford who must arrange for the engine to proceed direct to Castle Cary. The empty milk tanks must then be detached into the down refuge siding and berthed by No. 1 Castle Cary bank engine the following morning. Returns at 4.20am. Relieved at 4am by engine ex-Yeovil shed at 3am. Latter engine works 9.20am Castle Cary to Durston.

Engine No. 3. (Westbury duty) Saturday and Sunday, total of 8 hours, (3hrs Sat, 5 hrs Sun.) Works 6.50pm Westbury to Castle Cary (arr 8.40pm). To Westbury shed at 5am.

The Bombing of Castle Cary – Thursday, 3rd September 1942

Tom Whittle had started as an engine cleaner at Yeovil, was then made up to fireman and moved to Swindon and then transferred back to Yeovil. He recalled 'I shouldn't have been fireman on this turn'. In fact he had been booked on an earlier firing duty but had swopped it with fellow fireman Stan Eaton in order for Stan to attend a dental appointment that same afternoon. It was a misty morning as Tom made his way to the GWR locomotive shed at Yeovil Pen Mill to book on duty at 8.15am. Meanwhile, driver Jack Shergold was saying goodbye to his wife and daughter Joyce at their home in Sherborne Road which was just a few minutes walk to the engine shed. As he left, Jack turned to his family and told them that when he returned from work he would wash his overalls in the bucket. This was a time honoured fashion to wash coal and oil stained overalls in the days before the age of washing machines (even in my firing days during the 1950's this practice was still adhered to by many footplate crews).

Jack Shergold had started as an engine cleaner at the GWR shed at Salisbury, then moved to Leominster shed and had been a driver for ten years before being posted to Yeovil on 10th October 1941. The footplate duty being worked by the two men this day involved travelling to Castle Cary on a Weymouth–Bristol train which was booked off Yeovil at 8.40am. At Castle Cary they would relieve another Yeovil crew who had started earlier with pannier No. 1729. Then, after a bout of shunting at Cary they would set forth with about 12 or 15 wagons shunting at every station and yard until they reached their destination at Durston which was situated on the Bristol–Taunton main line. Jack Shergold and Tom Whittle, when they had booked on at the shed, had already been advised that a 'red' air raid warning alert was in operation and after studying the working notices for the day, they collected their kit and walked across the tracks to the station to await the arrival of the train.

The Bristol bound train arrived on time and the footplatemen climbed aboard with their tin boxes which contained everything from tea and coffee supplies and food to rule books, working timetables and special notices, soap and towels, newspapers, and spare gauge glass tubes. Tom and Jack made themselves comfortable for the short journey to Castle Cary. They sat there chatting away as footplatemen are inclined to do as the train rolled through the wartime Somerset countryside. When they arrived at Castle Cary the two men, after alighting from the train, strolled across the tracks to the down platform where 1729 was awaiting them at the end of the platform. It had just arrived from Brewham after banking an up freight train and they relieved the other Yeovil crew, Jack Rogers and Jack Reeves and traded the usual bout of banter which is customary amongst footplate crews, especially so if they all come from the same shed. No. 1729 was one of the 0-6-0 pannier tanks fitted with the half cab, a feature which, Tom Whittle recalled, probably saved his life. No. 1729 was one of the 1854 class and was built to lot 88 at Swindon in July 1892. As with all of the class it was constructed as a saddle tank and had been fitted with pannier tanks in July 1922. Having relieved their counterparts and stowed their boxes away, Jack Shergold and Tom Whittle were now ready to start the day's work. The signal was 'off', the regulator was opened and the pannier tank, which was standing with its bunker facing towards Yeovil, reversed along the down main line and stopped just past the scissor points in order to cross onto the up main line to perform shunting duties before forming the Durston goods. Unknown to them, a lone Junkers 88 was approaching the area, flying very low to escape radar detection; death and chaos at Castle Cary was now only a few minutes away.

Meanwhile, back at Yeovil, the air raid sirens had sounded just after 9 o'clock and Jack Shergold's daughter, Joyce, then aged 17 and working at the Mark's &

Spencer store, made her way to the roof of the shop with other members of staff for firewatching duties. The barrage balloons were just rising as Joyce reached the roof, and with a tremendous roar from their engines, two German bombers swept fast and low over the roof of the store heading in the general direction of Castle Cary. (It is not known if these two enemy bombers were involved in the air raid at Castle Cary, as there were many alerts in the area that day, and from contemporary accounts only one aircraft was involved in the attack on the junction). Mr George was thatching a straw mow (a 'mow' is a circular rick made out of wheat sheaves that had come out of a binder, and was thatched with a circular pointed top to keep the weather out of the rick) at Lower Farm, Sutton near Castle Cary. He heard a rat-tat-tat of machine gun fire from the Sparkford direction, and a few seconds later watched the bomber following the railway line with its bomb doors open over the Clanville Sawmills.

Back at the junction, 1729 with its crew was waiting to proceed onto the up main line, when, at 9.15am with a tremendous roar from the aero engines and the rattle of machine gun fire, the bomber appeared over the small garage next to the railway bridge over the Yeovil line. 'As we spotted him, so the bombs fell out'. The first bomb had wedged in the ballast between the wheels on the driver's side, with about four foot of casing sticking out complete with tail fin. Tom turned around with the intention of jumping out from his side of the engine as far away from the bomb as possible, then there was an almighty explosion and Tom found himself falling through the air before blacking out. (Tom Whittle believes that thanks to the half cab design of the locomotive, he was blown over the bunker, and this saved his life.) Tom came to, and found himself lying in the bomb crater with steam and water blowing everywhere. He was very lucky to escape with his life, suffering from scalding to his stomach, plus a couple of bits of shrapnel, his hair was singed, his clothing had been blown away by the blast and all he was wearing was the shoulder of his jacket plus one sleeve, and the waistband of his trousers was connected by a thread to a small piece of trouser down his right side. Driver Jack Shergold was dead, caught by the blast under the cab of the locomotive, and 1729 lay to one side damaged and beyond repair.

The scene at Castle Cary that day is beyond belief. Within a few seconds, a country junction had been turned into a scene of carnage with the smell of cordite and smoke hanging in the air, track destroyed and cratered, and buildings destroyed and burning. The bomber had struck with deadly pin point accuracy, approaching fast and low from the direction of Clanville Sawmills and following the main railway line. The aircraft had banked slightly to the right when it had approached the junction and then banked left to approach the station over the small garage that still stands today beside the road bridge over the Weymouth line. Four 500kg bombs had been dropped, the first crippled 1729 and killed Jack Shergold, wrecked eight trucks, brought down the telephone wires and blocked the main line. The second bomb hit the signal box destroying it, the goods shed and the parcels office behind it reducing them to a pile of rubble and killing the signalman, Mr Sibley. Other trucks near the goods shed were destroyed, and the third bomb pitched onto the main Castle Cary–Shepton Mallet road and demolished the

A view of No. 1729 at Castle Cary after the air raid by the Luftwaffe. The picture speaks for itself; no words of mine can convey the horrors of war inflicted on innocent workmen going about their everyday job. No. 1729, an 1854 class engine was built at Swindon in July 1892 to Lot 88 as an 0-6-0 saddle tank, it being fitted with pannier tanks in July 1922. Being too badly damaged to repair, No. 1729 was cut up at Swindon one month after the air raid.

R. C. Riley Collection

Railway Hotel, damaging Prideaux's milk factory and three cottages. The fourth bomb fell into the River Brue. After the bombing run, the Junkers 88 turned and flew back over the station, raking the area with machine gun fire before leaving the scene, and a toll of three dead and ten injured.

Tom vaguely remembers being carried to the ambulance which carried him and Jack Rogers who was suffering from shrapnel wounds, to Yeovil Hospital. Tom Whittle spent a total of three weeks in hospital. Fate moves in strange ways. David George was aged 7 years old in 1942, and was preparing to cycle to Castle Cary from Sutton with his mother to do the shopping. It was fortunate that he had a flat tyre on his bike and it took some time to repair, otherwise, both he and his mother would have been passing the station at the same time as the raid took place. He remembers seeing the "pub, signal box, and a train all wrecked in the station, and the road was covered in bricks, glass, and branches from the trees that had been blown off".

The bomber had delivered its deadly cargo, and one of the GWR's most important junctions was now crippled, albeit temporarily. The sound of the air raid had been heard at the ammunition depot of Dimmer camp three miles away and the men of the 82nd Company of the Royal Pioneer Corps with their Commanding Officer at their head, double marched to the station to give what assistance they could with filling in craters and clearing debris. Permanent way gangs and Signal & Telegraph staff from all over the district began to arrive to repair the damaged track and broken telephone wires and signalling. Bill Whittle (Tom's father), the Inspector's Timekeeper had arrived with the Yeovil permanent way gang, and was surprised to find Tom's tin box had been blown by the blast to the embankment alongside the Castle Cary–Shepton Mallet Road. The box was intact and standing upright, and upon opening, it was found that Tom's sandwiches and bottle of coffee were in good order, and enjoyed by Bill later! By eleven o'clock that very evening, trains were travelling to Weymouth on a single line, being supervised by hand signalling arrangements through the station with temporary speed restrictions. With Swindon giving priority to the junction which was opened as soon as possible, the GWR signal works at Reading delivered a small wooden signal box to Castle Cary by a special train. This was installed with a 22-lever frame and opened on 5th September. Work proceeded on a new signal box on the site of the bombed box, by McAlpines, using bricks from the nearby brickworks at Evercreech. The new box opened on 27th October 1942, and was equipped with an 85-lever frame and VT5 interlocking.

This one was one of four daylight raids which occurred in Somerset during September and October 1942, each raid being made by a lone bomber flying at roof-top height. In each case four bombs were dropped with great accuracy, and all four targets were railway junctions and milk factories or both. The second raid occurred on September 5th when Templecombe station and village was hit, with 13 people killed and 17 injured. The third raid took place on 29th September, when the Cow & Gate milk factory at Somerton received a direct hit with nine people being killed and 37 injured. The fourth raid occurred on 23rd October at Chard Junction on the Southern Railway main line, when the Wilts United Dairy complex was the target. Here, the bombs bounced over the factory which escaped serious damage, but one person was killed, and 33 injured, of which five, were seriously hurt.

Long up and down loops were provided to the east of the station lying alongside the up and down main lines and were brought into use on 28th March 1943. The loops were a useful addition to the West of England main line over the years until the end of steam, as they were used by through freight trains to stop and allow following express trains to overtake. In the 1957 summer timetable, the 3pm Wood Lane–Plymouth (SX), milk empties was booked to stop in the down loop from 7pm until 7.45pm to allow the 5.30pm Paddington–Plymouth to pass at 7.32pm. Whilst in the loop, the Plymouth milk empties detached milk tanks for the Weymouth line, which were later collected by the 8.50pm Westbury–Weymouth and detached at Yeovil Pen Mill. West of England express trains did not stop at Castle Cary, and passengers from the station intending to travel to Taunton had to use the local

151

Castle Cary, looking east on 25th April 1984. A three-car dmu (set No. B428) forming the 09.05 Weymouth–Westbury is signalled into the 'up' loop line in order to allow an approaching Paddington bound High Speed Train to pass. The 'down' loop and sidings can be seen to the right.

John Day

Class 43 HST formed of power cars Nos 43124 and 43010 heads through Castle Cary with the 09.25 Plymouth–Paddington on 25th April 1984. The signal box and lower quadrant signals are still in place.

John Day

services to the county town. These were either auto fitted trains hauled by pannier tanks, or if not auto fitted, the trains were formed of 'B' sets hauled by Prairie or pannier tanks. There was a daily local service of five Taunton trains, the first down being the 6.28am from Westbury which arrived at Castle Cary at 7.07am, was shunted in order to connect with the 5.45am Bristol–Weymouth (arr 7.53, dep 7.54,), the 6.28am ex-Westbury then formed the 8.10am Castle Cary–Taunton, (arr Taunton 9.11am). The 5.10pm Melksham–Taunton arr 6.24pm, dep 6.52pm, was shunted in order to connect with the 5.02pm Bristol–Weymouth arr 6.41pm, dep 6.42pm, before resuming its journey to Taunton. Most of the Weymouth line trains stopped at Castle Cary, with the first down Weymouth train from the station, (rail motor) leaving at 7.13am. From the 1970s certain West of England trains to and from Paddington were scheduled to stop at Castle Cary.

Siding accommodation began to be reduced from 1963 when the up siding on the Weymouth branch, and the connection from the down loop into the down Weymouth main line were taken out of use on 15th December. The station was closed to goods traffic from 3rd October 1966, and connections from the down main line to the goods yard were removed in May 1968. With the singling of the Weymouth line on 12th

May 1968 the junction of the Weymouth and Taunton lines which had been designed for the steam locomotive was removed and remodelled, up trains from the Weymouth line entered Castle Cary on the down main line for a short distance before gaining the up platform line. The goods shed road was removed on 22nd June 1969, the short spur and the back siding to the rear of the goods shed being taken out in 1970.

With the Westbury Panel box extending its operating area between Castle Cary and Somerton, colour light signals with their distinctive white crosses, denoting that they were not in use, began to appear in the area. Major alterations to the trackwork and signalling took place in February 1985 when the signal box was abolished and all lower quadrant signalling was dismantled. The down platform was rebuilt in order that Weymouth trains could call at either face of the remodelled structure. From the date of the layout alterations, all up and down Weymouth trains now use the remodelled down platform. Up Weymouth trains are routed along the down main line until they reach the island platform, then they proceed along the down main for a short distance before gaining the up main via a facing crossover east of the station. Down Weymouth line trains use the remodelled down loop which is signalled for reversible working. From 4th February 1985, all

152

Class 50 No. 50002 *Superb* rumbles past the Castle Cary 'down' inner home signal with the relief for the 11.45 Paddington–Penzance on 25th April 1984. The once busy loop and sidings to the right, now stand empty and deserted.

John Day

Class 50 No. 50015 *Valiant* in large logo livery takes the Weymouth line at Castle Cary on 19th October 1985 with the diverted 13.10 Waterloo–Exeter St Davids. The train will regain Network SouthEast metals via Yeovil Pen Mill and Yeovil Junction. A dmu on a Weymouth line service stands at the new platform in the distance. The signal box in the background was an empty shell when this photograph was taken and was demolished shortly afterwards.

John Day

Passengers await their Weymouth line train on the 'down' platform, as Class 43 HST power car No. 43033 brings the 06.00 Plymouth–Paddington into Castle Cary on 19th August 1992. The signal box and lower quadrant signals have now been removed as have the chimneys from the station building.

Peter Nicholson

Class 150/2 'Sprinter' No. 150273 formed of cars Nos 52273 and 57273 approaches Castle Cary on the single line from Yeovil Pen Mill with the 06.56 Weymouth–Bristol Temple Meads service on 19th August 1992.

Peter Nicholson

signalling at Castle Cary came under the control of Westbury Panel box. The goods shed still survives today in spite of "being knocked about by Corporal Hitler's Luftwaffe", and an engineers siding provided with a trailing connection to the up main line occupies part of the old goods yard. The former coal sidings have now been converted into a car park.

Dimmer Signal Box
130 miles 37 chains from Paddington

Dimmer signal box was situated between Castle Cary and Sparkford, approximately one mile from Castle Cary and was opened on 24th June 1908. The box, which was equipped with a six-lever frame did not remain in use for long as it was switched out from 1st September the same year. All signals were removed on 3rd February 1909, and the box was abolished on 24th February 1910.

Sparkford
134 miles 29 chains from Paddington
Opened 1st September 1856
Gauge conversion 18th/22nd June 1874
Signal box opened May 1877
Line doubled Castle Cary–Yeovil Pen Mill 1881
Raymond's Saw Mills siding, into use 16th February 1929
Milk sidings added c1932
Sparkford Vale Co-Op Dairy Society Ltd PSA 5th February 1936
WD sidings, North ground frame, north crossover, into use 28th May 1944
Closed to goods 7th January 1963
Station closed 3rd October 1966
Signal box closed 30th November 1966
Line singled Castle Cary–Yeovil 12th May 1968

The station, when opened on 1st September 1856, formed another one of the passing places on the then single broad gauge line. After the gauge conversion of 1874 the station remained a passing place until the doubling of the line in 1881. The large, former broad gauge goods shed was situated on the up side of the layout and lasted until closure. A dock siding, cattle pen, coal wharves and head shunt completed the siding layout on the up side, and a crossover was situated

between the up and down platforms. The station consisted of two platforms, with the main stone built buildings complete with the Station Master's office located on the up platform, and there was a large stone built waiting shelter on the down platform. The signal box, opened in May 1877, was positioned off the down platform at the Castle Cary end. Opening times were from 6am to 10pm weekdays, and 10.45am–6.45pm Sundays, and a switch was provided. The box which was equipped with 22 levers and later extended to 23 and was closed on 30th November 1966. Signalmen at Sparkford included Arthur Bicknell, Ted Hartnell and Norman Kibby. Freight traffic for the station included coal for Messrs Perrys, and later Messrs Snows, large tree trunks arriving on flat trucks for Raymond's sawmills, agricultural machinery, and cattle feed. Raymond's Saw Mills siding was connected to the down refuge siding and was brought into use on 16th February 1929. The public siding agreement dated from 21st October 1929.

To the west of the station, past the A303 road bridge, was situated the large creamery lying alongside the up main line. Two sidings were added c1932 for rail milk tankers, and a public sidings agreement dated 5th February 1936 was provided between the GWR and the Sparkford Vale Co-op Dairy Society. The creamery was later owned by United Dairies. The milk tanks were despatched to Kensington Olympia and were attached to an up Weymouth train, empty tanks being detached from the 8.50pm down Westbury by the night Cary banker, as per the 1954 working timetable.

Station staff at Sparkford included a Station Master, one porter/shunter and three signalmen. A light engine from Pen Mill shed (ex-shed 7.40am) was rostered in the 1954 working timetable to shunt at Castle Cary from 8 until 9am whilst en route to Castle Cary. Another light engine from Yeovil (ex-shed 9.30pm) was booked to stop at Sparkford en route to Castle Cary and detach and berth empty milk tanks from the 8.50pm Westbury–Weymouth. Extensive War Department sidings connected to the down refuge siding and the down main line, plus a north ground frame worked by an Annetts key, and a new north crossover, were brought into use on 28th May 1944. The WD sidings were also used by the Sarmac Agency Ltd sawmill. These sidings, North ground frame, and north crossover were all taken out of use

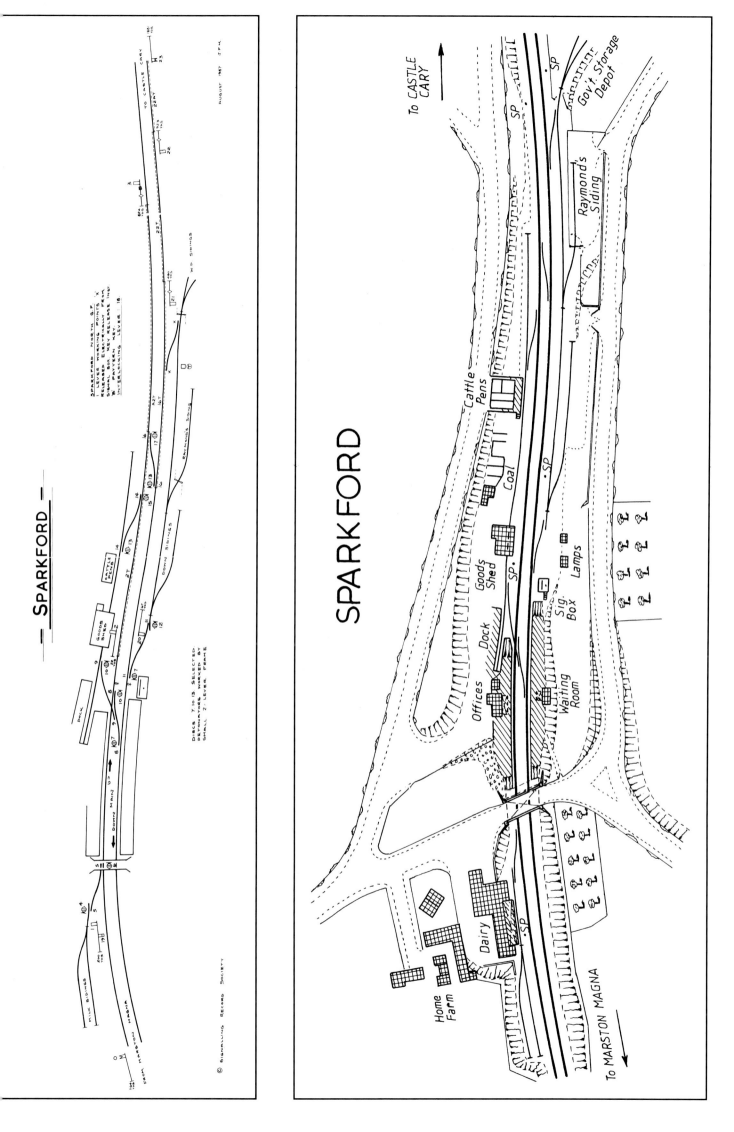

— SPARKFORD —

SPARKFORD

Sparkford as viewed from the A303 road overbridge on 1st October 1966. The main station buildings are situated on the 'up' platform to the left, with a waiting shelter provided on the 'down' platform. As always with the WS&W stations a cast iron gents urinal was provided and can be seen in the foreground standing on the 'up' platform. Note how the goods shed portal has been 'squared' compared with the 1915 view (page 19). The sidings on the 'up' side, including the goods shed line, have been removed. The station was closed to goods traffic on 7th January 1963. *C. L. Caddy*

Class 150/2 'Sprinter' No. 150272 is the first train to work under the new road bridge following the official opening of the A303 Sparkford bypass on Wednesday, 25th October 1989. This is the 11.45 Weymouth–Bristol Temple Meads and is seen from High Street bridge, Sparkford, which, until earlier that morning, had carried the A303, and almost unbelievably, overlooking the site of the former Sparkford station. *Peter Nicholson*

The 24-lever lever Sparkford signal box standing off the London end of the 'down' platform on 1st October 1966 complete with the signalman's bicycle leaning against the locking room door. Note how the steps have been altered compared with the 1915 view of the box, a porch has been erected around the entrance to protect the signalman from the elements, and the attractive brick chimney has also been replaced. The box closed on 30th November 1966. *C. L. Caddy*

A three-car dmu forming the 14.30 Westbury–Weymouth service, enters Sparkford on 1st October 1966. The station closed two days later on 3rd October. Note how the signal arms have been altered to upper quadrants utilising the same GWR post to be seen in the 1915 view.

C. L. Caddy

No. 1012 *County of Denbigh*, allocated to 82C (Swindon), storms through Sparkford with the 'up' Channel Islands boat train on 31st August 1959.

H. B. Priestley – Derek Phillips Collection

on 11th February 1962. The station was closed to goods traffic from 7th January 1963, and the the milk sidings, plus the up goods yard sidings, were taken out of use on 12th December 1963. This followed by the down sidings being taken out of use from 27th July 1964. The signal box was closed on 30th November 1966, and all signalling removed. The crossover between the up and down platforms, and the remaining short down siding were removed at the same time. The station closed on 3rd October 1966 and nothing now remains. The line today, singled since 12th May 1968 with the removal of the former up main line, is now crossed by an overbridge carrying the A303 Sparkford by-pass. The former creamery is now occupied by Haynes Publishing with its vast printing works, publishing offices and warehouse distributing the famed Haynes car manuals and the railway books of the Oxford Publishing Company etc.

Route Learning Car No. 975540 (ex-W55016) from Tyseley runs past the editor's window at Haynes/OPC and heads north through Sparkford on the afternoon of 17th May 1991.

Peter Nicholson

157

Marston Magna

136 miles 76 chains from Paddington
Opened 1st September 1856 as Marston
Re-named Marston Magna 9th May 1895
Gauge Conversion 18th/22nd June 1874
Signal box opened May 1877
Line doubled Castle Cary–Yeovil Pen Mill 1881
Ammuniton Depot Sidings into use 16th December
  1940
Signal box closed 16th February 1964
Closed to Goods 5th November 1962
Station closed 3rd October 1966
Line singled Castle Cary–Yeovil Pen Mill 12th May
  1968

Opened on 1st September 1856 and originally named Marston, the station was not equipped with a crossing loop as at other stations on the then single broad gauge line. The broad gauge era for the Weymouth line ended over the weekend of the 18th and 22nd of June 1874, and the line witnessed increasing traffic, especially after doubling in 1881. The station buildings were constructed of stone under slate roofs with the main buildings including the Station Master's office being located on the down platform and a large stone built shelter was provided on the up platform. The platforms were 290ft long, but a footbridge was not provided, with access to the up platform being gained by a footpath running down from the Rimpton road. Passengers to the down platform crossed the road bridge on the Rimpton road and walked down the railway owned access road to the station. The distinctive tall signal box, standing off the Yeovil end of the up platform, opened in May 1877 with a 12-lever frame, which was enlarged in later years to 22 levers. It was extended finally to a 23-lever frame. Signalmen at Marston Magna included Les Giles, Jim Maidment and Ron Whittle. In 1945, the signal box opened from 11am to 7pm on weekdays, and the signal lamps were not lit between 1st April and 1st September. As at all stations, Marston Magna had its own Station Master, and over the years, the following have served in that post: Mr Gilbey, Mr Almond, Mr Lush and Mr Shapley who became the last man to hold the post at the station. The following station staff were at the station in 1947: Mr Lush (Station Master), Joan Sibley (booking clerk), Ralph Bartlett (porter) Bill Chant (porter), Jim Maidment (porter), Ron Whittle (signalman). The Marston Magna permanent way gang working area, or 'Length', extended from Hummer bridge to Sutton bridge. As well as maintaining the track, the men cut the grass on the banks using the tools of the trade including the sickle, hook, bandy and scythe.

Another vanished feature from the railway scene are the huts used by the gangers to store their tools and have their meals, not forgetting the cider! The gang in 1925 included: Jim Miller, Harry Whittle, George Bryan, Arthur Pullman and Mr Parsons. Before the

Marston Magna station, looking west on 1st October 1966 after removal of the sidings and signal box. The station closed to passengers two days later on 3rd October.
C. L. Caddy

Marston Magna, looking east on 1st October 1966, two days before closure to passenger traffic. Weeds and grass are now taking control over the once well kept platforms and buildings.
C. L. Caddy

— MARSTON MAGNA —

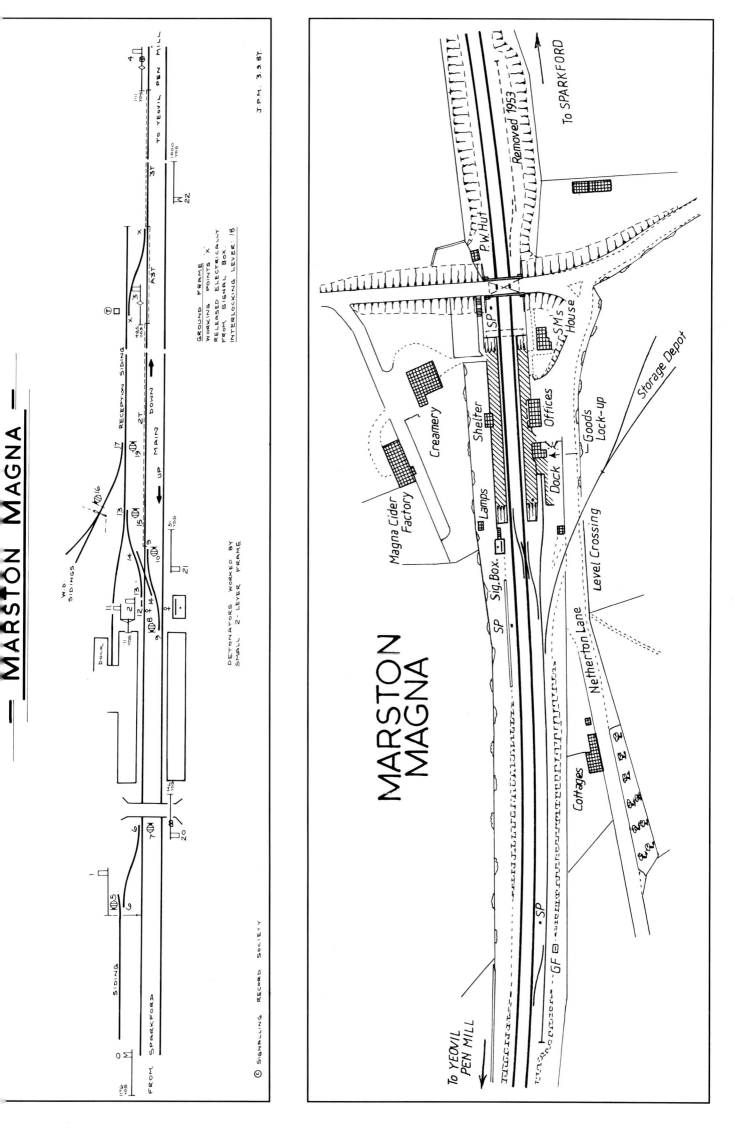

W.D. SIDINGS

RECEPTION SIDING

UP MAIN DOWN

FROM SPARKFORD

TO YEOVIL PEN MILL

SIDING

GROUND FRAME
WORKING POINTS 'X'
RELEASED ELECTRICALLY
FROM SIGNAL BOX.
INTERLOCKING LEVER: 18

DETONATORS WORKED BY
SMALL 2-LEVER FRAME

J.P.M. 3.9.87.

© SIGNALLING RECORD SOCIETY.

MARSTON MAGNA

To SPARKFORD

P.W. Hut

Removed 1953

Magna Cider Factory

Creamery

Shelter

Lamps

Sig. Box.

SM's House

Offices

Dock

Goods Lock-up

Storage Depot

Netherton Lane

Level Crossing

Cottages

To YEOVIL PEN MILL

Station staff at Marston Magna in 1948. Back row standing left to right: Jim Maidment (signalman), B. Chant (porter), Ralph Bartlett (porter), front row: Joan Sibley (booking clerk), Mr Lush (Station Master).

R. Bartlett

Second World War c1937, there was Mr Brown (ganger), Stan Apsey (2nd man), Edward White, Bill Dabinett, Jim Miller, George Bowden, Tim Milverton and Reg Trim. Members of the gang after the war included Tom Doel and Fred Patten. The station was lit by oil lamps until closure and their welcoming warm glow at night, especially the lamps which lit the pathway to the up platform, are still remembered.

Marston Magna, like all stations before the mass onslaught of road transport, was very busy with freight and livestock being delivered by rail for the local traders and farms. Cattle would arrive from Yeovil on market days, and would then be herded by drovers to the local farms. Some cattle came from Ireland, making the long journey by boat and train. Cattle feed and horses were also handled. The station was unusual in the fact that no sidings were provided on the up side, all sidings being on the down side of the station layout and comprised a dock siding holding eleven wagons, and a mileage siding which held 13 wagons. A down refuge siding was situated east of the station.

Coal for the local traders from the Somerset mines on the North Somerset line was delivered, and was also delivered for the Aplin & Barrett Creamery (originally named Western Counties Creamery). Their building was located behind the up platform, and the coal was required for the boiler house which supplied hot water and steam for the creamery. Farmers from the local farms and beyond would bring their milk in by horse and cart and would back their carts up to the platform of the factory to unload. Milk in churns from the factory went by rail to London, and full churns awaiting the next train, or empty ones waiting to be taken back to the creamery would be a common sight on the platforms. Butter and cheese were also produced at the creamery while surplus milk was turned into powdered milk.

The once-a-year Sunday school outing to Weymouth was very popular, and the village of Marston Magna was left practically empty on the day of the outing. The Magna Cider Company was also a good user of the railway, and the huge cider casks used in the factory for the storing and fermenting process would arrive by rail. Many 18-gallon wooden barrels would be loaded onto passenger trains for delivery to London and seaside towns. The cider factory also used coal delivered by the railway. An accident one day, gave one of the porters the fright of his life. He was pulling a platform trolley across the sleepered crossing to the down plat-

Cider casks destined for the Magna Cider Company await unloading in the 'down' yard at Marston Magna station. The wooden three-plank wagons belonged to various railway companies including, North British, Great Western, Great Central and Great Eastern. The casks were used for storage purposes in the cider making process, and were moved from the station yard to the cider company premises one at a time by a small lorry.

P. J. Marden

form when a down train running non stop through the station hit the trolley loaded with milk in 17-gallon cans. The story goes, that he did not stop running until he reached his home in the nearby village of Rimpton! Luckily nobody was injured, and the train eventually came to a halt, and the wreckage was removed.

Marston Ammunition Depot

The station was transformed during the Second World War when a large fan of sidings was laid to serve a huge ammunition depot. The sidings were opened on 16th December 1940. The former down mileage siding was extended to form a large down reception siding, and a trailing connection at the Yeovil end of the reception siding operated by a ground frame was also provided. A new facing connection was provided from the down main line. The Royal Engineers were known to have been in the depot at this time but later in the war the United States Army had many hundreds of soldiers billeted in the village to work at the ammunition depot. There were 500 soldiers encamped in Nissen huts at the village hall alone, besides many others. American officers at the depot included Major Zimmerman, Major Littlewood and Captain Bennett.

With the preparations for the coming D Day landings, train after train, day and night would arrive packed with ammunition. The trains were unloaded into American army lorries and the ammunition was distributed and stacked in fields, under hedgerows, and in peaceful country lanes in a five mile radius from the depot. Many country lanes were prohibited areas for the local villagers, and a special pass had to be issued for the inhabitants needing to use these areas. The villagers soon became used to large convoys of American army trucks rumbling through the village, and the soldiers themselves are well remembered by the older inhabitants. With the approaching invasion of France, especially during the days leading to the actual D Day itself, the area was a scene of frenzied activity as the ammunition was loaded on to freight trains. Train after train would pull out of the depot and head for the embarkation areas. As well as the trains, vast convoys of American and British army lorries would rumble through the narrow country lanes and the village of Marston Magna, heading for the embarkation ports well laden with their deadly cargo. Forty-eight hours after D Day the vast depot was emptied, and then the Americans vanished, never to be seen again. The village became quiet as it was emptied of troops, much to the sadness of many local people who had taken the 'Yanks' to their hearts.

Chester Eugene Denby

Chester Denby was 18 years old when he arrived at Liverpool in September 1943 being part of the huge United States Army build up to the D Day landings. On arrival at Marston Magna he was billeted with Mr & Mrs Stanley Apsey and his memories of the warm welcome and kindness that he received in the village is still as fresh today as it was in the grim days of the war. Mr Stanley Apsey was second man on the permanent way gang based at Marston Magna.

Here, in his own words is Chester's account of his wartime days in England:

In the first part of September 1943 I arrived and disembarked at Liverpool, England. At the age of 18 I had my first experience of being a passenger on the

Corporal Chester Eugene Denby. Fourth Group Regulation Station. Transportation Segment US Army. Stationed at Marston Magna from September 1943 to March 1944.

Mrs B. Darch

British railway system going from Liverpool to Bristol. My eyes were agog to see the British countryside for the first time in my young life. I was a member of the Fourth Group Regulation Station which comprised a part of the newly formed Transportation Segment of the US Army. Our particular function was to be an information center to help other American soldiers in need of direction. Several days before I received my travel orders, I was promoted to corporal. My travel orders specified that I was to be in charge of my detachment, and that I was to report to a Sgt Brooks at Marston Magna, Somerset, England. I found out, that I was in charge of one person who was a Frenchman named "Loui".

Here I was, a frightened youngster in charge of a man who had difficulty in understanding English. Thanks to the British railway, I arrived in Marston Magna safely. Prior to leaving Hampton Rhodes, Virginia. We were put through intensive sessions of bayonet practice in temperatures of 100 degrees. Most of the Company thought for sure that we would land in Africa, as the battle against Rommel's troops was in full force. I never thought that in a hundred years, I would end up as guest of a Mr & Mrs Stanley Apsey. My memory of their kindness and considerate care has remained with me through the last 49 years. Stan and Hilda exemplified the true British spirit of fortitude and patience which turned those early dark days of the war into England's greatest shining hour. It was here at Marston Magna, that I was one of a group that included a Welshman, Cockney Londoner, Frenchman, Southerners and Northerners.

The American men represented Groups 1st, 3rd & 4th Regulating Station Companies. Here many rail cars of 105mm shells and other ammunition were unloaded by a British Pioneer Battalion which was replaced by a black American Battalion, but I do not know their army unit numbers. I will never forget seeing the many mounds of destruction. It is my understanding that within 48 hours after D Day, the British railroad moved everything that took months to unload and store. Our Transportation unit also met and directed incoming American troops at all hours of the day. There was one train that we met at 2am in Yeovil, on which most of the passengers were sleeping and we were not too gentle in issuing commands to "hit the deck" or yelling "rise and shine". Much to our embarrassment most of the passengers were nurses, all officers being assigned to a station hospital at Sherborne, England. Whilst it is common knowledge that it took

161

Allied soldiers stand in front of the Railway Transportation Officer's nissen hut at Marston Magna during the Second World War. Left to right are: Sergeant Allen, Sergeant Macdonald (Mac), Sergeant Sprungs (Pop), Sergeant Black (Bill), Private First Class Alice (Frenchie), Lt Francis.

Mrs B. Darch

many brave deeds and the personal sacrifices of millions of people to achieve victory, it was in great part, those silent unsung heroes of the British railroad. It is my privilege and honour to say "I knew one of those men".

Chester E. Denby
South Bend Indiana U.S.A.

Many years later, when I became a fireman on the railway, I was booked on an empty pigeon train from Marston Magna to Salisbury. We arrived at Marston with our engine from Yeovil, the engine that day being one of our Southern U class 2-6-0 tender engines. Upon arrival at Marston we were shunted across to the down main line and then reversed our engine on to the long train of bogie parcels vans which was standing on the down siding. After coupling the train to our engine we had to wait in the siding for a down passenger train to clear the section, so I lit a cigarette and left our engine singing away to itself with a whisper of steam from the safety valves, as I wandered over to the edge of the goods yard. There, with the sounds of blackbirds chattering and whistling away, and with just a whisper of a summer breeze to disturb the hedgerows, almost hidden by the long grass, lay the rusty, grass covered rails leading across the road to the former ammunition depot. One could imagine the long trains of ammunition pulling away from the depot with wheel flanges squealing and rumbling away into the night during the war, and the various American accents from New York, Chicago, and the deep

South resounding around the depot in the heart of Somerset.

The down refuge siding lying to the east of the station was taken out of use on 12th April 1953, with all other sidings and the ground frame being closed on 5th November 1962 and removed on 16th December 1963. The signal box which had been switched out in its later years was eventually closed and the signals removed on 16th February 1964. The station itself lingered on until closure on 3rd October 1966. The main line between Castle Cary and Yeovil was singled on 12th May 1968 with the former up line being removed. The station has been completely demolished, although the Station Master's house is still there to give us a reminder of a once busy country station, which has now passed into history. The site of the former ammunition depot is now occupied by Messrs Gibbs Bros, agricultural engineers and the former Magna Cider Co. premises has now become the vast Magna Winery which is part of the Gaymer Group.

Yeovil Pen Mill

141 miles 27 chains from Paddington
Opened (Frome–Yeovil) 1st September 1856
Engine shed opened September 1856
Line opened to Weymouth 20th January 1857
Line opened from B&E Railway station at Hendford 2nd February 1857
Doubling of broad gauge line Yeovil–Evershot 1858
Gauge conversion 18th/22nd June 1874
Doubling of line Castle Cary–Yeovil Pen Mill 1881
No. 1 (North) signal box opened 1877. Closed 14th February 1937
No. 2 (South) signal box opened 1877. Closed 21st February 1937
New signal box (replacing North and South) opened 14th January 1937
Engine shed closed 5th January 1959
Pen Mill–Langport West closed to passenger traffic 15th June 1964
Line singled Castle Cary–Yeovil Pen Mill 12th May 1968
Line singled Yeovil Pen Mill–Maiden Newton 26th May 1968

Opened on 1st September 1856 the station became the temporary terminus of the line whilst construction of the route onwards to Weymouth was in progress. A daily service of five passenger trains each way, with two on Sundays was provided. When the line to Weymouth was opened in 1857 the daily service was increased to six trains each way per day. Bristol & Exeter trains used the station from 1857 arriving via the single line from Durston when the connecting link between Pen Mill and the B&E station at Hendford was opened. In 1869 there was a service of five trains per day on the Weymouth line, plus two on Sundays. The station was originally provided with an overall roof to a smaller design, as provided at Frome. After the construction of the Westbury and Frome avoiding lines in 1933, Yeovil Pen Mill was the only station between Westbury and Dorchester West which was subject to severe speed restrictions, especially through the 'dog leg' at the west end of the up platform. The station was protected by 'fixed' distant signals on the up and down main lines approaching the station, the only 'movable' distant signal being the Yeovil South Junction down distant. This shared the same post as the Pen Mill down main

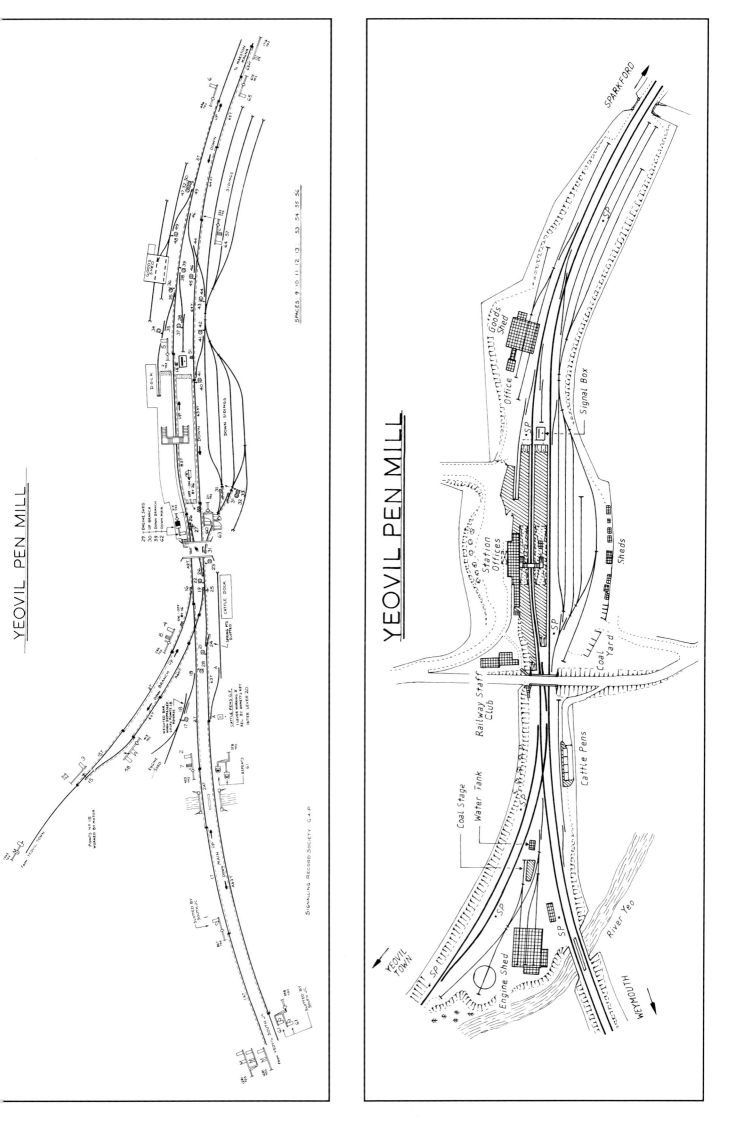

YEOVIL PEN MILL

YEOVIL PEN MILL

SIGNALLING RECORD SOCIETY G.A.P.

Yeovil Pen Mill looking east from the A30 roadbridge on 9th July 1956. Passengers await trains on both of the platforms – a 'down' train is imminent as both the starting, and South Junction distant arms are lowered.

R. C. Riley

starting signal and the down starter for the branch to Yeovil Town.

Pen Mill was also unique in the fact that with an ex-GWR right hand driven engine, it was the only station on the down main line, that passengers alighted from and boarded trains on the driver's side of the engine. Water columns were provided at the east end of the island platform for up trains, and alongside the down main line at the west end of the island platform for down trains. The column there was so positioned that engines could also refill their tanks whilst standing in the down goods yard. An inspection pit was provided in the down main at the west end of the island platform, but in later years this was filled in.

The main buildings are constructed of the local mellow Ham stone and are situated on the up side. A large 65ft long stone built goods shed containing a 30cwt crane lay to the east of the station alongside the up main line. In its later days the goods shed was used for storing animal skins, and the smell at times was quite atrocious, especially when shunting wagons for the shed. The station layout consists of two platforms, which are unusual, as the up line has platforms both sides of the track, although there are two platforms, the platform for the down line is located between the two main lines. The up platform is interesting as it is signalled in both directions. In steam days this was for the use of Taunton bound trains as they arrived and

'Hymek' No. D7000 in Brunswick green livery growls past the Yeovil Pen Mill goods shed with the 15.10 Weymouth–Bristol on 1st October 1961. Note the two-storey office attached to the former broad gauge goods shed to the right. No. D7000 was introduced to traffic in May 1961 being allocated to 82A (Bristol Bath Road). The final allocation for this diesel hydraulic was Old Oak Common before being withdrawn in July 1973, and cut up at Swindon in October 1975. Nos D7000-D7002, when new, had their air horns fitted below the buffer beam, while all the subsequent 'Hymeks' had theirs positioned on the cab roof, and eventually the three stalwarts had their air horns moved to the standard position.

John Day

departed from the up platform. However, in busy times, when track occupancy was at its peak, Taunton bound trains departed from the down platform. The up platform is still used by down trains today for the convenience of the staff and passengers, when they do not have to cross an up service. The difference today being that down trains can be routed direct into the up platform. Speed restrictions through the station at the time of writing are 15mph for up trains, and 20mph for down trains.

A house was purchased for £580 in 1931 for the Station Master. The overall roof was replaced in 1934, by individual platform awnings. Two signal boxes were provided in 1877, No. 1 box (renamed North) equipped with a 25-lever frame was situated east of the station alongside the up main. No. 2 box (renamed South) had a 26-lever frame, and was positioned in the fork created by the Yeovil Town branch and the Weymouth main line near the engine shed coaling stage. Both North and South signal boxes were closed in 1937, North box on February 14th, and South box had its points and signals disconnected on February 17th, but was retained as a block post until closure on February 21st. A new signal box situated off the London end of the down platform was brought into use on the 14th/21st of Febuary, and was equipped with a 65-lever

frame with VT 5-Bar locking, 4in Centres. Box size 38ft 2in x 12ft 2in elevated 8ft. The resignalling works costing £6,070 were utilised as part of the 1935 Government Relief of Unemployment Scheme. Platforms were lengthened and trackwork modified at the up end of the platforms at the same time. The signal box is still in use today. Signalmen working in the box during steam days included Jim Bant, Freddie Knibbs and Reg Hunt, with relief signalmen Jack Bishop and Dick Leighfield. Signal linesmen were: Bill Froude and Ted Keen.

The large down goods yard lying alongside the down platform was a busy one, handling large amounts of freight traffic to and from the main shunting yard at Hendford, and transfer traffic to and from the Southern at Yeovil junction. More down sidings were provided from 1924 alongside the down main line east of the station. Sidings were also located alongside the up main line serving the goods shed, and there was a bay line alongside the London end of the up platform which normally stabled the odd van or one of the 'B' sets used on local passenger services. To the west of the station past the A30 road bridge lay the cattle siding (into use 21st February 1937) serving the cattle pens alongside the down main line. Access to this siding was provided by a ground frame, with both the siding and

The GWR Type 11 signal box at Yeovil Pen Mill, looking east and still in use in 1994. The lowered arm on the 'up' starter, giving clearance to the single line section to Castle Cary, can be seen in the distance.

Peter Nicholson

With the signal box in the background, station staff at Yeovil Pen Mill pose for the camera in front of the running in board on the island platform in the late 1940s. Seated from left to right: Norman Kibby (senior porter), Mary Seal (ticket collector), Fred Matterface (yard foreman). Standing left to right: J. Henderson (porter), Tony Whittle (telegraph boy).

Norman Kibby

Class 3MT 2-6-2T No. 82040 from Taunton locomotive depot, shunts the 'down' goods yard at Yeovil Pen Mill on 20th May 1964. No. 82040 had arrived at Yeovil with a goods train via Langport West and the old Bristol & Exeter branch, and after marshalling wagons at Pen Mill the locomotive will return to Taunton, stopping at the branch stations en route to pick up and drop off wagons.

John Cornelius

ground frame being taken out of use on 2nd February 2nd.

An engine spotter on a summer Saturday in 1957 would have had a field day as a grand variety of locomotives worked through on the main line to and from Weymouth. Most of the locomotives would be of the ex-GWR classes including 'Castle', 'County', 'Grange', 'Hall', 'Manor', and Moguls with a sprinkling of BR Standards, and also pannier, Prairie and auto tanks would be fussing about on local services and banking duties. It would be a common sight for anyone standing on the A30 road bridge overlooking the station, to see a down train waiting for the road at the down starter, another one standing at the down outer home signal, and by turning to look over the other side of the road bridge, another down train could be seen waiting at the South Junction home signal. Such was the traffic on a summer Saturday, and Yeovil Pen Mill was the bottle neck with its speed restrictions, and engines stopping at Yetminster to pick up the banker. So let the years roll back as we take a look at the passenger timetable for that era more than 30 years ago:

dep of the 7.05am to Taunton
dep of the 7.37am rail motor to Weymouth
arr at 7.57am of the 6.52am from Taunton
arr at 8.16am of the 5.45am Bristol to Weymouth
arr at 8.29am of the 7.17am Weymouth to Chippenham
arr at 8.56am of the 6.00am Cardiff to Weymouth
arr at 9.02am of the 8.15am Weymouth to Bristol
arr at 9.49am of the 9.00am Weymouth to Paddington
arr at 9.50am of the 8.05am Bristol to Weymouth
dep of the 9.58am to Taunton
9.25am Weymouth to Wolverhampton booked to pass Yeovil at 10.19am
arr at 10.28am of the 9.27am Westbury to Weymouth
arr at 10.41am of the 9.10am Bristol to Weymouth
arr at 10.42am of the 9.35am Weymouth to Yeovil rail motor
10.00am Weymouth to Birmingham Moor St. booked to pass Yeovil 10.48
dep of the 10.50am rail motor to Yeovil Town
8.20am Paddington to Weymouth Quay booked to pass Yeovil at 11am
arr at 11.09am of the 10.05am from Taunton
8.30am Paddington to Weymouth Quay booked to pass Yeovil at 11.16am
arr at 11.17am of the 10.20am Weymouth to Wolverhampton
arr at 11.26am of the 11.24 rail motor from Yeovil Town

arr at 11.36am of the 8.30am Weston-super-Mare to Weymouth
arr at 11.47am of the 10.37am Weymouth to Yeovil rail motor
arr at 11.55am of the 8am Birmingham Snow Hill to Weymouth
arr at 12.03pm of the 11.12am Weymouth to Paddington
dep of the 12.10pm Yeovil to Weymouth rail motor
arr at 12.32pm of the 9.34am Reading General to Weymouth
11.50am Weymouth to Westbury ECS booked to pass Yeovil at 12.37pm
dep of the 12.38 to Taunton
arr at 1.20pm of the 11.25am Chippenham to Weymouth
arr at 1.35pm of the 12.40pm Weymouth to Bristol
dep of the 1.35pm Yeovil to Weymouth rail motor
arr at 1.54pm of the 12.35pm from Taunton
arr at 2.01pm of the 12.50pm Weymouth to Yeovil Town rail motor
dep at 2.08pm of rail motor to Yeovil Town
1.35pm Weymouth to Cardiff booked to pass Yeovil at 2.23pm
arr at 2.26pm of the 2.24pm rail motor from Yeovil Town
dep of the 2.32pm to Taunton
arr at 2.37pm of the 1.45pm Weymouth to Bristol
arr at 3.03pm of the 12.45pm Bristol to Weymouth
arr at 3.20pm of the 2pm from Taunton
arr at 3.39pm of the 12.30pm Paddington to Weymouth
arr at 3.41pm of the 2.32pm Weymouth to Westbury
dep of the 3.59pm to Taunton
dep at 4.15pm empty rail motor to Yeovil Town
arr at 4.27pm of the 11.05am Wolverhampton to Weymouth
arr at 4.30pm of the 4.28pm rail motor from Yeovil Town
dep of the 4.40pm Yeovil to Weymouth rail motor
3.45pm Weymouth Quay to Paddington booked to pass Yeovil at 4.52pm
arr at 5.05pm of the 4.14pm Weymouth to Paddington
arr at 5.05pm of the 3.22pm Thorney Milk
arr at 5.12pm of the 4.18pm Weymouth to Cardiff and Birmingham
arr at 5.20pm of the 4.14pm Westbury to Weymouth
arr at 5.30pm of the 4.45pm Dorchester West to Yeovil
arr at 5.35pm of the 4.15pm from Taunton
dep of the 5.47pm to Taunton
arr at 6.09pm of the 4.25pm Bristol to Weymouth
arr at 7.00pm of the 5.50pm from Taunton
arr at 7.10pm of the 5.02pm Bristol to Weymouth
arr at 7.15pm of the 6.10pm Weymouth to Westbury
arr at 7.48pm of the 6.35pm Weymouth to Westbury milk train
dep of the 7.50pm to Taunton
arr at 8.22pm of the 7.30pm Weymouth to Bristol
arr at 9.19pm of the 6.00pm Paddington to Weymouth
arr at 9.25pm of the 8.20pm from Taunton

dep of the 9.45pm to Taunton
arr at 10.05pm of the 9pm Weymouth to Yeovil rail motor
arr at 10.09pm of the 8.50pm Westbury to Weymouth
arr at 10.30pm of the 9.30pm from Taunton
dep of the 10.45pm to Maiden Newton
9.30pm Paddington to Weymouth Quay booked to pass
   Yeovil at 11.52pm

A vast array of engines from sheds far and wide including many 'namers' would arrive and depart or pass through Pen Mill in the final years of the steam locomotive. Lower quadrant signals would lower with a clang as each train approached, the platforms would shake as a mighty 'Castle' would rattle through with its exhaust crackling away from a copper capped chimney. The guard's whistle would sound shrilly along the platform and a stopping train would pull away with a blast on the whistle and a loud bark resounding around the station from the exhaust. A slow beat at first gradually getting faster as the reverser was knotched back, and the regulator opened wider until the train departed with its exhaust beat gradually fading in the distance, with signals rising to 'danger' in its wake. The hard pressed signalman would already be preparing to accept the next train. Late running trains would put the whole timetable into chaos, but most ran to time and delays, when they happened were rare.

One incident happened one day when a 'Castle', No. 5082 *Swordfish* failed at Yeovil when hauling the down 'Channel Islands Boat Express', and one of our U class, No. 31802, was despatched from Yeovil Town shed and hauled the express to Weymouth. *Swordfish* was hauled to the Town shed to have the fire dropped, and it stopped there for a few days before being collected and despatched back to the Western Region.

The station staff were kept busy with the hordes of passengers flocking on to the platforms, and the station bookstall would do a roaring trade in newspapers and magazines. Trains would be packed, and I well remember travelling as a passenger on a fast train to Paddington during those glorious years and having to stand in the corridor for most of the journey. Most stopping trains took advantage to replenish their tenders whilst awaiting the 'right away'. As well as the main line and branch services, there would be light engine movements to and from the shed as engines were changed on the Taunton services. A clank of buffers would resound from the down goods yard as a pannier tank acting as station pilot fussed about shunting wagons. When the shunting was finished the engine

would stand hissing gently with a whisper of smoke from the chimney as the crew enjoyed a cup of tea and a bite to eat. If one took into account the traffic movements at the Town station and at Yeovil Junction on the Southern Region main line which was just as busy as Pen Mill, all of this made Yeovil a major rail traffic centre. It seemed impossible at the time, but all of this was to change within a few years. In its heyday, the station had a considerable amount of staff, consisting of a Station Master, foreman, booking clerks, and 33 other ranks including guards, shunters, signalmen, carriage and wagon staff, platform staff, and signalmen. Staff included Mr Hole (Station Master), Fred Matterface (foreman), Reg Bungay, Freddie Brawn, Roy Vowles, Mrs Chapman, Reg Thomas (ticket collector), C&W examiners Tom Setter and Vic Chick

Regular dmu workings had started on 6th April 1959, with a total of three up and down workings a day interspersed with steam workings. Fuelling points were provided at Westbury and Weymouth. The boat trains from Paddington stopped running over the route from 2nd November 1959, with transfer of the services to the Waterloo–Weymouth route, and through services from Paddington ceased in 1960. The old B&E branch from Yeovil to Taunton via Langport West closed to passenger working from 15th June 1964, the final passenger trains ceasing on the previous Saturday, 13th June, with track removed between Curry Rivel Junction and Hendford by October 1965. The remaining stub of the old B&E branch between Pen Mill and Hendford goods was closed on 6th May 1968 together with Hendford goods depot.

On 16th September 1961 the first regular diesel locomotive workings appeared at Pen Mill with 'Hymek' diesels working the 10.10am SO Bristol to Weymouth and returning with the 3.25pm from Weymouth. When the neighbouring former joint station at Yeovil Town was closed to passenger services on 2nd October 1966, a passenger service between Pen Mill and Yeovil Junction via South Junction was operated from that date by a single unit railcar. This was the only regular booked passenger service to use the South Junction crossovers since the box opened, but this service only lasted until 4th May 1968 being replaced by a bus service.

The line was singled between Pen Mill and Maiden Newton on 26th May 1968, the up and down main lines were named up, and down loop, and signalled for two way working. The travel scene at Pen Mill today is very

2-8-0 "Long Tom" No. 3819 eases out of the 'down' goods yard and under the A30 road-bridge at Yeovil Pen Mill with a freight train for Weymouth on 27th June 1961. The 10mph speed restriction sign to the left refers to the curve through the 'up' platform.

John Day

Class 35 'Hymek' No. D7040 with a travel stained front end has just passed under the A30 roadbridge at Yeovil Pen Mill with a 'down' freight train on 31st July 1964. No. D7040 was introduced to traffic in July 1962 and allocated to 82A (Bristol Bath Road). Withdrawal came in January 1972, and the locomotive was cut up at Swindon in August of the same year.

John Day

Class 45 No 45101 leaves Yeovil Pen Mill and powers away along the single line towards Castle Cary with the diverted 06.40 Plymouth–Edinburgh on 4th May 1980. The locomotive entered traffic as No. D96 in April 1961 and was first allocated to 17A (Derby). It became No. 45101 in March 1973, and was finally allocated to Toton with withdrawal coming in November 1986. The signals in the background can route a 'down' train into either the 'down' or 'up' platforms.

John Day

different from the era described. By May 1974, train services had been reduced to seven daily and six Sunday trains, with a bare service of one train only on winter Sundays. From May 1989 the passenger services have been operated by two-car 'Sprinter' units, and the summer of the same year witnessed a service of nine trains Monday to Friday, twelve trains on Saturdays, plus seven on Sundays. The 'Sprinters' are supplemented by locomotive hauled trains in the summer timetable. For 1992 the following diagram was allocated to locomotive hauled trains:

SX	Class 37/0 (REJK)
2087	07.58am Cardiff Central–Weymouth
2V74	10.59am Weymouth–Bristol Temple Meads
2091	13.31pm Bristol Temple Meads–Weymouth
2V87	16.30pm Weymouth–Cardiff Central

As with all stations along the line Yeovil Pen Mill has not escaped modification and contraction. The down sidings alongside the station were reduced, with three sidings removed in 1966, after lying virtually unused and rusting for many years. The remaining sidings had become a hive of activity in 1993, being full of engineers' wagons being used in connection with new cable laying operations on the nearby Salisbury–Exeter main line. A staff coach resplendent in 'chocolate and cream' livery standing in the down yard brought back memories of former years.

A stroll around Pen Mill today finds the station with its lower quadrant signals still extant and although most of them are modern replacements that have been erected to suit the track alterations over the years, one signal in particular still stands as it did in the steam era. This can be found at the Weymouth end of the up platform, and carries a destination box and in my firing days would show four movements: Down Branch, Up Branch, Shed, Down Main. Nowadays it displays two movements: Main and Branch (the branch suffix now refers to the route to Yeovil Junction via the former up main whereas in my firing days 'Branch' meant the single line to the Town station). The station layout in 1993 had reverted back to the opening of the line to Weymouth in 1857, being now a passing place on a single line. The station buildings have remained unaltered over the years, but the old bookstall has long gone, the booking office has been renewed over the years, and the station underwent refurbishment in 1993. The platforms are still linked by a covered footbridge, the only one on the line in use today. Trains, leaving for and arriving from Weymouth use the former down main line, whilst trains for Yeovil Junction use the former up main line. The station still has its GWR feel about it, and one can still stand on the platform and imagine a gleaming 'Castle' or 'Grange' arriving in a cloud of smoke and steam, shaking the platforms with a thunder and a roar, with the exhaust crackling away from its copper capped

Yeovil Pen Mill, looking west from the 'up' platform to the A30 roadbridge on 5th September 1987. Showing the curving 'dog leg' which has bedevilled fast running through the 'up' platform ever since its opening. The station buildings have remained almost unaltered over the years and still have that special GWR atmosphere.
Peter Nicholson

chimney, and the slap of the vacuum pump echoing through the station whilst running in with the up 'Boat' during the 1950s.

Shunting Days at Pen Mill

Early, middle, and late turns were the norm for the shunting crews and in the days when Pen Mill shed was operating the turn was normally booked to a pannier or Prairie tank engine. The same rule applied when Yeovil Town shed operated the duty rosters, with the exception that in later years we would find ourselves with one of the U class 2-6-0 tender locomotives. Freight traffic was very heavy, with main line freights arriving daily from Bristol East Depot, Severn Tunnel Junction, and Westbury, plus the normal freight working on the Weymouth line. Local pick up goods would trundle in from the nearby yards and sidings, and freight would also arrive from Taunton via the branch. Yeovil Pen Mill was also a transhipment point for freight to and from the Southern Region at Yeovil Junction. Freight would also be tripped to the large goods yard at Hendford on the western edge of Yeovil. With a rumbling and a banging and clattering of buffers, the down freights would arrive and stop at the down platform. These trains would be hauled by a variety of motive power, of which the following were a common sight: 28xx 2-8-0, "Black Five", WD 2-8-0, Standard Class 5MT and Mogul 2-6-0. The freight train

crew would take water whilst the shunters walked the train and uncoupled the first 'cut', the carriage and wagon examiners would also walk the length of the train, tapping the wheels with their hammers to check that the train was free of defects. At this time we would have been standing out of the way with our pannier tank, the fire would be crackling away, with enough steam for the coming shunting movements. The cab would be hot as the firedoors would be open to keep the steam pressure from building up too much, water would be kept down to half a glass in the gauge tube, and some of my time would have been spent in oiling down the pipes and gauges. This had a two fold purpose, not only did the cab look nice and clean when it was oiled down, it also kept the dust down as well. Although I was trained as a Southern fireman, I must admit, that the ex-GWR pannier tanks were the best engine to have whilst shunting. They had an impressive steam brake, which was worked independently of the vacuum brake, the 'stick' reverser was a boon when shunting, much better than the screw reverser.

The freight engine was now ready to pull forward under the A30 road bridge, with a toot on the whistle the engine pulled forward taking with it twenty or so wagons and leaving the remainder of the train on the down main. A few seconds later, with a squealing of flanges the train reversed into the down yard until it was stopped by the shunter, who then uncoupled, the

Steam drifts from the safety valves of a pannier tank standing in the 'down' goods yard at Yeovil Pen Mill in the late 1940s. The engine would be awaiting its next duties as the station pilot/banker. The obligatory cast iron gents urinal complete with 'nameplate' can be seen to the right on the 'down' platform.
Norman Kibby

engine moved forward and then reversed into another siding to pick up more wagons. It then pulled onto the down main and reversed and coupled up to the waiting wagons of the freight train. If the down freight required a banker, then we would be pressed into service, if not, then we proceeded with the shunting, up and down the yard we would go, banging and thumping the wagons about, 'Ease up', 'hit 'em up', 'stop', 'back into the other road' so the commands would go on and on, sometimes the shunter would be on my side of the engine, and I would give the commands to him. At times the shunter would be on my driver's side of the engine, and if so, this would give me time to re-fill the boiler and hose down the footplate, or lean over the side and have a 'Woodbine'. Great care had to be taken when pulling down into the shunting neck near the road bridge, especially if the ground signals were at danger, as the catch points would be open protecting the down main line. At times the shunters would ask the signalman for the road if we had to pull out with a long train of wagons to shunt back into another road. The 'dummy' would clang over, and we would steam out with our wagons in tow onto the down main, and at times we would travel along and across the bridge over the River Yeo, before pushing back into the yard. Then it would be time to shunt the top yard, then over to the up side to shunt the goods shed, then time for a cup of tea, and a bite of 'pie' before resuming shunting. Carriages would have to be attached or detached to main line or branch trains, and the odd van or two would be tripped to Yeovil Town. A down train would need a banker, and if the bankers at Yetminster were busy, we would couple on at Pen Mill before our shift was over. Depending what shift we were on, we would either take the engine back to Yeovil Town shed, or be relieved by another crew at Pen Mill.

Yeovil Banking Engines. (Pen Mill Shed. Winter. 1954)
Engine No. 1.
starting time.   6.30am. Mon and Tues. 21 hrs.
...   ...   4.45am. Tues, Wed, Thurs, Fri, Sat. 91 hrs.
...   ...   4.45am. Sat and Sun. 26hrs 15m
...   ...   10.30am. Sun. 2hrs 20m

Yeovil Shunting Engines. (Pen Mill Shed. Winter. 1954)
Engine No. 2. *Pen Mill Shunter*. Starting time. 6.30am. Mon, Tues, Wed, Thurs, Fri, Sat. 23hrs. Performs passenger shunting when required

Engine No. 3. *Pen Mill Shunter*. Starting time 5.30pm. Mon, Tues, Wed, Thurs, Fri, Sat. 18hrs. Works 3.15pm. SX Langport West–Yeovil (P.M.) (arr 5.10pm). 3.32pm. SO Thorney–Yeovil (P.M.) Milk (arr 5.05pm). and 8.45pm Transfer, Yeovil (P.M.) to Yeovil Junction and back.

Engine No. 4. *Hendford Shunter*. Starting time 5.45am. Mon, Tues, Wed, Thurs, Fri. 64hrs 45m. (Starting time Sats 2pm, 1 hr 30 m). Works 6.15am Yeovil (P.M.) to Hendford (arr 6.25am.) and 7pm. SX, 3.35pm SO Hendford–Yeovil (P.M.), also on Saturdays 11.57am Yeovil (P.M.)–Yeovil Town and 1.08pm Yeovil Town to Yeovil (P.M.)

Yeovil Pen Mill 8th August 1913
August 8th 1913. Started off as a normal day for the staff at the station as they busied themselves with the workings of the day. Main line and branch services

arrived and departed, with passengers coming and going along the platforms. But this was to be no ordinary day, as tragedy was to strike in the early evening, making it the worst day that the station has ever known. At 6.03pm, (booked to arrive at Yeovil 5.33pm) the late running 2.45pm excursion from Paddington to Weymouth arrived at the down platform after being stopped at the North box inner home signal from 5.55pm until 6pm. The train consisted of the following vehicles attached to the engine in the order given: one milk van, six third class carriages, one brake third and one third class carriage, all fitted with the vacuum brake. Apart from the milk van which was a six-wheeled vehicle, all of the carriages were eight-wheelers. The total length of the train was 498½ft, the island platform was 360ft long, and the engine was one of the 'City' class 4-4-0 locomotives. The crew replenished their tender at the water column whilst their passengers de-trained, and unknown to the crew, the rear coach and half of the coach ahead of it were standing off the end of the platform. At least twenty passengers were stranded in the rear coach. The excursion was not the only late running train that day, as the 5.45pm Yeovil–Durston was standing in the up platform and eventually left at 6.08pm. The intention, from instructions left by the Station Master who had gone to Yeovil Town station on business, was that after the Durston branch train had departed the down excursion would be diverted onto the branch in order for the fast approaching 3.30 Paddington–Weymouth express to pass. However, the excursion was found to be too heavy for the Evershot bank, and as soon as the engine had been watered (the driver stated that this took about three minutes) the shunter uncoupled the milk van and leading coach from the train, the excursion engine then pulled up over the points in order to reverse into the down goods yard to detach the leading coach.

However the station foreman had contacted the North box and was told that the down express was off Marston Magna, and following the instructions left by the Station Master, immediately requested the shunter to back the excursion engine onto the train with the two vehicles it had just removed, in order to cross over to the branch, and then remove the leading coach when the express had passed. During this confusion when the shunting movements were going on, no one had thought about the passengers stranded in the rear coach, as it was found out later that some of them had intended to catch the Durston train.

Meanwhile, the 2.28pm Paddington–Weymouth express, which had been checked by signals at Castle Cary and Marston Magna, was now approaching the North box signals. The engine was 4-4-0 No. 3710 *City of Bath* and its train comprised one brake van, one first class saloon, two third class carriages, a brake van, one slip composite and one composite. All were eight-wheel vehicles and the total length of the train was 454ft. The engine was crewed by Driver Thomas Dowler and Fireman Richard Carver from Old Oak Common shed, both men being very experienced footplatemen. Dowler had been employed by the GWR for 40 years, 30 years as a driver, and Carver had been in the service of the Company for eleven years, and had served nine years as a fireman. Both men had reported for duty at 11.20am that day. Yeovil Pen Mill at that time was controlled by two signal boxes, South box situated 440ft beyond the west end of the island platform, and North box located 600ft to the east of the end of the up platform. North box was provided with the following signals relating to the down main line:

A down distant signal situated 1.586 yards to the east of the signal box.

An outer down outer home signal, situated 552 yds east of the signal box.

An inner down home signal, situated 100 yds east of the signal box.

A down starting signal, situated 112 yds to the west of the signal box.

Relief signalman Reginald Prosser was on duty in North box, and he had been a Company servant for eight years, and a signalman for $3^1/2$ years. On the day in question he had started work at 8.20am at Marston Magna box and worked until 12 noon. After a two-hour break he caught the 1.59pm down train to Yeovil where he took up his post at North box at 3.30pm and his shift finished at 7.30pm that night. His nearest signal box was Marston Magna 4 miles and 16 chains to the east. At 6.03pm, as the rear of the excursion train passed his box, Prosser sent the 'train out of section' message to Marston Magna. At the same time, 6.03pm, Prosser was offered the 'is line clear' from Marston Magna for the express. He accepted it at once. He was within the rules to accept the express, as his clearing point as regards the down main, was his down inner home signal, and the rules allowed him to accept a train from Marston Magna, providing the line was clear to the down inner home signal. He could not offer the train to the South box, because he had not received 'train out of section' from the South box. At 6.04pm he received 'train entering section' from Marston Magna, and at the same time he sent the 'shunt' signal to South box, indicating for the South signalman to shunt the excursion out of the way of the express. All of the North box down signals were now standing at 'danger'.

The view of the North box signalman as regards the down outer home signal was not a good one, and therefore track circuiting was provided for a distance of 200 yards behind the signal. An indicator in the signal box showed where any vehicle was standing on that portion of line. The North signalman was now watching the track indicator box to see when it indicated 'train track occupied', thus indicating the arrival of the express at the down outer home signal. Driver Dowler was now approaching Yeovil, his last stop had been at Frome, and he had been having a good run until being checked by signals at Castle Cary and Marston Magna. As he approached the North box down distant signal, which was standing at 'caution', he shut off steam and applied the brake. Trains entering the environs of Pen Mill on the down main run in on a left hand curve of $17^1/2$ chains radius, and on account of the curve, the driver on the right hand side of the engine, does not obtain a good view of the line ahead of him. The outer home signal was at 'danger' as he approached, and his speed was about six to eight miles an hour. The indicator in the North box showed 'train track occupied', and in his evidence, the signalman, Prosser, stated that he watched the track occupied indicator for about twenty seconds before lowering the outer home signal, in order for the train to approach the inner home signal. Driver Dowler, on the other hand, stated that the

signal was lowered when he was about twice the length of his train away. The inner home signal was then lowered when the train was about twenty yards from it, and travelling at a little over walking pace as it approached the North box starting signal which was standing at 'danger' protecting the excursion train.

Signalman Prosser watched as the train approached the starting signal, and he noticed that the driver was looking back at him, and thinking that the driver was about to pass the signal at danger, held up both his hands to attract the driver's attention. The signalman then watched in horror as the train passed the signal at 'danger' at an estimated speed of three miles an hour. Driver Dowler stated that he always made a practice of looking at any signal box that he was passing, and on this occasion he noticed that the signalman 'was motioning', and wondered what he was doing, but before he could make out what the signalman meant, the train had passed the danger signal. Fireman Carver backed up his driver's evidence at the inquest, and stated that after passing the inner home signal, he was attending to his engine and turning his injector on, and he noticed that the North box signalman 'was making a motion, as if something was wrong with the engine'. As soon as the fireman returned to his side of the footplate, he noticed that they had passed the danger signal, he shouted out to his mate, who had noticed it at the same time and applied the brake. He estimated the speed of the train at this moment at no more than four miles per hour, and the fireman screwed the handbrake on, but it was too late.

At the exact moment that the excursion train locomotive was reversing its two leading vehicles on its train, there was a splintering crash and a terrible bang as the down express rammed the rear of the excursion train. After a momentary silence the screams of the injured and trapped passengers resounded around the station and the down platform resembled a battlefield as the shocked station staff struggled to rescue the passengers from the debris of the rear coach. The fireman of the express was knocked out by the collision, but came to in the tender of the engine. The rear end of the excursion coach was stoved in causing the deaths of two people instantaneously, and injuring ten, of whom, one died later. At the following inquest, a verdict of accidental death through the momentary distraction of the driver's attention, and not of culpable negligence, was recorded. In his report to the Board of Trade Lt Col P G von Donop R.E. put the responsibility for the accident on the driver, for passing the danger signal, but at the same time added the following comments at the end of his report. 'Yeovil Station is a comparatively old one, and its arrangements cannot be regarded as entirely satisfactory; the platforms have not sufficient length to completely accommodate the trains, and owing to the curvature of the lines, the driver of a down train does not obtain a good view of the line in front of him when he is entering the station. The Company state that the question of remodelling this station has been for some time under consideration; it is, I consider, desirable that this should be taken in hand at an early date'.

Damage to Rolling Stock
2.45pm Paddington–Weymouth Excursion train. (via Berks & Hants)
Third No. 1902:- Coach completely wrecked.

The front end of No. 3710 *City of Bath* is embedded in the rear coach of the excursion train at Yeovil Pen Mill on 8th August 1913. Rescuers try desperately to rescue the injured passengers in the rear compartment.
Author's Collection

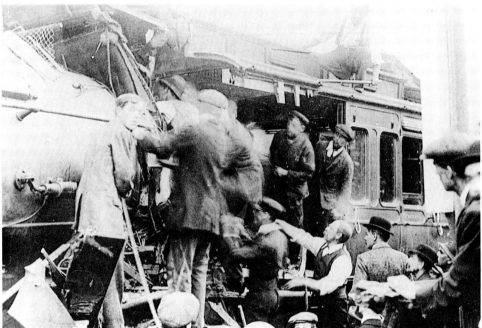

Another view of the tragic collision at Yeovil Pen Mill on 8th August 1913, showing the efforts to rescue the trapped passengers. The damage caused to the rear coach of the excursion train, even at the slow speed of the impact, was very considerable.
Author's Collection

Brake Third No. 2184. End and bogie badly damaged; one pair of wheels damaged; headstock bent; screw connection and one buffer broken; also gas cylinders, vacuum cylinders, lights, brake shaft and pull rods broken.
Third No. 1789:- One broken quarter light.

2.28pm Paddington–Weymouth (via Swindon)
Engine No. 3710:- Front vacuum pipe broken; step under smoke-box, trailing buffer and leading axle box damaged; front hand rail bent; and front end of footplate bent up.
P.B. Van No. 1057:- Two badly bent buffer guides and bent iron head stock.
Corridor First. No 3038:- Two broken C.I. buffer guides and one bent buffer rod.
Third No. 3616:- Two broken C.I. buffer guides.
P.B. Van. No 638:- One broken C.I. buffer guide.
Slip No. 7697:- Two badly bent buffer rods and damaged end panel.
Third No. 1316:- Headstock bent.
Third No. 1165:- One drawbar plate bent.
Third No. 3269:- Headstock and six quarter lights broken.
Third No. 3015:- One buffer guide and three quarter lights broken.

4-4-0 No. 3710 *City of Bath*
The engine, one of the famous 'City' class, was built at Swindon in March 1903, and when built carried the number 3433. This class of locomotive rapidly established a name for speed and was very popular with footplate crews. They first monopolised the express trains to Cornwall via Bristol for a year or two, and after serving on the Birmingham and South Wales routes, appeared on the Weymouth route from 1912 working fast trains. On 14th July 1903, *City of Bath* worked a five-coach Royal train conveying the Prince and Princess of Wales from Paddington to Plymouth. The speed of the engine was staggering, covering the distance from Paddington to the Bristol avoiding line (117 miles) in 102 minutes. The train had streaked through Chippenham at 80mph, and the total journey length of 246½ miles in 3¾ hours was a magnificent piece of enginemanship by the driver and fireman. One year later, on 9th May 1904 another member of the class, *City of Truro* made her now legendary run from Plymouth to Bristol with the up 'Ocean Mail' which had been disembarked from the *SS Kronprinz*. *City of Bath* was allocated to Chester in 1921, Barnstaple in 1922, and her last shed was Stafford Road before being withdrawn from service in September 1928.

Class 37/0 No. 37167 approaches Yeovil Pen Mill signal box with the 10.40 Radyr–Exmouth Junction coal train on 22nd March 1989. The signalman has the single-line token for the section to Yeovil Junction in his hand, and stands in readiness to pass it to the driver of No. 37167.

John Day

With the 'road' set for Yeovil Junction Class 37/0 No. 37227 rumbles through Yeovil Pen Mill with the 04.37 Washwood Heath–Exeter coal train on 12th August 1988. Note the reduced sidings to the right, now devoid of freight traffic.

John Day

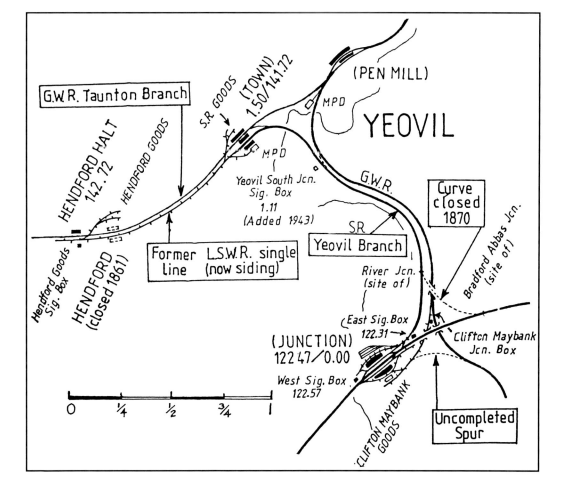

Yeovil South Junction

141 miles 66 chains from Paddington
Opened 13th October 1943
Route from South Junction to Yeovil Town closed 1st
  March 1967
Signal box closed 26th May 1968
Route from South Junction–Yeovil Junction singled
  26th May 1968

During the Second World War a series of junctions and signal boxes were constructed at strategic locations, and Yeovil South Junction was built at a position where the GWR Weymouth main line ran alongside the Southern Railway Yeovil Town–Yeovil junction branch. The new junction would enable trains to run from Westbury to Exeter via the Southern main line at Yeovil junction in the event of the GWR main line between Castle Cary and Taunton being disabled by enemy bombing. The signal box and layout, costing £9,045, was installed by Canadian troops in three days, working around the clock, and was opened on 13th October 1943. The new box had a 33-lever frame with VT 5-Bar locking with 4in centres. The lever frame was designed to control another junction facing the other way which would have allowed through running from Weymouth to Taunton via Yeovil Town and Langport but this connection was never installed.

Taunton driver W. J. (Jack) Gardner had cause to remember South Junction and the awkward turntable at Pen Mill during the war years, when he worked a troop train bound for Weymouth over the branch from Taunton to Yeovil. "One of my most memorable occasions of working over the Yeovil–Taunton line occurred on the 8th and 9th August 1944. D Day had

happened on 6th June, and after that there were hundreds of trains run to coastal ports with troops heading for the Continent. On the two days that I have mentioned, I was, as a fireman booked to work a troop train from Taunton to Weymouth packed full with ATS girls 14 coaches each day hauled by two 63xx class locomotives. I was fireman to George Smith, and this was straightforward enough until we reached Yeovil Pen Mill and the train was too long to do much with. We were the lead engine with No. 6343 and we stopped short of the crossover at the Sparkford end of Pen Mill and detached our engine and went on to the down line. Then the other engine pulled the train forward to allow us to get into Pen Mill Loco to turn. After doing this we came out onto the rear end of the train. The other engine detached and we pulled the train on to the branch from Yeovil Town, and when the other engine had gone into the shed to turn we pushed the train back into Pen Mill station far enough for the other engine to come out onto the front of our engine and couple up, and away we went for Weymouth. We had to return from Weymouth to Taunton light engines, so we turned again at Weymouth and came back as far as Yeovil South Junction. Whilst we were stopped by signals at South Junction I motioned to the signalman to let us back across the crossovers on to the Yeovil Junction to Yeovil Town line which he did, and so away to Taunton we went, very pleased at not having to use that pig of a turntable at Pen Mill shed. The next day we tried to do the same, but the South Junction signalman would not permit it. Why, I never knew, but as that day was fine weather we did not bother to turn and ran from Pen Mill to Taunton tender first".

Yeovil South Junction, looking towards Yeovil Town and Yeovil Pen Mill on 29th July 1961. The brick built, Type 13, war time signal box which opened on 13th October 1943 can be seen in the background. The Yeovil Town–Yeovil Junction tracks are in the foreground, and the Weymouth lines to the right. No. 4909 *Blakesley Hall* rounds the curve from Pen Mill with a 'down' Weymouth express.

John Day

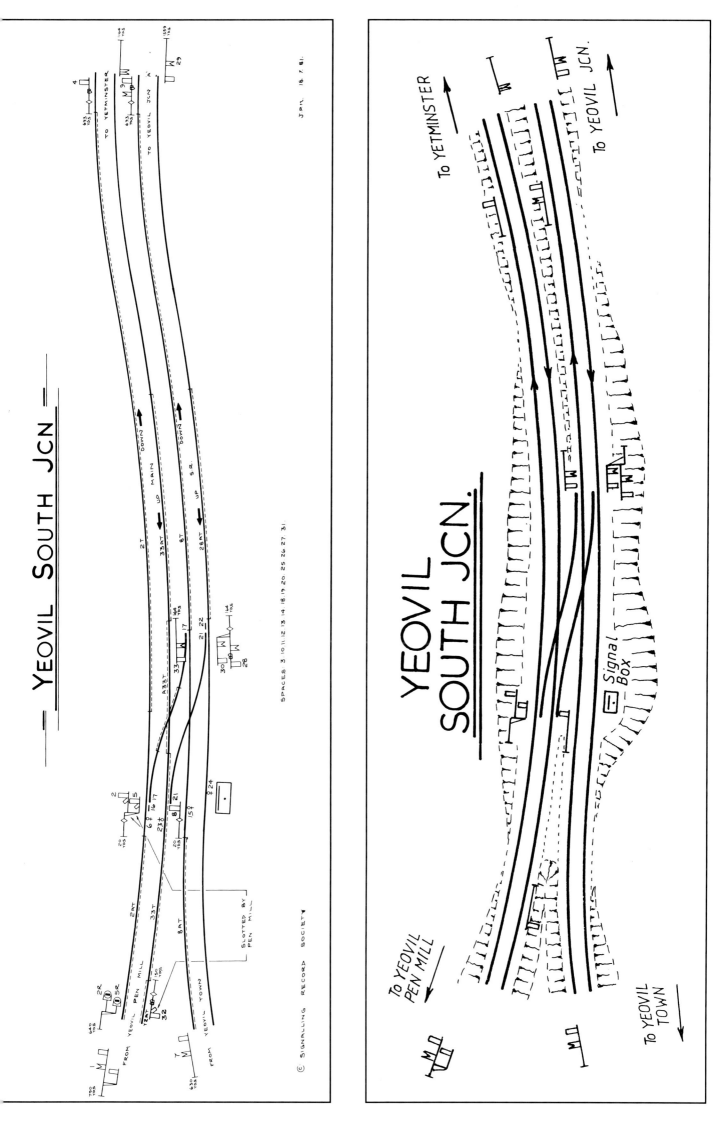

— YEOVIL SOUTH JCN —

SPACES 3. 10, 11, 12, 13, 14, 18, 19, 20, 25, 26, 27, 31.

© SIGNALLING RECORD SOCIETY

J.P.N. 18. 7. 81.

TO YETMINSTER

TO YEOVIL JCN A

2T

33AT

8T

28AT

UP MAIN DOWN

UP S.R. DOWN

FROM YEOVIL PEN MILL

FROM YEOVIL TOWN

SLOTTED BY PEN MILL

A33T

33

17

21 22

30

28

2

5

16 17

8 21

24

6

23

8

15

2AT

33T

8AT

12AT

32

2R

5R

YEOVIL
SOUTH JCN.

To YETMINSTER

To YEOVIL JCN.

Signal
Box

To YEOVIL
PEN MILL

To YEOVIL TOWN

George Pryer has recollections of the box in peacetime, but for a very different reason than Jack Gardner. "As a relief man, some pretty strange jobs came my way, but none stranger than the saga of Yeovil South Junction. This box had been installed in 1943 for wartime traffic, and had long been switched out of circuit. However, a railtour was booked to use the connection one Saturday, and with commendable foresight somebody decided that, as it had not been used for several years, the Signal & Telegraph Dept should visit it on the Friday to clean up all the contacts and see that everything worked. I was ordered to go with them 'in case of any difficulties' and to help make the box habitable.

We walked along the line from Pen Mill, and as we approached South Junction box we became aware of a buzzing sound which seemed to be coming out of the building. The cause soon became apparent; having

been shut up and silent for a long while, the place had become a breeding ground for flies! There were millions of them. The S&T team promptly announced that they had no intention of entering the box until something was done about the fly population, and I was despatched with all speed back to Pen Mill to explain the situation to the Station Master. I was duly given some money out of the booking office till to buy four cans of fly spray, which meant an even longer walk to South Junction via the nearest shop. When I eventually arrived back at the junction, about two hours after I first left it, I found the S&T gang happily sunning themselves on the grassy slopes of the cutting. I unlocked the signal box door and hurriedly pumped the contents of two of the cans up the internal staircase, then shut the door again to allow the spray to do its lethal work. After about twenty minutes I decided

No. 4941 *Llangedwyn Hall* runs cautiously through Yeovil South Junction with the regulator closed and steam issuing from her safety valves on 29th July 1961. No. 4941 is heading the 9.25am Weymouth–Birmingham Moor Street formed of Eastern Region stock. The train was reported as passing Tyseley 28½ minutes late that day, although that appears to be nothing unusual for this train.

John Day

A three-car dmu on a Westbury–Weymouth local service has just passed the Yeovil South Junction 'down' Weymouth line advanced starting signal on 17th July 1961. The signal post in the centre carries the South Junction–Yeovil Junction 'down' advanced starting signal with the Yeovil Junction 'A' signal box 'down' branch fixed distant arm.

John Day

The site of Yeovil South Junction, looking towards Yeovil Pen Mill on 22nd August 1981. The signal box and Yeovil Town branch have long gone, and the former double-track Weymouth line on the right, now forms two single lines. The nearest track is now the Yeovil Pen Mill–Yeovil Junction branch, and the furthest one is now the single line to Dorchester West. The lower quadrant signal to the left is for the Yeovil Junction–Pen Mill line, and the signal to the right is for 'up' Weymouth trains.

John Day

to survey my handywork and went up into the box. There were dead flies all over the stairs and at the end of the box nearest to them, but as those at the other end still looked healthy I used the remaining cans on them. In about half an hour it was possible to work in the place. Once a couple of windows were opened the survivors quickly flew away, but I managed to pick up five or six good heaped shovels full of carcasses and dump them in the concrete ash bin outside.

Of course, all the equipment was rusty and dirty, and the S&T had quite a hard time getting some of it to function properly. When they were satisfied with their efforts it was decided to try the block bells and indicators by obtaining the co-operation of the signalmen at Pen Mill, Yeovil Town, Yetminster and Yeovil Junction 'A' so that the block switches could be eased in for a quick 'waggle' when there were no trains about. As I was not passed for the box we couldn't open it in the normal way but this was duly done – and immediately we caused a block failure over half of Dorset! Eventually everything was put into working order, and the S&T must have carried out their testing efficiently because the railtour apparently used the junction the following day without incident."

Signalmen at the junction, have included Alan Barnett, Ray Byatt and Bill Froude. In BR days the box was little used, being switched out most of the time, and the 1954 working timetable shows that the box was 'switched in when required'. The connection was mostly used when the ex-GWR main line was blocked at times and a succession of Western Region trains would stop at Pen Mill to pick up a pilotman to guide them through South Junction and down the Southern Region main line to Exeter. Diverted up trains from Exeter would also need the services of a pilotman as far as Pen Mill. The Yeovil Town branch from South Junction was closed and taken out of use on 1st March 1967. South Junction box was closed on 26th May 1968 when the ex-GWR main line was singled. The connection to Yeovil Junction was also singled from the same date. Trains leaving Pen Mill for Yeovil Junction today use the former up Weymouth main line which is now known as the branch, using a single line token under the control of Pen Mill and Yeovil Junction signal boxes. Western Region trains still use the conection when the West of England main line is blocked, or closed through engineering work.

Clifton Maybank Junction

142 miles 60 chains from Paddington
Opened 13th June 1864
Closed 7th June 1937
Signal box (1) opened 1877. Closed 1896
Signal box (2) opened 1896. Closed 1st November 1937

In order to improve efficiency of exchanging goods traffic between the GWR and the LSWR at the congested goods depot at Hendford, the GWR, under powers obtained on 25th May 1860 opened a broad gauge single track branch to a goods transfer station at Clifton Maybank on 13th June 1864. Access to the branch was gained from the GWR main line, and the junction was situated between the bridge carrying the former Salisbury & Yeovil Railway original curve to Yeovil Town (closed 1st January 1870 but bridge was not removed until 1937) over the GWR main line, and the bridge carrying the LSWR Salisbury–Exeter main line over the GWR main Line. The branch burrowed underneath the LSWR main line curving and rising up a gradient of 1 in 85 before terminating in exchange sidings and a transhipment shed adjoining the London & South Western station at Yeovil Junction. There was

Although this is not the best of photographs, in fact it is quite poor, it is included for its importance, as it shows Clifton Maybank Junction and signal box in 1925. The line to the left is the goods line connecting the GWR main line with the goods transhipment depot at Yeovil Junction.
Adrian Vaughan Collection

Class 5MT 4-6-0 No. 73029 runs past the site of the former Clifton Maybank Junction with the 14.00 Weymouth–Yeovil Pen Mill on 31st August 1964. The Salisbury–Exeter main line can be seen passing over the Weymouth line in the background.
John Scrace

CLIFTON MAYBANK JCN

1932

FROM YEOVIL PEN MILL SOUTH

TO YETMINSTER

TO CLIFTON MAYBANK GOODS

UP MAIN

DOWN MAIN

751 YDS

160 YDS

207 YDS

1182 YDS

121 YDS

18 YDS

22 YDS

SPACES: 5. 6. 7. 8. 12. 13. 14. 15. 16. 21.

No. 47487 runs past the site of Clifton Maybank Junction with the 16.22 Bristol–Weymouth on 2nd April 1983. The Yeovil Junction–Yeovil Pen Mill branch can be seen to the left.

John Day

'Hymek' No. D7021 heads towards Weymouth past the site of Clifton Maybank Junction on 24th February 1962 with the 9.15am Swindon–Weymouth parcels.

John Day

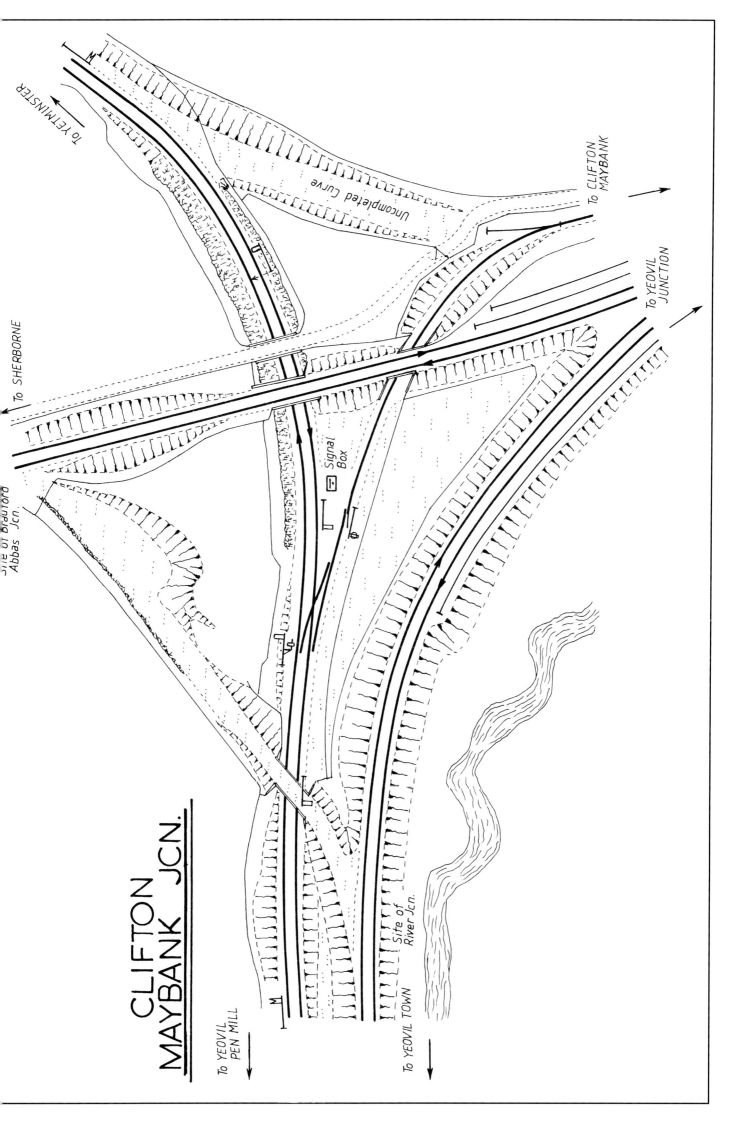

CLIFTON
MAYBANK JCN.

To YEOVIL
PEN MILL

To YEOVIL TOWN

Site of
River Jcn.

Signal
Box

Site of Bradford
Abbas Jcn.

To YETMINSTER

To SHERBORNE

Uncompleted Curve

To CLIFTON
MAYBANK

To YEOVIL
JUNCTION

no physical connection between the two companies' tracks until the gauge conversion in 1874.

After the gauge conversion, transfer trips were worked by LSWR and GWR locomotives. A second spur, west of Clifton Maybank junction giving access from the Weymouth direction to the transfer sidings, was authorised, but the earthworks only were constructed. In the early years of this century prior to the First World War, a total of 1,500 freight wagons were exchanged monthly. The branch was closed on 7th June 1937 and track removed by December 1937. After closure of the branch, exchange traffic between the GWR and the SR reverted to travelling via Yeovil Town.

The first signal box (not a block post) was in use from 1877 to 1896. It was replaced by a second box equipped with a 21-lever double twist frame situated alongside the up Weymouth main line. Clifton Maybank Junction signal box closed on 1st November 1937. The transhipment shed still stands today near the turntable at Yeovil Junction but the arches of differing sizes have long since been blocked up.

From the Southern Railway General and Working Appendice 1934:

Clifton Maybank Siding. Traffic to and from the S.R. is worked locally between Yeovil Pen Mill and Clifton Maybank.

The guard will be responsible for securing the train or wagons while standing on the running lines at Clifton Maybank, and the S.R. shunter will be responsible for the shunting, assisted by the guard of the train. Care must be exercised to properly secure vehicles (two spare sprags in addition to brakes to be always used) when standing on either of the lines at Clifton Maybank and between there and Clifton Maybank signal box, as there is a gradient of 1 in 85 falling towards the G.W. Weymouth main line. The S.R. Shunter will be responsible for working the signal to admit trains to the sidings from the G.W. single line, and also for working the points and wheel stops.

The connection between the Clifton Maybank line and the Southern Company's down siding at Yeovil Junction enables G.W.R. goods trains to run direct to the Southern Company's sidings intact. The points leading from the Southern Company's sidings through the connection to the G.W. line lie normally for the Southern Company's siding and have to be held for movements from the siding to the G.W. line. Owing to the steep gradient falling towards the G.W. line, the points to and from that line must be kept closed and padlocked when not in use, the keys of the points to be kept by the Southern Company's Shunter at Yeovil Junction. Wagons must not be propelled from the Southern Company's yard to the G.W. Company's line unless an engine is standing at the Paul's siding end of that road and a sufficient number of brakes have been pinned down on the leading wagons to control the movement over the falling gradient.

The points leading into Paul's private siding and the two facing points for trains coming from Clifton Maybank G.W.R. signal box must lie normally for the running line direction and be secured by padlock and key when not in use. The key of Paul's siding must be kept at Clifton Maybank signal box and handed to the Guard of each trip (Pen Mill to Clifton Maybank), who will be responsible for setting the points for that siding on arrival of the train and before shunting operations are commenced, and the points must remain in this position until the train is ready to return.

The S.R. Shunter must, before he goes off duty, see that the loop points at the goods office end and the G.W. transfer siding points are set and padlocked for the transfer siding. The points leading into the Mileage siding opposite the transfer shed must normally be set and locked to prevent access thereto. On arrival of a goods train at Clifton Maybank sidings the Guard must put down a sufficient number of hand brakes in addition to the van brake (two spare sprags in addition to brakes to be always used) until the train has been cleared from the arrival line.

Thornford Bridge Halt
144 miles 36 chains from Paddington
Opened 23rd March 1936
Beer Hackett sidings opened 30th September 1942
Beer Hackett sidings closed 15th October 1961

Opened on 23rd March 1936, the halt situated one mile from the village of Thornford comprised two staggered wooden platforms separated by a road overbridge. The platforms were equipped with small wooden shelters which were lit by oil lamps in the dark winter months. War Department sidings serving an army store located 24 chains from Thornford Bridge Halt were opened at Beer Hackett on 30th September 1942. The sidings lay alongside the up main line and were worked by a ground frame released by Yetminster signal box, and were taken out of use on 15th October 1961. The staggered wooden platforms were replaced by a single concrete version from Cattistock when that halt was closed in 1966. Trains today stop 'by request' at Thornford.

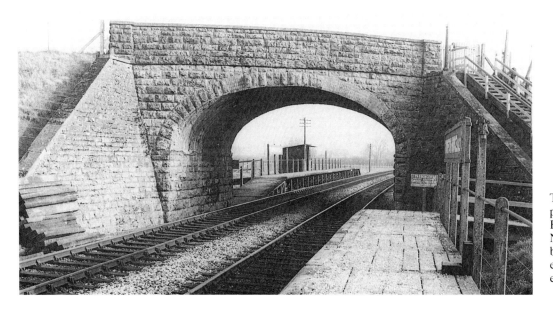

The staggered, timber built platforms at Thornford Bridge Halt on 12th February 1967. Note how the adjacent road bridge has been utilised to enable passengers to reach either platform.

C. L. Caddy

The basic platform and shelter at Thornford on 3rd April 1988, showing the single line stretching away to Yeovil.
Peter Nicholson

Yetminster

145 miles 45 chains from Paddington
Opened 20th January 1857
Broad gauge line doubled. Yeovil–Evershot 1858
Gauge conversion 18th/22nd June 1874
Signal box opened 1877
Down refuge siding extended 4th March 1901
United Dairies (Wholesale) Ltd PSA 18th July 1932
Closed to goods 5th April 1965
Signal box closed 26th May 1968
Line singled 26th May 1968
Unstaffed Halt from 6th October 1969

The station, opened with the line on 20th January 1857, stands at the foot of the bank which climbs for 5½ miles at an ascent of 1 in 51 to the summit at Evershot station. Stone built station buildings in the WS&W style were situated on both platforms, with the main offices being located on the up platform, and a waiting shelter on the down, behind which, stood the Station Master's house. There was no footbridge at the station, and steps were provided between the adjacent road bridge and the platforms. The goods yard serving the local traders was also located on the up side of the line. A loading dock complete with a 30cwt loading crane at the rear of the up platform was connected to the goods yard and two feed stores also stood in the goods yard. A down refuge siding was also provided. Various alterations to the layout occurred over the years, the down refuge siding having extended on 4th March 1901. A siding serving the United Dairies (Wholesale) Ltd was added in 1932.

A 27-lever, brick built signal box stood alongside the down main line near the entrance to the down refuge siding. Originally equipped with a stud frame, the box was converted to a VT3 Bar in 1912. Signalmen on duty at various times in the box have included Reg Francis, Bert Hull and Norman Kibby. Former station staff included Station Master Mr Ricketts and yard porter Stan Jessup.

Mr J. S. Perry remembers his father's working days at the station. "My father, H. J. Perry was the last Station Master at Yetminster and was appointed to that station, which also included supervision of Evershot station and the unstaffed halts at Chetnole and Thornford Bridge. In the late 1950s when my father took up this post, the staff consisted of two signalmen, two leading porters and a motor driver at Yetminster, and three signalmen and two leading porters at Evershot. In the absence of any bus service, passenger traffic at Yetminster was quite good, with some 50–70 people commuting daily to work in Yeovil. Throughout the day there was a steady stream of passengers joining trains, most of them to Yeovil, where most of the shopping was done. Yetminster village possessed only two or three shops.

The goods yard had the usual few wagons of coal to be unloaded by the local merchant, and a small animal feed warehouse was also there, which provided a local distribution point to the surrounding farms. The motor driver delivered this with other parcels picked up from the station. There was a steep gradient from Yetminster towards Evershot and the principal

'Modified Hall' No. 6977 *Grundisburgh Hall*, allocated to 82B (St Philip's Marsh), and heading the 3.10pm Weymouth–Paddington, sweeps down the bottom of the bank and into Yetminster on 6th September 1959.
H. B. Priestley – Derek Phillips Collection

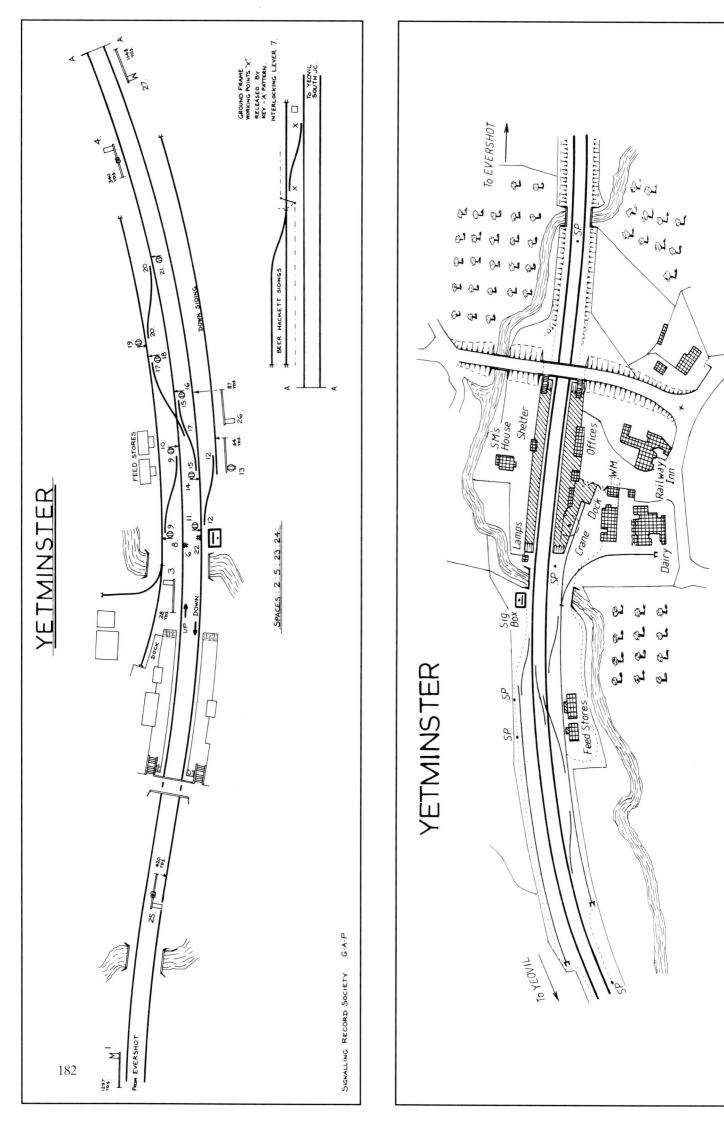

YETMINSTER

GROUND FRAME
WORKING POINTS 'X'.
RELEASED BY
KEY - 'A' PATTERN.
INTERLOCKING LEVER 7.

BEER HACKETT SIDINGS

To YEOVIL
SOUTH JC.

SPACES: 2·5·23·24.

SIGNALLING RECORD SOCIETY.   G·A·P·

FROM EVERSHOT

DOWN SIDING

FEED STORES

DOCK

UP

DOWN

YETMINSTER

To EVERSHOT

SMs House

Shelter

Lamps

Sig. Box

SP

Feed Stores

Crane   Dock

WM.

Offices

Railway Inn

Dairy

To YEOVIL

SP

Yetminster, looking east on 7th July 1962. The 'up' platform with the main station buildings is to the left. A Prairie tank engine stands in the goods yard while the Type 7D signal box can be seen to the right at the far end of the 'down' platform. A U class 2-6-0 tender engine on banking duties lifts her safety valves whilst standing in the bankers' siding. A Weymouth bound train is expected as the inner home signal is raised in the clear position.

C. L. Caddy

function of the signal box situated on the down side, was for the release of banking engines where there was a siding for banking purposes. Heavily loaded trains, especially freight trains, were assisted up the bank by banking engines which were not attached to the rear, and on summer Saturdays in the late 1950s three banking engines could regulary be seen in the Yetminster down refuge siding carrying out such duties. On 14th February 1966, my father retired when responsibility for Yetminster and other stations was assumed by the Area Manager at Yeovil."

The goods yard was closed on 5th April 1965, and sidings taken out of use on 7th July of the same year. The down refuge siding was taken out of use on 23rd November 1964 and removed in February 1965, and with the singling of the line from 26th May 1968, the signal box was no longer required and was closed from the same date. From October 1969 the station became unstaffed, and today the up platform only is in use and is provided with a basic modern bus stop type shelter. As with all the reduced stations on the route, trains stop by request, with passengers wishing to alight from the trains informing the guard, and those intending to board a train must give a hand signal to the driver

Maximun loads of passenger trains and empty coaching stock worked by one engine unassisted between Yeovil Pen Mill and Yetminster and reduced loadings for the Evershot bank.

BR Standard 4-6-2 Class 7 (70000)
'Castle' 4-6-0
'County' 4-6-0
Yeovil Pen Mill–Yetminster 440 Tons.
Yetminster–Evershot 315 Tons.*
Yetminster–Evershot 278 Tons.†
Evershot–Weymouth 455 Tons.

47xx 2-8-0
Only on local services at speeds not exceeding 60mph.
Yeovil Pen Mill–Yetminster 440 Tons.
Yetminster–Evershot 315 Tons.*
Yetminster–Evershot 278 Tons.†
Evershot–Weymouth 455 Tons.

BR Standard 4-6-0 Class 5 (73000)
'Hall' 4-6-0
'Grange' 4-6-0
Yeovil Pen Mill–Yetminster 420 Tons.
Yetminster–Evershot 288 Tons.*
Yetminster–Evershot 260 Tons.†
Evershot–Weymouth 420 Tons.

BR Standard 4-6-0 Class 4 (75000)
BR Standard 2-6-0 Class 4 (76000)
'Manor' 4-6-0
43xx 2-6-0
31xx 2-6-2T
41xx 2-6-2T
51xx 2-6-2T
81xx 2-6-2T
56xx 0-6-2T
66xx 0-6-2T
Yeovil Pen Mill–Yetminster 400 Tons.
Yetminster–Evershot 260 Tons.*
Yetminster–Evershot 232 Tons.†
Evershot–Weymouth 392 Tons.

BR Standard 2-6-2T Class 3 (82000)
45xx 2-6-2T
55xx 2-6-2T
57xx 0-6-0PT
94xx 0-6-0PT
Yeovil Pen Mill–Yetminster 345 Tons.
Yetminster–Evershot 204 Tons.*
Yetminster–Evershot 175 Tons.†
Evershot–Weymouth 336 Tons.

22xx 0-6-0
32xx 0-6-0
Yeovil Pen Mill–Yetminster 320 Tons.
Yetminster–Evershot 180 Tons.*
Yetminster–Evershot 152 Tons.†
Evershot–Weymouth 308 Tons.

0-6-0PT A Group.
16xx, 20xx, 54xx, 64xx and 74xx classes.
Yeovil Pen Mill–Yetminster 300 Tons.
Yetminster–Evershot 152 Tons.*
Yetminster–Evershot 134 Tons.†
Evershot–Weymouth 280 Tons.

14xx 0-4-2T
58xx 0-4-2T
Yeovil Pen Mill–Yetminster 250 Tons.
Yetminster–Evershot 132 Tons.*
Yetminster–Evershot 110 Tons.†
Evershot–Weymouth 176 Tons.

* When not stopping at Chetnole Halt.
† When stopping at Chetnole Halt.

Local Instructions June 1961.
**Assisting Passenger and Empty Coaching Stock Trains
Between Yeovil Pen Mill or Yetminster and Evershot.**

Whenever possible an assisting engine must always be sent to Yetminster in advance of the train to be assisted. Trains requiring assistance must be brought to a stand at Yetminster on the Evershot side of the down siding points to enable the assisting engine to be attached or draw on to the rear. At Evershot the assisting engine must be detached from stopping trains in the platform, running forward to the signal box only after the home (platform starting) signal has been replaced and again lowered. On trains not stopping at Evershot the assisting engine will not be coupled to the train, and it must cease to assist and its speed will be reduced so that it can be brought to a stand at the signal box.

When it is not possible for the assisting engine to be sent to Yetminster in advance of a train requiring assistance, it may be attached at the rear at Yeovil Pen Mill. In such circumstances, if the train is booked to stop at Evershot it must be coupled to the train and detached at that station. If however the train is not booked to stop at Evershot, it must stop at Yetminster, specially if necessary, for the assisting engine to be uncoupled, the subsequent working at Evershot being in accordance with the instructions contained in the previous paragraph. It is not necessary for the Guard of a passenger train which is being assisted from Yetminster to ascertain the number of the assisting engine. The actual load of the train to be assisted will be communicated to the Driver of the assisting engine by the signalman at Yetminster signal box.

Chetnole Halt
147 miles 52 chains from Paddington
Opened 11th September 1933
Up platform replaced by concrete platform from
  Cattistock. 1959
Line singled 26th May 1968

The halt situated some two miles from Yetminster, opened on 11th September 1933 for an estimated cost of £410. As at Thornford the timber platforms measuring 150ft x 7ft 6in were staggered and located either side of an adjacent road bridge, and basic shelters were provided. The former wooden up platform (as at Thornford) was replaced by a redundant concrete platform from the former Cattistock Halt which closed in 1966. With the singling of the line in 1968 the down platform at Chetnole was abolished. Trains stop today by request only.

Yetminster, looking east on 3rd April 1988, showing the basic facilities extended to passengers on the former 'up' platform.

Peter Nicholson

The platform and shelter at Chetnole as viewed from the nearby fields on 3rd April 1988.

Peter Nicholson

No. 5094 *Tretower Castle* heads up Evershot bank at Chetnole on 14th August 1960 with the 9.35am Bristol–Weymouth.

S. C. Nash

A Hawksworth 'County' No. 1009 *County of Carmarthen*, with a leaky front end, storms up Evershot bank at Chetnole with the 9.38am Parson Street–Weymouth on 14th August 1960.

S. C. Nash

Evershot

149 miles 76 chains from Paddington
Opened 20th January 1857
Broad gauge line doubled Yeovil–Evershot 1858
Gauge conversion 18th/22nd June 1874
Line doubled Evershot–Maiden Newton 1882
Signal box opened 12th October 1913. Replaced earlier
  box
Signal box closed 3rd January 1965
Goods yard closed 7th September 1964
Unstaffed from 7th September 1964
Closed to passengers 3rd October 1966
Line singled 26th May 1968

Standing 500ft above sea level the station is at the summit of the climbs from Yetminster and Maiden Newton. The attractive station buildings were unusual for the WS&W line in that they were constructed of timber instead of stone with the main offices located on the up platform. A footbridge connected the two platforms and in its early years this had an ornate roofing complete with valances. Evershot was one of the stations where the local gentry, in the persona of Lord and Lady Ilchester, had the right to have an ordinary passenger train stopped at the station either by themselves in person, or by an order signed by themselves, or by special request. Other persons qualified to stop passenger trains included The Hon John Fox-Strangeways, Lord Stanondale and Lord Ilchester's agent.

The goods yard was situated on the up side of the station, and a cattle pen was served by a small dock siding behind the up platform. Alterations took place over the years, including the lengthening of the platforms and additions and alterations to the sidings and crossovers during 1913/14. A solitary down relief siding was provided on the down side which ran behind the down platform. The original signal box, which stood at the Maiden Newton end of the station on the up side, was closed on 12th October 1913 and replaced on the same date by a new box standing alongside the down main line at the Maiden Newton end of the station. The new box had a 23-lever stud frame and measured: 25ft x 11ft x 8ft. Up until the mid 1940s the station had its own Station Master, but when the Southern Region took over the responsibility of the Castle Cary–Dorchester Junction section of the line in 1950, the post was abolished and Evershot became the responsibility of the Station Master at Yetminster, until 1966 when control was taken over by the Yeovil Area Manager. During the 1950s staff at Evershot consisted of two leading porters, and three signalmen.

The station was the point where the banking engines giving assistance to down trains from Yetminster ceased assisting, and after taking water at the column on the up platform they returned down the bank to Yetminster or back to Yeovil, 22 minutes being allowed for a light engine to run back to Pen Mill. A water column was also provided off the end of the down platform and a large water tank fed by an underground spring stood behind the station alongside the down relief siding. Vast quantities of water were consumed

185

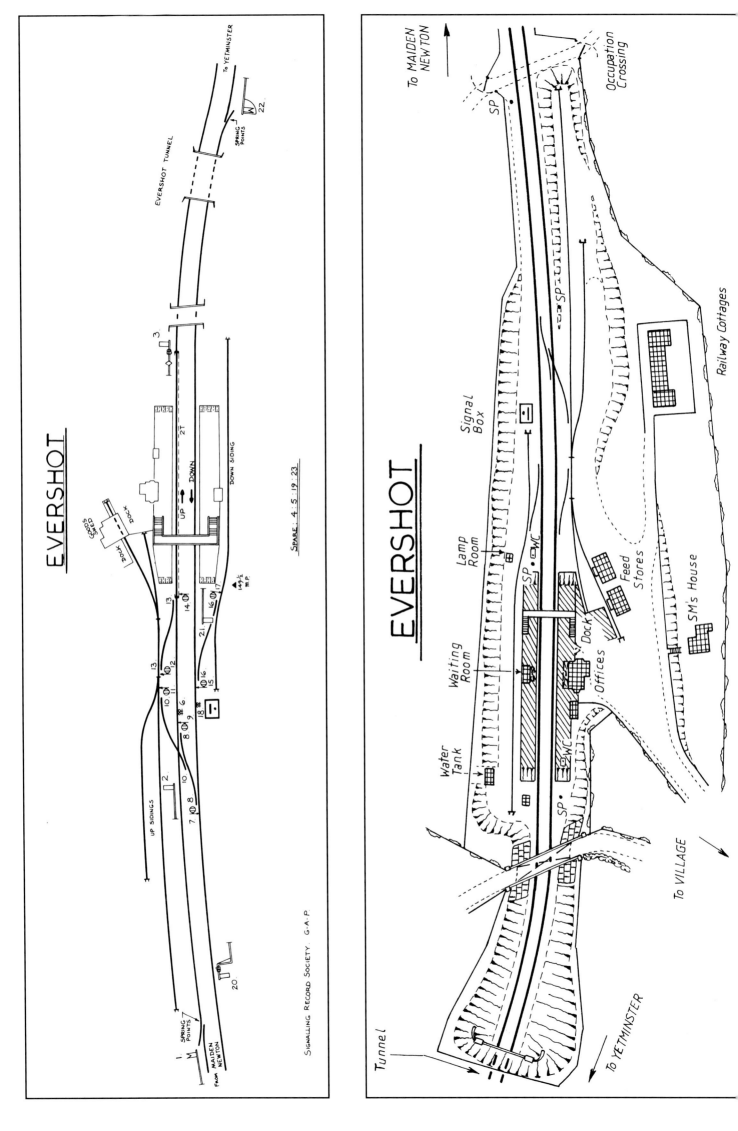

EVERSHOT

To YETMINSTER

EVERSHOT TUNNEL

SPRING POINTS

22

DOWN

UP

DOWN SIDING

GOODS SHED

DOCK

DOCK

2T

14½ m.P.

UP SIDINGS

SPRING POINTS

MAIDEN NEWTON

FROM MAIDEN NEWTON

20

SPARE. 4:5:19:23

SIGNALLING RECORD SOCIETY. G-A-P.

EVERSHOT

To MAIDEN NEWTON

Occupation Crossing

SP

SP

Signal Box

Lamp Room

Waiting Room

Water Tank

WC

SP

SP WC

Dock

Offices

SP WC

Feed Stores

SM's House

Railway Cottages

To VILLAGE

Tunnel

To YETMINSTER

Class 8F 2-8-0 No. 48431 from 82B (St Philip's Marsh), clanks cautiously through Evershot with the Bristol East Depot–Weymouth freight on 14th August 1958. The plume of steam at the rear of the train is issuing from 0-6-0PT No. 3671 which has assisted the train up over Evershot bank. Note the fireman looking down from the cab at the injector overflow. The train will stop here to detach the banking engine, and to pin down wagon brakes for the descent to Maiden Newton. This locomotive is now preserved on the Keighley & Worth Valley Railway.

H. B. Priestley –
Derek Phillips Collection

Evershot station, looking towards Maiden Newton on 18th April 1964. The large water tank which supplied the two water columns at the station can be seen to the left, standing behind the 'down' platform. The water column standing on the 'up' platform to the right was used to slake the thirst of locomotives and footplatemen alike!

C. L. Caddy

The signalman has already swiftly placed the inner home signal to 'danger' as the fireman of Class 5MT No. 73017 waves to the camera whilst approaching Evershot station with an 'up' vacuum fitted fruit train ('Per Pot') from Weymouth on 28th May 1960. Note the superb lower quadrant signal standing at the end of the 'down' platform and the brick built GWR Type 7D signal box in the distance, while the cattle pens and railwaymens' cottages can be seen to the right.

John Day

by the banking engines, especially during the busy summer months. All up freight trains were stopped to pin down brakes at the stop board before descending the bank to Yetminster. Various sidings in the goods yard including the up relief siding were taken out of use by 18th December 1963, leaving a solitary siding in the goods yard, and the down relief siding. The station became unstaffed and was closed to goods traffic from 7th September 1964, the remaining siding in the goods yard, the down relief siding, and the main line crossover were taken out of use, and the signal box was closed on 3rd January 1965. The station closed completely on 10th October 1966, and was demolished the following year.

The 308-yard long Holywell Tunnel, situated 27 chains east of the station, was the location for watching locomotives on down trains giving maximum effort as they reached the last portion of the bank. Let us now

A Swindon type cross-country dmu enters Evershot on 18th April 1964 forming a Bristol Temple Meads–Weymouth service.

C. L. Caddy

walk to the eastern portal of the tunnel. It is a glorious summer's day in 1957, we sit on the top of the cutting leading to the gaping tunnel mouth, smoke and steam from a preceding train drift lazily into the sunshine, birds dart and fly in their search for food, rabbits abound on the grassy edges of the trackside, the distant hum of traffic on the nearby main road breaks the silence. Below us in the cutting the gleaming rails shine in the midday sunshine, the catch points on the down main line gape open, and the down distant signal stands at caution. There is a blast on a whistle in the tunnel as an up train headed by a 'Hall' bursts out of the tunnel and runs panting down the bank, its long train of carriages with their bogie wheels clicking along the rail joints, rounds the curve and out of our sight. With a rustle of signal wires, the down distant signal arm lowers with a metallic clang, and for a few minutes there is no sight or sound of the approaching train, but then suddenly, wafting up on the summer breeze comes a faint sound of a barking exhaust growing louder by the minute. Then a second exhaust beat is heard, sometimes it merges with the other beat, sometimes not, the exhaust beats grow louder as the train approaches, at this moment the train is still out of sight, hidden by the curvature of the track, but the beat of the exhaust is unmistakable, only one type of engine can make a coughing beat like that, it is the beat of a GWR main line locomotive. The rails are quivering with the progress of the oncoming train, and now, rounding the curve with her exhaust beating out a tremendous bark from the chimney comes a mighty 'Castle' in her coat of green with copper capped chimney, brass safety valve, and bearing her nameplate on the third splasher, the pounding beat of the engine abounds around the cutting, cinders and steam are thrown out of the chimney as the locomotive advances slowly towards the tunnel.

The fireman has his back to us as he tends to the needs of the firebox, the driver is leaning over the side of the cab listening to the beat of his steed, with one hand on the reverser, ready to give another notch forward if it is required. There is a loud blast on the whistle as the engine nears the tunnel mouth, the exhaust beat becomes muffled as the 'Castle' enters the tunnel, another whistle as the engine wends its way through the darkness. The cutting lapses into a temporary

silence as the coaches rumble by at a walking pace, each compartment packed with passengers and suitcases, then another exhaust beat approaches around the curve, and the banker looms into view. A pannier tank shoving and pushing for all its worth at the rear of the train, the sound is ear splitting as with a blast on the whistle, the banker and rear coach enter the tunnel. The beats of the banker's exhaust are muffled by the tunnel roof, but the engine is still pushing and will not stop until the Evershot road bridge comes into view. The cutting lapses again into the sounds of the country, as clouds of smoke and steam billow out from the tunnel. A short time later the pannier tank emerges from the tunnel and runs down the bank towards Yetminster. The down distant is again lowered as we await another train coughing and barking up the bank – what will it be? 'Castle', 'Grange', 'Hall', 'Manor', or Mogul? In steam days, one never knew what type of locomotive would be approaching in those far off days of 1957, unlike today when two-car 'Sprinters' are the norm, with occasional forays by Class 37 and 47 diesel locomotives.

George Pryer now recollects Evershot station in the early 1960s: "If one could choose just two places as typifying the Westbury–Weymouth line, I believe Evershot and Bincombe Tunnel box (of which, more anon) are the best examples. Evershot was a remote country station actually located at Holywell, which was little more than a crossroads and a couple of houses, and a long walk from Evershot village. Passenger business was thin, but the place was so well kept it was almost a showpiece. There were rambling roses and other climbing plants around the platform railings, and the grass of the embankments always looked as if it had been cut with a lawn mower. One of the staff had a couple of goats which could be seen tethered at the lineside whenever one passed in a train, and these ensured that the undergrowth was kept in check. Furthermore, the ganger obviously took great pride in his section, and the cess beside the running lines and sidings was neatly filled and levelled with grey Meldon dust, as was the space beneath the rodding run from the signal box to the points. Modern practices do not allow time for such niceties, but Evershot in the early 1960s looked a treat and was a tribute to the staff who worked there."

No. 4918 *Dartington Hall* with her paintwork absolutely gleaming in the summer sunshine, approaches Holywell Tunnel at the top of Evershot bank with the 10am Swindon–Weymouth excursion on 14th August 1960. The locomotive is passing over the catch point which was located to derail any 'down' train breaking away and stop it running back down the bank.

S. C. Nash

No. 1024 *County of Pembroke* lifts her safety valves whilst pounding up Evershot bank on the approach to Holywell Tunnel on 14th August 1960 with the 10.10am Bristol Temple Meads–Weymouth. The Evershot 'down' distant signal can be seen to the right, standing near the platelayers' hut.

S. C. Nash

Cattistock Halt

153 miles 18 chains from Paddington
Opened 3rd August 1931
Closed 3rd October 1966

The timber built two-platformed halt located four miles from Evershot was built to an estimated cost of £636 and opened on 3rd August 1931. The platforms were re-built with concrete pre-cast sections in 1959 upon the introduction of dmu services. Cattistock closed on 3rd October 1966, and the platforms were re-erected at Chetnole and Thornford respectively.

Cattistock Halt, looking towards Evershot on 18th April 1964.

C. L. Caddy

Maiden Newton

154 miles 8 chains from Paddington
Opened 1st September 1857
Bridport branch opened 12th November 1857
Gauge conversion 18th/22nd June 1874
No. 1 signal box (North) opened 1877, closed 1885
No. 2 signal box (South) opened 1877, closed 1885
Extension to West Bay on Bridport Branch opened 31st March 1884
Signal box (3) opened on down platform 1885, closed 1921
Doubling of main line Evershot–Maiden Newton 1882
Doubling of main line to Grimstone & Frampton 1884
Signal box (4) opened 1921
Bridport–West Bay closed to passenger traffic 22nd September 1930

Bridport–West Bay closed to freight traffic 3rd December 1962
Bridport branch closed to freight 5th April 1965
Maiden Newton closed to Goods 5th April 1965
Line singled Yeovil–Maiden Newton 26th May 1968
Line singled Maiden Newton–Dorchester West 9th June 1968
Bridport branch closed to passenger traffic 5th May 1975
Signal box closed 15th May 1988

The station, which was also the junction with the Bridport branch, comprised two platforms serving the main line and a terminal bay for the use of branch trains. Here, as at Witham the branch bay was provided with a timber train shed. The station build-

Maiden Newton, looking towards Dorchester in 1931. To the right can be seen the timber built train shed for the Bridport branch trains, and two superb lower quadrant signals, complete with square wooden posts topped by finials, stand at 'danger'. The signal to the left is the "up" main starter, sited on the "down" side for sighting purposes due to the curvature of the track through the station. Beyond the attractive lattice footbridge connecting the two platforms, a goods train can be seen at the end of the 'down' platform with the signal box in the distance.

National Railway Museum

Maiden Newton looking towards Evershot in 1931. The main station buildings constructed in knapped flint stand on the 'up' platform to the left, with a waiting shelter provided for the 'down' platform on the right. The smoke vents for the Bridport bay over-all roof can be seen to the right of the station chimneys on the 'up' platform, and advertisements for Sutton's Seeds, Bovril, Nestle's Milk and the *Daily Telegraph*, decorate the platform. This photograph must have been taken during a lull in traffic, as there is no sign of passengers or staff. The curvature of the main line can be seen in the distance as it passes under the road bridge in the distance.

National Railway Museum

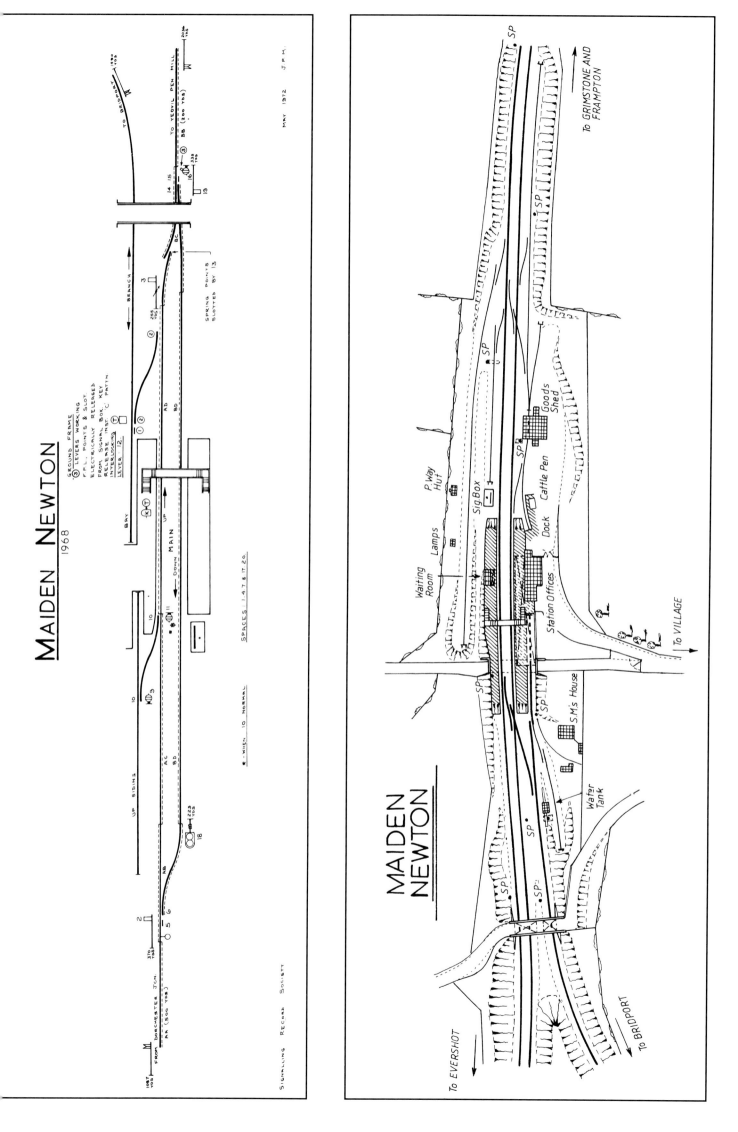

MAIDEN NEWTON
1968

GROUND FRAME
③ LEVERS WORKING
F.P.L, POINTS & SLOT.
ELECTRICALLY RELEASED
FROM SIGNAL BOX. KEY
RELEASE INST. 'C' PATH
INTERLOCKING
LEVER 12.

SPACES : 1·4·7 & 17·20.

※ WHEN 10 NORMAL

SPRING POINTS
SLOTTED BY 13.

TO BRIDPORT

TO YEOVIL PEN MILL

BRANCH

BAY

MAIN

DOWN   UP

UP SIDING

FROM DORCHESTER JCN.

SIGNALLING RECORD SOCIETY   MAY 1972   J.P.M.

MAIDEN
NEWTON

SP

To GRIMSTONE AND
FRAMPTON

SP

SP

Goods
Shed

P.Way
Hut

Waiting
Room

Lamps

Sig. Box

Cattle Pen

Dock

Station Offices

S.Ms House

Water
Tank

To VILLAGE

SP

SP

SP

SP

SP

To EVERSHOT

To BRIDPORT

To GRIMSTONE AND
FRAMPTON

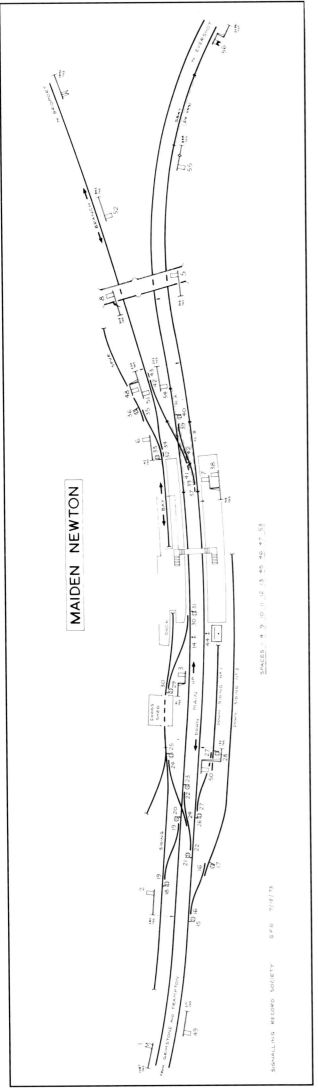

MAIDEN NEWTON

SPACES - 4 9 10 11 12 13 45 46 47 53

SIGNALLING RECORD SOCIETY   GFG   7/12/73

Maiden Newton, looking towards Evershot on 9th May 1965. The GWR Type 7D signal box to the right is standing alongside the 'down' main line. Note the attractive waiting shelter on the platform.

C. L. Caddy

Signalman W. L. Kenning relaxes on his chair inside Maiden Newton signal box in 1955. As always, the interior of the box is spotless, and the ever boiling kettle is perched ready for use on the stove to the right.

Adrian Vaughan Collection

ings constructed of knapped flint had the main offices on the up platform and a waiting shelter on the down. A lattice footbridge connected the two platforms, but this was replaced in later years by a Southern Region concrete version. The goods shed, and traders' sidings were situated at the Dorchester end of the station on the up side. Two signal boxes were opened in 1877. The 22-lever No. 1 box (later re-named North) was positioned alongside the down line of the passing loop opposite the junction with the Bridport branch. The 14-lever No. 2 box (later re-named South) was sited south of the station near the down goods siding. The two boxes were closed in 1885 and replaced from the same date by a 30-lever box positioned on the Dorchester end of the down platform. This box in turn was closed in 1921, and replaced by a box sited off the south end of the down platform, and was equipped with a VT 3-Bar 56-lever frame. Box size, 33ft 6in x 12ft x 9ft 6in. A down refuge siding was brought into use on 27th January 1906.

The Bridport branch services in the 1950s were worked by pannier and Prairie tanks, but the latter did not arrive on the branch until 1941 when No. 5555 was used for the first time. When the branch train had arrived at Maiden Newton and its passengers had disembarked, the engine would propel its 'B' set into the gravity siding, and after uncoupling, would then run forward and reverse out of the way of the coaches which rolled back into the bay under the control of the guard using his handbrake. The engine would take water whilst the coaches were being 'shunted' by the guard.

Freight at Maiden Newton between the war years and up until the late 1950s consisted of coal for the local traders, and milk from the branch which arrived in churns for the Wilts United Dairies and after processing was sent to major towns and centres by rail. After 1932, six-wheel 'Ro-Tank' wagons were introduced, upon which, road milk tankers were loaded via the end loading dock situated behind the up platform. Cattle were transhipped in quantity at Maiden Newton and on the branch. Freight traffic on the branch included petrol, coal, milk, cattle feed while items exported from the branch included, watercress, pit props and wooden boxes for fruit traffic from Galpins at Toller, gravel and shingle from West Bay, and nets and twine from the factories in Bridport.

Passenger services on the branch at first consisted of four or five trains each way daily but with the opening of the extension to West Bay on 31st March 1884, the service was increased to seven, with three of these running to West Bay. By 1906 the daily service of passenger trains had increased to eight north of Bridport and ten to the south. On Sundays there were three services between Maiden Newton and Bridport only, and one service to West Bay. The Sunday trains were worked by the railmotor that was used for the weekday Abbotsbury service. Passenger services were withdrawn from West Bay on 22nd September 1930, but freight lasted until 3rd December 1962. In 1934 the branch had nine weekday and five Sunday trains. By 1959 there were twelve trains daily and eight on Sundays. The Sunday service was withdrawn in September 1962, and in 1974 a service of nine daily trains was in operation. On 15th June 1959, Weymouth based diesel units worked the regular trains on the branch, and the final steam locomotives to be based at Bridport, Nos 4507 and 4562 departed for Weymouth on the same day. Bridport shed was closed at the same time, and after the arrival of the diesels the daily goods service and the sole remaining steam passenger service were hauled by pannier tanks from Weymouth shed until 1964. Steam passenger services on the branch had ceased by this time, and ex-LMS 2-6-2 tanks continued to work freight trains to Bridport until the closure of the goods yard in 1965. At first, the diesel units on the branch were formed of three-car units, but with declining passenger traffic, the sets were reduced to two-car units, and finally in 1965 had been reduced to a single car.

When Weymouth shed closed in 1968, the diesel unit was supplied by Westbury. The junction between the Bridport branch and the main line was altered on 28th April 1968, this preventing through running onto the branch. The new connection was via a trailing connection from the up main line operated by a ground frame. Closure of the branch finally arrived on 5th May 1975, with the last services operating on Saturday 3rd May. Such was the passenger traffic that day, that the single railcar was coupled to a three-car set, with two guards provided on each train to issue tickets. At 8.40pm the last train left Bridport to the usual sound of exploding detonators. The track was lifted in November 1975,

Maiden Newton on 16th August 1960. Dmu car Nos 50742 and 50689 stands in the bay to the left, forming the 12.12pm to Bridport. Dmu car Nos 50665 and 50719 can be seen in the distance, heading towards Evershot with the 11.40am Weymouth to Westbury.

H. B. Priestley – Derek Phillips Collection

A three-car dmu formimg a Bristol–Weymouth service glides into Maiden Newton on 4th February 1967. The curving nature of the track can be seen in the distance, passing under the road bridge. This is the reason why the 'down' inner home signal, (which can be seen in the 'off' position) is situated alongside the 'up' main line.

C. L. Caddy

Maiden Newton looking towards Dorchester on 9th May 1965. A 'down' train is signalled, and the Bridport branch line can be seen to the right running towards the covered train shed in the distance. Note that the gravitational siding to the right has now been removed. Relics of the Second World War in the shape of concrete tank traps can be seen to the left and right of the photograph.

C. L. Caddy

Two lone passengers await a Weymouth bound train at Maiden Newton on 3rd April 1988. The attractive waiting shelter on the 'down' platform is still in place and looks well cared for. The two-lever ground frame in the foreground controls the entrance/exit to the siding which has been retained for the permanent way department.

Peter Nicholson

and the ground frame and connection to the main line removed on 14th November 1976.

The gravity siding at Maiden Newton, and the down siding near the signal box known as the 'Bridport' siding, were taken out of use on 20th December 1963. The down refuge siding was taken out of use on 1st September 1967, as were the up sidings on 29th March 1963. With the main line converted to single line in 1968 and the layout reduced to a passing loop the signal box frame was reduced to 20 levers. In 1968/69 the overall roof was removed from the bay line, at the same time the old lattice footbridge was replaced by a Southern Region preformed design from a station on the former LSWR Salisbury–Exeter line. The signal box closed in May 1988. Today the section from Maiden Newton to Dorchester is controlled by Dorchester panel, and from Maiden Newton to Yeovil by Yeovil Pen Mill box. Drivers of up trains collect the token for the Yeovil section from a small cabin positioned on the up platform. There is another cabin containing a token machine on the down platform for the use of drivers on down trains to return the token from the Yeovil section. The section from Maiden Newton to Dorchester is worked by tokenless block. Maiden Newton is now an unstaffed halt, a far cry from the days when the staff consisted of the Station Master, two porters, lad porter, two shunters, three signalmen, parcel porter, booking clerk and a junior clerk.

The days are long gone of a pannier tank coupled to its 'B' set standing under the overall roof in the branch bay with smoke drifting lazily from the chimney and a faint breath of steam swirling from the safety valves. The driver would be wandering around the engine complete with his oil feeder giving the straps and glands a top up, and the scrape of the shovel on the footplate as the fireman puts a few rounds of coal around the firebox whilst waiting for the rumble and roar of an approaching main line stopping train. Carriage doors would slam as passengers disembark and head for the branch train, the 'boards' would be 'off' and with a roar from the chimney as the vacuum ejector was opened, and with a toot on the whistle, the pannier tank would pull away on the journey to Bridport, leaving a lingering smell of hot oil and steam in its wake.

Grimstone and Frampton

157 miles 56 chains from Paddington
Opened 20th January 1857 as Frampton
Renamed Grimstone July 1857
Renamed Grimstone and Frampton 1858
Gauge conversion 18th/22nd June 1874
Line doubled Maiden Newton–Grimstone and Frampton 1884
Line doubled Grimstone & Frampton–Dorchester 1885
Signal box (1) opened 1885. Closed 1904
Signal box (2) opened 1904. Closed 5th April 1966
Open to goods August 1905
Closed to goods 1st May 1961
Unstaffed Halt from 11th April 1966
Station closed 3rd October 1966
Line singled 9th June 1968

The station, situated on the side of the Frome valley, opened with the line on 20th January 1857. Known as Frampton at the opening, the name was altered to Grimstone in July 1857, and renamed Grimstone and Frampton from 1858. At first the station was on the single line with a crossing place at Evershot, but the gauge conversion in 1874 was followed by the doubling of the line from Maiden Newton in 1884 and southwards to Dorchester in 1885. The station comprised two platforms connected by a footbridge. Station buildings were constructed of brick with the main offices situated on the down platform, and a waiting shelter on the up platform. The 20-lever frame signal box was situated off the Dorchester end of the up platform. Box size, 21ft x 12ft x 8ft. Goods facilities were not provided until 1905, when a crossover, and a single siding on the down side ending in a loading dock behind the down platform, were brought into use on 31st January. The station was opened for goods trafic from August of the same year. Here, as at many country stations, coal for the local traders was delivered by the local pick up goods. The 1938 summer timetable shows a total of nine down (ten Sats), and ten up (eleven Sats) calling at the station on weekdays, with four down and five up trains on Sundays. In the 1966 summer timetable, services at the station had not altered much with a weekday service of eight down and ten up trains on weekdays, and six and eight

Hertfordshire Rail Tours' 'The Royal Wessex' makes its return leg through Maiden Newton on 10th December 1988 behind Class 33s Nos 33114 *Sultan* and 33113. The train consists of the 'raspberry ripple' VIP Mark 1 FOs and worked from Waterloo–Weymouth, and on to the Quay (empty). The train has passed the station and is now entering the single-line section to Yeovil Pen Mill, the lower quadrant signals have been swept way and the abandoned trackbed of the Bridport branch can be seen to the right.

Peter Nicholson

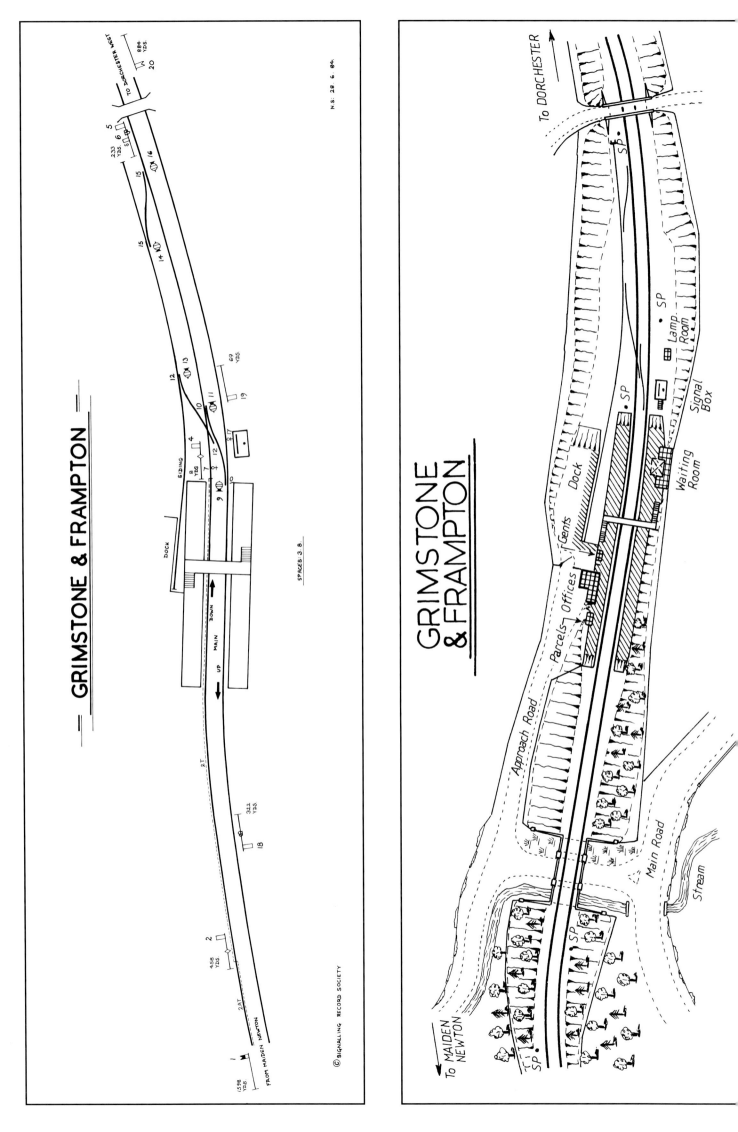

— GRIMSTONE & FRAMPTON —

TO DORCHESTER WEST

884 YDS.
20

5
6
SIDING
15
16

233 YDS.

15

14

15

12

13

SIDING
10
11

69 YDS.

19

DOCK

8 YDS.
4
7

12

17

9

DOWN
MAIN
UP

2T

322 YDS.

18

2
458 YDS.

2AT

1598 YDS.

1

FROM MAIDEN NEWTON

SPACES: 3.8.

N.S. 28. 6. 84.

© SIGNALLING RECORD SOCIETY

GRIMSTONE & FRAMPTON

To DORCHESTER

SP.

Lamp. Room

Signal Box

Waiting Room

SP.

Dock

Gents

Parcels Offices

Approach Road

Main Road

Stream

SP.

SP.

To MAIDEN NEWTON

Grimstone & Frampton signal box pictured here on 9th September 1961, was equipped with a 20-lever frame. The brick built coal bunker can be seen to the right at the bottom of the box steps. The box measured 21ft x 12ft x 8ft and was closed on 5th April 1966.

C. L. Caddy

respectively on peak summer Saturdays. In 1945 the signal box was opened from 9am to 5pm on weekdays only and because the box was switched out at night and on Sundays, the signal lamps were not lit between 1st April and 30th September each year. The station was closed to goods traffic from 1st May 1961, with the siding and crossover taken out of use by 31st December of the same year, leaving the box to function as a 'break section' block post until closure on 5th May 1966. The station was unstaffed from 11th April 1966, closed on 3rd October 1966, and demolished in 1967.

"If railways could be beautiful, interesting and stimulating, they could also at times have an ethereal quality. Stand on the dimly oil-lit platform of a remote country station like Grimstone and Frampton on a gusty night when the lamps flicker and the wind moans in the telephone wires, and the signal box is switched out, the office is unmanned, and there is nobody around. Then, borne on the wind, swelling and dying, the sound of an approaching train, invisible in the inky darkness save for the winking yellow eyes of the engine headlamps. Perhaps the sky would suddenly be flooded with a dancing red glow as the fireman opened the firebox door to add a few shovels of coal, and the train would

rush by into the night leaving nothing but the faint sulphurous smell from the engine and the sight of the red tail lamp rocking and swaying until it vanished into the distance. Of scenes like this is the romance of railways made." (G. Pryer)

Bradford Peverell & Stratton Halt
158 miles 72 chains from Paddington
Opened 22nd May 1933
Closed 3rd October 1966

The halt, situated near to the A37 main road and half a mile from each village, was opened on 22nd May 1933. The 150ft platforms were staggered and timber built and were replaced by concrete versions in 1959. Closure came on 3rd October 1966, but although very overgrown, the platforms are still in place today. In 1955 two temporary signal boxes and crossovers were installed in connection with engineering work east of the halt. Single line working in the winter timetable only was introduced between the two boxes known as Viaduct 199 signal box, and Viaduct 202 signal box. Opening and closing dates for both boxes: opened 14th January 1955, closed 5th April 1955, re-opened October 1955 and closed 18th May 1956. In addition,

Grimstone & Frampton station, looking towards Maiden Newton on 9th May 1965 showing the brick built station buildings and signal box. A 'down' train is signalled. The small goods yard, closed on 1st May 1961 had been previously situated in the foreground.

C. L. Caddy

Bradford Peverell and Stratton Halt, looking south on 18th August 1963 showing the staggered platforms. Authorised on 23rd March 1933, with 150ft long timber platforms, shelters, gates, lighting, and a footpath to the road, the halt opened on 22nd May 1933 at an estimated cost of £575.

C. L. Caddy

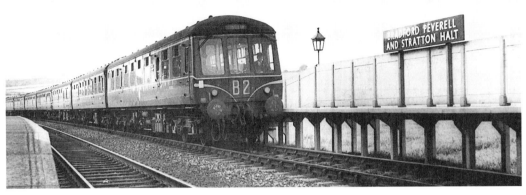

A nine-car dmu forming the 2pm Bristol Temple Meads–Weymouth is seen here passing Bradford Peverell and Stratton Halt on 18th August 1963. The original timber platforms were replaced by concrete cast sections in 1959 upon the introduction of dmu services.

C. L. Caddy

box 199 only was reopened on 29th December 1957 for single line working to Grimstone, and was closed again in March 1958. The crossovers and temporary signal boxes provided for the single line working were removed upon completion of the work.

Dorchester West

161 miles 63 chains from Paddington
Opened 20th January 1857 as Dorchester
Line doubled Grimstone and Frampton–Dorchester 1885
Station signal box (1) opened 1885 closed 14th May 1908
Re-named Dorchester West 26th September 1949
Station signal box (2) opened 14th May 1908, closed 24th March 1968
Closed to Goods 6th September 1965
Line reverted to single track Maiden Newton–Dorchester 9th June 1968
Unstaffed from 2nd January 1972

This once fine station designed by Ritson and opened on 20th January 1857 has been witness to a period of neglect in recent years. The main building on the down side is constructed of cement rendered stone under a broad hipped roof, window openings are round headed, reminiscent of the Italian style. Passenger accommodation was sumptious for this GWR station in the county town of Dorset, first and second class passengers had separate waiting rooms, there was also a first class ladies' waiting room and a gents' toilet. Staff offices comprised a booking office which was also divided for the benefit of first and second class passengers, and a superintendent's office. A lamp room and store were housed in a separate building. A fine timber built overall roof train shed strengthened with iron trusses (as at Frome) covered both platforms, but the roof was removed in 1934 and replaced by glazed

canopies. Many local people still remember Wymans bookstall which stood on the down platform. With the growth of the local populace and railway services, a new brick built building was constructed in the early years of the present century on the up platform and comprised a general waiting room, a gents' urinal, and a ladies' waiting room with toilet. A signal box (No. 1 box) equipped with an 18-lever frame, opened in 1885 and was situated alongside the down line near the road underbridge north of the down platform. Alterations took place in 1908 with all work completed by May of the same year. Both station platforms were extended northwards by 160ft, part of the down refuge siding was removed for the alterations, and the former No. 1 signal box was removed and replaced by a new signal box located 40 yards to the north. The new signal box had a 29-lever frame. Box size, 25ft x 12ft x 8ft. Other alterations to the layout in 1908 included re-siting the down refuge siding exit and the nearby main line trailing crossover. As the down platform was to be widened, advantage was taken of the former broad gauge clearances between the platforms by slewing the down main slightly towards the up.

Vast siding accommodation was provided at Dorchester. Stopping freight trains arrived from Bristol East Depot, Swindon, Severn Tunnel Junction and Paddington plus the local freight services from Yeovil, Weymouth and Bridport. Apart from the down refuge siding located north of the station, the main sidings were confined to the Weymouth end of the station. The former broad gauge stone built goods shed (similar in style to the goods shed at Yeovil Pen Mill), traders sidings and cattle pens were on the down side of the layout. Traders operating out of Dorchester included Silcocks, Dorset Farmers Ltd and coal merchants Bryer Ash. Long sidings lay alongside the up line including the 250-yard long cemetery siding. Transfer of freight wagons between the two stations at Dorchester took

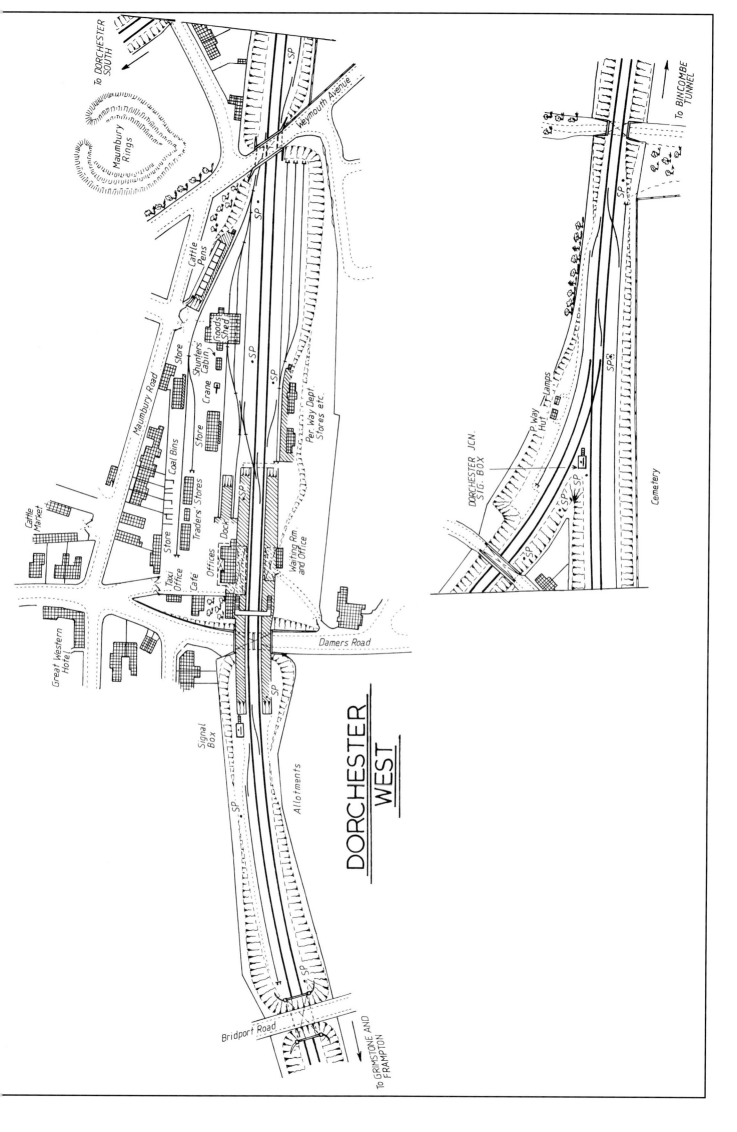

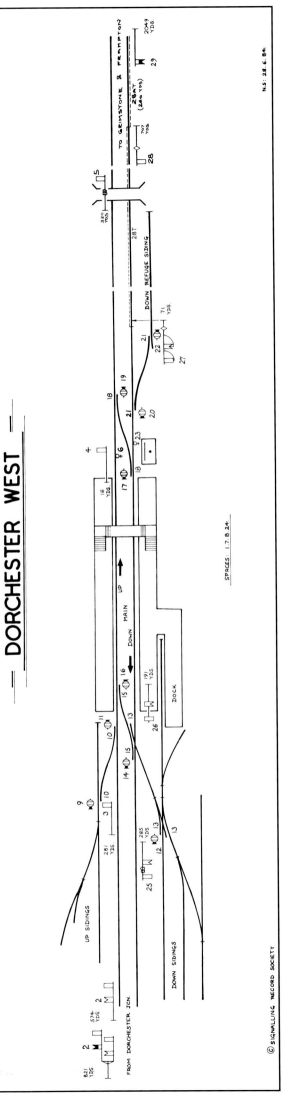

— DORCHESTER WEST —

© SIGNALLING RECORD SOCIETY

N.S: 28.6.84.

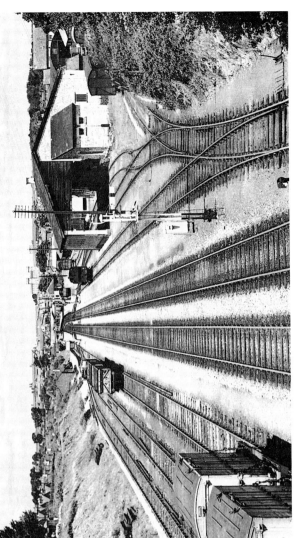

The Dorchester West Type 7D signal box which was located at the Yeovil end of the 'down' platform is pictured here on 4th November 1961. It was opened on 14th May 1908 and closed on 15th March 1968.

C. L. Caddy

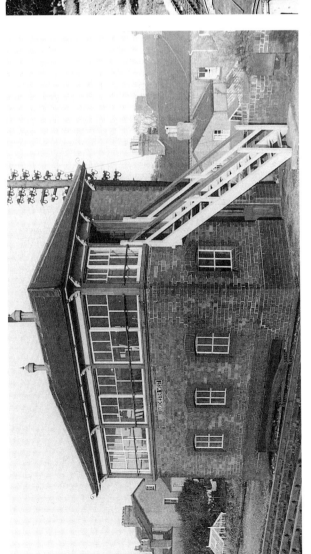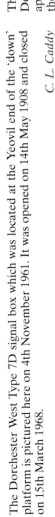

The station stands in the distance in this view of the shunting yard and goods shed at Dorchester West on 10th July 1956. A SR rail built signal in the foreground guards the approach to Dorchester Junction, various goods wagons stand on either side of the layout, and the station pilot stands near the goods shed to the right. The former broad gauge goods shed is very similar in style to the version at Yeovil Pen Mill.

R. C. Riley

place daily. (In the broad gauge era a daily transfer train was worked by a broad gauge engine to the L&SWR goods yard, which was equipped with mixed gauge rails adjoining a standard gauge siding.) By the late 1920s freight exchange traffic was made at Dorchester Junction, with wagons from the GWR to the Southern Railway being worked to the down sidings at Dorchester Junction for acceptance by the Southern. Exchange wagons from the Southern to the GWR were tripped to the up cemetery siding for clearance by the GWR.

From the Southern Railway Working Appendice March 26th 1934.

TRANSFER OF WAGONS The exchange point is Dorchester Junction for both Companies.

The SR must put traffic for the GWR in the up cemetery siding and the GWR must put traffic for the SR in the down junction siding.

Each Company must see that their traffic from the exchange sidings is cleared by 5pm daily to enable the night trains to put off traffic.

When it is necessary to work full trains from one Company's system to the other, the following instructions must be observed:

The train from the GWR station to the SR station must run on the down line from the GWR station clear of the crossover road on the main line at Dorchester Junction and must then be propelled to the SR station on the up line, but it must stop well clear of the SR main line until signalled forward into the station.

The train from the SR to the GWR station must be drawn out to the junction and propelled to the GWR station on the up line under the protection of the fixed signals.

The train must always have a Guard or Shunter in charge who must ride in the Guard's brake van, which must be the rear vehicle when the train is drawn and the leading vehicle when propelled. The engine of such train must always lead towards Weymouth on account of the gradient falling in that direction.

The exchanging of goods wagons at Dorchester Junction terminated in 1956 and the Dorchester shunting engine worked trip freights between the two stations. A daily shunting engine was supplied from Weymouth shed, which would arrive with a staff train formed of a single coach, usually an auto trailer. The engine would shunt the Dorchester West yard before returning to Weymouth and making two further journeys to Dorchester to resume shunting and making transfer trips to the Southern Region station. With the declining goods traffic in the 1960s the goods yard closed on 3rd March 1965 with coal traffic lingering on until 6th September 1965. The down siding north of the station was taken out of use on 1st November 1965 and most of the down yard was removed by September 1968, with the rest of the sidings taken out of use on 11th May 1969. The up mileage sidings were also taken out of use on 20th August 1968. The main line north of the station to Maiden Newton was reduced to a single line from 9th June 1968, and a crossover at the northern end of the platforms was restored with the singling of the line. The line today through the platforms is still double track as far as Dorchester Junction. The station became unstaffed on 2nd January 1972.

Mr J. S. Perry now recalls his working days at Dorchester: "I joined the service of the Great Western Railway Company in Dorchester as a temporary junior clerk on 13th August 1945, almost at the end of World War II which had but two days to run before peace was declared. The county town of Dorset can boast two separate railway stations served by the Great Western

'Hymek' No. D7020 arrives at Dorchester West on 7th July 1971 with the 17.07 Westbury–Weymouth. No. D7020 was introduced to traffic in February 1962 and allocated to 82A (Bristol Bath Road), the locomotive being withdrawn in January 1972 and cut up at Swindon in September 1972.
John Scrace

No. D1002 *Western Explorer* arrives at Dorchester West on 26th May 1973 forming a Weymouth–Bristol service. No. D1002 was introduced to traffic in March 1962, was withdrawn in January 1974 and cut up at Swindon in June of the same year.
C. L. Caddy

Three-car dmu set No. C820 arrives at Dorchester West off the single-line section from Maiden Newton, forming the 12.00 Swindon–Weymouth on 2nd March 1988.

John Scrace

Dmu set No. C820 stands alongside the 'down' platform at Dorchester West on 2nd March 1988 with the 12.00 Swindon–Weymouth, the destination board on the front car has not been changed and reads, 'Cardiff Central'.

John Scrace

and Southern Railways respectively. They were about ½ mile apart but merged at Dorchester Junction. Both were very busy stations used heavily by passenger and goods traffic as of course there was little road traffic, the use of motor vehicles being curtailed by petrol rationing. Dorchester GWR station had quite a large staff. In addition to two booking clerks, there were five signalmen, three at the junction box open 24 hours, and two at the smaller station box, four goods yard shunters, a goods yard checker and a goods yard porter. Platform staff consisted of a foreman (who also supervised the goods yard), two lady ticket collectors, a leading parcels porter, two parcels porters and three platform porters.

Unlike all the other stations along the line, we did not have a permanent Station Master but were supervised by the Southern Railway Station Master from the other station. By contrast the Chief Goods Clerk who supervised all the goods clerks who were Southern Railway employees and were employed at the Southern Railway station, was a GWR employee. This practice had been in operation for many years and the sharing of facilities did not end there. The collection and delivery of goods and parcel traffic was carried out by horse and cart, the horses being owned by the Southern Railway, the horse drivers being SR employees yet the horses were kept in stables situated in the GWR station goods yard! There were a total of 14

stations and unstaffed halts between Weymouth and Yeovil Pen Mill together with two branch lines, one to Abbotsbury from Upwey Junction and the other to Bridport from Maiden Newton. There were intermediate stations at Upwey and Portesham on the Abbotsbury branch and Toller and Powerstock on the Bridport branch. Services on these two branch lines were operated by railmotor cars, usually consisting of an engine and one railmotor coach capable of being pulled or propelled, control in the latter case being given by the driver from a small driving cabin at the front of the motor coach, leaving the fireman in the engine at the rear. These services operated from Weymouth to Abbotsbury and Bridport about six times daily. There were no Sunday trains on the Abbotsbury branch.

"In addition to the local railmotor coaches most of the trains running between Weymouth and Westbury stopped at all stations and halts. Two daily fast services ran in each direction between Weymouth and London (Paddington) at 9.15am and 4.25pm daily, while in the reverse direction, trains left Paddington at 12.30pm and 6pm due at Dorchester at 4.15pm and 9.55pm respectively. All passenger trains were well loaded, and at weekends there was a considerable volume of HM Forces leave traffic as there were several military camps in the area, plus the Naval base at Portland which generated traffic from Weymouth. With the end of hostilities, rail services were gradually increased, initially by creating an express service direct from Weymouth to Bristol to avoid passengers changing at Frome or Westbury. This ran twice daily in each direction, one service being worked by a three-coach GWR diesel rail car set.

Most of the passengers for destinations in the London area and the Eastern and Southern counties used the Southern Railway services from the other Dorchester station as the service was of a greater frequency to London than the GWR could provide and it was marginally quicker. Passengers for destinations in the Midlands and North used the GWR services to Bristol. For a short time, no doubt in an endeavour to attract some traffic, one of the Paddington–Plymouth services slipped a coach at Westbury for Weymouth which connected with the 4.25pm from Bristol–Weymouth. This gave an overall journey time via the GWR route from London to Dorchester of just over three hours, some 30–40 minutes quicker than any Southern Railway service between the same two locations. It was, however, little used and was soon withdrawn. In 1946, steamer services operated by the GWR resumed from Weymouth to the Channel Islands, a connecting boat train running to Weymouth from London and in the reverse direction, this was the only passenger train service which ran through Dorchester non stop. The majority of the stopping trains between Weymouth and Westbury were worked by 'Hall' or 'Manor' class engines. The express services to and from London were usually headed by the more powerful 'Castle' class, but the most powerful GWR engines, the 'Kings' could not be used between Castle Cary (where the Weymouth line diverged from the Paddington–Plymouth main line) and Dorchester.

"The booking office at Dorchester was one of the old glass passimeter type, about the size of a small garden greenhouse. It was only possible for three people to stand inside and it was not possible to accommodate a chair, so stools were provided for the clerks and which were kicked under the counter when not in use. The office was half timbered but the top half and roof were built of opaque glass, no ventilation, other than the booking windows was provided and this structure was enclosed with a large wall with windows and a skylight. Although a small gas fire was provided this was little used. The summer of 1947 was particularly hot and I can remember on some evenings well after 9 o'clock cashing up in temperatures of 100 degrees Farenheit. Conditions in which we had to work were at times very uncomfortable and not helped by the fact that booking clerks were required when issuing tickets to be dressed in a jacket, collar and tie! At the end of 1947 a new, much larger office was constructed which greatly improved our working conditions although the office, as was the station, still illuminated by gas lighting.

After about nine months I was transferred from the booking office to the adjoining parcels office to learn about parcels work. Parcels traffic both outwards and inwards was particularly heavy. The mainstay of our traffic was despatched on the 6.10pm Weymouth–Swindon train which left Dorchester at about 6.40pm having some eight minutes to load all the traffic. In addition to heavy GPO mails, upwards of 300 baskets of watercress were despatched nightly as well as industrial machinery parts and other general items. On many occasions the station time allowance was exceeded in spite of every available hand being used to help load. In those days two railway companies were competing for business, and working in a parcels office provided an excellent grounding in railway geography. Traffic was classiified into 'local' and 'foreign'. The former indicated that the parcels travelled for the whole of the journey over GWR lines and that company kept all the receipts. 'Foreign' meant that part of the journey was made over other companies' lines and the GWR kept only a proportion of the receipts based on the percentage earned on the GWR proportion of the total mileage. These adjustments were calculated in the Railway Clearing House based in London and it meant that when preparing the monthly accounts, traffic had to be divided into two groups. Exactly the same procedure applied to freight traffic but I did not gain any experience in this field while at Dorchester. The goods yard was busy with coal and animal feed as there was a large storage warehouse from which deliveries were made to outlying farms by railway vehicles. (The horses were confined to town deliveries.) Some scrap metal was forwarded but the general traffic was dealt with at the Southern Railway station. After $3\frac{1}{2}$ years at Dorchester I was transferred to the reservations office at Weymouth Quay as a summer clerk."

George Pryer had transferred from the locomotive department at Weymouth to the traffic department in 1961, and he has his own memories of the station. "I soon found that Dorchester West was a very busy station, handling as it did a heavy general parcels traffic, plus barrow upon barrow of watercress. The staff at the time consisted of a station foreman, leading porter, porter and booking clerk on early and late turns, with a junior porter working a middle shift. It shared a station master with Dorchester South, which by that time was considered to be the main station in the town as it dealt with most of the London traffic. There was indeed a certain amount of ill feeling between the staff of the two stations, probably dating back to the old days of company rivalry, and no opportunity was missed to collar each other's business. If a tradesman's van brought an assortment of parcels for despatch by rail, the leading porter would charge up those that were for obvious 'Western' destinations and then inform the sender that he could also deal with those addressed to Bournemouth or Poole which of course should have gone to the South station. This meant loading them into a down train for transfer via Weymouth, but at least the money found its way into the West station's cash till, rather than that of the enemy across the road!"

A summer Saturday morning at Dorchester West is recalled by Peter Foster. "Leafing through my spotting book of some 35 years ago I found the entry for 14th June 1958. This was a significant date because it was the first summer Saturday of the 1958 timetable. I was at Dorchester West in time for the 9.29am Maiden Newton–Weymouth local, this former rail-motor working was now a two-coach WR corridor set powered by a pannier tank from Weymouth shed, No. 7782. Hardly had the 9.29am departed when another Weymouth stalwart appeared and stopped at the up platform with a squeal of brakes and the roar of the vacuum from its chimney. This was a large 2-6-2 Prairie tank No. 4133 in black livery heading the 9.35am Weymouth to Yeovil Pen Mill and Town stations. Again this was a former

With the signal box in the backround No. 4918 *Dartington Hall* in ex-works condition and bearing an 84A shedplate (Stafford Road) stands alongside the 'down' platform at Dorchester West with the 9.15am Swindon–Weymouth parcels on 16th August 1960. This duty was often used by locomotives as a running in turn from the ex-GWR locomotive works at Swindon.

H. B. Priestley

rail-motor working, and with a toot on the whistle and a sharp beat from its chimney, the Prairie tank pulled away with the 'boards' slamming to danger in its wake. The next train to appear was the 10am Weymouth–Birmingham Moor Street (as opposed to Snow Hill) and with a long blast on the whistle, the train appeared, headed by 4-6-0 No. 6876 *Kingsland Grange*, 82D (Westbury) carrying the reporting number 383 on the smokebox door. The long train of packed coaches rumbled through the station gathering speed as the engine was opened up heading to the first booked stop at Westbury. (I believe the incoming empty stock for this service was listed in the special weekly notices as there is no trace in any working timetables.) The 8.05am Bristol–Weymouth was the next arrival which was usually rostered to a Bristol Bath Road locomotive, but on this day the train was hauled by 4-6-0 No. 5099 *Compton Castle* carrying the 81A Old Oak Common shed plate on the smokebox door. In between the 8.05am Bristol and the 9.27am Westbury–Weymouth was slotted a light engine, No. 5981 *Frensham Hall*, no doubt returning to her home base. The 10.20am Weymouth–Wolverhampton express drew into the up platform behind behind No. 5935 *Norton Hall*, and the 9.27am Westbury–

Weymouth stopper came to a stand at the down platform with a squeal of brakes. The train was headed by an immaculate Westbury Mogul, No. 6399, in BR lined out Brunswick green livery. This was a regular duty for No. 6399. Another summer Saturday treat was the 11.12am Weymouth–Paddington express which reached the Capital at 3.30pm, also with a Westbury engine at the head. This was No. 5982 *Harrington Hall* and another regular locomotive to appear on the Westbury–Weymouth route in the late 1950s. More or less at the same time, the down platform was occupied by the 9.10am summer Saturday extra from Bristol to Weymouth with No. 4988 *Bulwell Hall* of 82B St Philip's Marsh in charge, this engine being previously based at Weymouth.

Then it was all 'boards' off for the first part of the down Channel Islands boat train departing from Paddington at 8.20am for Weymouth Quay. The engine, unusually on this occasion, was No. 5942 *Doldowlod Hall*, which would come off at Weymouth Junction with the leading brake and resturant car, in exchange for the Weymouth tram engine, an outside cylinder pannier tank which would haul the express through the streets to the quay to connect with the sailings to the Channel Islands. The next train to appear was the 11.25am

Class 50 No. 50002 *Superb* leaves Dorchester West on 3rd August 1978 and heads towards Dorchester Junction with the 09.25 Bristol–Weymouth. Weeds and bushes now occupy the site of the former goods yard.

John Scrace

Chippenham–Weymouth with Weymouth based No. 5983 *Henley Hall*. I then climbed aboard to continue my day's spotting at Weymouth. This would be a small sample of the trains which traversed the Westbury–Weymouth route on that Saturday. 1958 was to be the last year of the all steam service between Westbury and Weymouth, as the following year witnessed the Bristol District dieselisation programme under way. A three-car dmu was allocated to Weymouth in February 1959, and diesel units replaced most, but not quite all of the steam worked Bristol–Weymouth services with the introduction of the summer timetable.

Dorchester Junction
Signal box 162 miles 8 chains from Paddington
First box opened 1866 described as a kind of
  'observatory' with levers
Second box (Dorchester No. 2 equipped with 16
  levers) opened 1877
Third box opened 1896

Controlling the junction between the former GWR and LSWR routes the 36-lever junction signal box was sited in the fork of the junction and was situated 33 chains south from its counterpart at Dorchester West. Dorchester Junction box had a 25-lever frame when opened in 1896 and replaced an earlier box dating from 1877. At first when opened, the LSWR made a single line trailing connection with the actual junction from the east, the track to Weymouth then being mixed gauge. The connecting spur to the LSWR station was

GWR property. The LSWR c1870 laid a second pair of rails from its station to the junction of mixed gauge tracks. An up refuge siding (known as Cemetery siding) was provided in 1901 at the junction and further improvements were made in 1908 when new trailing connections from the down main line to the up refuge siding were installed. A new down refuge siding connected to the down main was also provided with space for the new down refuge siding being accomplished by excavating the sides of the cutting. All the new connections and signals were controlled from the junction box and the frame was altered to 36 levers. Further advances to the junction arrived in 1913 with track circuiting and outer home signals being installed. Dorchester Junction box closed on 5th July 1986 when the junction was brought under the control of the Dorchester Panel. The Cemetery siding and its trailing connection with the down main line had been removed on 24th November 1972. Further alterations came into use on 7th December 1980 when the double track from Dorchester West was singled at the throat of the junction, and the double track connecting curve to Dorchester South was slewed to improve the track layout.

Part of the services which passed through Dorchester Junction on Saturday 22nd July 1961:-

No. 6925 *Hackness Hall* on 10am
  Weymouth–Birmingham Moor Street
43xx No. 7303 (71G) shunting
Class 4MT No. 76013 (71A) down light engine

Dorchester Junction and the GWR Type 5 signal box on 14th April 1968 with the ex-GWR route in the foreground and the SR lines to Bournemouth and Waterloo running behind the box. A solitary brakevan stands on the Cemetery siding in the foreground, and there is plenty of freight traffic standing on the Southern exchange siding in the background. Note the SR upper quadrant rail built signal standing adjacent to the signal box, and the GWR lamp hut standing in the fork of the junction.
C. L. Caddy

Dorchester Junction signal box on 4th April 1970 with the ex-GWR lines in the foreground. Note that the SR upper quadrant signal seen in the previous picture has now been removed, and electrical relay cabinets now stand alongside the box. The signal box closed on 5th July 1986.
C. L. Caddy

DORCHESTER JUNCTION

SIGNALLING RECORD SOCIETY   G A P

TO DORCHESTER WEST

GOOD'S
YARD

UP SIDING

UP MAIN

DOWN MAIN

DOWN

UP

To DORCHESTER SOUTH

UP BRANCH

DOWN BRANCH

DOWN SIDING

SPACES 30 37

FROM BINCOMBE TUNNEL

UP

DOWN

The interior of Dorchester Junction signal box pictured here on 17th February 1985 showing the lever frame, box diagram, and instruments. The box floor is spotless, with a nice piece of carpet to give some home comforts to the signalmen.

M. Marshall

'West Country' No. 34094 *Morthoe* (71B) on 10.10am
  Weymouth–Waterloo
Class 5MT No. 73041 (71G) on 10.20am
  Weymouth–Wolverhampton
'West Country' No. 34040 *Crewkerne* (70A) on 7.57am
  Waterloo–Weymouth
'West Country' No. 34041 *Wilton* (71B) on down boat
  train Waterloo–Weymouth
Class 4MT No. 76058 (71B) on 11am
  Weymouth–Waterloo (via the 'old road')
No. 4941 *Llangedwyn Hall* on 11.12am
  Weymouth–Paddington
No. 6957 *Norcliffe Hall* on 9.10am Bristol Temple
  Meads–Weymouth
57xx No. 9620 (71G) down light engine
No. 5994 *Roydon Hall* on 7.50am Birmingham Snow
  Hill–Weymouth
No. 5993 *Kirby Hall* on 9.43am Bristol Temple
  Meads–Weymouth
'West Country' No. 34043 *Combe Martin* on 12.20pm
  Weymouth–Waterloo
Class 5MT No. 73085 on 9.24am Waterloo–Weymouth
Plus dmus on various workings.
  Shed codes: 71A Eastleigh, 71B Bournemouth and
  71G Weymouth.

Monkton & Came Halt
163 miles 8 chains from Paddington
Opened as Came Bridge Halt 1st June 1905
Re-named Monkton & Came Halt 1st October 1905
Closed 7th January 1957

The two-platformed timber built halt was opened on
6th June 1905 with the introduction of railmotor
services between Weymouth and Dorchester. The halt
was intended to serve the golf playing public travelling
to the nearby club at Came Down, but as it was of
more use to the inhabitants of the nearby village of
Winterborne Monkton, the halt was renamed Monkton
& Came Halt from 1st October 1905. A total of seven
return trains a day were plying between Weymouth
and Dorchester by 1907. Steam railmotors were used
initially, with auto fitted trains appearing in 1911,
working at least one of the return services. The halt
was closed on 7th January 1957.

Bincombe Tunnel Box
164 miles 32 chains from Paddington
Signal box (1) opened 1876 closed 1896
Signal box (2) opened 1896
Engine siding into use 1896
Engine siding taken out of use September 1969
Signal box closed 1st March 1970
Engine siding removed October 4th October 1970
Down line slewed over site of siding December 1980

The signal box situated alongside the up main line at
the summit of the climb from Weymouth at the north
end of Bincombe Tunnel. It is an interesting fact that
Brunel had put forward in 1844 the suggestion that the
WS&W should be worked on the 'Atmospheric'
system with its gradient problems, and Captain
Moorsom, engineer to the Southampton & Dorchester
Railway had favoured using the system between
Weymouth and Dorchester, but the idea did not come
to fruition. The box was opened in 1896 and replaced
an earlier signal box. The new box was equipped with a
13-lever frame. The engine siding between the up and
down lines was provided from the same date. Until the
end of steam this was the place to watch up trains,
complete with the banking engine at the rear, come
storming out of the tunnel showering cinders and
steam up into the sky. The banking engine would come
to a stand just past the signal box whilst the train it had

The disused Monkton &
Came Halt looking north
towards Dorchester on 11th
August 1963. The halt had
been closed since 9th June
1957.
  C. L. Caddy

No. 6985 *Parwick Hall* heads a
troop train near Dorchester
just south of the closed
Monkton & Came Halt on
11th August 1963.
  C. L. Caddy

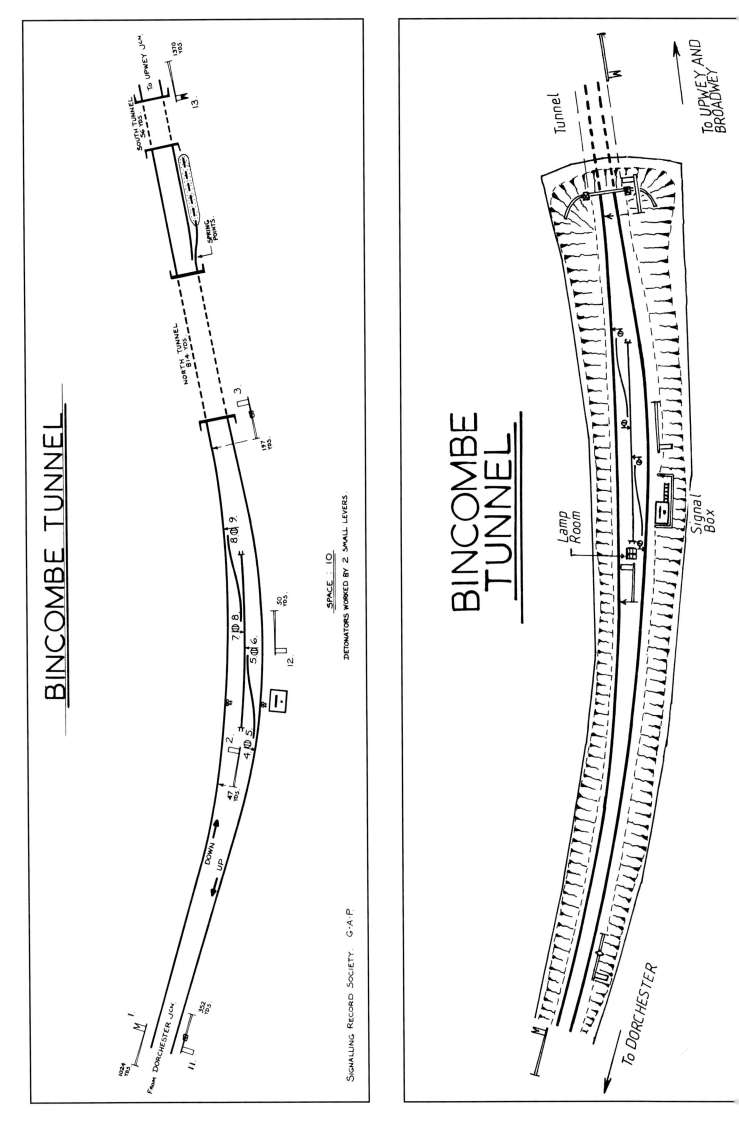

BINCOMBE TUNNEL

SOUTH TUNNEL 56 YDS.

To UPWEY JCN.

1370 YDS.

13.

SPRING POINTS.

NORTH TUNNEL 814 YDS.

197 YDS.

3.

8. 9.

7. 8.

5. 6.

50 YDS.

12.

DOWN

UP

47 YDS.

2.

4. 5.

1.

FROM DORCHESTER JCN.

352 YDS.

11.

1024 YDS.

SPACE :: 10

DETONATORS WORKED BY 2 SMALL LEVERS.

SIGNALLING RECORD SOCIETY. G·A·P.

BINCOMBE TUNNEL

Tunnel

To UPWEY AND BROADWAY

Lamp Room

Signal Box

To DORCHESTER

Bulleid 'West Country' class No. 34004 *Yeovil* heads past Bincombe Tunnel signal box and engine siding on 11th June 1967 with a 'down' rail-tour special.

S. C. Nash

Class 4MT 4-6-0 No. 75068 has just passed through the short tunnel carrying the Weymouth to Dorchester road over the railway and now plods towards Bincombe Tunnel on 20th May 1967 with the 16.46 Weymouth–Bournemouth.

S. C. Nash

been assisting raced away to Dorchester Junction. The banker, with its injector singing away, would reverse into the engine siding which was situated between the up and down tracks, and if the road was clear would trundle back to Weymouth. A banker, running light engine, was allowed ten minutes to travel from Bincombe box to Weymouth. If up traffic was heavy that day, the banking engine would find another up train waiting for assistance at Upwey Junction. The engine siding was taken out of use in September 1969 and the signal box was closed on 1st March 1970 with removal of the engine siding on 4th October of the same year. The down line was slewed over the site of the former engine siding in December 1980.

George Pryer now recalls his signalling days at Bincombe and gives us the signalman's viewpoint at this lonely box: "Bincombe Tunnel was one of those places that could truly be called 'atmospheric'. To begin with it was something of a challenge to reach the place, the official access being via Monkton & Came Halt which involved a long walk beside the line. Of course, generations of signalmen had long since aban-

doned this idea and reached agreement with the farmer who owned the field which separated the railway from the main road to cross his land, and some rough steps had been cut into the side of the steep cutting. Surprisingly for a place so isolated, the box had electric light when I knew it, and it was a cosy little building. The lever frame was not large, a mere 13 levers, but it could be much more interesting to operate than its modest size suggests, for this was the point at which the bank engines which assisted heavy trains out of Weymouth 'dropped off' and returned light. The view from Bincombe box was better than one would expect from a place stuck in a cutting. Towards Dorchester one could see well beyond the up starter, and because of the rolling nature of the surrounding land, it was possible to look out over quite a wide vista of waving pasture, sometimes dotted with cows and sheep. Towards Weymouth the view was of course cut short by the tunnel, out of the mouth of which issued whisps of smoke and steam long after the passage of a train. Indeed on busy summer Saturdays there was a continuous issue of gases, as out of the gates of Hades!

With steam billowing everywhere, an unidentified Bulleid Pacific and a Class 4MT Standard head towards Bincombe Tunnel with a Weymouth–Waterloo train in Easter 1966, whilst a 'Hymek' diesel glides out of the tunnel with a 'down' train from the ex-GWR route.

D. E. Canning

Class 5MT 4-6-0 No. 73110 *The Red Knight* bursts out of Bincombe Tunnel and runs down the bank with the Waterloo–Weymouth Quay 'Channel Islands Boat Train' on 5th May 1965.

C. L. Caddy

It was possible to see just one farm from the box windows, so at night it was inky dark except for the red or green lights in the signals, and there was a real feeling of isolation. But to see a heavy up train approaching was to experience all the romance of the traditional railway. Having received 'entering section' from Upwey, followed by 2 pause 2 – the code for engine assisting in rear – asked 'line clear' to Dorchester Junction and pulled off, there followed that kind of expectant silence that one could only experience in a mechanical signal box. A period marked by the slow ticking of the clock, the singing of the kettle on top of the iron stove, and the chirping of the birds outside. Then, suddenly, one was aware of a sort of rhythmic vibration in the air; the train had entered the far end of

the tunnel and the force of the engine's exhaust striking the brick arch of the tunnel roof sent shock waves through the ether. Eventually the leading engine would emerge into the daylight wreathed in steam and sending clouds of it high into the air as it conquered the last few yards of that gruelling gradient, and as it passed the box, followed by the now accelerating train, the banker would come out of the tunnel and drift to a stand nearby, the smoke drifting lazily in at the box windows. If there was a pathway the banker would return immediately to Weymouth and disappear into the smoke of the tunnel within a couple of minutes, but very often it was necessary to hold it in the engine siding that was provided between the two running lines until a down train had gone. Banker crews preferred this, as a down train running at a good speed ventilated

The lonely GWR Type 5 Bincombe Tunnel signal box, measuring 17ft x 10ft elevated 10ft which was situated alongside the 'up' main line is pictured here on 4th April 1970.

C. L. Caddy

the tunnel and cleared away some of the fumes before they travelled through it tender first. Again, on busy days it was no easy task getting rid of bankers without causing delay to down trains, and the signalman at Bincombe needed to develop a good relationship with the engine crews so that he could persuade them to run at something rather more than the booked speed. Bincombe Tunnel box today is now an untidy pile of bricks in the lonely cutting."

Upwey Wishing Well Halt
165 miles 18 chains from Paddington
Opened 28th May 1905
Closed 7th January 1957

The two-platformed timber built halt, complete with corrugated iron pagoda shelters, was opened on 28th May 1905. The nearby tourist attraction of the 'Wishing Well' brought many visitors by rail in the early years of the halt, but increasing competition from road transport and buses which could drop their passengers nearer to the attraction meant an ever dwindling railborne custom. The halt eventually closed on 7th January 1957.

Upwey Station
165 miles 75 chains from Paddington
Opened 21st June 1871
Closed 19th April 1886
Signal box opened 1876 (former Weymouth Junction box)
Signal box closed 9th November 1885 (retained until 19th April 1886)

In 1870, following a memorial from the local populace, the GWR agreed to open a station, providing the residents subscribed the sum of £150 towards the costs, and by December of the same year a total of £100 had been collected. The station opened on 21st June 1871. Two platforms were provided and LSWR trains called at the station from 1st February 1872. No goods facilities were available. The former signal box from Weymouth Junction, dating from 1866, was sited off the Weymouth end of the up platform and used as an intermediate block post. The signal box closed on 9th November 1885 but was retained until 19th April 1886 when the station was closed and replaced by a new station at Upwey Junction, located 35 chains south of the old station.

No. 35028 *Clan Line* hauls the 16.00 Weymouth Quay–Waterloo up the 1 in 50 bank near the site of Upwey Wishing Well on 18th May 1967, with Type 3 diesel giving assistance at the rear.

S. C. Nash

Upwey Junction
166 miles 30 chains from Paddington
Signal box opened 9th November 1885
Abbotsbury branch opened 9th November 1885
Station opened 19th April 1886
Station re-named Upwey & Broadwey 29th November 1952
Abbotsbury branch closed 1st December 1952
Line to Upwey Goods (on branch) reduced to siding December 1952 for freight facilities
Freight withdrawn from Upwey Goods 1st January 1962
Station unstaffed from 1st March 1965
Signal box closed 1st March 1970

The six-mile long branch line between Abbotsbury and Upwey Junction opened on 9th November 1885. A 22-lever signal box (Upwey Junction) was provided from the same date standing off the Weymouth end of the down platform. The new station at Upwey Junction was not ready when the branch opened in 1885 and trains from Abbotsbury had to proceed to Weymouth for passenger and goods circulation. The new station at Upwey Junction opened on 19th April 1886, the station buildings being constructed in timber. No freight facilities were provided at the main line station as freight traffic was dealt with at Upwey station on the branch. Abbotsbury trains arrived at the branch platform which was situated at a lower level than the main up platform. The branch from Upwey station ascended at 1 in 44 on an 11½ chain curve to reach the platform at the main line station. Passenger services on the branch were worked at first by steam railmotors until their replacement by push and pull trains. In its early years and until the growth of road traffic, the branch was popular with visitors travelling to the sub tropical gardens at Abbotsbury and the famous swannery. Most branch trains terminated at Weymouth, although some of the stock worked through to Portland. Track alterations took place on 9th February 1911 when a new crossover was installed south of the junction, and from 6th March 1917 the headshunt from the branch was taken out of use. Part of the original junction was removed on 8th December 1929 with all trains entering the down main from the branch using the new connection installed in 1911.
Passenger services to Abbotsbury:
1890 4 daily services
1906 7 daily services. 2 Sundays
1925 5 daily services. 2 Saturdays
1934 8 daily services. 4 Sundays
1952 6 daily services. 1 Saturdays

The Abbotsbury branch closed on 1st December 1952 with most of the track removed by 1955 except for the section from Upwey Junction to Upwey station which

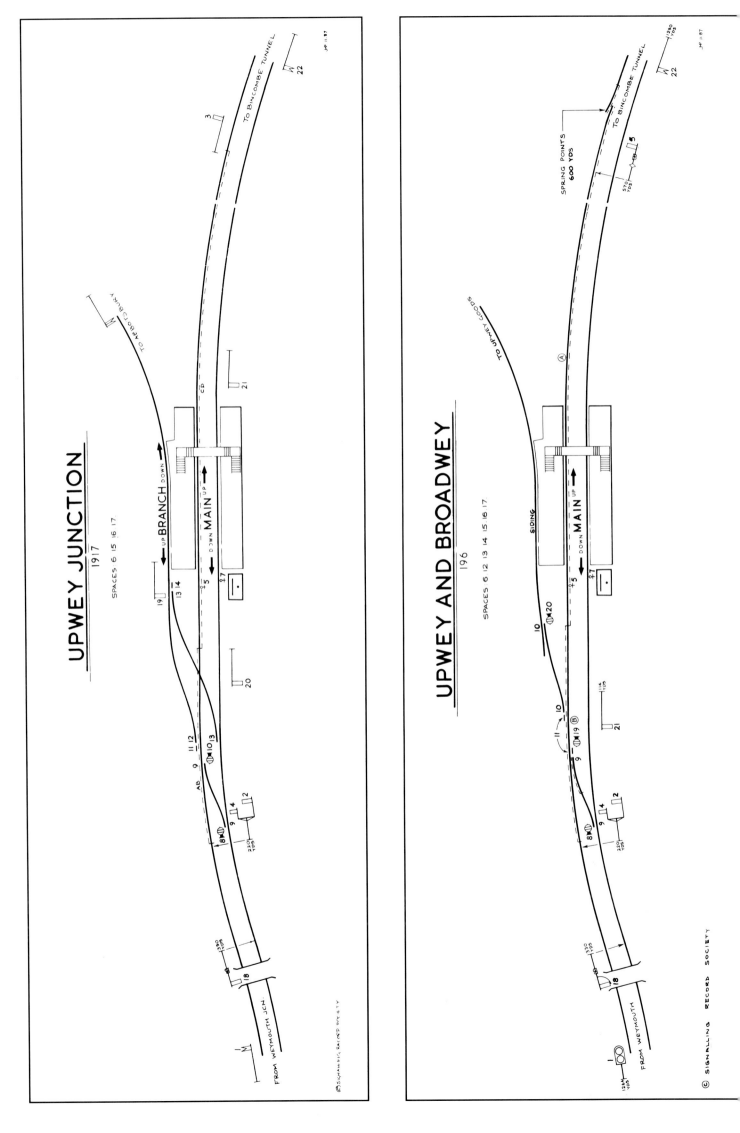

UPWEY JUNCTION

1917

SPACES 6 15 16 17

UP BRANCH DOWN

DOWN MAIN UP

TO ABBOTSBURY

TO BINCOMBE TUNNEL

FROM WEYMOUTH JCN.

© SIGNALLING RECORD SOCIETY

UPWEY AND BROADWEY

1966

SPACES 6 12 13 14 15 16 17

SIDING

DOWN MAIN UP

TO UPWEY GOODS

SPRING POINTS 600 YDS

TO BINCOMBE TUNNEL

FROM WEYMOUTH JCN.

© SIGNALLING RECORD SOCIETY

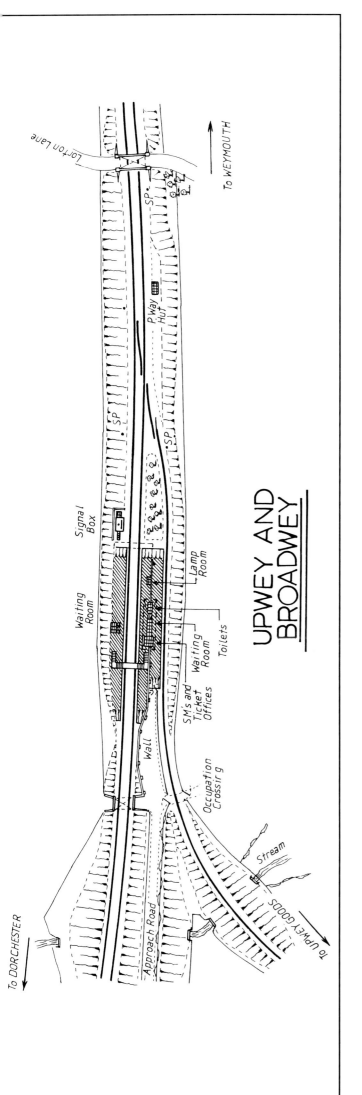

UPWEY AND BROADWEY

To DORCHESTER

To WEYMOUTH

Lorton Lane

Signal Box

Waiting Room

Wall

Occupation Crossing

Approach Road

Stream

To UPWEY GOODS

S.M's and Ticket Offices

Waiting Room

Lamp Room

Toilets

P.Way Hut

SP.

SP.

SP.

SP.

No. 4927 *Farnborough Hall*, with steam issuing from the safety valves after running down the bank, with its non taxing load of two coaches, runs through Upwey and Broadwey on 22nd May 1963 heading the 3.20pm Bristol Temple Meads–Weymouth.

C. L. Caddy

Upwey and Broadwey station and its attractive footbridge and station buildings, seen here looking towards Weymouth on 7th July 1966. The signal box can be seen to the left at the end of the 'down' platform.

John Scrace

A three-car dmu forming the 15.00 Weymouth–Westbury runs past the GWR Type 3 signal box and into Upwey and Broadway station on 5th January 1963. The signal box was named Upwey Junction until 29th November 1952.

C. L. Caddy

Class 5MT 4-6-0 No. 73018 is seen here running into Upwey and Broadwey on 11th August 1963 with the Weymouth–Eastleigh goods. The line leading to Upwey Goods on the former Abbotsbury branch can be seen in the foreground. Note the 15mph sign to the left, this being for the trains from Upwey Goods gaining the 'down' main line. The station 'down' main starter can be seen in the 'off' position above the cab of the engine.

C. L. Caddy

was reduced to a siding, renamed Upwey Goods and retained for freight traffic which lingered on until 1st January 1962. The remaining portion of the branch to Upwey and the connections to the main line were taken out of use on 7th July 1963.

The branch station at Upwey is still standing today and is now part of an industrial estate. The main line station was renamed Upwey & Broadwey on 29th November 1952, and became unstaffed from 1st March 1965. The signal box was closed on 1st March 1970. Upwey & Broadwey is still in use today although the original buildings have been replaced by bus stop shelters, stopping services from the former WS&W line still call, and since the electrification from Bournemouth in May 1988, there is now an hourly daytime service to Waterloo.

George Pryer now delights us with his boyhood memories of Upwey. "A particular schoolboy pleasure was to save up the fourpenny train fare and take a return ticket from Weymouth to Upwey Junction (by then renamed Upwey & Broadwey), and spend a whole day watching trains from the platform of the latter. It was the ideal spot! Down trains would be travelling at tremendous speed as they free-wheeled down the 1 in 52 gradient from Bincombe Tunnel, whilst in the up direction the engines would be labouring mightily with even the lightest loads, heavy trains being assisted in the rear with a 'banker'. Furthermore, it was a very pleasant location. It was possible in those days to sit on the platform and not see a house, there was a wonderful view of the hills with Hardy's Monument

An unusual pairing of a 'Warship' diesel No. D842 *Royal Oak*, and Bulleid Pacific No. 34021 *Dartmoor* powering the 17.41 Weymouth–Bournemouth towards Upwey and Broadwey on 3rd July 1967. Only a few days are left before the end of steam on the Southern Region.

S. C. Nash

and Culliford Tree standing out against the skyline to the North, and looking back towards Weymouth, the great hump of Portland was clearly visible in the distance.

Here one could listen to the bells in the little signal box at the end of the platform and watch the semaphore signals clatter 'off' in response to the signalman's movements. And if one tired of watching trains, how enjoyable it was to take a stroll along what remained of the Abbotsbury branch to 'Upwey Goods', where there was the grass-grown remnant of a passenger station, a massive stone goods shed with the doors always firmly closed, and a couple of weedy sidings usually containing a few coal wagons. Beyond these sidings the rails continued for about thirty chains, becoming progressively more rusty, until they reached a buffer stop literally in the middle of nowhere. Beyond that again, the deserted ballast curved away into the distance in the general direction of Abbotsbury.

In the 1950s closed railway lines were enough of a novelty to have a strange appeal of their own, and I can remember being fascinated by Upwey Goods. My visits were invariably made on a Saturday afternoon when the coal merchant (for whose sole benefit the place seemed to operate) was not working, and one could stand in that remote little goods yard and hear nothing but birdsong, the drone of bees and the tinkling of the infant River Wey, and breathe the sweet aroma of wild flowers mingled vaguely with the smell of warm creosote drawn from the wooden sleepers by the warm sunshine. It was a world apart, a place tenuously connected to the transport system of Britain whilst managing to remain detached, timeless, silent. We did not know it then, but Upwey Goods

was already an anochronism in the 1950s, a product of the horse and cart era and a throw back to the time when nobody owned a motor lorry reliable or powerful enough to do anything but very local deliveries.

Economists, who have no time for the picturesque unless it is sufficiently spectacular to be commercially exploited, were to deliver the death blow to such places within the next few years, but meanwhile a diminutive 14xx 0-4-2 tank continued to trundle a wagon or two of coal out from Weymouth on about four mornings per week. Briefly the sounds of shunting would drift down the lovely Waddon Valley–the valley for which the optimistic promoters of the Abbotsbury Railway had forecast such vast mineral riches. However, it must not be thought that the whole of Dorset consisted of deserted railway sidings. The main lines of the county were still very busy, and were often worked to absolute capacity on summer Saturdays.

Radipole Halt
167 miles 59 chains from Paddington
Opened 1st July 1905
Closed 6th February 1984

Served at first by steam railmotors, and later by auto fitted trains plying between Weymouth and Dorchester, and Weymouth–Abbotsbury trains, Radipole Halt was built to serve the developing northern suburbs of Weymouth, and opened on 1st July 1905. With timber built platforms and typical GWR cast iron pagoda waiting shelters it was one of a total of 51 'Halts and Platforms' opened in 1905 by the GWR. The last service train called on 31st

With the imposing bulk of the Isle of Portland in the distance, Class 4MT 2-6-0, No. 76011 approaches Upwey with the 16.46 Weymouth–Bournemouth on 3rd July 1967.

S. C. Nash

Three-car DMU set No. C577 forming the 10.24 Swindon–Weymouth arrives at Upwey on 16th March 1988. Note the 'third rail' in position in readiness for the commencement of electric services to Bournemouth and Waterloo on 16th May of the same year.

John Scrace

Upwey station on a bright, but bitterly cold 16th February 1992 with 'Wessex Electric' No. 2407 approaching on a 'down' working to Weymouth.
Pauline Nicholson

43xx Mogul 2-6-0 No. 6319 runs through Radipole Halt with a 'down' train on 11th May 1963.
C. L. Caddy

December 1983 with the halt closing on 6th February 1984.

Weymouth
168 miles 62 chains from Paddington
Opened 20th January 1857 GWR and LSWR
Open to goods 2nd March 1857

At long last, twelve years after the Act was granted on 30th June 1845, and almost nine years after the opening to Westbury in 1848, the 27½ mile extension of the WS&W line to Weymouth from Yeovil was opened to traffic on 20th January 1857. On the same day the LSWR also began operating from its own station at Dorchester, both companies using the double mixed gauge track from Dorchester Junction to Weymouth.

The timber built terminus with its overall roof and glazed end screens designed by T. H. Bertram was constructed by a local builder, T. Dodson for an estimated cost of £10,000. The first up GWR train on the opening day left at 6.15am, arrived at Dorchester at 6.30am, and ran to time as far as Yeovil (7.10am) and Chippenham with a booked arrival time of 11.25am at London. No knowledge of the locomotive used on the first train is known, but *Otho* was used on the second train, the 8.30am up, and *Arrow*, and *Comet* were used on other trains during the day. The

No. 6814 *Enborne Grange* heads the 5.20pm Weymouth–Bristol Temple Meads just north of Radipole Halt on 22nd May 1963. The halt can just be seen past the bridge in the background.
C. L. Caddy

Bulleid Pacific No. 34023 *Blackmore Vale* thunders through Radipole Halt with the 17.30 Weymouth–Waterloo on 17th May 1967.
S. C. Nash

Radipole Halt, looking towards Weymouth in the late 1970s, showing the GWR pattern 'Pagoda' standard corrugated iron shelters in use on both platforms. Note how the platforms have now been equipped with electric lighting.
C. L. Caddy

Southern Times of 25th January reports on the opening day:

"The first train… departed at 6.15am. We are informed that the train arrived in Yeovil precisely at the time advertised (7–10), being fifty five minutes, an evidence of punctuality, which, in a first attempt, is rather extraordinary. The next train started at 8.30, and while waiting its departure, we will take a glance at the station, in which the *Otho* 'with dulcet simmerings, singeth a quiet tune,' and waits the touch that will wake him into snorting and vigorous life . . ."

There was no grand opening ceremony at the station for the first train as had been the norm for other openings, but there was of course, a large crowd of inhabitants ready to cheer the train on its way. The second GWR train from Weymouth left at 8.30am, with the first LSWR up train departing at 11.55am and passing Dorchester Junction at 12.25am. GWR trains used the main train shed, with the South Western trains arriving and departing at the west and east side platforms. It is recorded that the mixed gauge points and trackwork were quite a complicated affair as the LSWR locomotives in Indian red livery with black bands and white lining, hauling their varnished teak coaches, mingled with the green broad gauge engines of the Great Western on the opening day. Due to the very short notice given by the GWR with regard to the opening of

the line, celebrations in the town did not occur until 27th January. The day was declared a public holiday, the streets were decorated, and two triumphal arches decorated in evergreen and bearing the words 'WELCOME' surmounted by flags displaying the word 'FREEDOM' were erected near the King's statue at the approach to St Mary Street and St Thomas Street.

The mayor and municipal dignitaries walked in procession with the townspeople, from the town hall to the railway station with the band of the 15th Hussars at the head playing a selection of tunes including 'Hail the Conquering Hero'. The GWR had been generous in donating 300 tickets for an excursion to Yeovil which was enjoyed by all. The festivities continued throughout the day with other bands playing to the enjoyment of the populace, and the opening day came to a close with a splendid ball being held at the Victoria Hotel. A sumptuous dinner was celebrated at the Royal Hotel with many toasts and counter toasts being given in honour of the arrival of the railway. At the opening the GWR had a daily service of six trains, and the LSWR provided five down and seven up trains. By omitting certain stops the fastest down train from Westbury to Weymouth achieved the journey in 2 hours 8 minutes, with the fastest of the up trains taking 1 hour 55 minutes. The best of the LSWR trains at the time made the journey from Weymouth to Waterloo arriving at the Capital five minutes earlier than their rival. The

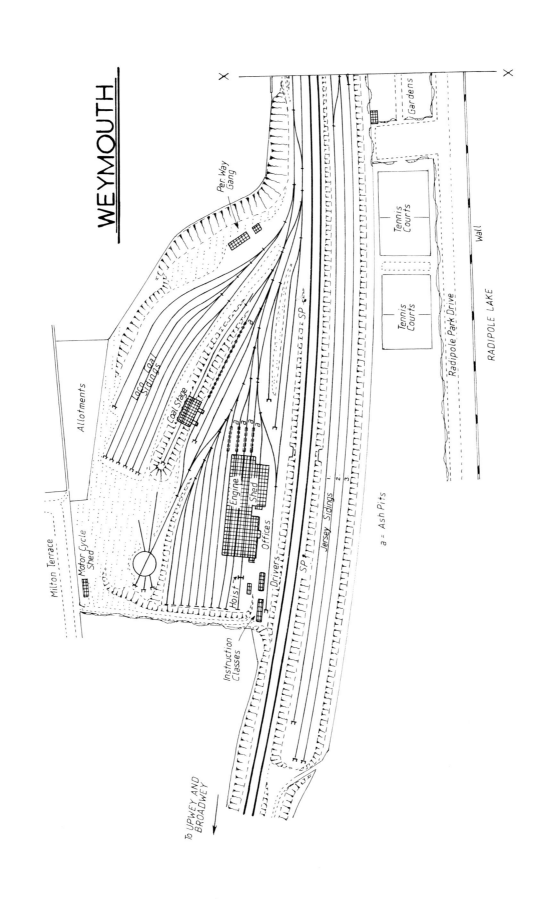

WEYMOUTH

To UPWEY AND BROADWEY

Milton Terrace

Allotments

Motor Cycle Shed

Per Way Gang

Loco Coal Sidings

Coal Stage

Instruction Classes

Engine Shed

Offices

Hoist

Drivers

SP

SP

Jersey Sidings

1
2
3

a = Ash Pits

Tennis Courts

Tennis Courts

Gardens

Radipole Park Drive

Wall

RADIPOLE LAKE

X — X

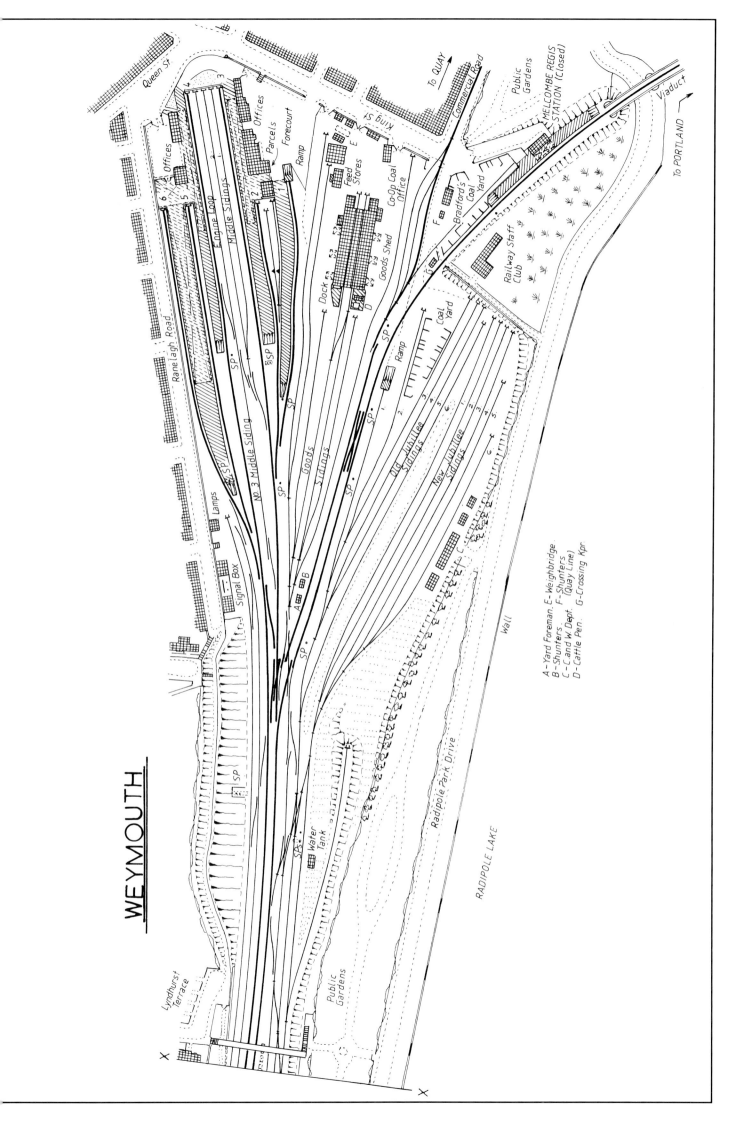

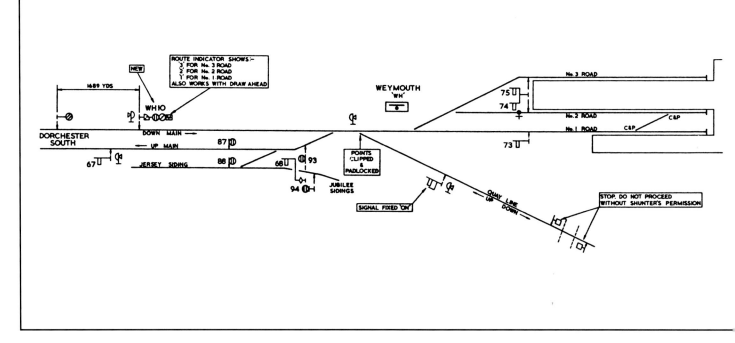

station was opened to goods traffic from 2nd March 1857 and a large wooden goods shed was served by both the GWR & LSWR. The standard gauge tracks (two) were situated on the left hand side of the shed, and the broad gauge (two) located on the right. Space was provided through the centre of the shed for the provision of an exchange platform or mixed gauge track, each company having their own cranes for the ease of loading/unloading. The shed was replaced in 1884 by a substantial brick built version containing two tracks and sited further west, which enabled the up

departure platform to be lengthened, together with the provision of a new excursion platform.

The financial crisis of 1866/7 was to hit the GWR hard, bringing many economies to its train services. The Weymouth line service in particular was cut from five London connections to four, and 1868 was even worse with London services cut to three. Even with the gauge conversion of 1874 the absymal service on the Weymouth line continued with the best trains taking over five hours to reach Paddington, which was one hour longer than by the LSWR to Waterloo. The one

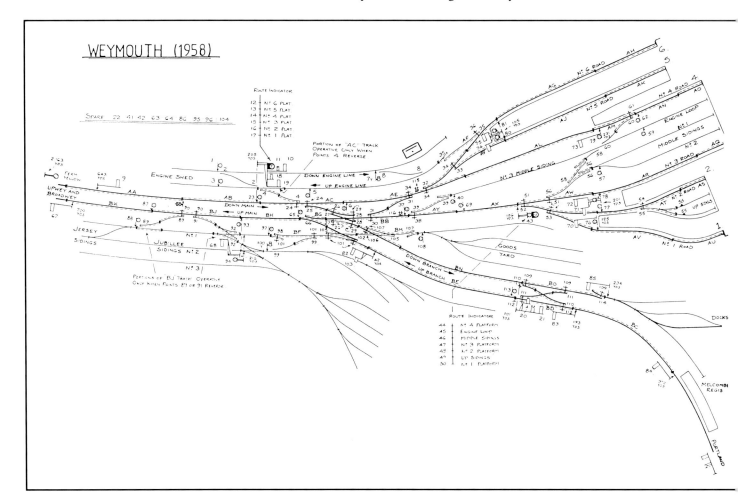

bright hope with the gauge conversion was that the GWR could compete in a more efficient way for the Jersey potato traffic. By 1887, with improving conditions, the GWR was now working six daily down trains from Paddington, seven from Bath to Weymouth, (two each way Sundays) and six Weymouth to Bath. The LSWR on the other hand provided twelve down trains from London, with timings being roughly equal for the rival services. The 5.50pm ex-Waterloo arrived in Weymouth at 10.53pm, whilst the 5.45pm ex-Paddington arrived in Weymouth at 10.45pm. The fastest LSWR train reached Weymouth from Waterloo in 4 hours 5 minutes, beating the best GWR timing of five hours.

However by 1889, with the Channel Island traffic developing and expanding, the Weymouth–Paddington service was reduced to 4 hours 30 minutes. In 1891 an up train named the 'Channel Islands Express' ran independently from the quay to Swindon and there joined the Weymouth Town portion. The following year the GWR began running a special train from the quay at the earliest moment after the Channel Islands boat had berthed. The train was advertised for Trowbridge and Swindon and connecting with express trains to Bristol, London and the North. The LSWR however, was also competing well, and cut the distance between Waterloo and Weymouth by three miles, and the journey time by 40 minutes by opening the Holes Bay Curve (connecting Poole with Hamworthy Junction) and by using the Bournemouth direct line (opened 1888) on 19th May 1893.

By 1892 the through coach services between Paddington and Weymouth were still rostered with London–South Wales trains, with all involving the attaching and re-attaching of coaching stock taking place at Swindon. The South Wales services involved, included the 11.55am Paddington–Swansea, 3.15pm Paddington–Swansea, 5.45pm Paddington–New Milford and the 9.15pm Paddington–New Milford, all this shunting adding to the timings of Weymouth services. By 1899 two trains from Waterloo reached Weymouth in 3 hours 4 minutes. The steam railmotor services running between Weymouth and Dorchester, and Weymouth and Abbotsbury, began on 1st June 1905. From 1st July 1901 the GWR reduced the mileage from Paddington to 147 miles by using the new line from Patney to Westbury, which accelerated the service to Weymouth. The best timings then being achieved in 3 hours 40 minutes, but this was still half an hour longer than the quickest service to Waterloo.

By 1924 the best GWR train to London was timed at 3 hours 40 minutes which was 15 minutes longer than the Southern Railway journey to Waterloo. The fast down GWR trains made the journey in 3 hours 10 minutes, against the Southern's 3 hours 20 minutes. Also in 1924 the GWR were running through coaches daily to Birmingham and Worcester, with four daily expresses to Paddington, one up train of which conveyed through coaches for Birmingham. The up boat train departed at 3.45pm, and the down 'boat' left Paddington at 9.15pm. Three trains each way terminated at Westbury, with through trains running to Bristol via the Trowbridge or Durston routes.

The Southern Railway's, all Pullman 'Bournemouth Belle' began running on 5th July 1931. At first the 'Belle' was extended to Weymouth in its first year of operation, but the Weymouth extension was found to be uneconomic and was withdrawn from the 1932 summer timetable. The 'Bournemouth Limited' had a

timing from Waterloo to Weymouth of three hours in 1934, this timing being reduced to 2 hours and 58 minutes in 1935. The summer timetable of 1939 was to see the weekday passenger services on the GWR route to Weymouth at their zenith before the outbreak of war. We start with the down trains. Times given are the individual starting times from their respective stations and the order which they arrived at Weymouth.

From	
6.15am Westbury	(Passenger & Milk empties)
6.00am Bristol	
7.35am Westbury	
6.35am Parson St	SO (Excursion)
6.45am Swindon	WO (Excursion)
8.10am Bristol	SX (Diesel Car)
10.25am Dorchester	(Auto)
9.27am Westbury	
8.30am Paddington	(to Weymouth Quay)
9.30am Bristol	SO (to Weymouth Quay)
9.23am Bristol	SX
11.20am Yeovil	SO (Auto)
11.35am Yeovil	SX (Auto)
8.30am Birmingham	SO (to Weymouth Quay)
9.40am Paddington	SO
1.23pm Dorchester	ThSO (Auto)
11.38am Chippenham	
9.30am Birmingham	SO
2.12pm Dorchester	(Auto)
11.42am Bristol	
2.53pm Dorchester	SX (Auto)
3.08pm Maiden Newton	SO (Auto)
1.35pm Chippenham	SX (Diesel Car)
12.30pm Paddington	
1.10pm Cardiff	SO
4.35pm Dorchester	(Auto)
11.15pm Wolverhampton	
4.32pm Yeovil	SO (Auto)
4.10pm Westbury	SX (Diesel Car)
4.35pm Yeovil	SX (Auto)
4.10pm Westbury	SO
4.25pm Bristol	
6.35pm Dorchester	(Auto)
7.27pm Dorchester	
5.03pm Bristol	
7.50pm Yeovil	(Dsl SX Pass SO)
8.45pm Dorchester	(Auto)
6.00pm Paddington	
9.55pm Dorchester	(Auto)
9.55pm Yeovil	ThSO
10.20pm Yeovil	
11.30pm Dorchester	(Auto)

Up passenger trains from Weymouth 1939:

To	
6.50am Paddington	MTHSO
7.20am Westbury	
8.30am Bristol	
9.00am Paddington	
9.30am Yeovil	(Auto)
10.07am Birmingham	SO
10.10am Bristol	SX (Diesel Car)
10.30am Wolverhampton	
11.00am Dorchester	SO (Auto)
11.03am Dorchester	SX (Auto)
11.25am Bristol	SX (Diesel Car)
11.45am Paddington	
11.55am Bristol	SO
12.42pm Dorchester	ThSO (Auto)
12.55pm Yeovil	SX (Auto)
1.02pm Yeovil	SO (Auto)
1.20pm Dorchester	(Auto)
1.52pm Westbury	SO
2.00pm Westbury	(Parcels)

221

2.10pm Dorchester	(Auto) (to Maiden Newton SO)
2.40pm Westbury	
3.45pm Dorchester	
3.40pm Paddington	(from Weymouth Quay)
4.15pm Paddington	
4.05pm Cardiff	SO (from Weymouth Quay)
4.30pm Taunton	SX (Diesel Car)
4.45pm Birmingham	SO
4.55pm Yeovil	SO
5.40pm Dorchester	(Auto)
6.05pm Yeovil	SX (Diesel Car)
6.20pm Bristol	
6.50pm Dorchester	(Auto)
7.15pm Swindon	
7.40pm Yeovil	
8.10pm Bristol	
8.15pm Dorchester	(Auto)
8.38pm Parson Street	SO (Excursion)
8.38pm Swindon	WO (Excursion)
9.00pm Yeovil	
9.20pm Dorchester	(Auto)
11.00pm Yeovil	ThSO
11.00pm Dorchester	ThSX (Auto)

Of interest in the above timetables are the diesel rail-car workings introduced on the line in 1936. Bristol–Weymouth services worked by the streamlined diesel railcars were the fastest in the country at the time. The single ended GWR built sets, with a coach between, appeared at various periods until the arrival of the single unit cars, and they stayed on the line until the arrival of the BR dmus in 1959.

By the summer of 1956, slip coaches were still being dropped off from the 'Cornish Riviera' and the 3.30pm down Paddington at Heywood Junction, where coaches were attached to a down service. Passengers on the down 3.30pm slip, hauled to Weymouth on the 4.25 ex-Bristol semi fast from Westbury, reached Weymouth in 3 hours 27 minutes, compared with the best Southern Region express which made the journey in 3 hours 31 minutes. The last Channel Islands boat train to and from Paddington ran on 26th September 1959, although a portion from Weymouth Quay to Paddington was conveyed on the 4.10pm Weymouth–Paddington on Tuesdays, Thursdays and Saturdays from 29th September–31st October 1959. The down portion from Paddington arrived on the 6pm ex-Paddington on the same dates. From 1960 the boat trains were switched to the Waterloo route thus beginning the gradual run down of services on the former GWR line. The two daily return trains between Paddington and Weymouth were reduced to one each way from 13th June 1960, and to a down train only from 12th September 1960. This service was withdrawn completely on 11th September 1961. The March 1961 timetable shows twenty weekday and seven Sunday, steam hauled trains still operated between Weymouth and Bristol, mingling with the dmus. Excursion traffic still plied to and from Weymouth, plus a Saturday 8am Birmingham Snow Hill–Weymouth Quay working. In 1965 an 06.10 Saturday buffet car express from Derby to Weymouth via Bristol was introduced, but the writing was on the wall for the old WS&W line and from 1974 services were reduced to seven daily, and six on Sundays, with one service only operating on winter Sundays. The Weymouth–Bristol dmus connected with Paddington trains at Westbury, as do the present day 'Sprinters' which arrived on the line from 15th May 1989. In the 1989 summer timetable there were nine daily services Monday–Friday, twelve on Saturdays and seven on Sundays.

Excursion traffic, which is part and parcel of any seaside station, came from the GWR and the LSWR soon after the opening. In April of the same year regular cheap excursion trains arrived on Monday, departing on the following Saturday or Saturday week, and for the first time the mass of the population had cheap fast travel to Weymouth, and they used it.

Dorset County Chronicle, 16th April 1857 reported: "In addition to the regular visitors by the regular trains, we have had abundant arrivals by two excursion trains on the GWR, the first of which (from London) reached here late on Saturday bringing upwards of 200 persons, that of Monday however was comparatively a 'monster' consisting of 18 carriages conveying more than 1000 passengers from Bath and other towns along the line."

The Weymouth, Portland, & Dorchester Telegram, 1st August 1861: "On Monday last an excursion train of 22 carriages containing 850 passengers arrived from Bath and Bristol." 29th August; "For the last few weeks, the excursion trains have brought into the town several thousands of visitors and although their stay in many cases is of very short duration, the lodging houses are pretty nearly always full."

No. 4919 *Donnington Hall* hauling a 'down' excursion runs into Weymouth on 23rd June 1962. *C. L. Caddy*

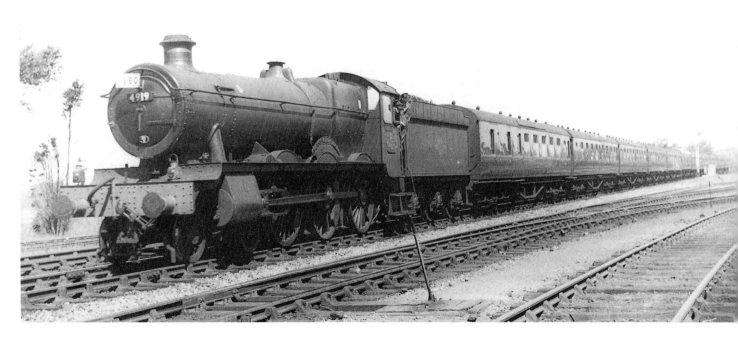

Showing the state that main line locomotives were reduced to in the final years of Western Region steam. Travel stained No. 4082 *Windsor Castle* hauls the 17.20 to Bristol Temple Meads, formed of four coaches only, out of Weymouth on 30th April 1964.

C. L. Caddy

Wimborne Journal 1873: "On Saturday morning the Esplanade and St Thomas St. were startled from their propriety by the spirited sounds of a brass band playing with more than common liveliness, everybody rushed out and Behold! About 300 men with their wives and families marched in grand procession down the street. They were connected with Vobster Quarries, Somerset, and the holiday treat was given by their employers, they started out about 5 in the morning from Vobster in 12 wagons and arrived at Frome about 20 past eight, hence they left by train and arrived at Weymouth about 10, most of them left by the Portland Steamer for the Isle of Stone."

A half day excursion from Waterloo on 4th June 1906 (Whit Monday) cost four shillings and three-pence, this particular LSWR excursion train to Weymouth running via Wimborne, possibly to evade the old Act of 1871 which stipulated: "No train should pass through Poole without stopping." By 1880 the number of lodging houses in the town had almost

Class 4MT 2-6-0 No. 76026 stands ready to assist Bulleid Pacific 4-6-2 No. 35027 *Port Line* with a train for Waterloo out of platform 3 at Weymouth.

D. E. Canning

During the last few days of steam operation on the Southern Region Bulleid Pacific No. 34087 *145 Squadron* runs towards Weymouth Junction with the 08.10 Waterloo–Weymouth Quay on 5th July 1967.

S. C. Nash

With the locomotive shed in the background rebuilt 'Merchant Navy' Pacific No. 35007 *Aberdeen Commonwealth* approaches Weymouth with the 08.35 from Waterloo on 5th July 1967.

S. C. Nash

doubled, such was the demand of the travelling populace. The excursion traffic grew more popular to the resort with its station placed just a stone's throw away from the pleasing sandy beaches and sea front. The Swindon Works trains were also popular visitors to the resort over the years and in 1912 a total of five trains arrived on one day packed full with workers and their families to enjoy the seaside air for a week. The Swindon Works trains were a mammoth undertaking for the Great Western with over 21,000 members of staff and their families departing for destinations far and wide. More than 500 coaches, plus locomotives and train crews had to be assembled for the outward and return workings, the most popular destinations being, Weymouth, Weston-super-Mare, Minehead and the Devon resorts. When excursion trains arrived at Weymouth in the late 1940s and 1950s the streets leading to the sea front would be packed with people as they swarmed in droves from the station and I, like many young boys in our earlier years, still remember the thrill of arriving at Weymouth by train and walking excitedly past the shops with their buckets and spades, sunglasses and sun tan lotion, 'kiss me quick hats', hanging on racks outside, and the aroma of fish and chips from the nearby cafes drifted in the air as we crossed the road by the famous clock to view the blue

sea (if it was a nice day!), walk on the golden sands, smell that lovely sea air, and watch, and listen to the squawkings of 'Punch and Judy'. Happy days.

The Quay tramway opened on 16th October 1865, but there were no facilities until a landing stage and crane were brought into use in 1876. Freight traffic was drawn by horses, and passengers had to make their own way to the quay. Like the Portland branch, the tramway was to be run jointly by the LSWR and GWR but in practise it was always operated by the GWR. After representations to the town council, a trial run accomplished by a small locomotive and coach was made on Tuesday 19th March 1878, although locomotives were not introduced on a regular basis until June 1880. With the raising and widening of the town bridge and a new landing stage, complete with a platform for passenger trains being brought into use in 1889, the tramway was then opened for the through working of trains in the same year. One train ran daily from London connecting with the night boat and at the same time the GWR took over the running of the Channel Islands Packet service from the local company who had been operating it on their behalf.

Traffic began to increase enormously with up to 300 freight wagons being dealt with in 1908, the main traffic being flowers, new potatoes, tomatoes from Jersey

The old order on the Quay tramway as remembered by many visitors to Weymouth over the years. 0-6-0PT No. 1367, complete with its warning bell on the framing, has a gaggle of vans in tow near the cargo stage on 7th June 1961.

C. L. Caddy

and Guernsey, and broccoli from France. In April 1910 an up express departed from the landing stage at 4.10pm on Tuesdays, Thursdays and Saturdays. On 13th July 1933, HRH The Prince of Wales officially opened the major improvements at the Quay station which had been started in 1931 at a cost of over £150,000. The improvements included the berthing pier being extended by almost a quarter of a mile, the terminus enlarged to two platforms and the track at the new quay station doubled and able to hold 36 coaches at the two platforms. New berths, five electric cranes and other modern facilities were also provided. The new terminal improvements were used from May 1933 prior to the official opening, and a regular boat train to Birmingham was introduced from the same month.

On the tramway itself, the quay was widened and a new larger radius curve was laid at Ferrys Corner, thus doing away with the practice of using special 48-inch 3-link loose couplings between coaches. Regular services were suspended during World War II and a new train ferry terminal was installed for the invasion of Europe.

The wooden cargo stage dating back to the 1870s was reconstructed in 1950/1. Holiday traffic and vegetable traffic increased during the summer seasons of the 1950s, and an extra platform was constructed at the Quay station in 1961 upon the cessation of sailings from Southampton. At this time four or sometimes five boat trains could be seen on summer Saturdays, and two or three trains were also required for the night sailings, although night boat trains seldom ran after 1962.

A dmu service was run from the quay in the summer seasons of 1983/4, but declining traffic witnessed the final service to Waterloo on 26th September 1987. The tramway, although unused, has seen a variety of enthusiasts' specials over the years, and on 25th March 1993 a test train formed of a TC unit was propelled to Weymouth by electro-diesel No. 73109, where No. 37038 was put on and travelled along the tramway to the quay.

This was the first recorded use of a Class 37 on the tramway, and the heaviest class of locomotive to have

No. 5091 *Cleeve Abbey* runs cautiously into Weymouth with a boat train from Birmingham on 25th July 1964. A locomotive, fresh off shed and awaiting permission to run tender first into the station can be seen to the right on the engine line near the signal gantry.

C. L. Caddy

The 'Wessex Wanderer' rail-tour, organised by the Plymouth Railway Circle from Plymouth to Weymouth Quay via Yeovil, runs into difficulties with a parked car outside the Sea Cow bistro en route to the Quay on 3rd April 1988. The five-car dmu comprised Set Nos P468 (Car Nos 51325, 59482, 51310) and P870 (Car Nos 53200, 53638.)

Peter Nicholson

Class 37/0 No. 37038, weighing over 100 tons, becomes the heaviest locomotive ever to traverse the Quay tramway on 25th March 1993 with a trial train to test clearances for Class 37s. This was in preparation for the Wednesday only 1993 summer service from the Quay to Yeovil Pen Mill and return.

C. L. Caddy

been used on the quay line. May 31st 1993 witnessed the start of the Bristol–Weymouth excursions worked by a Class 37, and on 3rd June this train worked the first of the Weymouth Quay–Yeovil specials (with lunch served). The train ran from July 19th until 2nd September (FX) and on Wednesdays only operated the Weymouth Quay–Yeovil trip before returning to Bristol later in the day. Locomotives seen on this duty included Nos 37408 *Loch Rannoch*, 37407 *Loch Long*, 37012, 37035, 37191, 37223, 37230, 37263, 37421, 37425, 37429 and 47414.

Mr J. S. Perry who gave us his memories of Dorchester, now recalls his days at Weymouth Quay. "After 3½ years at Dorchester I was transferred to the office at Weymouth Quay as a summer clerk. This office dealt exclusively with reservations on the Weymouth–Channel Islands service which had resumed a few years previously. The service was worked by two steamers, the old *St Helier* and *St Julian*, supplemented at weekends by the much larger and newer *St Patrick*, and whilst the two smaller ships had a capacity of 950 passengers, the *St Patrick* could take 1,300. The

Class 37/4 No. 37408 *Loch Rannoch* heads the empty coaching stock to Weymouth Quay on 3rd June 1993 in preparation for the Wednesdays only, charter train to Yeovil Pen Mill.

C. L. Caddy

basic service, Monday to Friday was the 8am ex-Jersey, due Weymouth Quay at 3pm, and the 1pm Weymouth Quay due Jersey at 7pm. On Saturdays there was an additional 1.30pm service from Weymouth Quay to Jersey which returned overnight and arrived at Weymouth at 6am. There was no outward service from Weymouth on a Sunday. The control of passengers was achieved by the issue of free sailing tickets up to the capacity of the ship demanded by the Board of Trade. Needless to say the greatest demand was on Saturdays for the 1pm service from the quay which was the connection out of the London boat train. The reservation office consisted of eight clerks including a clerk in charge. Correspondence was heavy and was filed, and was dealt with, always, by return as it was essential to close applications for sailing tickets as soon as the boat's capacity had been reached, so that alternatives could be offered. If we were unable to offer space, then intending passengers could turn to the opposition, as Southern Railway services operated out of Southampton. During the summer of 1949 when I was at Weymouth Quay, it was decided that mid week excursions be operated to Guernsey, usually on Wednesdays by the *St Patrick* which was utilised during midweek. The fare was 25 shillings (£1.25) return. The boat left Weymouth Quay at 9.30am due Guernsey at 1.30pm and the idea was a success from the start. I remember on the first day arriving for work at 9am to be greeted by a long queue stretching from the Quay station some hundreds of yards along the Weymouth Promenade! No pre-booking was possible, and as it was a fine day in June, hundreds turned up and it was estimated that 500–600 people were turned away. Arrangements were hastily revised for the following week but the demand was maintained throughout the summer and this proved an excellent source of revenue. At the close of the summer season it was decided that the regional boundaries were to be adjusted, and the Southern Region took over the line exclusively to Weymouth. As I was a GWR employee, I had the option of transferring to the Southern Region or returning to the Western Region, which I elected to do, and in mid September 1949 transferred to Holt Junction in Wiltshire as a general station clerk."

The Portland branch opened on 9th October 1865 to goods, and to passenger traffic on 16th October of the same year. This was a mixed gauge line and leased jointly by the GWR and the LSWR, but was initially worked by the latter only until 1st February 1877. Thereafter it was worked by both companies in alter-

nate years until 1931, when the Southern Railway took responsibility for working the line. In 1878 a line was opened on to Admiralty property at Portland and at first was mainly used for carrying fuel to the then coal fired ships of the Royal Navy. Initially the branch trains started from Weymouth station and reversed, before gaining the branch. The line was extended to Easton in 1900, for goods only from 1st October, and for passengers also on 1st September 1902. Melcombe Regis station was opened west of the main station on 30th May 1909, the new station being located at the northern end of the viaduct which crossed the Backwater. From the date of opening it was used by the branch trains, thereby eliminating the awkward reversal at the already congested main station. A new steel viaduct, west of, and replacing the original wooden viaduct was constructed across the Backwater and opened on 7th February 1909, the branch being re-aligned in connection with the new station and viaduct.

Passenger services over the years:
1869 8 daily trains, 5 Sundays.
1914 23 daily trains, 1 Saturday, 7 Sundays.
1934 20 daily trains, 12 Sundays.
1952 18 daily trains, 8 Sundays.

A large variety of motive power was used on the branch including: GWR 850 class saddle tanks, Beattie well tanks, Drummond M7 class 0-4-4 tanks, steam rail-motors Nos 12 and 13, O2 class 0-4-4 tanks, including the following Nos, 177, 179, 185,189, 193, 197, 207, 213, 229, 221 and 233. Also, C14 class 2-2-0 motor tanks, GWR pannier tanks, and Ivatt 2P 2-6-2 tanks. Freight traffic included general goods, Portland stone, and supplies for Whitehead's torpedo works. Supplies to the Naval base at Portland were heavy, especially in wartime, and vast quantities of coal and armaments were conveyed along the branch to the dockyard in the First World War. The same applied to the Second World War when ammunition and oil were conveyed by train. Special passenger trains conveying servicemen to their respective warships would trundle along the branch, and with the build up to the D Day invasion with Weymouth and Portland being one of the major embarkation areas, troop trains, petrol trains, and trains carrying every type of fighting vehicle would rumble over the Backwater Viaduct heading for Portland.

Passenger traffic was withdrawn from the branch on 3rd March 1952, with the final trains having run on 1st

March. Although closed to passenger traffic, a few specials used the branch in its fading years, the Railway Enthusiasts Club visiting the line on 7th June 1958 in a red two-coach push & pull set, No. 738 hauled by M7 No. 30107, for example. The special had started at Bournemouth taking its passengers to Hamworthy, Upwey, Portland, Bridport and West Bay. An RCTS railtour arrived on 14th August 1960 using pannier tank No. 3737. Melcombe Regis station, although closing with the branch was used to some extent by excursion traffic avoiding the congestion at the main station. Freight traffic continued trundling across the branch until withdrawal on 5th April 1965. The track south of Portland was removed in 1966, and from Weymouth to the Admiralty sidings in 1970.

Weymouth station was staffed by both the LSWR and GWR, each company having its own Station Master and staff. A similar situation arose at many joint stations including Yeovil Town, but the LSWR staff were withdrawn from Weymouth in October 1912, the GWR platform staff then being responsible for working the station. As part of the Government's Relief of Unemployment Act of 1935, it was decided to reconstruct the station which was, by this time, cramped and congested due to the vast amount of increasing traffic. The scheme was deferred in 1937, but the alterations were authorised in 1938, and more additions to the plan were added in 1939. The whole

was valued at £78,275 to include a new signal box to replace the junction and station boxes, but with war being declared, the plan was shelved, except for the Jubilee and Jersey sidings. £6,300 was authorised to provide additional carriage and goods sidings which formed part of the Jubilee yard (1935 being the Silver Jubilee of King George V). Nos 1–6 Jubilee sidings were added in 1935, Nos 7–12 Jubilee, and Nos 1–3 Jersey sidings were opened in 1938/9. Alterations took place in the goods yard, and South (1935) and North (1938) ground frames were installed. The only other part of the station rebuilding plan to be completed before the onset of war was the removal of the Southern Railway engine shed but the glass was removed from the station roof in 1939 as a precaution against air raids.

The much needed improvements began in 1951 with the removal of the overall roof, followed by the opening of the improved platforms and new signal box on 14th April 1957. Platforms 5 and 6 were introduced at the same time, but up until the new works the platforms had been numbered 1–5 from east to west, although for some reason they were now reversed. With the opening of the new signal box in 1957 all platforms were available for both arrivals and departures, but it remained the practice to use Nos 1, 2, and 3 for departures and 4, 5, and 6 for arrivals. No. 3 was the main departure platform, with No. 2 dealing with most

The brick built Weymouth signal box, opened on 14th April 1957, replacing the time worn Weymouth Junction and station boxes. The new box was equipped with a 116-lever Westinghouse A3 frame. Having a life span of 30 years, the box was closed on 19th September 1987.

John Morris

Rebuilt Bulleid 'Merchant Navy' class 4-6-2 No. 35017 *Belgian Marine* stands alongside platform 3 at Weymouth on 24th March 1965.

C. L. Caddy

Class 4MT 2-6-4T No. 80066 stands ready to leave Weymouth with the 4.50pm to Bournemouth Central on 29th September 1962.

C. L. Caddy

of the Southern Region trains. No. 1 was devoid of shelter and inconvenient for the ticket collector, and was only used about three times per day.

On the arrival side, as many trains as possible ran into No. 4 with No. 6 being the next choice. No. 5 was the 'parcels' platform, and was partially occupied for much of the day with vans. This was altered about 1961, and for some odd reason, No. 6 became the parcel platform. Thereafter it was only used by arriving passenger trains when excursions were pouring in at weekends. When the local service went over to dmu working, the units tended to arrive at 1, 2, or 3, ready to form their next service. Much additional traffic both passenger and freight arrived when Southampton was closed as a Channel Islands port in 1960, and traffic was concentrated at Weymouth. Vegetable trains ('Per Pots'), numbering up to five a day departed from the quay. Additional sidings were laid for the new traffic in 1961, with Jersey sidings 1 and 2 being extended, New Park sidings, and Jubilee 6A siding added. However, the new traffic only lasted a few years and the layout was trimmed from the late 1960s, the up sidings being taken out of use on 18th January 1966 and removed on 23rd June 1968. No. 1 platform was demolished over the period from 23rd May to 5th June 1966. The cargo service between Weymouth and the Channel Islands

was withdrawn in the 1970s making the vast siding areas redundant. The goods yard was taken out of use on 23rd July 1972 and removal was completed by May 1973. No. 12 Jubilee, No. 3 Jersey and New Park sidings were all taken out of use on 17th December 1972, Nos 1 and 2 Jersey followed on 18th May 1973 and the middle sidings between Nos 3 and 4 platforms, the No. 2 platform line, and No. 1 siding were all taken out of use on 8th May 1978. The signal box was closed on 19th September 1987 and the area is now controlled from Dorchester. On 16th November 1987 all Jubilee sidings were removed.

Engine Spotting at Weymouth During the 1930s

Phil Rendall now takes us back to the 1930s and his engine spotting days: "The best place to spot engines over the years was known as the 'bank'. This was the banked public footpath from Ranelagh Road to the Alexandra bridge, on which there were banked seats. From this vantage point could be seen the main passenger and goods stations, the sidings, the Southern Railway shed adjacent to Ranelagh Road, the old signal box, Melcombe Regis station and the arrival/departure lines under the bridge, plus the important access line to the Great Western shed and turntable, now the sight of a housing estate.

229

Summertime Saturdays were quite exciting, especially with the arrival of the GWR highlight of the day namely, the summer 'Channel Islands Boat Express' especially as on a summer Saturday when it sometimes ran in six 'parts', the first one or two hauled by 'Castles', then two 'Halls,' and the remainder by 4300 class 'Moguls'. The trains normally consisted of 14 coaches on each train. The locos returned to the shed to be watered, coaled, and turned. The trains were then pulled along Commercial Road to the Harbour by 0-6-0 saddle or 'match-box' tank engines (eg No. 1331 ex-Whitland & Cardigan Bay) or supplied with Welsh names (eg *Kidwelly* or *Cwm Mawr*) equipped with a bell, and a man out front carrying a red flag to clear the route of cars and pedestrians.

Initially, due to the tight radius of the harbour route at Ferrys Corner, around to the Town bridge, the standard couplings were removed from the coaches and replaced by chain links. In later years, the harbour wall was rebuilt in an outer curve to provide a larger radius. The trains queued in Commercial Road forming a captive audience for us lads when we were playing tennis in the Melcombe Regis Gardens. The other activity allied to the harbour was the cargo trade from the Channel Islands, Jersey potatoes, tomatoes, cauliflowers etc, with a return trade in the needs of the islands. Ships at the harbour in the 1930s included *St Helier*, *St Patrick*, *St Julian*, also the cargo ships *Roebuck*, and *Sambur*. I also remember *Reindeer* from my early days.

Weymouth had its own goods station and sidings. Rail borne Portland stone was also transported by the GWR. There was also the frequent 'motor-train' service hauled by 0-6-0 pannier tanks running between Weymouth and Dorchester and onwards to Yeovil. Motor-trains also worked from Weymouth to Abbotsbury via Upwey. The Yeovil 'motor' stopped at all stations and halts before reaching Pen Mill. Excursion traffic arrived from all parts including Wales and the Midlands, and brought a new lot of "namers" to Weymouth that otherwise we would have not seen. Saturdays were so busy with all the extra trains that Melcombe Regis station was often used for the discharge of passengers. There were also daily trains to Wolverhampton, Birmingham, Paddington and Bristol. Frequent visitors to Weymouth in the 1930s were:

'Castles': Nos 4098 *Kidwelly*, 5005 *Manorbier* (including the time when the engine was streamlined), 5018 *St Mawes*.
'Halls': Nos 4932 *Hatherton Hall*, 4958 *Priory Hall*, 4962 *Hagley Hall*.
'Saints': Nos 2927 *St Patrick*, 2931 *Arlington Court*, 2971 *Albion*.
'Stars': Nos 4016 *Knight of the Golden Fleece*, 4022 *Belgian Monarch*, 4071 *Cleeve Abbey*.
'Bulldogs': Nos 3306 *Armorel*, 3330 *Orion*, 3408 *Bombay*.
'Duke': Nos 3283 *Comet*.

The 6.30pm departure of a mixed passenger/goods was always worth a walk 'up the bank' even on a wet evening, because this train arrived in the early hours of the morning, hid in the shed all day and then emerged to glide into the station in the evening. It was usually hauled by a 'Saint' class, *Lady of Lyons*, *Saint Ambrose*, *Bibury Court*, or *Bride of Lammermoor*. Two regular visitors to Weymouth were, *Ivanhoe* and

With plenty of steam to spare in readiness for the climb to Bincombe Tunnel, Class 4MT 2-6-0 No. 76006 departs from Weymouth with the 11.18 to Waterloo on 5th July 1967. The two tracks in the foreground are the engine arrival and departure lines for the locomotive shed.

S. C. Nash

This photograph sums up everything that most holidaymakers remember about Weymouth: Steam trains on the Tramway and Channel Island Steamers moored alongside the Quay. September 4th 1959 finds Class 57xx 0-6-0PT No. 7780 at the head of a passenger train at the Quay station. Behind the train can be seen the framework for the new theatre under construction, to replace the earlier version which had been destroyed by fire. Berthed alongside the Quay is the well known Channel Island Steamer *St Julien*, that was used on the route for many years.

H. B. Priestley – Derek Phillips Collection

Waverley. From the 'bank' and other locations I have seen 45 of the 73 'Star' class (eg Knights, Monarchs, Queens, Princes, and Abbeys): 'Castles' and 'Halls' too numerous to mention: 'Bulldogs' named from Cornish origins, rivers, birds, famous people, and the countries of the Commonwealth. We often saw *Sir Watkin Wynn*, *John G. Griffiths*, *Tor Bay*, and *Severn*. Of the Southern Railway locomotives, the 'Lord Nelson' class were frequent arrivals, especially, *Sir Richard Grenville* and *Lord Howe*. Also 'King Arthurs', especially the engines with long nameplates, such as *Sir Mador de la Porte*, and *Sir Urre of the Mount*. A school teacher once asked me what was the good of my hobby. I replied that I knew all the Kings of England, famous Castles and Halls, and the Knights of the Round Table. Even now I can be quite casual when on holiday visiting a castle saying 'Oh!, I've known about it for years!' All thanks to watching the locos go past the bank."

Engine Spotting at Weymouth, Saturday 14th June 1958 and August 1960

After a morning's observations at Dorchester West Peter Foster had now arrived at Weymouth on board the 11.25pm from Chippenham, hauled by No. 5983 *Henley Hall*. "A good variety of steam locos were on view as we passed Weymouth locomotive shed. Amongst them was the single chimneyed No. 5093 *Upton Castle*, 'Battle of Britain' Pacific, No. 34090 *Sir Eustace Missenden*, and No. 7914 *Lleweni Hall* from Reading shed, plus two Weymouth regulars, pannier No. 7780, and Churchward Prairie No. 4507 with the straight side tanks often to be seen on the Bridport

branch. Among the parade of trains on that 1958 summer Saturday was the 1.10pm from Bournemouth Central running to Melcombe Regis station because of intense platform occupation at the main Weymouth station, and on this occasion, it was 'Chonker' No. 30484 in charge. Later, No. 6966 *Witchingham Hall* of 82C (Swindon) appeared rounding the bend into the station by the newly opened signal box, with the Saturdays only, 12.45pm stopper from Bristol Temple Meads. I noted another delightful Churchward Prairie tank, No. 5563 from Yeovil Pen Mill shed, and the second London District 'Hall' of the day, No. 5918 *Walton Hall* from 81C (Southall) heading the 7.30pm express to Bristol in the cool of the evening. This time of day on a summer Saturday had a very special atmosphere for me, with the Weymouth shed yard filled with a mix of familiar and foreign engines simmering away after a busy day's operations, and amongst them I noted Mogul No. 7323 from 82B (St Philip's Marsh).

Two years later my log book of August 1960 reveals a summer Saturday's train observations at Weymouth, beginning with No. 5935 *Norton Hall* from 82D (Westbury) storming out from platform 3 with the 10am to Birmingham Moor Street. The train was packed full with returning holidaymakers and occupied the whole length of the platform. The 10.20am to Wolverhampton Low Level was filling up on number 1 platform, and standing alongside at platform 2, was 'Lord Nelson' class, No. 30864 *Sir Martin Frobisher*, at the head of the 10.10am departure, which in the week was a stopper to Bournemouth Central. However, on summer Saturdays this train was extended to Waterloo,

231

Class 5MT 4-6-0 No. 73029 leaves the environs of Weymouth with the 18.15 to Bournemouth on 17th May 1967.   *S. C. Nash*

calling at virtually all stations to Woking, then fast to Waterloo reaching the Capital at 3.42pm! By 1960 dmus were part of the Weymouth railway scene and an interesting combination of Gloucester and Swindon built units formed the 6am from Cardiff General. Pannier tank No. 9756 of 71G (Weymouth) appeared on the 9.32am local from Maiden Newton, and No. 5974 *Wallsworth Hall* arrived with the down parcels. The next highlight on the departure side was the 11.12am to Paddington which was in the charge of No. 4957 *Postlip Hall* of 82A (Bath Road). This train gave an excellent mid morning service for returning visitors, calling at Dorchester West, Maiden Newton, Yeovil Pen Mill, Marston Magna, Sparkford, Castle Cary, Bruton, Witham, Frome, Westbury, Hungerford, Newbury, Reading General and Paddington. Time now for a rapid sprint along the length of platform 5/6 to view the arrival at Weymouth Junction of the 'Channel Islands Boat Express' hauled by No. 34093 *Saunton* of 71B (Bournemouth), and shortly afterwards the second part of the boat train arrived behind No. 35005 *Canadian Pacific*. The two Bulleid locomotives were exchanged for Weymouth's outside cylinder panniers, Nos 1367 and 1369, for the remainder of the journey along the Tramway to Weymouth Quay. There were numerous Southern Region departures during the late morning and early afternoon, among them being the 11am and the 1.20pm to Waterloo, both of which were routed via Wimborne and Ringwood on summer Saturdays to avoid Bournemouth. The final treat of the day was to watch the 4.18pm to Cardiff General hauled by a Hawksworth 'County', No. 1014 *County of Glamorgan* pick up its portion from Weymouth Quay at Weymouth Junction, the whole long train then being banked out of Weymouth for the climb up through

Ridgeway and through Bincombe Tunnel. Happy Days!"

'Hymeks', and 'Western' class diesels were to be seen on the former WS&W line and following the elimination of steam traction in 1967, Class 47s were in frequent use. Class 50s were introduced on the route prior to the introduction of Class 37s. Following the electrification of the line from Waterloo to Bournemouth in 1967 trains to and from Bournemouth were comprised of two 4TC sets push-pulled by Class 33 diesels. The final remains of the old station were demolished in the spring of 1986, and the handsome modern station of today is vastly different from the steam era version of thirty years ago. The final link in the electrification between Bournemouth and Weymouth came into use on 16th May 1988, with the handsome 'Wessex Electrics', the Class 244 units powering the services to and from Waterloo. Other types of electric traction now appear at Weymouth including 4VEP and 4CIG units, plus Class 73 electro diesel locomotives. In 1989 on summer Saturdays a Class 33 with two 4TC sets worked one return trip between Bristol and Weymouth forming the 13.30 down service, and returning with the 17.05 ex-Weymouth. On Saturday 14th November 1990 an HST 125 appeared for the first time working an InterCity special train from Birmingham to Weymouth formed of eight coaches with power units Nos 43010 *TSW Today* and 43188 *City of Plymouth*. The ex-GWR route, now a pale shadow of its former self, still has Class 37 locomotive workings to bolster its 'Sprinter' services in the summer services.

The Hawksworth County Class
Before finishing the chapter on Weymouth I would like, once more, to recall steam operation on the ex-GWR line in its final years and I am indebted to

Class 47 No 47080 rumbles past Weymouth signal box with the 08.12 from Leeds on 11th September 1978.   *John Scrace*

Richard Woodley for furnishing me with his log of the journey. The line between Westbury and Weymouth, with its undulating gradients, demanded engineman-ship of the highest order especially with the faster timed and heavily loaded trains. The Hawksworth 'County' class took to this line like a duck to water as they were extremely powerful and free steaming engines. Our engine this day, on 6th July 1963 is No. 1006 *County of Cornwall* from 82C Swindon shed hauling the 4.15pm Weymouth to Cardiff. The load was made up of three coaches Weymouth Quay–Birmingham, two coaches Weymouth Quay–Cardiff and six coaches Weymouth Town–Cardiff, a total of eleven vehicles, weighing 342/360 tons. (All the coaches had arrived at Weymouth earlier on the 7.05am Birmingham–Weymouth Town hauled by No. 6971 *Athelhampton Hall* which returned light engine to Westbury, and was observed at Yetminster at 1.15pm.)

Pannier tank No. 3633 had departed with the portion from the the Quay at 4.09pm, (six minutes early!) arriving at Weymouth Junction at 4.27pm, where the 'County' was waiting. After the portions had been coupled together and Class 5MT No. 73041 had buffered up to the rear to give banking assistance, the train was now ready for the off. Up on the footplate of the 'County' the fireman had his fire just right, the steam pressure was high on the clock, the vacuum gauge was registering 25 inches of vacuum and the engine was throbbing away with steam cascading from her safety valves. The way ahead was clear, the long cock-a-doodle whistle from the leading engine was answered by the banker at the rear of the train and with a loud bark from her exhaust the 'County' moved forward slowly at 4.33$^{1}/_{2}$pm this was against the sched-uled timing of 4.35pm. The coaches started to gather speed as they rumbled over the points, the banker was

Class 47/4 No. 47831 *Bolton Wanderer* in immaculate main line livery stands at Weymouth on 7th August 1993 with the 09.35 to Manchester.
Norman Kibby

The most famous locomotive of them all – No. 4472 *Flying Scotsman* LNER A3 class Pacific, is shown here on the over girder turntable at Weymouth shed in 1965 after working a special train. The amount of effort needed to turn an engine of this size on a hand operated turntable can be judged by the straining efforts of the footplatemen in the foreground. Most of the ex-GWR sheds I had occasion to visit were equipped with hand operated turntables, with the exception of Taunton which had an electric version. Fortunately, our Southern Region sheds had vacuum fitted tables, which made a footplateman's task much easier.

D. E. Canning

LNER A4 class 4-6-2 No. 4498 *Sir Nigel Gresley* is turned at Weymouth on 4th June 1961 having worked a special 'down' from Waterloo.

Peter Nicholson

chugging along at the rear as they gained the main line and then opened up to give maximum assistance. Up ahead the 'County' was striding away as the reverser was eased back and the regulator opened wider. Radipole Halt was passed in 2 mins 15 secs at 29mph, the train stormed through Upwey & Broadwey (4 mins 30 secs) heading into the bank, Bincombe Tunnel signal box was passed in 7 mins 45 secs at 24mph, and the banker now dropped off the rear and *County of Cornwall* was now picking her heels up. Dorchester West was achieved in 13 mins 30 secs against the scheduled 15 minutes. Five minutes after leaving Dorchester the train was whistling through Bradford Peverell at 52 mph, two minutes later the platforms at Grimstone & Frampton shook with the passage of the train at 46 mph, (at Grimstone, No. 1006 passed No. 5948 *Siddington Hall* on the 11.10am Wolverhampton–Weymouth, which was running to time.

Speed was now dropping with the climb to Maiden Newton which was reached in 12 mins 45 secs against the timing of 12 minutes. Cattistock Halt was passed two mins 45 secs from Maiden Newton with speed now dropping to 31mph on the climb to Evershot, the summit at Evershot being passed at 23mph in 9 mins (scheduled 7 mins) – two minutes down. This was recoverable running down the bank and Chetnole Halt shuddered as the train tore through at 64mph (11 mins 30 secs). Yetminster was passed 2 mins 15 secs later (13 mins 45 secs) at 58mph, but speed restrictions brought to an end for the moment any more high speed running. The train ran through Thornford Bridge Halt 1 min 15 secs later at 58mph and a severe PW slack brought the speed down to 35mph, and this dropped further, down to 25mph as the train threaded its way through Yeovil South Junction and its fixed distant signals, and the Yeovil stop. The train was now down the pan for timing, (21 mins 30 secs) against the scheduled 17 mins.

The crew now had the bit between their teeth, and after leaving Yeovil stormed through Marston Magna at 60mph (6 mins 30secs after Yeovil), Sparkford was achieved at 58mph (9 mins 15 secs)

and arrived at the next stop Castle Cary spot on schedule! (14 mins) The train was so long that it had to draw up in order for its passengers to disembark. After leaving Castle Cary the train was timed at 43mph as it passed under the S&D underbridge at Cole, and it whistled through Bruton at 39mph (6 mins 15 secs after leaving Castle Cary), still going well up the bank, with the 'County' and crew giving all they had. The summit at Brewham was topped at 32mph (12 mins), and with the climb now over, the engine could fly, and fly she did through Witham, 2 mins 30 secs (14 mins 30 secs), later at 53mph increasing to 62mph. Running under clear signals, with power still on, Blatchbridge Junction was passed at 62mph as the train took to the Frome avoiding line and rocketed past Clink Road Junction (20 mins against the scheduled 23 mins) at 62mph, increasing to 64mph! As the train approached Fairwood Junction the speed would be reduced for the Westbury stop. Fairwood was passed at 42mph (23 mins 30 secs against the scheduled 26 minutes), and arrived at Westbury 25 mins 30 secs against the schedule of 30 minutes, the train was seven minutes late with nil time booked to the loco. At Westbury the Birmingham portion was made up to five coaches and went on with No. 6961 *Stedham Hall*.

Earlier in the day No. 1011 *County of Chester* had been on the 10.30am Weymouth to Wolverhampton calling at Yeovil from 11.27am–11.30am. This engine also made a good strong start from Yeovil and appeared to be going well, though it was on a slower schedule with a lighter load of ten coaches than No. 1006. The 10.30am was allowed eight minutes longer than the 4.15pm to Westbury. In fact the schedule of the 4.15pm was faster than some dmus like the 1.50pm Weymouth–Cardiff. It was also a lot harder than the 'Channel Islands Boat Express' timing to Frome and Westbury with a similar load. Yet another 'County' was working the 9.30am Reading–Weymouth. It was too far away to identify but was probably No. 1028 *County of Warwick* which was later seen standing on Weymouth shed at 2.21pm.

'Steam returns to Weymouth'. The first steam locomotive to visit Weymouth since the 1960s. Rebuilt 'West Country' Pacific No. 34027 *Taw Valley*, hauling the 'Dorset Phoenix' departure, storms past the Safeway car park in apalling weather on Saturday 13th November 1993. The train was assisted at the rear by class 73/0 No. 73003 *Sir Herbert Walker*.

Peter Nicholson

Index

July 1994 saw the rare appearance of Class 165/1 'Network Turbos' on the Westbury to Weymouth line. Weymouth was the start of the Tall Ships Race and attracted a vast number of visitors during the few days the ships were in harbour. One of the extra trains run on Monday 18th was the 08.40 from Westbury, comprising Nos 165134 and 165110, seen (above) from the Sparkford bypass (A303) bridge with Sparkford Sawmills and Haynes Motor Museum in the right, background.

The following day the train, which returned from Weymouth at 18.00, was made up of Nos 165128 and 165103, and is shown going down in the morning, arriving at Castle Cary. Due to industrial action by RMT signalmen there were no trains on this line on the Wednesday, the day many people would have gone to Weymouth to see the ships setting sail for the 430-mile race to Spain.   *Peter Nicholson*